# FAR AND NEAR

### ON DAYS LIKE THESE

# FAR AND NEAR

## ON DAYS LIKE THESE

**NEIL PEART**

ECW Press

Cover design: Hugh Syme
Text design and typesetting: Tania Craan
Editor: Danny Peart, Paul McCarthy
Editor for the press: Jennifer Knoch
Proofreader: Crissy Calhoun
Producer: Jack David
Printing: Friesens   5   4   3   2   1

Published by ECW Press
2120 Queen Street East, Suite 200
Toronto, Ontario, Canada M4E 1E2
416-694-3348 | info@ecwpress.com

Library and Archives Canada
Cataloguing in Publication

Peart, Neil, author
Far and near : on days like these / Neil Peart.

Issued in print and electronic formats.
ISBN 978-1-77041-257-6 (bound)
978-1-77041-266-8 (special edition)
978-1-77041-267-5 (pbk.)
978-1-77090-487-3 (PDF)
978-1-77090-673-0 (ePUB)

1. Peart, Neil—Travel.  2. Motorcycling.
3. Drummers (Musicians)—Canada—
Biography.  4. Lyricists—Canada—Biography.
5. Rush (Musical group).
I. Title.

ML419.P362A3 2014   786.9'166092
C2014-904504-2   C2014-904505-0

The publication of *Far and Near: On Days Like These* has been generously supported by
the Canada Council for the Arts which last year invested $157 million to bring the arts to
Canadians throughout the country, and by the Ontario Arts Council (OAC), an agency of the
Government of Ontario, which last year funded 1,793 individual artists and 1,076 organizations
in 232 communities across Ontario, for a total of $52.1 million. We also acknowledge the
financial support of the Government of Canada through the Canada Book Fund for our
publishing activities, and the contribution of the Government of Ontario through the
Ontario Book Publishing Tax Credit and the Ontario Media Development Corporation.

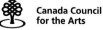

PRINTED AND BOUND IN CANADA

To Andrew and Steven
Every day is Memorial Day
To those who live on
Every day is Thanksgiving Day

Table of Contents

INTRO: **ON DAYS LIKE THESE**   ix

1 **TALKING DRUMS IN DEATH VALLEY**   1
FEBRUARY 2011

2 **EASTERN RESURRECTION**   13
MAY 2011

3 **SINGLETRACK MINDS IN THE SCEPTERED ISLE**   27
JUNE 2011

4 **THE FRYING PAN AND THE FREEZER**   46
JULY 2011

5 **AT THE GATE OF THE YEAR**   76
JANUARY 2012

6 **WHERE WORDS FAIL, MUSIC SPEAKS**   89
JUNE 2012

7 **THE BETTER ANGELS**   107
OCTOBER 2012

8 **WITNESS TO THE FALL**   133
NOVEMBER 2012

9 **ADVENTURES IN THE WILD WEST**   154
DECEMBER 2012

**10** **WINTER LATITUDES** 183
MARCH 2013

**11** **THE SWEET SCIENCE** 205
MAY 2013

**12** **DRUMMER WITH A SINGLETRACK MIND** 231
MAY 2013

**13** **SHUNPIKERS IN THE SHADOWLANDS** 238
JUNE 2013

**14** **ON DAYS LIKE THESE** 257
JULY 2013

**15** **IT'S NOT OVER WHEN IT'S OVER** 279
AUGUST 2013

**16** **ANGELS LANDING** 300
NOVEMBER 2013

**17** **BUBBA AND THE PROFESSOR** 321
FEBRUARY 2014

**18** **NOT ALL DAYS ARE SUNDAYS** 343
MARCH 2014

**19** **TELESCOPE PEAK REVISITED** 358
APRIL 2014

OUTRO: **ON NIGHTS LIKE THESE** 381

# ON DAYS LIKE THESE

**Like the first volume** in this series, *Far and Away: A Prize Every Time*, these stories grew over three years of my life, work, and travels. Likewise, the manner of relating them, the voice, still aims at the feeling that someone you know took the time and care to write the best letter he could—to share his life, work, and travels.

Several thoughts along those lines have come my way recently. One was the inventive short-story writer George Saunders, who defined the difference between all the informal writing that fills our world (and its ether) and what he could only call "literary" writing. His was a one-word distinction: "Revision."

An avant-garde fictionist from an earlier generation, David Markson, never owned a computer, right up to his death in 2010, at age eighty-two. As reported in the *New York Times* during a late-life correspondence with a younger poet, Laura Sims, she printed out and mailed him some of the online comments about his work. Though they all intended admiration, Mr. Markson was not impressed.

"'Hey, thank you for all that blog stuff, but forgive me if after a nine-minute glance I have torn it all up,' he wrote back. 'I bless your furry little heart, but please don't send any more. In spite of the lost conveniences, I am all the more glad I don't have a computer. HOW CAN PEOPLE LIVE IN THAT FIRST-DRAFT WORLD?' Later he wrote: 'I have just taken the sheets out of the trash basket and torn them into even smaller pieces.'"

Both authors were talking about the simple act of taking care, of offering any potential reader plain *courtesy*. Judging from the online chatter they both decried (this reporter's number one rule: "Don't Read the Comments!"), many people find sloppy writing genuinely offensive, an assault on one's eyes and brain while trying so hard to absorb *meaning*.

Carelessness is obvious, but care is better if it's not, as per the Roman poet Ovid: "If the art is concealed, it succeeds." When I am asked about the technical aspects of drumming or lyric writing, it is possible to get analytical, but only for professional, academic purposes. For the *real* audience, the listeners and readers who find pleasure in my music, lyrics, and stories, they don't need to be aware of flams and paradiddles, intricate rhyming schemes, and elaborate metaphors. The underlying quality I would like them to sense in a Rush song, a concert, or one of my stories is simply that "Care has been taken here."

That could be a decent metaphor for life—investing your time with care, selectively, to the work, play, and people sharing your life. Also investing that time with care *emotionally*—doing those things, *living* those things, as well as you can, for yourself or for others.

In helping me to take care, I am greatly indebted to my brother Danny for editing feedback and encouragement ("symbiotic nepotism," I call it) on most of these stories. Jen Knoch at ECW also shared editorial qualities I define as "devoted" and "trustworthy," and I will always benefit from the earlier guidance of Paul McCarthy.

A notable upgrade in this second volume is that my motorcycling partners Michael and Brutus both stepped up to SLR cameras during this period. I continued to learn what made a good photo setup, taking note of scenery, light, traffic, the absence of ugly intrusions like powerlines and guardrails, that sort of thing, and "directed" them. (There was some grumbling about always having to climb hills for the overview I wanted, but they eventually appreciated the results.) Together we ended up with a much richer choice of images to illustrate these tales, and in another form of revision, friend Craiggie helped fine-tune them in his digital darkroom.

My drive to write and revise with such care is always based on a wish to share as deeply as possible what it was like to live "on days like these"—these places, these experiences, these people. Few activities in my life seem more important than finding a way to put life into words and pictures. Sharing all that in a letter to a friend as well as I can gives me a clear vision of where I'm aiming—at *you*, dear reader.

After publishing *Roadshow* in 2006, I received a letter from a motorcyclist in Georgia who was inspired by my quest for the national park passport stamps. He wasn't able to roam that far himself, but he was creative—over a series of weekend trips, he and his riding buddy decided to collect all of the state parks in Georgia. He wrote humorously about tracking down bemused staff members in each park to give them *some* kind of documentation—even a check-canceling stamp.

If any readers are inspired that way, to set out on their own little shunpikers' quests, that is high praise indeed. I hope you will enjoy these stories half as much as I enjoyed the journeys, and will treasure your own even more.

Rider's repose, Gardiner, Montana

# TALKING DRUMS
# IN DEATH VALLEY

FEBRUARY 2011

**The setting of the opening photograph** is Death Valley National Park, California, near the site called Natural Bridge. The snow-topped Panamint Mountains form the backdrop, while I am gesticulating and (no doubt) pontificating in the middle, surrounded by the people and cameras of the Hudson Music crew. The subject of my little speech was drumming—specifically, drumming in front of an audience.

So that explains the title, but suggests a number of other questions. Starting with, I suppose, "Um . . . why?"

Well, it started in 1995, when I made an instructional video about composing drum parts and recording them, called *A Work in Progress*. My collaborators on that project were Paul Siegel and Rob Wallis, and we had enjoyed working together, sharing our ideas and realizing them on film. Paul and Rob were both drummers who had gravitated to the educational side, founding the Drummer's Collective in New York City, then later Hudson Music, to make instructional DVDs. They were around the same age as my bandmates and me, and likewise had enjoyed a long, productive partnership of close to the same duration, so we understood one another.

In 2005, the three of us made another instructional video (this time "straight to DVD"), *Anatomy of a Drum Solo*, which investigated the title subject, based around my solo from the *R30* tour. That solo had been filmed and recorded in Frankfurt, Germany, and thus was titled "Der Trommler" (the drummer). (On *Rush in Rio*, it was "O Baterista!" while the *Snakes and Arrows* version, filmed in Rotterdam, was "Die Slagwerker.")

The theme for our next collaboration seemed obvious: live performance, preparing for it and *surviving* it. In early 2010, we began collecting material, now augmented by a new member of the Hudson Music team, Joe Bergamini. "Jobee" is a drummer well schooled in several fields, as well as an educator and journalist, and has been particularly successful in the orchestra pits of Broadway—first-call drummer for many of the hit shows, including such richly percussive and challenging scores as *In the Heights*. (I loved that show.) Jobee has a frighteningly detailed knowledge of my work, my methods and influences, and thus his inputs and questions were insightful and inspiring.

In April 2010, the Hudson Music crew joined me at Drum Channel in Oxnard, California, and filmed several days of my rehearsals for the *Time Machine* tour. In July, they filmed an entire Rush show, in Saratoga Springs, New York, with supplementary "drum-cams" on me. They also captured the soundcheck and pre-show warm-up, when I did a bit of talking to the camera, as I had during the Drum Channel filming in April. However, we would need to shoot some more "talkie bits" to go before each of the songs from the live show, explaining the special problems or challenges in a particular song and noting technical highlights.

So, I thought, why not go somewhere really nice to shoot those?

*A Work in Progress* had been filmed in May 1996 at Bearsville Studios, in New York's Catskill Mountains, so we had plenty of nice outdoor settings for the narrations around the neighboring woods and lakes. Same with *Anatomy of a Drum Solo*, which was shot at nearby Allaire Studios in the summer of 2005.

This filming session was scheduled for January 2011, so we were limited in choices for outdoor shooting. Winter in Quebec might have been pretty, or not—you can never tell about winter weather. We might get bright, clear days with glittering snow mounded all around, or we might get gray skies and gloomy rain. I thought of Big Sur, a rugged stretch of California's Pacific coast with dramatic ocean views among redwood forests and state parks and beaches. It is one of my favorite parts of the world, but at that time of year we might be interrupted by rain there, too.

So . . . I suggested Death Valley. Being the driest place in North America, averaging less than two inches of rain a year—and sometimes none—the chances of clear weather were good. I have been enchanted by that region of desolate splendor since my first visit, in the fall of 1996, when Brutus and I rode in under a full moon on what remains one of the great motorcycle rides of my life. (See "December in Death Valley" in *Far and Away*.)

I returned many times after that, notably on the *Ghost Rider* journey in 1998 and '99, and every year or two since, so I had explored the area pretty thoroughly. The better I came to know it, the more I loved it.

It seemed to me that if we could combine such splendid natural backgrounds with the existing rehearsal and stage footage, it would elevate the show enormously. I was glad when the Hudson Music guys agreed. They set about getting the necessary permits (filming in a national park has certain "conditions") and making the arrangements. Here I am riding toward Death Valley on January 10, on my way to meet the Hudson crew at Furnace Creek.

I rode through the Panamint Valley, on the western side of the Panamint Mountains. The opposite, eastern aspect of that range is shown in the background of the opening photograph. From both views, the highest, snowiest summit is Telescope Peak (11,049 feet), which was the climactic setting in *Ghost Rider*. Its neighbor just to the north, Wildrose Peak (9,064 feet), was featured in the "December in

Death Valley" story. That day my hike up Wildrose had led me into snow in the higher elevations, and so it was when I came riding in this time. Not long after the above photo was taken, the road veered left and led northeast into the Panamints, and I began ascending the little-used road toward the Wildrose Pass. The narrow, winding track got rougher all the way, the pavement often crumbling into gravel as it twisted steeply upward.

Then, as I rounded a bend, a sheet of white lay ahead of me in a shadowy canyon, a north-facing curve covered with snow. A few four-wheelers had slithered through, and their tracks were compacted into slick ice. I stopped right there and carefully turned my bike around to head back down. I *might* be able to tiptoe through that one icy stretch, but there would likely be more snow higher up, and I was alone. People were waiting for me, expensively. It was no time to take silly risks.

Once safely turned around, I straddled the bike at the edge of the snow, watching as a 4x4 pickup eased up and stopped beside me. The driver lowered his window, and we greeted each other. I told him I was heading back down, and he said, "Maybe I'll try it a little farther." But when he went to accelerate upward, all four tires started spinning, *zing, zing.*

I smiled and said, "Maybe not."

He chuckled and nodded agreement. "Maybe not." He reversed carefully down the road until he could turn around.

I followed his truck down through the rough part of the road, then passed him with a wave as the pavement smoothed out. Now I would have to take the longer but more well-traveled and lower-elevation route over Townes Pass—which was fine, but with that unexpected dead-end detour, and no gas until Stovepipe Wells, I would have to stop and pour in the extra gallon of gas I carried on the back of my bike.

When I had loaded the bike the previous day, I had almost decided to leave that accessory behind. I felt I knew where all the gas stations were around Death Valley, and how to plan my stops, so I shouldn't have any problem.

However, the Roadcraft lesson would be that sometimes you encounter . . . the unexpected. So you'd better be ready.

The next morning I was waiting at Furnace Creek when Rob, Paul, and Jobee arrived with their crew—director Greg McKean and cameramen Dan Welch, Jeff Turick, and Nate Blair. They had all flown into Las Vegas, and drove up in a rented Suburban and Ford sedan, carrying a ton of camera gear and plentiful snacks for the perpetually peckish

Jobee. Over an intensely action-packed day and a half we filmed my "talkie bits," prompted by Jobee's questions, in six or seven spectacular locations. I also encouraged them to capture some "gratuitous riding footage," as I hoped to bring as much variety to this drumming DVD as I could.

My dream would be to create a show that even non-drummers would enjoy watching, and now, thinking ahead to the coming months, it will be exciting to see all of those parts, from the rehearsal studio, the live stage, and Death Valley, edited together into what we hope will be an entertaining and instructive program. The working title is *Taking Center Stage: A Lifetime of Live Performance*.

This story will return to Death Valley and the film shoot directly, but I have to explain that even while I was engaged with that adventure, another big project was filling my days—a new book. I have long wanted the stories I write for this department to be "dignified" and made permanent by appearing in print, and at last I made it happen.

Typically, it turned out to be a much bigger job than I anticipated, but everything does, if you aim high enough. Once I had found a publisher and stipulated that the book had to be in print before the tour's continuation in late March, they gave me a list of requirements.

I needed a title and subtitle, which would help direct the design of a cover, which I would develop with Hugh Syme, as usual. I would have to write a new introduction and afterword, supervise various copy elements for the jacket and flaps, choose photographs for them, find all the text and photograph files for each of the twenty-two stories, then read over the copyedited text, the typeset text, and finally the corrected text. All in all, it was a solid two months of work, but I was delighted to see it truly coming *together*—a collection of stories that had been written and published independently now took on a *unity*, becoming a single narrative that spanned almost four years of my life. At first I had been daunted by having to write the "Intro" and "Outro," but they proved to be the keystones in framing the twenty-two individual stories to make them feel like one.

During that process of putting it all together, it occurred to me that there are few activities more enjoyable than *making things*. When I was young, it was car models, go-karts, then later pop-art mobiles and laughably inept carpentry. A couple of years ago, I ran across a wall-mount "drumstick holder" I had dreamed up in my teens. It had been inspired by my dad's cue rack by his pool table, but it was a crudely shaped assemblage of gray-painted plywood, with holes drilled by an old brace-and-bit—it looked like it had been crafted by a troglodyte. But still—I had *made something*.

It is stimulating and satisfying to write stories, or play the drums, but most gratifying of all to me is creating a physical object: a book, a CD, a DVD. Of course it remains the *content* that gives the mere object its value, but many would agree, I hope, that owning such a carefully crafted object is more pleasing than just acquiring the content by whatever means. That urge may sustain the existence of things apart from their content, and that would be good, methinks.

The cover photograph I chose was taken by our Master of All Things Creative, Greg Russell, while he and I were riding together in Central California in 2008, on the *Snakes and Arrows* tour. The setting is the Westgard Pass, between Nevada and California, and at the time of using the photograph in a story called "South by Southwest," I remarked that it was the kind of spacious photo you didn't often see in motorcycling magazines. (They tend to focus on the *hardware*.) However, this panorama certainly captured an element of what I love about motorcycling, and nicely exemplified the title and the subtitle.

The other big event lately has been our appeal on behalf of the Chilean Red Cross in "The Power of Magical Thinking." In a way, that episode led to the making of the book.

When I finished writing that story in November 2010, I was wondering if that might be the time to start trying to generate some revenue from these stories. Given the time and effort I spend on them, plus paying editor Paul McCarthy for his input and Greg Russell for his design, not to mention manager Brutus over at Bubba's Bar 'n' Grill, I had been looking for a way to make the site more self-supporting. The excellent Bubba's merch had not caught on as wildly as Brutus and I had hoped, and it had been hard for us to find a way to introduce advertising *tastefully*.

Greg, Brutus, and I tossed around ideas for selling "The Power of Magical Thinking," like maybe asking for a nominal charge of one dollar. Even if only some of the readers kicked in, it wouldn't take much of a fraction. (With the eventual posting of that story in November, plus a new edition of Bubba's Book Club, we set a new record of over 63,000 visitors—two *million* hits.) That solution was defensible rationally, ethically, and even economically (on both sides), but it remained hard to feel *good* about—getting all uppity and demanding people start paying for what they had been getting for free. Oh, I knew it was the right thing to do, especially in terms of setting an example for others in the "Slow Blogging" fraternity—those who, like me, found the medium creative and rewarding in every way except for the minor detail of earning a little money. Back in the '70s, the clever English pop group 10cc had a song that went, "Art for art's sake/ Money for God's sake." Or as my riding partner Michael likes to point out, "A girl's gotta eat."

Jamie LeSueur,
Andres Gutierrez, Brutus

Then I hit on the idea of making those contributions *charitable*, and the story itself pointed to a deserving recipient: the Chilean Red Cross. Greg designed a cool little appeal, in which we asked for a minimum donation of one dollar, with the option to skip straight to the story. Brutus coordinated the fundraising, which was a surprisingly complicated undertaking. (As I have learned from observing Don Lombardi's struggles in launching Drum Channel as an online resource for drummers, anyone who is truly interactive with the Interweb, even in the second decade of the twenty-first century, is still among the "pioneers" in that brave new world. As a consequence, obstacles and complications seem endless.)

We managed to get it all "active" in early November, and by the time we closed the appeal in early January, a couple thousand people had willingly chipped in, many at more than the minimum. We had raised almost $5,000, and I decided to match that, so Brutus was able to pose with a "novelty check" ("cheque" in Canada, which I think is a useful distinction, but it doesn't translate into American) for $10,000.

So, a turning point of sorts had been reached, in my mind. Somehow the idea of having a story generate some income, even for charity, fired up my ever-growing wish to see those stories in print, as a published book. Thus was born the desire to create *Far and Away: A Prize Every Time*.

Some questions lingered, however. As I worked with the publisher to assemble and groom the stories for print, that edition was becoming the definitive one, with its more generous and asymmetrical layout, its larger format, and its sheer existence as a *thing*. Now the online versions felt like "demos," and I really wanted to take them down, to have the book take their place, in every way. I decided to leave up the most recent year's worth of stories. That way we would still offer a nice variety on the site, and it happened that those stories were all part of the same "chapter" of the larger tale.

Speaking of matters of scale, I call this photo *Death Valley Bonsai*, because the skeletal, gnarled tree was actually only about a foot tall—a lovely example of the miniaturization of desert life (and death). The shot was taken near Badwater Basin, the lowest spot in North America, at 282 feet *below* sea level. It is also the hottest place in the Western Hemisphere, with a record temperature of 134°F in 1913.

It was nowhere near that hot on the days we filmed in Death Valley, however (the snow in higher elevations is a clue). The morning temperature was 37°, barely rising to 60 through the day.

The water in the background is another illusion. A recent rainfall had flowed down from the rocky canyons and alluvial fans, *bajadas* (the debris fields at the base of the mountains, eroded into perfect angles, called the "angle of repose"—Wallace Stegner used that as a metaphor in a fine novel with that title), and at the lowest point, an inch or two of water had collected over the usual white mineral flats. Desert landscapes are hard, impermeable surfaces, like natural concrete, with little vegetation, so any water from rain or snowmelt just goes hurtling downhill, carrying everything before it. That's why flash floods are so dangerous in the desert. (Though they also fulfill a needed function in nature: certain seeds only germinate when their hulls are worn away by the stones carried in a flood, the water increasing their chances of survival.)

Our film crew set up right at the edge of the shallow lake, where director Greg wanted to capture the mountains reflected on the water behind me. We all hiked down to the point cameraman Jeff had scouted, but the salt-crusted soil was sodden, and people's boots started sinking—some to their ankles. Being posed at the very edge of the water, I had been given three two-by-fours to stand on, but as I watched cameraman Dan sinking before me, lamenting his "one pair of shoes," I gave one of the boards to him.

"A flotation device," I said.

The rest made do as well as they could, dancing and sloshing around to find firmer footing.

After I had introduced the setting on camera, Dan remarked that it was funny to hear me describe being in the lowest, hottest, and

driest place in the Western Hemisphere, with a great big *lake* behind me. (Also, I know now I should have said lowest and driest in *North America*, because there's a lower point in Argentina, and the Atacama Desert in Chile is drier. Live and learn.) Dan was right, and I redid the speech to explain the "lake."

We had already shot segments in front of the Artist's Palette and Natural Bridge, from Badwater and different views of Zabriskie Point, and of me riding past the sand dunes and along the valley floor. The final location I was hoping to get was Dante's View, overlooking the length of the valley and distant mountains from 5,475 feet. The park ranger who had been assigned to "watch over us" (one of the conditions imposed by the national park) reported that the road up to that peerless viewpoint was presently closed due to snow. He said he could get us through the locked gate, but that only his 4x4 truck, and maybe the film crew's Suburban, would make it to the top—not the Ford sedan or my motorcycle. I was disappointed to hear that, as I had visions of filming my ascent on the bike as a possible way to introduce the whole show—but "it is what it is." At least we could get up there some way.

Late in the afternoon of the second, final day, we headed for that location. Leaving Badwater, I told the guys I was going to gas up in Furnace Creek, then would meet them at the locked gate. But as I climbed that narrow, winding road (and as the temperature fell), no barrier appeared—until a natural one occurred, a belt of snow across a sheltered loop of road.

Knowing I had other people around to help pick up the bike (and/or me) if necessary, I decided to chance it. Slowly I crept along the road's edge, where the snow was softest, with my feet down like outriggers. I made it through that stretch, but soon there was another one, this one even deeper and icier. Again, I tiptoed through, and ahead I saw the parking area for Dante's View above the final set of steep, snowless loops.

But, there was no one else there. We had less than an hour of daylight left, as the sun descended toward the Panamint Mountains, so I felt anxious. We wouldn't have another chance. What if the others were waiting for me farther down? I really didn't want to ride down and find them, and have to traverse those snowy patches twice over, so I could only wait. It seemed such a long time, the orange sun inching ever downward, before I finally saw the ranger's pickup, the Suburban, and the Ford making the ascent. They had been waiting for me lower down, some of them of little faith (Dan), sure I would *never* have made it through that snow.

It was a perfect moment for that Hollywood cliché *"People—we're losing light!"* Quickly we set up and filmed me riding down and up that last bunch of loops, with scattered snow in the scrub behind me, then set up at the viewpoint's edge for my introduction to the program, in the kind of light photographers call "the magic hour."

Now I would be racing the light in another way—to get downhill through the snowy patches and flooded washouts, with gravel strewn across the pavement, before dark. Even then, it would be another thirty miles or so back to the motel at Stovepipe Wells, in the chilly evening air, so I quickly put on all my cold-weather gear and headed down.

Artist's Palette–crew in middle distance setting up

Back on the main highway, I could relax, knowing it was an easy cruise now. Usually twilight is a scary time to be riding, with visibility fading for the rider and surrounding drivers, and wildlife more active. But there was little to fear on that road—clear vision on every side for many miles and, perhaps most important, NO DEER.

I paused at an overlook to watch the light fade across the valley, then rode on, cruising slowly, keeping warm, and feeling good now—looking forward to the Macallan waiting for me in my room.

# EASTERN RESURRECTION

**"Eastern" can refer to this pagoda,** with its Chinese design, and in a different way, to its location—not in the Orient, but in the eastern United States. It stands atop Mount Penn, overlooking Reading, Pennsylvania, where Michael and I stayed a night in late April. We were on a long backroad ride between the Adirondacks in upstate New York—where a few deep snowbanks lay in the woods, and flying snow filled the air—and Baltimore, Maryland, where flowers carpeted the woods, and spring filled the air.

The pagoda was built in 1908 by William Abbot Witman, a local quarrier who wanted to beautify the city whose hillsides he had been stripping bare. He planned the edifice to be a landmark hotel and restaurant, but it was never opened—the need for a suitable access road up almost 900 feet of steep mountainside being the biggest apparent obstacle.

In the background of this photo, the streets and hillsides of Southern Pennsylvania are beginning to show sprays of green among the trees—an effect I've come to think of as "The Airbrush of April." Those first signs of post-winter rebirth, the radiant bursts and washes of spring color, are so expressive of returning *life*, and are one reason why the word "resurrection" occurred to me for this story. Even as the band was reviving the *Time Machine* tour, bringing it to a new series of North American cities and countries outside North and South America (heading to Europe in May), and I was resurrecting my drumming and motorcycling skills and endurance, all around me the world was being reborn.

My April travels with Michael on this sequel to last year's *Time Machine* tour carried us from Florida up to Quebec—thirteen shows and 3,800 miles of motorcycling between them. The weather varied from warm and blossoming across Tennessee to a polar wasteland in Ontario.

We traced thousands of miles of eastern backroads in April, weaving north and south and north again. Through different zones of latitude, I witnessed every stage of spring, in Tennessee, Kentucky, and West Virginia, and gradually farther north. Sometimes we looped south again through Ohio or Pennsylvania a week apart (seeking warmer weather on days off, usually in vain), where we saw markedly different phases of spring rebirth in the same countryside.

Locally, that progress was clearly represented by a series of natural stages. First was the greening of the lawns and roadsides, as the grass recovered its living color and the daffodils and crocuses emerged in people's gardens. Then the first blossoms flared in vivid sprays of color, those that flower before they leaf, like the bright yellow forsythia bush that was familiar to me from my youth in Southern Ontario, flaming along driveways and housefronts in early spring.

The following photo was taken on the road down from that pagoda atop Mount Penn (the road's complicated engineering a testament to Mr. Witman's problems over 100 years ago). Among the green washes at the roadside, a spray of forsythia glows yellow, while to the upper right, among the mostly bare, gray branches, a magnolia tree flowers in pink and white.

In the fifteen years I have been traveling on concert tours by motorcycle, the band has never toured in the East at that time of year, and it truly was a revelation to me. On April 4, our first ride led through the open woods of Tennessee, on the way from a show in Greensboro, North Carolina, to one in Nashville. While Michael and I followed

the gentle curves and contours of two-lane roads, passing fields and lawns fresh with green, the woodlands remained a stark gray-brown network of bare trunks and branches. But I started to notice increasing numbers of small trees that glowed with vivid magenta blossoms, standing out all the more for being the only bright color amid the gray pavement, greening roadside, bare woods, and blue sky.

Those bright flourishes of purple decorated the open woods across Tennessee, though on the next day's ride, north into Kentucky, we didn't see them. Curiosity piqued, I started asking local friends and browsing websites, and learned that they were called redbud trees. I was surprised to learn that they are very common throughout the eastern U.S.—they are even the state tree of Kansas. In summer, the redbud trees trade their blossoms for leaves and become just another small, unremarkable tree among the dense green foliage. But in April, the redbuds glorify the woods with an Easter-egg shade of purple. (Add the yellow of forsythia and robin's egg blue, and you've got a fine palette for Easter—a possible pun in the title, I confess.) I soon observed that the northward spread of redbud blossoms was a sure herald of approaching spring across the East.

So again, all of that "spring fever" blazing in my eyes, and in my mind, was part of the reason why "Resurrection" demanded to be part of this story's title. Also, the states through which most of our travels led us—Tennessee, Kentucky, Ohio, Indiana, West Virginia, even Pennsylvania—are among the most vehemently, *loudly* Christian parts of the country. The bible belt becomes the bible *bellow*, shouting at you all over the place.

The church signs I have often cited, like the generic "FREE TICKET TO HEAVEN—DETAILS INSIDE," were common and mostly unoriginal. Several gigantic billboards towered high above the road, urging us to "BE AN ORGAN DONOR—GIVE YOUR HEART TO JESUS."

On another vast billboard, the left half was scrawled with huge ragged letters slashing out the word "SIN," while on the other half was a block of text in quotes, "IT SEEMED LIKE A GOOD IDEA AT THE TIME."

Michael laughed and said, "It always does!"

In the temperate regions of the Northern Hemisphere, April is a time of rebirth—celebrated since prehistoric times by the good old pagans. In the same way that Christianity co-opted the pagan midwinter festival as a good fit for their own celebration of their savior's birth (for which there was never any seasonal evidence, biblical or historical), naturally the return of life to fields and forests after the ravages of winter made a perfect metaphor for their savior's crucifixion and resurrection. Again, the pagans had celebrated that spring equinox since time immemorial.

Some church signs in April reminded us that "JESUS IS THE REASON FOR THE SEASON," as they do around Christmas, but I guess it's not really true. You might as well say, "THE SEASON IS THE REASON FOR JESUS."

One moderately clever church sign read, "JESUS PAID THE PRICE—YOU KEEP THE CHANGE."

A modestly sized sign set low in front of a small-town church particularly caught my eye, then occupied my reflections for many miles down the road. It read, "THE EASTER BUNNY DIDN'T RISE FROM THE DEAD."

Setting aside the sign's scolding piety, I couldn't help but think of one Easter Sunday when I was about seven, brother Danny four, and sister Judy three. That morning the three of us looked into our back-yard and saw the bloody remains of a rabbit near the doghouse of our beagle mix, Trixie. Dad shooed us away and went outside with a shovel, leaving us kids traumatized that our dog had killed the Easter Bunny. Soon after that, Trixie (who apparently had other behavioral problems than childhood-icon-slaying) "moved to a farm" (Danny has never forgiven Mom and Dad for that euphemism), but for Danny, Judy, and me, the Easter Bunny didn't rise from the dead.

Over our post-ride cocktails and dinners, Michael and I discussed all of those church signs and billboards, and the mentality behind them, as well as all the variations on the theme of resurrection. One time we must have startled a Christian friend, who was standing by and listening silently as these two apparent heathens discussed the last sayings of Christ on the cross. For reasons I can't begin to imagine, I remembered the Aramaic of the only saying substantiated in two gospels, when Jesus shouts to the sky, *"Eli eli, lama sabacthani?"*—"My God, my God, why hast Thou forsaken me?" Michael and I know our Judeo-Christian theology pretty well—we both had that kind of upbringing and have always been interested in matters philosophical and supernatural—matters which obviously combine most strongly in religion.

Among Michael's other security tasks, he keeps an eye on the mail that comes my way, and he shared one message from a reader that he thought was humorous. It was from someone who enjoyed my writing, but admonished me not to be a "faith-basher."

That gave me pause—the *name*, not the idea.

I don't want to be *any* kind of a "basher" (except on the drums), and thinking over that concept launched a train of thought—a train hauling boxcars full of mental freight that will need to be unloaded sometime soon (on *you*, patient reader).

But first, here's a lovely little valley in Southern Ohio, just over the river from West Virginia. I saw a bluebird on the wing that morning—always a happy sight. We were returning from a two-day ride from Cleveland southeast through rural Ohio and West Virginia (just incidentally, I am sure that state has more one-lane paved roads—the rarest in the land—than any other) to overnight in Charleston, then back up to Cleveland for the show. I really ought to be able to *sell* that route to other riders, it was so good—a million-dollar ride that would surely be worth, oh, ten dollars . . .

A minor scene in a book by Paul Theroux has stuck in my mind for many years and, until recently, I could never figure out why. Now I realize that the scene is a portrait of the psychic response to being called names by strangers, especially in print. The book is *My Other Life*, one of Theroux's "fictionalized autobiographies," about a writer named Paul Theroux who, in one chapter, is traveling on a book tour in Australia. (I laughed out loud when he had a hotel bellman call him "Mr. Thorax.")

As I remember the scene (from reading it fifteen years ago), the "other" Paul Theroux meets an attractive Australian journalist, impeccably groomed and sophisticated, and when their flirtation reaches its tipping point, she suddenly pulls out one of the author's books about a train journey, in which he described a scruffy Australian girl rutting in the berth below him. Pointing at that passage in the book, she says emphatically, "That's not me."

Of course, Mr. Thorax and the reader are intended to understand that it *was* her, but she could not live with being described in such a way, at such a moment, for all time. The character's intent was a deliberate desire to change the author's perception of her.

What made the passage stay with me, I think, is that it's such a human response to being categorized, especially in an unflattering way. Many of us spend a lifetime receiving others' impressions of us, and thinking, "That's not me." (Also the title of a great old Brian Wilson song, but with lyrics by Tony Asher that are more about self-reflection than one's reflection on others.)

Recently I read a theory that the way others saw us in high school has much to do with the adults we become. That notion offers a deep well of reflection, and definitely has some truth to it, but I would say most of our imprinting comes even earlier, as small children. If as a child you were told you were dumb, incompetent, thoughtless, and selfish, say, or made to feel that way, you might spend the rest of your life trying to prove "That's not me."

Even in grown-up life, when you learn that someone has a bad impression of you that you feel is unjust, you might set out to show that person a different you. It has happened to me, in both directions.

But alas, I may have to live with being called a "faith-basher." I simply can't think of a way to prove it untrue. And in any case, in today's world there are many more people who will bash you *with* faith than *for* it.

I think of a large sign I saw on a lawn in Harrisburg, Pennsylvania, that made my eyes pop in my helmet: "AFRICAN-AMERICANS MURDER 60% OF THEIR UNBORN CHILDREN IN NYC."

I had to slow down and read it again to believe what I was seeing—at first I literally did not believe my eyes. It wasn't the *message* that so shocked, but the *messenger*—and those racially specific words. (Like when we rode Interstate 68 out of West Virginia and across Maryland, and passed the sign for Negro Mountain. Michael and I both had to look twice to be sure of what we were reading.)

In this case, it amazed me to think that one individual had decided that displaying that particular message in front of his or her home was a good thing to do—to express their disapproval of other people's actions and beliefs, and tacitly express their own faith in a god-given right to *control* those actions and beliefs.

Around the bellow-belt, there was a lot of that kind of finger-wagging self-expression, and I wonder if being appalled by that arrogance is really faith-bashing. When people ram their beliefs down your throat, you can't help but spit them out.

Among the ultimate faith-bashers, in the best sense, are Trey Parker and Matt Stone of *South Park* fame, and on a night off around our show at Madison Square Garden, my wife, Carrie, and I went to see their Broadway musical, *The Book of Mormon*. The next day I wrote to thank my friend Matt for the tickets, under the title "When only one word will do." That word was "GENIUS!"

(I laughed when Matt replied, "It's a great date night, right?")

The show is a brilliant piece of musical theater, and I also loved one quote Matt gave in an interview about it, which particularly went to the faith-basher accusation: "We figure God can take it—because he sure can dish it out!"

The above photo was taken on a particularly nasty April day, and as I rode along the backroads of Ohio and Indiana, I was trying to figure out how to capture a photograph of such riding conditions. I was hoping for one of those little bus shelters for children you sometimes see in rural areas, figuring I could put Michael there, and have him photograph me riding by through the rain.

However, such a setup never appeared. In one small town, I pointed and signaled us into a spray-wash (previously imparted Roadcraft—rare shelter for a motorcyclist on a rainy day). We parked inside, out of the rain, got off the bikes, and smoked a Red Apple, while Michael, as usual, thumbed his handheld device. (One female friend calls him "Texty McTexterson, from Textybrook, Texas.") I looked at the driveway behind, with rural fields beyond blurred in the steady rain, and saw the photograph I wanted. Michael and the camera stayed dry while I rode slowly past in each direction. (Sometimes you just have to give those secrets away.)

Toward the end of last summer's series of shows, the first go-round of the *Time Machine* tour, my bandmates and I agreed that we were still pleased by that musical and visual presentation, and wanted to bring it to audiences in other places. Our manager, Ray, was quick to note that there were many cities where we hadn't performed that tour—Cleveland, Detroit, Montreal, Vancouver, and so on. Because the band's live shows have been so *popular* these days (something to be grateful for, all right), and the three of us feel that we are playing at a higher level than ever before (while recognizing that at our advanced ages, that upward curve cannot last forever), we decided that rather than locking ourselves away in a studio to finish *Clockwork Angels*, the album we have been chipping away at since, oh, 2009, we would do some more shows this year.

In the spirit of giving away the "secrets" behind some of the photographs I choose, I asked John ("Boom-Boom"—our pyro technician and photographer of daily events) how he captured this amazing image. He told me he had to scale the rigging behind us, then climb sideways along the truss above the video screen. Then he had to wait for the lighting to be right, and for the three of us to be facing each other. (The end of "The Spirit of Radio" is my guess.)

A few days ago I inscribed a print of this photograph to Boom-Boom with "This is *art*—the hard way." And the meanings are multiple: Those three guys down there, and that vast crowd in front of us, are the main reason why we had to do some more shows this year. Because we *could*!

But to quote another church sign, "GOD MAKES ALL THINGS POSSIBLE—NOT EASY." (That is a good one.) As I have mentioned plenty of times, touring is hard, both physically and emotionally—and that last effect is particularly wrenching for me these days, with

a darling baby girl, Olivia, only around a year-and-a-half, at home, without Daddy—and Daddy away, without Olivia. Grown-ups can miss each other while understanding *why* they're apart, but of course it's different for little ones.

Hoping to help Olivia understand why Daddy had "abandoned" her, I made her a little picture book called *Where's Daddy?* I explained how people have jobs (a difficult enough concept to simplify for a toddler, but I came up with what I think is a good definition, "It's how we all help each other"), and showed pictures of doctors, farmers, restaurant workers, tailors, and so on. Then I showed a photo of me playing onstage with the band, and wrote, "Daddy's job is different— Daddy plays the drums for people."

I introduced her to Uncle Alex and Uncle Geddy, with photos of them waving to her, and then pictures of how Daddy travels—an airplane, a bus and trailer, and a motorcycle. Then I assured her that Daddy would be home soon, and showed pictures of all the things we would do together, ending with "Because Daddy LOVES to be with Olivia," then a photo of me alone on a dock in Minnesota with the satellite phone (from the story "Cruel Summer" found in *Far and Away*), with the caption, "And Daddy HATES to be away from Olivia."

The first time I read the book to Olivia, as we have read so many other picture books together, nestled close on the sofa with my arm around her, I really could feel her taking it in.

Turning the page, we then looked at a photo of a newborn Olivia, clutching my finger in her tiny fist (from "The Ballad of Larry and Suzy," also in *Far and Away*), with the caption, "But right from the first day Olivia was born, she could see that life was going to be *complicated*."

Then I included this photograph by my friend Craiggie, as a necessary distraction from all that *seriousness*.

So . . . let's look at a bunny!

When it comes to discussing our working schedules, these days each of us bargains with Ray separately, which helps to avoid any unnecessary disagreements before Ray can "broker" a consensus among us. For my part, I wanted to be home this summer with my family, but offered to tour in May and June.

Ray countered by saying that the other guys were keen to bring this show to Europe, and I was not against that idea (the *motorcycling*!), so we'd really need another month to accomplish that. Ray proposed working in April as well as May and June. I knew the motorcycling weather in April could well be dicey, but Ray promised to keep that month's itinerary to the southern states.

Well . . . we did *start* in Florida, North Carolina, Kentucky, and Tennessee, but then all of a sudden we were in Ohio, Pennsylvania, New York, Chicago, Detroit, and even Ontario and Quebec. (Though admittedly, *southern* Ontario and Quebec . . . )

Here is an early April day in Kentucky, but apart from the green grass, the photo could as well have been taken in November. The day's temperatures were November-like, too, in the forties and fifties Fahrenheit. Further north, it would be worse . . .

However, back in January, when I noticed how Ray had tricked me with the itinerary, I told Michael we had better look into some heated riding gear. For many years, in cooler weather I had used an electric vest—made with an electric-blanket type of technology, it is wired into the bike's electrics and helps to warm your core. Our bikes have heated grips, too, so our gloved hands stay fairly warm—but I had always found that in chilly weather, no matter how well my feet were socked and booted, they got cold. If your feet are cold, you're never going to be happy. I wanted electric socks! (More than one friend has commented on that good band name: the Electric Socks.)

A company called Gerbing makes a variety of heated clothing, mainly for motorcyclists but also for the U.S. Department of Defense (special ops, Michael and I guess—winter-motorcycle-ninjas), and we ordered their combination of vests, socks, and gloves.

Revelation!

*Warm feet!*

("Winning!")

At the end of our first long ride on a cold day, on April 4, up through Kentucky to Lexington (an unplanned refuge from the violent weather that rocked the eastern U.S. in early April), we raised our glasses and toasted, "Gerbing—blessèd be thy name!"

Now it seemed that *wind* was our worst enemy, especially added to rain. On a few rides, like when we had to make some miles on an interstate across Ohio and Michigan on a day of fierce quartering winds, the riding was more like a wrestling match. Four or five hours of fighting against the steady wind, the sudden lulls in underpasses, momentary stronger gusts that were almost overpowering, or the bow waves of the semis as we passed them, left us with aching shoulders.

But we had one more weather extreme to face. On April 18, I awakened in a Best Western in Sarnia, Ontario, and what I saw through the open curtains was unbelievable—once again, I literally did not believe my eyes. I closed my eyes, rubbed them, opened them again, then got up and stepped closer to the window. Sure enough—about four inches of snow covered the ground, the trees, and our bikes.

Every morning on tour it is my joyful responsibility to awaken Michael, usually with a drum pattern tapped on his door, or a rattle of the curtains over his bunk, and "Wake up, Wendy! It's time for school!"

That morning I ran to Michael's connecting door and pounded on it, calling out "Michelle! For once you don't *have* to get up—but you *have* to get up. Come and see this!"

And what to his wondering eyes did appear . . .

Well, obviously there would be no motorcycling that morning, but it was a day off, so we didn't have to go anywhere. I had planned a backroad ramble around Ontario for the day, ending up in Hamilton for the following night's show, but if the snow remained, or increased, we might need to be rescued by the bus and trailer. I sent a photo of our snow-covered bikes to bus driver Dave's phone (he was in Toronto, taking my other bike in for service), and texted him, "There might be a change of plans."

Michael and I took a "snow day," lazing around and going to see a movie (the *Arthur* remake—we thought it was a good "date movie"). We adjourned to Norm's Pub and Grill next door, and watched the Montreal Canadiens game (I had to explain to Michael what a "body check" was) on the usual six or eight flatscreens in such "sports-bar" establishments.

"The Airbrush of April"–Maryland

Through the day and evening, the snow melted on the pavement, and eventually off the bikes, and the following morning we were able to ride to the show in Hamilton, but it was *bitter* cold, barely above freezing and gloomy gray.

Riding a motorcycle on a day that's even just moderately cool—say 45°F—gives you a windchill at 75 mph that is, literally and palpably, freezing. (I have noticed over many long rides in hot or cold weather that I can feel a difference of two degrees, up or down.)

On days like that, electric socks are way better than prayer, and generally technology is superior to superstition in counteracting a day's weather, roads, or medical problems. However, I do suspect no human is completely immune to superstition.

I have written before that as a child of five or six, I devoutly believed I could alter reality—escape punishment—if I *worried* about it enough. That was prayer. In *Ghost Rider* I wrote about the stunningly accurate tarot reading I had from a Vietnam veteran on Venice Beach, California.

Recently a Harley-riding friend gave me a "freedom bell" for each of my two motorcycles. I hadn't heard of them before, but they are small metal bells embossed with a motorcycle (an old Indian, by the look of it), and a tinkling clapper inside. The freedom bells are to be hung from a low point on your motorcycle, near the road, to capture Evil Road Spirits before they can cause you mechanical ills or crashes. According to the packaging,

Road Spirits can't live in the presence of a bell. They get trapped in the hollow of the bell. Among other things, their hearing is supersensitive. The constant ringing of the bell and the confined space drives them insane. They lose their grip and eventually fall to the roadway. (Have you ever wondered how potholes are formed?) The bell has served its purpose.

Apparently the magic is doubled if the bells are given to you, and I thought, "Why not?" While I was working on my new 1200 GS before the last American show of this run, in Baltimore (draining the gas and oil for its journey to Helsinki with the band gear), I carefully tied a freedom bell (with a reef knot) from the centerstand crossbar. There it will dangle above the roads of Europe while I ride and capture those Evil Road Spirits.

Along the Maumee River, Indiana

Brutus will be riding my second bike over there, while Michael will be traveling with the crew and concentrating on security, so I'll see if Brutus wants the second bell on his ride.

Another superstition I find irresistible is fortune cookies, and on one of our first rides of the tour last summer, at a Chinese buffet in Artesia, New Mexico, Michael and I received some interesting fortunes.

Mine read, "You are soon going to change your present line of work." (On the day before the first show of a tour that continues almost a year later, no points there.)

Michael's fortune was more prescient: "You are about to become $8.95 poorer. ($6.95 if you had the buffet.)"

And it *all came true! Doubled!*

(Plus tax and gratuity.)

One superstition I do cling to is that when I'm home for a break in a tour, I don't look at *exactly* what day I'm leaving. Sometimes I have a feeling it's a Tuesday, and live and take care of chores accordingly, then find out I don't leave until *Wednesday*, and it is the sweetest of bonus days. Better even than the "snow day" in Sarnia. (Michael insists on calling that day "The Chronicles of Sarnia," but I refuse.)

When I opened my motorcycling journal to start this tour's notes, I noticed a lone entry on the last written page. It was from after I returned home last October, from South America, after having been away touring for most of the previous six months. I remembered the moment I wrote that entry. Jet-lagged, I had been up very early, even before fourteen-month-old daughter Olivia's usual 6:00 wake-up

call, and the house was dark and quiet as I stood in the downstairs hall. Upstairs, Carrie was asleep, Olivia was asleep, and our golden retriever genius-love-sponge, Winston, was sprawled in the hall, and all of them were safe.

I had a sudden feeling of *peace*—"everything is all right"—and realized that I never get that feeling on the road. I fetched my journal and recorded my new understanding of what *home* means. "Feel more *complete* here—because those who matter most are right here. On the road, maybe feel more *alive*—more fiercely in the moment—but never as if 'everything is okay.'"

That is a feeling I can only experience at home, when I *know* from moment to moment that my loved ones are all right.

Because the Easter Bunny didn't rise from the dead.

# SINGLETRACK MINDS IN THE SCEPTERED ISLE

JUNE 2011

This royal throne of kings, this scepter'd isle,

This earth of majesty, this seat of Mars,

This other Eden, demi-paradise,

This fortress built by Nature for herself,

Against infection and the hand of war,

This happy breed of men, this little world,

This precious stone set in the silver sea,

Which serves it in the office of a wall,

Or as a moat defensive to a house,

Against the envy of less happier lands,

This blessed plot, this earth, this realm, this England.

—William Shakespeare, *Richard II*

**That was Will talking through John of Gaunt,** set six or seven hundred years ago, and he obviously liked his country. These days, Brutus and I like it, too. The motorcycling is fantastic, through lovely and occasionally magnificent scenery, and the day-off destinations, the country hotels, are wonderful. The weather can be . . . variable (I once described "the three Rs" of motorcycling in Britain as "rain, roundabouts, and the wrong side"), but that's one lesson I learned from the English, living there in my youth. If you make plans for an outing, a picnic, a hike, or a motorcycle ride, whatever the weather on that day, you *go*.

That was a valuable life lesson, among the many I have learned from other people, other cultures, in my travels. That kind of "press on regardless" attitude is not only particular to Britain's rainy climate, but powerful as a metaphor—about pursuing happiness and enjoying life even when the conditions seem unfavorable.

In those weathered isles, the relatively small and densely populated countries of Great Britain and Ireland, it is wonderful to discover how much open space remains to be explored. Most notable for us Scooter Trash types, a multitude of tiny one-lane roads wind through the lush forests and farmlands, and across the stark beauty of the rolling moors and barren mountains. The British call those little roads "singletracks," and for thousands of miles they weave through the countryside of England, Wales, Scotland, and Ireland.

For three European Rush tours now, R30 in 2004, *Snakes and Arrows* in 2007, and *Time Machine* in 2011, Brutus and I have been doing our best to explore as many of those singletracks as we can. This tour would also be our first European ramble in spring, which naturally gave us a whole new palette of landscapes. In a story that now lives in *Far and Away*, "Shunpikin' It Old Skool," I explained the word for the deliberate avoidance of all major roads: "shunpiking." It could be said that this pursuit of singletracking represents Extreme Shunpiking.

In an area like the North Yorkshire moors pictured above, you can ride miles through vast open country, on a network of paved singletracks. Occasionally you might have to stop at a livestock gate, open it, pass through, then close it again (to keep the sheep on one side or the other), but traffic is rare, and villages and crossroads far between. In farmed or wooded areas, the narrow lanes were often tightly hemmed by stone walls or tall hedges on both sides, so the riding was necessarily slow. We would putter along in first or second gear, often in the rain, ever watchful for sheep, cows, equestrians, their droppings (you don't want to hit cow pats or horse buns in a

rain-slick corner), occasional cars or Land Rovers, and gigantic tractors towing fragrant manure spreaders.

When any kind of oncoming traffic appeared, animal or mechanical, we would stop and pull over as tight to the hedge as we could (on
days with a lot of that kind of action I called us "hedge-huggers") to
let the cow, sheep, horse, car, or tractor through. One time a tandem-
wheeled tractor towing huge fertilizer wagons so completely filled
the lane that Brutus and I had to turn our bikes around, with difficulty, and retreat to a driveway to let the monster by.

Many times I reflected on how nerve-wracking it would be to travel
those roads by car, but our singletrack motorcycles were perfect for it,
and we have come to love traveling that way, over hundreds of miles
of those little lanes. The scenery could range from delicately pretty to
breathtakingly vast, and the riding was often technically challenging.
Experienced motorcyclists know that riding slowly can be difficult,
especially near the edge of balance, and it requires deft smoothness
on the controls and body movements on the bike. For Brutus and me,
the necessarily slow pace could make a more relaxing journey than
the kind of "sporting" speeds we would adopt on larger, faster roads.

Not that there's anything wrong with that, either—we also like the
so-called "B" roads in Britain, the next step up from the singletracks,

but not as big or busy as the "A" or "M" roads (motorways). I particularly remember some of the B roads in Wales as entertainingly twisty, framed in spring woodlands, and lightly traveled.

Brutus had done his research on famous motorcycling roads in Britain, too, and he routed us along one called the Cat and Fiddle Road, after a pub at its peak, in Derbyshire and Cheshire. Winding and fast, it is regularly listed as "the most dangerous road in Britain"—though the sad fact is that if you subtract the motorcycle fatalities, it's actually one of the safest. So the real danger, alas, is the motorcyclists, not the road itself. Riding into that area, I had never seen more warning signs for motorcyclists, including many gruesome posters placed by an organization called "The Shiny Side Up Partnership." I noticed their website address at the bottom of their posters, and it says they are "working to reduce the number of sportsbikes involved in crashes on our roads." (Brits say "sportsbikes," while North Americans drop the middle s: "sportbikes.") Their yellow, black, and red signs pictured fast-moving motorcycles with slogans like "To Die For?" and "Bends—Dead Ahead." Anywhere Brutus and I rode in England with that kind of high-speed, winding road popular with sportsbikers, we saw those signs.

North Yorkshire B road

On the Cat and Fiddle Road, the local authorities have posted their own warning signs, lowered the speed limit, installed many speed cameras, maintain aerial enforcement, and something called an "average speed detector." They even claim to have "motorcycle-friendly barriers" (yikes). But the grim toll continues—thirty-four motorcyclists killed on that one road between 2006 and 2008 alone.

A large part of the motorcycling culture in Britain centers on superfast repli-racers—purposeful, cutting-edge machines that really belong on racetracks. As such, they require expert, even professional riders. Like those professionals, these wannabes of varying talents and experience wear bright-colored and armored leather racing suits, helmets, boots, and gloves—but even those are little enough protection for the riders who miscalculate the combination of speed and angles, and throw themselves down the road.

As I know myself, having once owned a Ducati 916, riding a high-performance, competition-focused motorcycle seemingly *compels* you to ride it hard—but it's easy to get over your head. (One reason I don't have that bike anymore.) Racetracks these days are relatively safe places to go fast, on a bike or in a car, but on public roads, bad things can happen really fast.

Add to that the tendency for the British sportsbike boys, like the cruisers in the U.S., to go out and ride in bunches. One can imagine the peer pressure and testosterone-driven egos when the boys hit a famous motorcycling road like the Cat and Fiddle and try to "outdo" each other. Leaning way over in corners to rub the "chicken strips" off the edges of their tires, maybe even trying to "get a knee down," like the racers do. But they are not racers, and they are not on a racetrack.

Each of them who loses it big leaves a terrible wake of pain behind—for their companion riders who watch them die (how awful to carry that for the rest of your life), and for the families that have to hear it later—from the police. All of those individual tragedies are sad to contemplate, and one reflection I often had on the singletracks was that if anything bad did happen, it was going to happen very *slowly*.

In the same way that racebikes make their riders want to *race*, our adventure-touring bikes make us want to, well, adventure-tour. So a sign like the above is a challenge, not a hindrance. Ahead there may be broken pavement, gravel and stones, rutted dirt, water crossings, puddles of mud and/or manure—but we can usually get through.

Another name I came up with for our unhurried but highly "detailed" mode of singletrack travel is "Slow Touring." Like the Slow Food or Slow Blogging movements, it reflects a focus on quality and character over speed and masses of "content."

And where the riding is smooth and easy, with good visibility ahead, it gives you time to think. One day in the mountains, I was thinking about all of the barren peaks in England, Scotland, Wales, and Ireland, wondering why they are not forested. It finally occurred to me that those mountains were not *always* barren. It is apparent from thick stands of spruce in manmade plantations that trees willingly grow there, but when the original forests were cut down, centuries ago—even millennia ago, back when the Romans occupied the British Isles—the trees didn't grow back. Those bare mountains remain spectacular, carpeted in low grasses and heather, and the millions of sheep obviously like them, but it is melancholy to imagine the towering canopies of oaks that must once have graced those peaks.

These are the Wicklow Mountains in Ireland, on our way to the band's first-ever show in Dublin. The plantations of pulpwood are dark patches in the distance, while the foreground is a rare photograph of me taking a photograph—one of my "Action Self-Portraits," with the camera held out in my left hand. Brutus tried taking a few shots looking forward from his bike, a series he called, "Got Your Back."

The focus of my camera angle is the yellow-blossomed shrubs at the roadside, which I had been noticing since we landed at the southeast corner of Ireland, on a ferry from France (after the first three shows, in Finland and Sweden). Like the redbud trees in the eastern U.S. that sent me on a botanical quest in the previous story, "Eastern Resurrection," these yellow blossoms stood out so brightly against the greenery around them, in hedges and along the roadsides, that I wanted to know what they were called.

When we crossed by ferry from Northern Ireland to Troon, Scotland, and I noticed them along the golf course in front of our hotel, I asked the young bellman what they were called. He shrugged and said, "We just calls 'em 'jags,' like when we lose our golf balls in 'em and that." Next morning I asked the hostess at breakfast, and she didn't know either, but must have called the groundskeeper. As we left she handed me a little note reading "gorse," as well as what must be a local name, "wind bushes." (Later I learned it should have read "whin" bushes, which is another ancient name for gorse.)

Further research taught me that they were also called "furze," and a light went on. In Thomas Hardy novels and such, there were characters called furze-cutters, and apparently the wood is oily and burns very hot when dried. In areas where the trees were already clear-cut, shrubs like that would have been the only available fuel. Archaeological studies in Britain have shown that the Romans burned gorse 2,000 years ago, for industries like refining salt. When you see those images of peasants with bundles of sticks on their backs— like that Led Zeppelin album cover—it's gorse, or furze, they were gathering. In another twist, the shrubs were brought to the Pacific Northwest as an ornamental, and soon spread out of control. Like the similarly bright yellow Spanish broom I have written about before, gorse bushes are now considered a pest—a "noxious weed"—in that part of the world.

It seems that throughout Britain, the various strains of gorse are almost always flowering to some degree, leading to a cute old expression, "When the gorse is out of bloom, kissing's out of fashion."

Northern Ireland, yellow gorse
in foreground and behind me

Time and again in our travels around England and Wales, the Roman occupation was brought to our minds. A simple piece of information like the name of a plant, gorse, and learning of its use by the Romans in their local industries like mining, and reflecting on all of those deforested mountains, somehow made the ancient history of Britain seem more real, more relatable—the Romans were destroying the environment for economic reasons 2,000 years ago. They were also building towns and roads, and many place names evoke that era ("*castra*" is Latin for "military camp," thus all of the English towns ending in "caster" or "chester" had Roman origins).

For almost 400 years, from around 43 CE until their empire crumbled, the Romans controlled, exploited, and developed England and Wales, their forces only repelled along a shifting northern border by the Caledonians—the Scots. The famous stone wall the Romans built across the width of England, Hadrian's Wall, had the same purpose as the Great Wall of China—a barrier against the "northern barbarians." (In both cases, those "northern barbarians" may have been equally happy to see that wall go up.)

Little is known about the Roman occupation of Britain, surprisingly, except through archaeological studies. (The Britons were not yet churning out their elegant histories and literary fiction.) However, one may also reflect that 400 years of Roman occupation meant 400 years of *slavery* for the locals, in the Roman mines, foundries, building projects, roadworks, camps, and farms. That long period of suffering and humiliation may help to explain the continuing distrust of continental Europe by the British.

At a remote mountain pass in the Lake District, Brutus and I paused for a break at a wide spot in the road. I read a sign describing the ruins of a nearby Roman fort that had housed a "cohort" of fifty soldiers. The fort was built there to command the Eskdale Valley, still a wild and lonely part of England, and I thought about all of those soldiers sent thousands of miles away from their homes in sunny Italy to hold so many distant corners of the empire, stationed in fortified outposts amid a hostile local population, and often hostile *weather*, too. On a practical level, I wondered how the Roman emperors had been able to find enough reliable and capable governors for all of that territory. (A similar thought had occurred to me earlier in our travels this May, in Scandinavia, when I thought of the Nazis overrunning all of those countries and more—how difficult it must have been to administer so many far-flung countries with hostile populations.)

Some of the oldest tracks in Britain predate the Romans with their penchant for engineering wide, straight roads, and plenty of slave labor to build them. The country lanes wind narrowly through valleys and across mountainsides, simply laid on top of the landscape, like a ribbon, rather than cutting and blasting through it, in the modern fashion. Those roads were designed to allow two horsemen to pass, no more, and most of the traffic would have been on foot—two legs or four. Still today, animal traffic could be more common than vehicles on such country lanes, and I collected a series of "roadblock" photos, when our progress was halted by herds of cows being driven across the lane to another pasture, sheep wandering across in their "free range" areas, and one time in Ireland when a pack of hounds came along, fanned out across the lane from hedge to hedge. Their keepers smiled and waved as we pulled over to let them by.

A quality I have ascribed to roads in North America applies equally well to Europe—perhaps to anywhere: The best roads are the ones no one travels unless they *live* on them.

Another collection I began in my journal and with photos of signposts was of amusing English place names. It is easy enough to look

Roman singletrack, with distance marker, North Yorkshire

at a map of England's villages and find such examples, but these were ones that Brutus and I actually passed through, or near—Dingle, Wincle, Froghall, Glutton, Swineside, Much Marcle, Middle Wallop, Hutton-le-Hole, Winkhill, Tintwistle, Bottomhouse, Foxt, Leek, and Wookey Hole. Those names have a quaint cuteness that is still characteristic of the English, giving each other nicknames like Gazza, Dickie, Deedee, and Pippa. But seriously, if you lived in a village called

Blubberhouses, or Uckinghall, or—I swear—Wetwang, wouldn't you change it?

Welsh place names have a different distinction: most of them are inscrutable to the foreign eye, or tongue. In previous journeys and writings I have listed some scary examples, and this time Brutus

Devon thatched roof

and I stayed in a village whose name seemed a little easier at first—Llandrillo, which could be said in an English or Spanish way. However, we learned that it is properly pronounced "Clan-drith-low." So . . . we give up on Welsh!

Perhaps nowhere in England are history, quaintness, and beauty blended as richly as the western shire of Devon. Viewed from the singletracks, the countryside seems manicured, low hills and cozy valleys in an ancient patchwork of rich green fields bordered in stone walls and hedges; dark, fairy-tale woodlands carpeted in bluebells; and tiny villages with thatched houses and pubs, intricate gardens, and apple-cheeked denizens. Except for the utility wires and cars, it could be 500 years ago.

Outsiders might think of England as London, Manchester, Liverpool, and so on, but away from the cities, the scenery can be richly varied and unexpectedly grand—the North Yorkshire moors and Dales, the Lake District, the Peak District in Derbyshire, and many other pockets of picturesque countryside. Famously, there are spectacular areas in Ireland, Scotland, and Wales, but the variety of landscapes in England is what sets it apart. Places I'd never even heard of, like the Cheddar Gorge (yes, birthplace of the cheese, traditionally aged in the caves under that gorge), proved to be unexpectedly impressive—and called for an immediate halt for Brutus and me to do some riding photographs through it.

Another pleasant aspect of Brutus's and my Slow Touring approach this time was that Brutus designed our daily routes to be fairly short in distance, so we always had time for photographs. We also tried a few different techniques for the inevitable motorcycle-in-landscape shots—including the long view pioneered by Greg Russell in the photograph that ended up being the cover of *Far and Away*. Brutus and I called those the "far and away" shots, and tried to capture such panoramas in places where the scenery was *big*.

Lately I have also been finding that I often prefer shots of landscapes with the rider pictured riding away, rather than toward the viewer. That way the viewer is seeing what the rider was seeing at that moment, and it seems easier to imagine yourself *into* the scene—following that rider.

However, there are some places where you might not want to be following me. (In the photo to the left, you can see the rear tire splashing water, and me leaning right, trying to see around the stone wall ahead—a typical posture on those curving one-lanes.)

The signpost, in the Lake District, points the way to the Wrynose Pass, which cuts off from a road known as "The Struggle" to the high, narrow switchbacks of the Hardknott Pass—the steepest road in Britain. The exclamation mark denotes a warning (someone has scrawled "sheep" in the dirt beside it), and the sign under it reads: "Extreme Caution, Wrynose and Hardknott Passes, Narrow Route, Severe Bends, Gradients Max 30% (1 in 3)."

Imagine a length of wood three feet long, with one end raised a foot high—that is a one-in-three gradient, and it is *steep*. The actual switchbacks climbed even more sharply to their apexes, slick with rain, and that short stretch of Extreme Singletracking was a severe test of riding technique. It demanded delicate balance, throttle control, clutch feathering, gentle rear-wheel braking, and careful leaning and steering to negotiate the nearly 180° bend toward the next sharp incline and turn.

When we had made it, and paused for a breath on the other side, I said to Brutus, "That took everything I know." Brutus replied, "It took some stuff I didn't even know yet!"

Across the Hardknott Pass was the Eskdale Valley, shown above ("far and away"), where I had read about the Roman fort. It was a

much gentler decline, the track looping down the mountain beside a waterfall (in the center) and slopes of grass and rock.

It should be noted that most of these photos were taken by Brutus. He had a new camera that produced great results, especially in the dim light of these rainy or overcast days, and we coined a new motto: "I pick the spots; he takes the shots."

Sometimes my camera and I got lucky and captured "the one" of the day—like descending into a Yorkshire village on another rainy day (a *different* rainy day—we had more than our share). This kind of view often worked well in practical terms, too, because I would be leading (following Brutus's route on the GPS), and if I saw a fetching scene coming up, I would wave Brutus to a stop behind me. Parking at the roadside, I would pull my camera out of the tankbag, then wave him ahead of me when I was ready.

I call these the "Along For the Ride" views, and there's a lot of "English spring" in this one, too.

Generally, though, it was Brutus who really nailed the riding shots this time. One of the most difficult techniques for us amateurs to capture is the "panning shot," taken from the side with the rider sharp in the foreground, and the background blurred by the motion. I have watched professional photographers work on those panning shots, say of racing cars or motorcycles, following their passage with their cameras again and again, just to capture one image that works. So I rarely even try that technique, knowing it is practically always doomed to failure. Brutus, though, is more daring and determined, and one day on a B road in Staffordshire, he managed to get the best

panning shot any of my riding partners have ever taken.

The Romans once claimed, "All roads lead to Rome," and coincidentally (or not), the English have long said the same about London. That makes a good segue to where all of these singletracks (and B roads, A roads, and occasional M ways) were leading us: to the cities where I had to show up and play the drums with Rush. (Why, some people actually thought that was the reason we were *there*!)

After the initial shows in Helsinki, Stockholm, and Malmo, Sweden, we played that first-ever show in Ireland, in Dublin, and that was a thrill. (In the comic movie that opens our *Time Machine* shows, I have a minor role as an Irish cop named O'Malley, and I was delighted when the audience cheered when O'Malley said, "Jesus, Mary, and Joseph—sounds like the damned howling in Hades," and they cheered again when Alex's "Slobovich" mentioned the name "O'Malley.") Then came some good shows in Glasgow, Sheffield, Manchester, Newcastle, Birmingham, and finally London. Rotterdam and Frankfurt would follow, and I always explain that *every* show is important to a dedicated professional, but somehow London, like Toronto, is always "a big one" for me—a kind of hometown show.

Perhaps the most significant time of my youth was spent in London, when I was nineteen and twenty years old, living away from home—so *far* from home—for the first time, and making my own way. I played in a couple of bands around the London pubs, and even at the famous Marquee, as well as some of the universities and dance clubs around the country. (Every time I visit the Lake District, I remember playing in Kendal and Whitehaven back in 1971 with a short-lived band called English Rose—just prior to my "starving artist" period, when that band ran out of work.)

And the shows I *saw* there in those years—like the Who at the Oval Cricket Ground on their *Who's Next* tour, with Rod Stewart and the Faces, Pink Floyd at the Rainbow Theatre, and Tony Bennett at the

London Palladium. ("One of these things is not like the other"—I know. But that *was* a great show, and the drummer, Kenny Clare, was *brilliant*.)

There were some great bands who seem long forgotten, like Hookfoot, made up of several of Elton John's frequent studio musicians, including another great drummer, Roger Pope. My flatmate Brad and I saw them backing Al Kooper at another famous venue, the Roundhouse, and Brad later bought their LP, and we both liked it.

In another connection of memories, on that ride into London from Devon, Brutus and I had a distance to cover and were forced to take the motorway most of the way. (As in the U.S., the "mileage disposal unit.") Out of nowhere I saw the giant stone circle of Stonehenge loom up to my left, right beside the motorway. The memories stirred started with Thomas Hardy's *Tess of the d'Urbervilles*, I guess, and its melodramatic conclusion in that setting. Then Hookfoot's song "Coombe Gallows" began to echo in my head, with some lines about Stonehenge—"Not too far from the Salisbury Plain/ Where the Stonehenge relics stand in vain." I haven't heard that song in nearly forty years, but the link was immediately forged. (Naturally the Spiñal Tap song was in that mix too . . . )

Brutus, in front
of Harrods

On our first tour of the U.K., around 1977, my bandmates and I got our driver, Bert, to take us to Stonehenge when we were traveling nearby. It was twilight, just before they closed the gates, and no one else was around. In those days you could still walk right up to the stones and touch them, and stand in the middle of them and sense their immensity and mystery. The place had the kind of power—of *energy*, if you like—that I have felt at the Mayan ruins in Palenque, the massive pyramids of Teotihuacán near Mexico City, the ruins of the Greek city Ephesus in Turkey, a chief's secret council house in West Africa, and even at NASA's Mission Control at Cape Kennedy or Houston—a lingering vibration in the air that "serious events have passed here."

Around that time, in the late '70s and into the '80s, the band often recorded in London for weeks at a time, and I would commute across the city by bicycle, getting to know it even better. In the late '70s, we played several times at the Hammersmith Odeon, before graduating to the "big barn" at Wembley, where we played many memorable shows. This time we would perform at London's new venue, the O2 Arena, for the first time.

It would also be the first time I had motorcycled in London. Brutus and I followed our GPS units (Dingus and Dick, in this incarnation) right through the center of town. The traffic was dense and aggressive, so it was "edge of the seat" riding, but we could take in the sights (and a few photographs) while standing at red lights. We rode through Kensington and Knightsbridge, past the splendidly rococo Victoria and Albert Museum and the enormous department store, Harrods, past Bond Street and the Ritz, around Piccadilly Circus and down to Pall Mall, passing the tower of Westminster and Big Ben, around Trafalgar Square, and along the Embankment past the Thames, St. Paul's Cathedral, and the Tower of London and Tower Bridge.

While we were stopped at a light, Brutus joked, "Is there a sight we've missed?"

Obviously, it was quite a contrast from the singletrack lanes of Devon we had left on that morning, or the North Yorkshire rambles of previous days. But we made it to work in time for me to do an oil change on my bike, for both of us to download and edit the photos from the past couple of days (sometimes taking forty or fifty shots *each* in that time), then to our "real jobs." Brutus had his route-planning and accommodation-booking for the upcoming days, and loading the bikes onto the trailer, with help from Michael and our excellent European driver, H.P. (for Hans-Peter—an amiable and conscientious German). After an interview with a drum magazine, I would head to the stage for soundcheck, then dinner with the Guys at Work, warm-up, and showtime.

In a previous story collected in *Far and Away*, "The Power of Magical Thinking," I concluded with a photograph of the audience I had taken from the stage in Santiago, Chile—the first time in my life I had ever done that, and a memorable occasion to capture that way.

I decided to do the same in London, as another memorable occasion, for all of the reasons outlined above. On my way back up the steps and across the stage to the drums for the encore, I had Lorne hand me my camera, and while Alex and Geddy were tossing out T-shirts to the crowd, I snapped this photograph.

Like the photo of the Santiago audience, this one tells many stories. First of all, it's of me and my bandmates headlining in front of 13,517 people in London, England—exactly forty years since I arrived there as an ambitious teenager.

To the right of my sixteen-inch cymbal is a girl at the barricade holding a pair of my drumsticks—sent out in response to the sign in front of her, referencing the "Prize Every Time" subtitle of *Far and Away*. In the middle, a guy holds up a banner reading "Kufi Swap"— one name for the African-style hats I wear onstage, which he is also wearing, wanting to trade. I sent him sticks and let him keep the hat.

Just out of view to my right were the audience "stars" of the night for me—a man with his daughter, aged around ten or eleven, I'd guess, in the second row. Both of them wore Rush T-shirts, and the girl was holding a sign that began with "My Dad Made Me . . ." but I couldn't read the rest. During the show I glanced their way from time to time and noticed that the dad was the obvious fan, while the girl had certain favorite Rush songs—ones she knew and could sing along with. Perhaps the sign referred to the moment during our performance of "Overture" from *2112*, near the end of the show—two crew members, Anson and Doug, appear in gorilla and chicken costumes, and act out some little absurdity. (I have noted before—"we entertain the crowd; the crew entertains *us*.")

On May 21, for example, the night of the "Rapture Fail" (some loonies, I mean people of faith, predicted the end of the world and ascension to heaven on that date), the guys presented an absolutely *brilliant* vignette in Newcastle. A third crew member named Grit, with messiah-like hair and beard, stumbled out onto stage left dressed in a bedsheet, looking bewildered and perplexed, and carrying . . . an oar. The gorilla and chicken crossed from stage right and escorted him away, gently and sympathetically.

Obviously the dad and his daughter were aware of those characters, because as soon as we started "Overture" and the lights came up, I looked out and saw the dad wearing a gorilla mask and the girl in a feathered yellow chicken mask. I guess that was what "My Dad Made Me" do—but that "gameness," her very presence with her dad, and her appreciation for the music, deserved the sticks I sent her, through Michael.

And you know, in an unprecedented break, I'm going to stop this story right here—with one final, favorite image, from the Vosges Mountains of Alsace, France. It was taken on a wonderful piece of road that made me think, "Why isn't this road *famous*?"

That kinetic moment, between the final two European shows in Rotterdam and Frankfurt, can hint at part of the next story, about Finland, Sweden, Estonia, Latvia, Germany, France, Belgium, Switzerland (ah!)—and the towns and cities, like Bruges, where Brutus, Michael, and I laughingly celebrated the movie *In Bruges*, and Paris, where Brutus had his first visit to the City of Light. We did honorable battle with the traffic of the Place de la Concorde and the Champs-Elysées, and with a seafood feast at La Coupole in Montparnasse.

So, I guess the sequel will cover the "left-hand-drive" part of Europe. That makes a good division point, and an obvious title: Singletrack Minds: The Other Side of the Road.

# THE FRYING PAN
# AND THE FREEZER

JULY 2011

**During the first run** of this year's continuation of the *Time Machine* tour (part deux) in April, Michael and I motorcycled between shows in the eastern United States and Canada. As described in "Eastern Resurrection," the weather was cold, wet, and windy—even snowy farther north. Verily, we did suffer most grievously, and there were great chatterings of teeth and shiverings of limb.

Likewise, as told in "Singletrack Minds in the Sceptered Isle," May in Europe was cold and wet for Brutus and me. (If not quite so biblical.)

However, back in the U.S. in June, riding with Michael again, all that changed. We went from the freezer to the frying pan—then back into the freezer.

Hence a couple of other titles I considered for this story: "A Season of Fire and Ice" (which felt too similar to an earlier *Far and Away* story, "Fire on Ice") and "A Season of Swelter and Snow." But the best metaphor seemed to be the frying pan.

The above photo was taken in Big Bend National Park, near the Rio Grande in South Texas. It shows me riding the remote and unpaved Terlingua Ranch Road through the Chihuahuan Desert. It was June 13, and the temperature was 112°F. It felt like an oppressive oven.

It felt *deadly*.

Apart from residents of the American Southwest, or the desert areas of North Africa, most sensible persons have never experienced such hellish degrees of heat. (I have long treasured a bit of weather trivia: which two states have never recorded temperatures above 100°? One is Alaska, not surprisingly, but the other is Hawaii—kept more temperate by its mid-ocean setting and steady trade winds.)

In any case, let me tell you: 112° is *brutally* hot. Especially on a motorcycle, on a dusty gravel road, under the midday sun, wearing full protective gear. But you would be suffering even if you were naked in the shade. (And if that isn't a fetching title for a painting, a song, a poem, or a story: "Naked in the Shade.")

The landscape around us was signature Chihuahuan Desert, a regular, seemingly patterned array of creosote bushes, grassy clumps, and spiky yuccas. It seemed impossible to imagine that I had once seen that same baking landscape covered with *snow*—in March 2003, when I spent a few days at Big Bend on the road trip that would become *Traveling Music*.

Beneath our wheels, the surface of Terlingua Ranch Road varied according to small degrees of elevation. Along the ridges and higher stretches, it was packed dirt and gravel, easy enough to navigate. However, the lower-lying areas were deep, loose gravel and sand—the worst possible conditions for big, heavy bikes like ours. A berm of soft gravel or a deep rut filled with sand can take control of your front wheel, send the bike slewing around, and easily put you down. You always have to be ready to roll the power on, to keep the front wheel light, and to put a foot down sometimes, too, to keep the bike upright. Like riding in crosswinds, it was a constant wrestling match, and in such withering heat, it was another reason we didn't want to have to start picking up bikes. That would soon drain us completely.

So we motored our way along in first gear, slowly and carefully.

This photo shows Michael in a section of loose gravel like that, creeping along with both feet poised like outriggers to "dab" the ground if necessary.

Two key sensory elements that photographs cannot convey are temperature and smell. I have written before about cold winter days and my belief that snow has a distinct fragrance. In extremely hot and dry places, I am equally sure that *heat* has a smell. And just as with very cold air, in such conditions it can seem difficult just to draw a breath.

It is the nature of dry air, whether hot or cold, to carry little scent—

a molecular thing—but there is a certain essence that seems to pervade every desert when the temperatures are extreme: baked rock, baked dust, baked vegetation—maybe just baked *planet*.

The American deserts vary greatly in their type and pattern of flora: for example, Joshua tree and creosote in the Mojave; mesquite and cactus in the Sonora; sage and juniper in the Great Basin. In each case, during rare spells of cool, wet weather the deserts become amazingly fragrant. Creosote actually gets its name from the way it smells in the rain, and that's also when sage most lives up to its characteristic spicy perfume. But in every desert, when the mercury gets above 100°F, those delicate aromas dull into a harsh, clanging monotone. When I think of what that smells like, I think, "Heat."

The world is an oven, and *you* are in the roasting pan.

Like extreme cold, extreme heat is dangerous, and when you feel the sheer oppression of it closing around you or the faintness brought on by the slightest over-exertion (like wrestling the bikes against the loose road with your shoulders, legs, and body, and even the *thought* of having to pick them up), you become aware of how tenuous your existence could be in such conditions.

By way of illustration, if I'm in Quebec in winter and the temperature falls below about –15°C (5°F), I don't go out snowshoeing or cross-country skiing alone. An injury from one of my frequent falls, or even a broken binding or ski tip, would likely be the end. The situation for Michael and me in this desolate place, in such intolerable heat, was similar. We had plenty of gas and water, yet remained only one mishap or misstep away from the edge of survival. We hadn't seen one other vehicle, or building, along that lonely road. If either of us had a mechanical problem or fell and hurt himself, we would both be stranded.

Perhaps we'd be able to summon help, maybe from the satellite phone (though it never seems to work when we need it most), but if not, the other would have to ride for rescue. I had experienced that kind of desperate situation before, in the Sahara when, mired in deep sand, Brutus's clutch had failed "way out there," where we had also lost the supposed "road." As I headed back alone toward Douz, Tunisia, hoping to arrange for a truck to rescue Brutus and his bike, I was sliding in the sand, trying to stay upright and keep moving, and nervously watching the bike's temperature gauge rise ever higher, toward the red zone. Tense and terrified, I believed that if anything happened to me or my bike then, *both* of us were going to die.

Terlingua Cemetery, 112°F

That story eventually had a happy ending, but in this case, I was not over-exaggerating the situation—not "catastrophizing," like I know I sometimes do. On the National Park Service website for Big Bend, there's a section called "How NOT to die in the desert." One caution reads, "This environment is not forgiving; hikers have died here after going just a few hours without water." Then it lists a few daunting cautionary tales from past years, grim accounts of lost or stranded people dying from heat and thirst.

That would be, without question, a *hell* of a way to die.

Still, that day in Big Bend may have been the hottest for Michael and me, and thus the most dangerous, but it was only one of a series of days that saw temperatures over 100°. Two days in Arizona, for example, topped out at 110. (My original plan to escape to the cooler mountains had been ruled out by the record forest fires raging along the Arizona–New Mexico line—talk about "extreme heat.")

Bottom line—we broiled in Arizona, too. And Nevada, where Vegas also hit 110 degrees.

Earlier that month, we also encountered high temperatures in the southeastern U.S., amplified by extreme humidity. Our first ride started at a truck stop in Montgomery, Alabama, then led us through

Selma. When I was designing that route the day before, looking over the map for possible "areas of interest," I remembered newspaper photographs and television stories about Alabama from my youth in the early '60s. And a number-one song from 1965, "Eve of Destruction," with these lines:

*Think of all the hate there is in Red China*
*Then take a look around to Selma, Alabama*

Ah, so many stories, just about that song from the summer before I turned thirteen—written by nineteen-year-old P.F. Sloan, recorded by Barry McGuire as a weary, late-night "guide track" that became the master, and the drummer—Hal Blaine, ubiquitous in those days, on records by everybody from the Beach Boys to the Byrds to Simon and Garfunkel.

I started taking drum lessons that fall, on my thirteenth birthday, and after school I would play along with the radio—often to Hal Blaine's drumming, though I didn't know it. Another drummer of my generation expressed his disillusion when he learned, "My six favorite drummers were all Hal Blaine!"

When "Eve of Destruction" made number one on the charts, an "answer song," "Dawn of Correction," was hastily released, with an optimistic, pro-American dialectic. One of its composers, John Madara, later dated proto-starlet Joey Heatherton and accompanied her on a Bob Hope tour to Vietnam. After seeing what American soldiers were going through, he felt "a little uncomfortable about those lyrics."

Anyway, with those stories and songs in my head, I titled that day's ride the "Civil Rights Tour"—always glad to include a little history along the way—as we meandered our way through the Deep South on our way to New Orleans.

That shameful time of upheaval and violence proved to be fascinating to reflect upon and deserves to be remembered. Segregation was apartheid, and the vote was denied to the African-American citizens by both political maneuvering and bullying.

Montgomery is the capital of Alabama, and its part in the story came early, in 1955. In December of that year, an African-American woman named Rosa Parks was arrested for refusing to give up her seat for a white person. (Today there is a section of Interstate 10 in Los Angeles, among others, named after Rosa Parks. Just a few years ago a stretch of Interstate 55 in Missouri was given her name in response to the KKK's wish to sponsor it. )

French Quarter,
New Orleans

Way down South

A year later, in December 1956, the Supreme Court declared seg-regated buses to be unconstitutional. That was the beginning of an historical "correction" of sweeping effect, but even a full decade later, the racist environment was little improved.

On March 7, 1965, a march was planned from Selma to Montgomery —a day that became known to history as "Bloody Sunday." State and local police attacked the 600 marchers with billy clubs and tear gas. A second march was planned for a few days later, but injunctions were levied, and more violence was threatened, so when Martin Luther King was confronted by a wall of "peace officers" on Edmund Pettus Bridge, outside Selma, he prudently declared that day to be a "cere-monial" march. He turned his people around—a courageous and wise choice, avoiding violence while continuing to fight.

There are many dramatic levels in that story—the white supporters from the North who were brutalized or killed, the Jewish rabbis in the "front line" of those marches, and the strict adherence the protestors paid to legal strictures, which allowed them ultimately to triumph.

The simple result was that on March 21, a five-day march finally reached the Capitol building in Montgomery—though protected by 2,000 soldiers, 1,900 members of the Alabama National Guard (under federal authority), and uncounted FBI agents and federal marshals.

So as Michael and I rode between Montgomery and Selma, I was considering all of that, and my mental radio couldn't help but play

Lynyrd Skynyrd's "Sweet Home Alabama," a title that now emblazons the state's license plates.

As one who regularly travels in all of the American states, filtering through traffic and looking at the different plates for many miles, I tend to notice their slogans. I used to like Pennsylvania's, for example: "You've Got a Friend in Pennsylvania." Then they changed it to a dreary web address. Same with Indiana, who used to have "Amber Waves of Grain" and "The Crossroads of America," but now offer a dot.com. Bah.

Alabama's license-plate slogan was once "Stars Fell on Alabama," the title of a romantic standard from 1934 by Frank Perkins and Mitchell Parish. Parish's lyrics are said to refer to a meteor shower in 1833, "when the stars fell," but of course they are a metaphor for . . . love. Or something like it.

> *We lived our little drama*
> *We kissed in a field of white*
> *And stars fell on Alabama*
> *Last night*

Much is implied by that "stellar metaphor," it seems to me, but it is a nice anthem for the state. No bragging about its skies being uniquely blue, as in "Sweet Home Alabama," and without any defensive bluster—like Skynyrd's attack on Canadian Neil Young, who had dared to criticize the state's racial backwardness in a couple of his songs. This "Sweet Home Alabama" verse speaks for itself:

> *Well I heard Mister Young sing about her*
> *Well, I heard ol' Neil put her down*
> *Well, I hope Neil Young will remember*
> *A Southern man don't need him around anyhow*

My taste in Classic Southern Rock might favor the more eclectic and nuanced Allman Brothers Band, but I don't presume to criticize a venerable institution like Lynyrd Skynyrd—especially because my good friend Michael Cartellone has been their drummer for many years (funny that his previous band was called Damn Yankees). But none of the three guys who wrote "Sweet Home Alabama" were even *from* there, and their producer, Al Kooper (born Alan Kuperschmidt in Brooklyn), couldn't have been too sympathetic to the song's redneck

ethos. (Though Kooper's voice appears in the background of the above verse, mimicking Neil Young singing "Southern Man.")

But when it came to songs of racial protest, Neil Young's "Alabama" and "Southern Man" could never approach the bitter fury of Nina Simone's "Mississippi Goddam."

*Alabama's gotten me so upset*
*Tennessee made me lose my rest*
*And everybody knows about Mississippi Goddam*

Nina Simone also recorded a song made famous by Billie Holiday, "Strange Fruit." In more recent times, a 1993 live recording by Jeff Buckley (whose early demise was another tragedy) is also unforgettable.

*Southern trees bear strange fruit,*
*Blood on the leaves and blood at the root,*
*Black body swinging in the Southern breeze,*
*Strange fruit hanging from the poplar trees.*

Another terrible fact that should be remembered forever is that in the early twentieth century, just 100 years ago, an annual average of 100 black men—one every three days—were being tortured and executed by mobs of white Americans. That is a reminder of how far we have come, which echoes the anthem sung by Martin Luther King and his followers, "We Shall Overcome." But it also illustrates how far we had to go—and what a journey is ahead of us yet, before there is justice for all.

Like the stories of William Faulkner or Flannery O'Connor, songs like "Sweet Home Alabama" and "Strange Fruit" are the text of the South, old and new. The great American songwriter Johnny Mercer was a Southerner, too, and one verse in his lyrics for "Blues in the Night" defines a certain geography of that region—that "distinct society," in the words coined for Canadians to refer to Quebec.

"Dem Old Cotton
Fields, Back Home"

*From Natchez to Mobile*
*From Memphis to St. Joe*
*Wherever the four winds blow*

Interestingly, St. Joe—St. Joseph, Missouri—might have stood for the route *out of* the South, being the westernmost point reachable by rail until after the Civil War, and thus a metaphor, a synecdoche, for "the West." The other three cities, Natchez, Mobile, and Memphis, basically triangulate the Mississippi Delta. Cotton and sugarcane country. Slave country.

As Michael and I rode across the sweltering farmlands of Alabama, Mississippi, and Louisiana, with all of those associations with civil rights and the racial strife in the "Old South" alive in my mind, I decided that the worst life imaginable must have been that of an African slave in the Mississippi Delta. To imagine the fear and misery of being wrenched from their homes and put into chains, surviving an unimaginably inhumane ocean journey, to end up laboring in the fields all day, every day, in that kind of heat, with no choice, no reward, no freedom, and no hope—it's hard to imagine anything worse. In the past, when I contemplated the "worst life" scenario, it seemed to me that being a coal miner must be about the worst life I could imagine. But slavery . . .

In cooking, "poached" means cooked in water—and here is a fine example. This image would seem to be about as far as possible from the arid Big Bend photos shown earlier, but it was only a few days before, and not that far—southern Louisiana. It was 98°F, and with the obvious "humidity"—above, below, and all around me—the sticky swampland air felt like a hot sponge, even more uncomfortable than the baking desert. Riding in from the Civil Rights Tour, Michael and I spent a full day in and around New Orleans, which is rare for us. We usually avoid the big cities except for show days, but New Orleans is worth it, for its uniqueness and charm—and the opportunity to stay in a good hotel and eat at a fine restaurant.

Also, because we were already in town for the next night's show, I could plan a show-day ride that didn't actually have to *go* anywhere. Perfect!

The official band itinerary showed the distance from the hotel to the arena as "0.9 blocks," but Michael and I managed to ride more than 200 miles between those two points. That might stand as a record for a shunpiker—those who avoid all "direct routes" to anywhere.

Scanning the map the day before, I saw a gray line that ran straight south from New Orleans and ended at a dot called Lafitte, and a memory bell sounded ("that rings a bell"). Some years ago, in *Smithsonian* magazine, I read a fascinating story about the pirate Jean Lafitte. Around the turn of the nineteenth century, Lafitte and his older brother Pierre had a fleet of ships working out of a stronghold called Barataria in the Louisiana bayous. From there they sold smuggled and plundered goods to the merchants of New Orleans—Jean the pirate, Pierre the dealer. During the War of 1812, Jean Lafitte and his Baratarians played a key role for the American side in the Battle of New Orleans against the British, and were pardoned by the American government for their previous crimes.

A dot at the end of a lonely little road, along with a little history like that, was lure enough for this shunpiker. The ride down to Lafitte carried us through typical Louisiana swampland, past trees draped in

Spanish moss, across a high bridge over the Intracoastal Waterway, and to the remote shrimp-boat harbor of Lafitte. From there we doubled back a short way and headed farther south—as far down the Mississippi as the road would carry us.

Farther, actually, because long stretches toward the bottom of that road were underwater. Anywhere else in the country, such roadways would have been classed as "flooded," and closed—but here, it just seemed to be accepted as normal.

Cars and trucks passed, pushing up bow waves and leaving wakes—just as we did—to and from the harbors for shrimp boats (inspiring quotations from *Forrest Gump* from Michael) and oil-rig outfitters. We saw many scary-looking industrial plants, like the one in the background of the earlier photo of me splashing along the road. Chemical and petroleum refineries seem to line the banks of the Mississippi all the way down from at least Missouri.

We also saw many relics from Hurricane Katrina, even more than five years later: prefab buildings erected beside the bare foundations of where a home had stood, and even a few standing ruins of larger buildings, their second-floor windows smashed and filled with debris. Another American tragedy.

When I stopped to take a photo of Michael's impressive fountain of spray, I put my boots down through the water to the road and straddled my motorcycle. As I toed the shifter into neutral and grabbed the camera from my tankbag, I happened to look down, and was amazed to see a dinner-plate-sized crab scuttling by. I just stopped and stared, in surprise and delight, while the crab paused beside me, as if to hold his ground, and gave me a baleful look. I learned later that he was a male blue crab, called a "Jimmy" (young females are "Sallys," and older females "Sooks")—but at that moment, the germane fact was that the "territory" Jimmy was so ready to defend was *the surface of the road*.

The dark green algae around him is convincing evidence that those stretches of road are flooded frequently, maybe always, and that algae was also very slippery under our wheels. In deeper stretches, the bow wave was strong enough to sweep my feet right off the pegs and splash high over my windscreen and helmet.

That was . . . interesting, but we were glad to get back to drier roads, heading north again to catch a ferry across the Mississippi,

then returning to the city on the other bank to catch a second ferry back into New Orleans.

There we had the hottest moment we, or our motorcycles, had ever experienced. Traffic on the bridge over the Mississippi into the city center was at a near standstill, and as we straddled the bikes in that 98° sponge, surrounded by waves of engine heat, exhaust fumes, and tortured metal, both of our instrument panels started flashing a red warning light, for "overheating." We knew just how they felt . . .

After a few days of that kind of swelter, Michael and I began riding out earlier, to put in some miles when it was cooler. Though that was relative—the above photo was taken a few days later, riding out of Lajitas, Texas (another echo of *Traveling Music*, in 2003), near Big Bend. It was around 6:00 a.m., and the temperature was already in the eighties.

(My original route for that morning had included another long stretch of gravel, but after the previous day's sufferings, Michael said, "You're not doing *that* again." I snorted huffily and pretended to resist, then agreed, "Hmpf—I'm not doing *that* again.")

After a glorious, roller-coaster ride along the river in the pre-dawn twilight, and breakfast in Marfa (I was sad to see that the diner where

I stopped in 2003, Mike's Place, was gone), by the time we reached El Paso just after noon, it was 107 scorching degrees.

The haze along the horizon and around the rising sun in this photo tells another story—about the forest fires devouring huge areas of Arizona. As we loaded the bikes that mid-June morning, my nostrils picked up the unmistakable smell of burning forest—from almost 500 miles northwest of us. Normally Big Bend country, like Death Valley or Grand Canyon, has air so supernaturally clear that you can see the folds in mountains and canyons from many miles away, but all over the Southwest we would notice that smoke fuzzing the skies.

After El Paso, when Michael and I were headed up toward a show in Phoenix, I had hoped to route us into the mountains of Eastern Arizona, up that amazing Highway 191, and maybe stay the night in Show Low—but now that area was smack in the middle of a record-breaking forest fire.

So instead we rode southwest from a truck stop in Casa Grande, Arizona, through the hot cactus desert (110°F) of the Tohono O'odham reservation. We were near the Mexican border again, and on the lonely backroads we traveled, we encountered a staggering number of Border Patrol vehicles blazing by in their green and white paint. There was also an equally staggering number of roadside shrines—crosses of wood or metal, with colored-glass candle holders and plastic flowers—like I had often seen in Mexico. At first I thought they were for victims of auto accidents, as usual, but I soon saw that there were just too many of those shrines, along straight stretches of road, and sometimes they seemed to commemorate entire families.

They were, I realized, memorials for people who had died trying to cross the desert to a new life in the United States. Sometimes groups of them were betrayed and stranded by their supposed guides, the "coyotes," to die in horrible ways. Sure, they were illegal aliens, or would-be undocumented workers, as you prefer, but—what to do? The great Western writer Edward Abbey's suggestion was to catch them, give them guns and ammunition, and send them back to fix the things that made them leave.

But Edward Abbey was a conservative pragmatist, and I am a bleeding-heart libertarian—who also happens to be fond of Latin-Americans. The "libertarian" in me thinks people should be able to go where they want to go, and the "bleeding heart" doesn't want them to suffer needlessly. In any case, such wrenching stories are surely part of another ongoing American tragedy. At one of our roadside stops,

Michael mentioned that a large part of the border patrol's duties was actually saving people like that, and I knew that was true.

But I still didn't like their quasi-military *presence* everywhere, and I sure didn't like their omnipotence—stopping our bus and searching it whenever they felt like it, for example. Under the Department of Homeland Security, they had too much power. I always think of a scene in Derek Lundy's *Borderlands*, when he described riding his motorcycle in Texas, in Big Bend country, near the Mexican border. He was stopped by the green-and-whites, and his motorcycle's luggage was thoroughly searched—with no probable cause whatsoever. When they let him go, he reported, "I got my constitutionally violated ass out of there."

Michael and I followed an enjoyable, deserted two-lane blacktop north through the Vulture Mountains (great name for that deadly

environment). Circling east, we climbed higher, into the Bradshaw Mountains, to Prescott (5,400 feet) for the night. As we followed the winding road upward in long sweeping bends, I watched the digital thermometer on my motorcycle fall, one or two degrees at a time, all the way down to a relatively cool 96°.

And you know—it *did* feel much better!

The following day led us down through the quirky little town of Jerome, Arizona, which is perched on the edge of a cliff. Nowadays it is a "ghost town for tourists," with only a few hundred inhabitants, but it is also somewhat of an artists retreat. And like many little places I encounter, Jerome has a rich and colorful history. Little-known places like Jerome (though among "famous residents," they list Maynard James Keenan from the band Tool) always tempt me to dash off on another tangent about their amazing histories—but I try to leave interested readers with a hint of where the stories live, and let them explore on their own if they wish. (Sounds like a good recipe for education!)

Three fun facts about Jerome:

1) In 1903, a New York newspaper dubbed Jerome "the wickedest town in the West."

2) The town was named after a New York financier who never visited the place, just invested in the mines—which brought in billions in copper, gold, and silver ore for seventy years.

3) In the early twentieth century, the miners were infiltrated by union organizers from the IWW (International Workers of the World, or the "Wobblies"). The "communist agitators" were rounded up, roughed up, shoved into railroad cattlecars, and dumped in Kingman under threat of death if they returned. It became known in labor history as the "Jerome Deportation."

From Jerome, Michael and I struck off along a remote National Forest road in the pinewoods (well west of the fires), and got our daily dose of off-pavement exploring.

Lately Michael and I have adopted the method Brutus and I used in Europe to get our riding photographs. Because both of us had cameras, one would ride by while the other photographed, then keep riding on while watching for another good background, where he would stop to shoot a few of the following rider. "Leapfrog photography," we called it. It also happened that the camera Brutus had—a Panasonic Lumix with a Leica lens—took particularly good pictures in dim light. That had been well proven in England, and after I bought the same camera for Michael, we would notice the same effect in the similarly gloomy light of the Pacific Northwest. With both of us taking photographs, we could collect plenty of them without taking too much time from the day's journey.

That day we got a double dose of off-pavement riding, as we worked our way southeast to the Apache Trail. We had ridden that road a few years before with Master of All Things Creative Greg Russell, and it might stand as a paragon for our kind of motorcycling. A little over twenty miles of gravel, decently graded and not too soft, followed by the same distance of twisty pavement, low speed and highly technical, following the Salt River down toward Phoenix.

It was almost enough to let you forget that it was 107°F all around you.

But you couldn't ignore that harsh reality.

During a series of shows in Southern California, I was able to "commute" from home, which was nice. Though I was only "half-home"—still mentally in mid-tour, in mid-flight—half was better than none.

Apache Trail

On the day of the next show, in Vegas on June 24, Michael and I left Los Angeles at 6:00 a.m., hoping that riding out early would help us avoid traffic—but we knew it wouldn't beat the heat. We crossed L.A. on Interstate 10, then cut off to Twentynine Palms and "the scenic route" to Vegas, through the Mojave Desert, with its Joshua trees, creosote, and low, wrinkled brown mountains. By 9:00 a.m., when we hit Old Route 66 and Roy's Motel at Amboy, the temperature had already topped 100°F.

What a relief, then, in the days of late June, to climb into the Sierra Mountains of California—the Range of Light. We rode west from Reno across the Ebbetts Pass, at 8,730 feet, surrounded by cool thin air, sweet-smelling pine forests, and lingering banks of snow at the road-side. Like many of the Sierra passes, that road was shown on the map as "CLOSED IN WINTER," because of the great amount of snow the area received—averaging over forty feet annually.

We were comfortable in our riding clothes, breathing fresh and fra-grant mountain air (often suddenly chilly from blowing across those

snowbanks), and curving our way through spectacular forested scenery below snow-frosted peaks. At such times I often think of an old expression of my dad's, "Now, this is a treat instead of a treatment!"

Still farther north, and still higher up, we would see a lot more snow—several times blocking our way, on National Forest tracks in Oregon and Washington State. As I have pointed out before, in the highest mountains of the West, June is still late winter. Our friend Tom Marinelli joined us in Ashland, Oregon, and we rode together up through central Oregon to Crater Lake.

Like Big Bend and Grand Canyon, the scale of Crater Lake is difficult to register when you stand before it, and even harder to carry away with you. No matter how many times I revisit majestic landscapes like that, I am freshly amazed. At over 6,000 feet of elevation, the lake itself is about five miles in diameter, and nearly *two thousand* feet deep—one of the deepest lakes in the world. Its water is nearly all snowmelt, and thus it is also one of the *clearest* lakes in the world.

Here is a glimpse of Crater Lake in passing, with Wizard Island (the original volcano's cinder cone) to the left.

Michael and I had ridden through Crater Lake National Park the previous summer, in the opposite direction, with Greg Russell. That had been in August, and we had been able to ride all the way around the lake that time. Now it was June, and much of that East Rim Road still lay under the vast snowfields that remained—from the average *forty-five feet* of snow the area received each winter. Another land of extremes.

(I would like to go snowshoeing there one day—to experience the sensation of walking across a landscape that is four stories below my feet.)

The highway running west of Crater Lake was open, but there was still plenty of snow around. The road was sometimes just a plowed trench between immense white cliffs.

My chosen destination for that night was Bend, Oregon, which I hadn't visited since my *Ghost Rider* ramblings, back in '98 and '99. Before that, the only thing I knew about Bend was that it was the hometown of a minor character in Jack Kerouac's *On the Road*. But again, any association—any memory bell—is enough to make a destination for me. I had liked the area and the town—especially the motel, with rooms right beside a swift little river, the most pleasant of night music. So I led us back to the same motel, the Riverhouse, and found it little changed (in a good way!).

Bend is also notable for being on the natural boundary between the Cascade Mountains and the desert they shadow: the Great Basin. I remembered riding east from there into the basin-and-range sagelands of Eastern Oregon and Nevada, treeless and vast, and this time I noticed that as we approached the town from the west, through the forested mountains, sage bushes began to appear under the pines—gradually fading from one vegetation zone into another.

From Bend, Tom, Michael, and I headed northwest, toward the next show near Portland, and now we were in the true Pacific Northwest—high mountains with dense forests of tall evergreens, hooded with cloud and dripping with rain.

Another American tragedy was present there, too—massive areas of ragged clear-cut forest, sometimes disguised by what are called "scenic corridors" (just enough trees left to frame the highway), or miles of uniform plantations—tree farms—with signs informing you when they were "harvested," and when they were replanted. They were *trees*, all right, but it didn't look like a *forest*.

In the Pacific Northwest, as in Canada's British Columbia to the north, logging was a major industry, and thus a source of many jobs. That's important, no question, and it is one threshold where I part company with organizations like Greenpeace. Speaking with one of their advocates once, I said I would find it hard to shut down any industry, even coal mining, when it would put so many blameless, hard-working people out of a job. The Greenpeace guy said he had no problem with bringing it all down, and he meant it, but . . . I'm a bleeding-heart libertarian.

In any case, it's hard for me to get *too* judgmental about lumbering, because I like things made of wood.

Drums, for example.

Houses.

Books.

But I am glad we have those national parks, at least, to protect some of it for the future—and even for the present. Because I enjoy visiting them *now*, and in the West, they are often reachable on days off.

After the Portland show, we said goodbye to Tom, and Dave drove Michael and me to a truck stop in Grand Mound, Washington, just south of the state capital, Olympia. We set out in the morning to circle Olympia National Park, passing through Aberdeen, the hometown

of Kurt Cobain—another American tragedy. As we waited at a red light, I pointed out a sign with the city's slogan: "Come as You Are," one of Cobain's many great songs—and a clever welcome to visitors.

Michael said Nirvana songs filled his helmet for the rest of that rainy ride.

The weather was the kind that created the temperate rainforest we were passing all morning: rain. The Olympic Peninsula contained the wettest region of the continental states, averaging 135 inches annually, and the landscape around us was a blurry watercolor of dark green and gray. Glimpses into the roadside woods showed lush ferns and moss among the gnarled pillars of the treetrunks.

The downpour was constant, with occasional heavier spells, and the air was damp and chilly. We sensed rather than saw some hints of spectacular views to the left—the Pacific—but mostly just concentrated on riding safely and getting by the slower traffic, especially the huge, double-trailer logging trucks. They threw up a cloud of spray all around that made trying to pass them treacherous. You had to hang a long way back, where you could see past the obscuring mist of their passage, and watch for a long, open stretch where you could make a safe pass.

From Port Angeles, at the north end of the Olympic Peninsula, I picked up my passport stamp at the Olympic National Park Visitor Center, and we crossed to Vancouver Island by ferry. Landing at Victoria, we rode another seventy miles to a second ferry, from Nanaimo to the city of Vancouver.

There we spent a pleasant evening at the home of my brother, Danny, and his family, feasting on a meal prepared by the third member of our Scooter Trash gang, Brutus. At the arena the next day, the last day of June, Michael and I were also joined by another frequent riding guest, Brian Catterson, editor-in-chief of *Motorcyclist* magazine.

Usually we take Brian riding in the rain—it has always seemed to

work out that way—but this time the weather gods smiled upon him. And us. With Brian riding my spare bike, after the Vancouver show the three of us rode south from a town in Washington called Sedro-Woolley (an irresistible name—though it should be noted that the town was originally called "Bug," which hints at another place with history). We curved along the foothills of the Cascades, then higher, toward the night's destination of Mount Rainier National Park.

It was July 1, Canada Day, but we were still in the "freezer," surrounded by vast amounts of snow that remained from the more than *seventy* feet that fell in that area over a typical winter.

Under bright blue sky and brilliant sun, the scenery was unparalleled—immaculate. Approaching Mount Rainier from the north side, its 14,400-foot dome appeared above the lower forested peaks as if luminous, lit from within, like an illusion created by a special effects generator.

This little gravel road led through a northern section of the national park, and I had seen on the map that it was going to end—one way or another. It turned out to be lingering snowfields on a northern loop around 4,300 feet that turned us back, but no matter—I had drawn that little side trip into the route as "optional," for if we had time. The sidetrack turned out to be well worth it, beginning with lunch at the "Historical" Carbonado Saloon, in the tiny village of that name on the northern edge of Mount Rainier National Park. Carbonado, true to its name, was a former coal-mining town—a *company* town—that once rivaled Tacoma for size, but now has dwindled to a few hundred residents. (Another worthwhile story for interested travelers—or armchair travelers.)

Oh yes—I mentioned that I had "drawn" that dirt road into the route. I chose that word literally, meaning drawn with pen on paper (traditional GPS: "Get a Pen Stupid"). That was because somehow the software maps for our master navigation program, "Mother," had a strange and inexplicable *gap* in that region. Mother didn't know *any* of the roads, even major ones, so Michael had been unable to translate my route, highlighted on the map, into data for our on-bike units, Doofus and Dingus.

So yours truly had to be Doofus for the next couple of days—the old-school navigational device guiding Michael and Brian across Washington State. I used the paper map for reference occasionally, but mainly followed one I had drawn myself. In the olden days, I had learned to sketch a simplified line-drawing of the day's route, showing only the relevant information of highway numbers, towns at junctions, and other town names that seemed as though they might be useful when I stood at an intersection, wondering which way to turn.

It made me very busy that first day—riding the ride (looking after my own safety and "place on the road"), *leading* the ride (making sure Michael and Brian always knew what I was going to do, and glancing back from time to time to see that they were always in view), and navigating, too. But it worked out fine. When a doubt appeared in my inner Doofus, I signaled the boys to the side of the road and had another look at the map.

By late afternoon, we were passing through the gates of Mount Rainier National Park, collecting another passport stamp, and heading for our accommodations at the Paradise Inn. It stood just below the mountain, at 5,400 feet, and was surrounded by high banks of snow. Photos inside the hotel showed aerial views of the building in midwinter, almost completely buried in snow.

Looking up at Mount Rainier's radiant white dome from the hotel parking lot, Brian remarked, "To think it goes up another nine *thousand* feet!"

Just before dinner, standing outside with Michael and Brian, I looked at the ten-foot pile of snow beside the lodge and decided I had to climb it. I traversed my way up the side, as I would on snowshoes, kicking the edges of my shoes in and side-stepping upward. Michael called up, "Hey, Icechucker!" (his name for us Canadians), and I saw a stranger's camera pointed at me, and Brian giving the photographer his card. Neither Brian nor Michael had their cameras, so Brian had asked a friendly tourist to capture this Icechucker Moment.

The man turned out to be a Rush fan from Minnesota, on his way, like us, to the next night's show. Yet he felt no need to intrude on my evening in any "fan" way, and later emailed this photo to Brian. (Thanks Patrick—for *both* of those favors!)

We headed out early the following morning, winding east and down through the rest of the park, then up again and across the White Pass, at 4,500 feet. We descended to the vast rolling grasslands of the Columbia River Valley, with irrigated farms looking well tended and prosperous.

Still navigating by my hand-drawn map, and occasionally asking

Afternoon setup

locals for directions, we found our way to a nice piece of gravel road, in the open sagelands now, then a final stretch of two-lane blacktop, and a few miles of Interstate 90. Our destination was The Gorge, an outdoor amphitheater on the banks of the Columbia, for the final show of the *Time Machine* tour.

Added to the forty-four shows and more than 23,000 miles of motorcycling from summer 2010, my bandmates and I had now performed a total of eighty-one shows, before almost one million people. With riding partners Michael and Brutus, I had ridden 36,729 motorcycle miles, covering North America, South America, and Europe.

Michael and I were glad to get in early that day to The Gorge, needing to pack up and move off the bus, while Dave (with welcome help from Brian) organized the trailer and loaded my California bike on a pallet, to ride in one of the equipment trucks back to Los Angeles.

I have written before that one of the things I like about playing outdoors is that I have a better view of the audience—especially in a location like The Gorge, where the crystalline twilight lingered into the beginning of the second set.

Just this year, the band instituted a new policy where we don't start a show until at least ninety percent of the ticket-buyers are

in the venue. We knew that in the past some people missed the beginning of the show through no fault of their own—gridlock traffic, crowded entryways—and we didn't think that was fair. With computerized ticket-takers these days, the arrivals are easy to calculate, and most nights, a half-hour or so before the scheduled show-time, the announcement came over the crew's radios: "Ten minute hold." Then sometimes a later one, "Add another five." We never held longer than fifteen minutes—considering all of the people who *had* made it to the venue on time, not wanting to make them wait, plus there were union and building curfews to consider.

Some nights the Powers That Be—production manager C.B. and tour manager Liam—would even cut five minutes from the intermission, and we didn't like that. As in one variation of Geddy's announcement at the end of the first set, "We have to take a break . . . because we're about a hundred! Don't go away!"

Even people who don't like our band have to appreciate our *audiences*. They simply enjoy themselves so much that it's contagious!

Some sing along with every word; some play air drums or guitar; most just smile and rock along with us. It's a wonderful thing to witness, especially from my vantage point.

Not that it makes my job any easier—quite the opposite. I feel I have to live up to that level of devotion, so I drive myself all the harder. The touring stories I write during the breaks tend to have much more to say about the journeys than the shows, because the basic "story"

of the show is pretty much the same: soundcheck at 5:00, warm-up thirty minutes before showtime, then go up there and try my best to reach my inner standard of "acceptable" (never judging higher than "good")— and either succeed or don't. That's the only variation to what is essentially the same story, eighty-one times.

A smiling moment like this is rare for me onstage and is usually directed at Alex's antics or crew members Anson and Doug appearing in the gorilla and chicken costumes. Mostly, I know, I manifest the "grim determination" it takes for me to do that job.

But it is true that when I am on a concert tour, if I'm not happy on the drums, then I'm not happy *anywhere*. That is a deep observation. And it also helps to illustrate why a guy like Lorne (Gump) Wheaton is so important to me. Every day, without fail or flaw, Gump sets up, tunes, and maintains those drums just perfectly. He is able to *feel* how each part of the complicated drumset should relate to the player, so my workspace is always comfortable. Nothing naggingly a little out of whack.

When there is an equipment failure during the show—a broken tom head, loose snare mount—we choreograph the change almost automatically. I pick the break between songs when it's possible, step down off the riser and out of the way, while Gump and Anson from the sound crew make the trade. Usually nobody else will even know anything happened.

These are some of the almost fifty people who deliver the show and put it all together every day. Drivers, riggers, band crew, lighting crew, sound crew, video and effects, security, nutrition—all that and so much more.

I try to show my special appreciation, daily and annually, to "my guys" on the crew, like Gump, who look after my *personal* world so well. Road manager Donovan seems to have a limitless, nearly *miraculous* stock of every specific traveling need I might have—whether it's Macallan, Mitchum, or a Montblanc refill. Bus driver Dave goes way

beyond that job description in taking care of bus housekeeping, motorcycle parts, supplies, and tools, service appointments, even restoring my fifteen-year-old motorcycle trailer on his own time last year.

Something Dave said to me at the end of one tour I will never forget: "You're the only artist I've ever driven that I feel I work *with* instead of *for*."

That meant a lot to me, and it's the way I want things to be.

Like a remark I once made to Michael, in response to some profane and insulting tirade, "I love that you feel you can talk to me that way—but I really wish you wouldn't."

He likes to quote that to others and thinks it's hilarious—in light of him enduring my abuse and slanderous banter while I drag him through frying pans and freezers. Or Brutus, following me through Brazilian rainforests and along Welsh cowpaths—designing adventurous routes and fantastic destinations, just so he can follow me around to them.

Thousands of people stand in front of the three of us when we're onstage—but a lot of important people stand behind us, too, a network

As many crew members
as we could round up
that afternoon

A reflective moment

that's almost immeasurable. And . . . let's not forget the ones who stand behind us at home.

That can be the loneliest and least-appreciated place of all—at least by outsiders. After I was home for a day off after the Phoenix show, then had to leave the next afternoon for a show in San Diego, little Olivia, almost two now, woke up from her nap and went running down the hall toward my office, saying, "Go see Daddy!" When she was told, "Daddy's gone to work again," she burst into tears. Hearing about that made me feel very bad. As I've written before, I can stand missing her, but I can't stand her missing me.

However, on the "happy side" of that equation, an audience of more than 13,000 people attended the final show of our *Time Machine* tour, on July 2, 2011. Most of them had traveled a considerable distance—The Gorge is a long way from anywhere (the nearest town, humorously, is George, Washington). But we too had traveled a long way to get to that stage. And despite how many shows we had played, our weariness, and our sheer *age*, we managed to pull off a magic show that night.

Roaring at Alex

We could feel it in our ensemble playing, tight and energetic, but these days an exceptional night is often apparent in our improvised sections— Geddy on his bass in the outro of "Leave That Thing Alone," Alex in the frenetic solo section of "Working Man," and for me, the first half of my solo (later titled "Moto Perpetuo," or perpetual motion). When the three of us are at the top of our individual games, we are able to elevate the whole to a sublime synergy.

At the end of the show, as we bowed and waved and Geddy thanked the audience for being so great, at that show and so many others, I heard him drop the f-bomb—for the first time in history. After saying, "It has been great," he repeated that phrase and added that emphatic modifier. It was definitely a case of "when no other word would do"—to express how successful the tour had been, how much it meant to us, and how much we appreciated the people who had *made* it great.

In that moment, the three of us knew that at

last we would be stepping away from the "frying pan" of live performance (the crucible) for a while, and would have some time off to chill: "the freezer."

And what a great way to mark that transition.

Sometimes things are so perfectly right that you can't help but get carried away in the moment . . .

# AT THE GATE OF THE YEAR

**It has been six months** since my last letter—and the time has been full. As ever, the more stories I have to tell, the less time I have to tell them.

I have never liked the clichés about time racing by, because I think you simply have to keep up with that pace—live your life at exactly the speed of time. Anyone asking, "Where did the time go?" obviously wasn't paying attention! Each day, week, month, or year is a vessel of fixed capacity, to be filled with memorable incidents and stories. Every day can be observed in a way that is worth sharing—a motorcycle tour in South America or a trip to the grocery store and a pleasant few words with the baggers.

Responding to a letter from a friend who claimed to have nothing to tell, Thomas Jefferson wrote, "Just tell me about the events passing daily under your eyes." Properly experienced and expressed, every life is of interest to another.

Now, at the pivot of another year (my sixtieth, I am proud to crow—how foolish to regret the passing years, if you consider the alternative), I am drawn to a kind of "reckoning," a time to pause and reflect. The title phrase has long resonated for me that way: "the gate of the year."

From the time I was small, I admired a framed piece of needlepoint that hung on my grandmother's wall. She had made it on the family dairy farm in Southern Ontario during the dark days of World War II—when my father was a boy. On a field of white linen, her deft needle had stitched colored threads in a precise, artful design. In one corner, a brown-robed arm raised a golden lantern, and beside it meticulously sewn letters traced out a few lines of poetry that had been quoted by Britain's King George VI in a December 1939 radio address.

More recently, the historical importance of that speech was re-created as the climax of the 2010 film *The King's Speech*, and it was the first royal Christmas Day radio broadcast in a tradition that continues with George VI's daughter, Queen Elizabeth II. Her televised speech from Christmas Day 1997 was a key theme in another film, *The Queen* (2006), and resonated sorrowfully in my own life. Referring to the devastating fire at Windsor Castle, and the death of Princess Diana, she described it as an *annus horribilis*, a disastrous or unfortunate year, and it had certainly been that for me.

Back in 1939, the king concluded his speech with the words, "I said to the man who stood at the gate of the year, 'Give me a light that I may tread safely into the unknown.'" He was quoting a poem by Minnie Louise Haskins, which then goes off into some "celestial guide" sort of stuff (you know, putting your hand in the hand of the Judeo-Christian skygod). But the image of "the Gate of the Year" from Grandma's needlework has stayed with me all my life—especially as a time for reflection and resolution. Right now I have no idea what's going to happen in 2012, or if I will "tread safely into the unknown," but 2011 has been quite a year to look back upon.

(I am reminded that exactly twenty-five years ago, I sat down at the Gate of the Year and made a list entitled "Why 1986 Was the Greatest Year." Nice to think that even then I knew enough to count my blessings—and now I know it even better.)

Just a few days before the Pagan Winter Festival in 2011, amid all the haste and urgency of that season, I suddenly discovered that I had a wonderful gift before me—an unexpected few hours that I could afford to "squander." Santa Bubba's job was done—gifts chosen, wrapped, and shipped off to Canada—and Chef Bubba's job was ahead—family feasts for Christmas Eve and Day. But that Wednesday afternoon I felt like I was miraculously facing an open window—a breathing space—and all at once I felt free, and I lit up inside.

Considering what I might do with that little wedge of freedom, a motorcycle ride would have been perfect, but my bike wasn't "at home" just then. So I gathered my jacket, cap, and shades, and headed for the garage. Starting up my old Aston Martin DB5, just past its own forty-seventh birthday, I let it idle out front for a little while. (Old cars, like old drummers, need careful warming up.) Then I climbed in and curved down through the canyon to the end of Sunset Boulevard, and turned north onto the Pacific Coast Highway. Accelerating hard to clear the carburetors (and for fun), I shifted up into third and fourth and into an easy cruise. The bright sunshine over the ocean and along the coastline was softened by a pale, misty haze, and lazy waves tumbled onto the sand in long white rollers. Pelicans glided low over the water, fan palms speared skyward in motionless elegance, and traffic was light on a December afternoon.

Having grown up in Southern Ontario, where days in late December were typically cold and snowy, or filthy with slush, I have never taken California's Mediterranean climate for granted. A permanent lesson was etched into my mind when I first moved there, in January 2000, and was riding back from a motorcycle journey to Death Valley. Winding down through Malibu Canyon, framed in rocky walls and chaparral green after the winter rains, the Pacific glittered before me, and I thought, "It's the last day of January. I'm on my motorcycle. And I *live here*."

One piece of Roadcraft lore I try to pass along to younger musicians, athletes, or actors is that when you're away from home for long periods of time, it is wise to make that home where your *spouse* wants to live. In 2000, I moved to California because that's where Carrie was from, and where she wanted to live, and I knew my traveling days were probably not over. Fair enough. I maintained a foothold for my Canadian roots with a second home in Quebec, where I would love to have been spending a white Christmas, but . . . for now our home was California.

For a touring musician, the only proper destination in time off is *home*—the recently defined "staycation." Toward the end of every tour, when people ask me where I am headed when the tour is over, I can only shrug and say, "Um, home?"

It's like when people ask me before I go away if I am excited about going on tour, and I can only look at them in wonderment. *Should* I be excited about leaving my wife, my baby daughter, my friends, my dog, my house, my toys, my desk, my kitchen, my grocery stores, and all that?

Not long ago I read an interview with a young musician just back from his first tour, and he remarked that one lesson he had learned was that while he was away, his friends and family just went on with their lives—without him. He realized it was up to him to reconnect with them again, to try to rejoin their lives. I once defined that process for myself as, "Putting it all back together." Meaning my *life*.

That morning had been my deadline for getting packages off to family members in Canada, and it ended a flurry of shopping, wrapping, and boxing. These days the American border paranoia complicates things terribly, and our assistant Adela spent three hours just filling out forms. Gift boxes coming the other way had been slower than usual to arrive, and I was stunned to see that some wrapped presents from Canada had actually been cut open. They were *books*!

Authorities are by nature cold and fearful, and one can see how they might feel they had to do that, but it still seemed sordid. (As it does when a customs agent ruffles through your laundry.) And in the dozen years I had been celebrating my Pagan Winter Festivals in the United States, it had never happened before.

That long frontier between the U.S. and Canada was once proudly hailed as "the world's longest undefended border." That notion has become a sad joke, especially on the "Homeland Security" side: drones patrolling the forty-ninth parallel from the sky, ubiquitous surveillance cameras, long lines to enter on the roads from Canada, and . . . vandalized Christmas presents.

This impromptu tableau of ornaments and lights was created in front of the pagan tree during decorating time by Olivia, the owner of the darling little feet in the background. At almost two-and-a-half, this is the first Pagan Winter Festival she has truly *experienced*, and possibly the first one she may remember, now that she has passed what is called "childhood amnesia." My own earliest memories start around that time, and in that season, so I would hope the same for her—and we tried hard to make this one unforgettable.

In recent years I have found the season to be difficult—because I used to love it so much, and the reasons I loved it so much had been taken from me. But now there was a new reason to love it again: for Olivia.

It is ironic that a religion that has historically co-opted prehistoric festivals for their own purposes would insist that pagans are unable to celebrate Christmas. Of course, it was ours *first*. The idea of grafting Christian festivals onto existing celebrations dates back at least to the eighth century, when Charlemagne massacred thousands of pagan Saxons for resisting his . . . "missionary zeal."

It is also arrogant to suggest that without religion we have no reason to feel "goodwill toward men." It isn't fear of godly punishment or promise of heavenly reward that makes generosity feel good—it's simple humanity. Any undamaged individual knows how good it can feel to help others.

I would love to avoid the taint of "faith-basher," as I have been called, but a further irony is that the most fanatical "Christians" today are the most vocal *against* the biblical example of, say, being good Samaritans. They would proudly (and loudly) deny even *mercy* to the less fortunate.

(The shortest verse in the Holy Bible may yet remain the truest: "Jesus wept.")

So the Pagan Winter Festival is mine, too, and my peaceful afternoon drive along the Pacific marked the brief nexus between getting all the presents out to people and provisioning and preparing the feasts for Christmas Eve and Day. Once again, I had visited Bubba's Bar 'n' Grill to check my recipes, to refresh the knowledge and instructions from past experience, and make lists of necessary "ingredients" (Brutus term). Shopping early for the non-perishables, able to scan the spice shelves for esoteric juniper berries and mustard seeds for the turkey brine, I had laid in most of the "grocerinos" (Brutus again).

So for that fleeting moment, I was feeling on top of the challenges ahead and good about the year behind me.

Most recently, I had been recording in Toronto with my bandmates, from mid-October until early December. We completed the songwriting and arranging for *Clockwork Angels*, the album we started back in late 2009—before going "on hiatus" for the *Time Machine* tour, and playing eighty-one shows in North America, South America, and Europe. (Some hiatus.) While Alex and Geddy were finishing the writing and arranging in one smaller room of the studio, over in the big room I was working with The Mighty Booujzhe, recording my drum parts. As we prepare to start mixing in the New Year, it is too early to say anything about the results. (I once described mixing as "the end of waiting," while Geddy calls it "the death of hope.") About the *process*, though, I can't resist spilling a little. It was our second time working with the production team of Nick "Booujzhe" Raskulinecz and engineer Rich "Tweak" Chycki. Beginning with a confident level of trust allowed us to reach higher, and I recorded my drum parts in a way that, for me, was completely different than ever before. Even right up to our previous album, *Snakes and Arrows* (2007), my method was to take a demo version Alex and Geddy had made of each song and play along with it many, many times. I would experiment with possible rhythms and decorations, and gradually organize them into an arrangement. At that point, I might start recording demos myself—often with Alex as engineer—and improve them over time, with input from my bandmates and coproducer (Booujzhe, in that case).

(A reminder about that nickname: Nick likes to suggest outrageous fills for me to play, and he will mime them with wild physical

gestures and sound effects: "Bloppida-bloppida-batu-batu-whirrrrr-blop-*booujzhe!*"—that last being the downbeat, with crash cymbal and bass drum.)

In recent years, I have been working deliberately to become more improvisational on the drums, and these sessions were an opportunity to attempt that approach in the studio. I played through each song just a few times on my own, checking out patterns and fills that *might* work, then called in Booujzhe. He stood in the room with me, facing my drums, with a music stand and a single drumstick—he was my conductor, and I was his orchestra. (I later replaced that stick with a real baton.)

Rush songs tend to have complicated arrangements, with odd numbers of beats, bars, and measures all over the place, and our latest songs are no different (maybe worse—or better, depending). In the past, much of my preparation time would be spent just *learning* all that. I don't like to count those parts, but rather play them enough that I begin to *feel* the changes in a musical way. Playing it through again and again, those elements became "the song."

This time I handed that job over to Booujzhe. (And he *loved* it!) I would attack the drums, responding to his enthusiasm and his suggestions between takes, and together we would hammer out the basic architecture of the part. His baton would conduct me into choruses, half-time bridges, double-time outros, and so on—so I didn't have to worry about their durations. No counting, and no endless repetition. What a revelation! What a *relief*!

There was this one song, though . . .

Here the music stand in front of my drums represents an historic event: the first time I have ever used written notes—or at least numbers. There were two sections of one song that were ridiculously complicated, and I didn't want to have to stop and learn them in my old way—I wanted to keep *playing*. So I wrote them down: one passage in which the rapid-fire snare accents went "4-2-4-2-3-2-4-2-3-2-1-y" (16th note push), and a series of staccato punches that went "1-3-1-5-1-4-1½." (Not *exactly* one-and-a-half beats, I guess, but a reminder that the last punch was also the downbeat into the next section.)

By these methods, each song's drum part was composed, arranged, performed, and recorded in just a few hours, rather than many days, as in the past. Also, each performance occurred only once, with magic—or lucky—moments from a few takes combined into one that was fresh and spontaneous. Now I can learn and reproduce that part, if desired, much as I did by the old process, but of course it's not the same. I like to believe that a listener can sense when a player is on the edge of his seat, so to speak, playing with urgency, invention, and excitement. Sometimes the listener may share the player's relief at having got safely back to "one."

Performing to that level was the satisfying culmination of several years of ambition, pursued through studying with Peter Erskine; practicing faithfully for months with just high-hat and metronome as part of my preparation for playing the Buddy Rich tribute concert back in

'08; making "The Hockey Theme" in '09; recording two new Rush songs, "Caravan" and "BU2B," in early 2010; and—perhaps paramount in the sense of working toward a goal—playing all of those shows on the *Time Machine* tour in 2010 and '11. Study, practice, experimentation, composition, and recording all reach their acme on the stage—nothing is more demanding than live performance, thus nothing does so much for my playing. (A fact about which I remain ambivalent, because until real-time holograms are possible, and accepted by audiences, it demands such long periods away from home.)

The "Hemispheres Chord" at the end of "Far Cry"

The year also had its share of tragedies, failures, and regrets. (Such different animals those be! Tragedies can be shared, but I have learned to keep my failures and regrets to myself. That is a deep kind of Roadcraft. Like our song, "Bravado," about burning our wings if we fly too close to the sun—the price of trying hard is occasional failure.)

One true tragedy was the passing of my drum teacher and friend of twenty years, Freddie Gruber. Freddie was eighty-four, and had lived life entirely by his own lights, so it was a natural time (alas), and his decline was mercifully brief. I am grateful that I was simply around during that time, to be able to *be there*, for Freddie and for his caregivers. In the patterns of my life, I could so easily have been away on tour, and thus Freddie's passing might have become more than a tragedy—it might have been a "regret," even a "failure."

Over the years, Freddie had become a close friend to Carrie as well, and when I was away on tour, they used to talk on the phone pretty well every night. When Carrie visited Freddie for the last time, she heard him say something I had heard, too. After telling one story or another from his long and active life, Freddie would nod, smile, and say, "I had quite a ride. I wish I could do it all again."

I was struck by that statement, because I had never felt that way myself. To the contrary—as much as I enjoy my life, I remain glad I *don't* have to do it all again. But I still appreciated that sentiment of Freddie's and, as a tribute, wove it into one of our new songs, with one character reflecting on his life in that fashion.

*Some days were dark*
*Some nights were bright*
*I wish that I could live it all again*

Another philosopher named Fred—Nietzsche—said something similar, "'Was that life?' will I say to death. 'Well! Once more!'"

I smiled at a comment mutual friend Rob Wallis posted the day after Freddie's passing: "The world seems a little less interesting today." That was a lovely way to put it, and the way I feel, too. I miss him.

In early November, more than 200 of Freddie's friends, including many former students, gathered for a Celebration of Life. Many stories were told, good music was played, and laughs were shared. Freddie would have approved. As I wrote in my obituary for him (something else I was grateful to be able to do), "He was smart, hip, warm, and funny, and although he kept himself insulated from the intrusions of what he called 'straight life'—the 'real world'—he was wise in its ways, always well informed, incisive, reflective, and caustic."

Jim Keltner, *moi*, Ndugu Chancler, Roy Haynes, Ian Wallace, Freddie– April 2006

Early that afternoon, I saw Ed Shaughnessy across the room and went over to pay my respects. A drummer with the *Tonight Show* band for many years in the Johnny Carson era, Ed had played on the Buddy Rich tribute album I produced in the early '90s. We chatted for a couple of minutes, then Ed said, "As a teacher myself, I have always wondered, what exactly did Freddie *do*? I asked Steve Smith, and he just said, 'It's complicated.' I asked Dave Weckl, and he said, 'It's complicated.' Then I asked Freddie himself, and he said, 'It's complicated.'"

We laughed, and I told him he had given me an idea for what I would say to the people that day. For I was determined to make myself get up and say a few words, although public speaking is always . . . challenging for me. ("Terrifying" might not be too strong a word.) Also, for the first time I would try improvising *that*, too. My few previous attempts at formal public speaking, in front of audiences and television cameras, had been carefully composed, largely memorized, but also depended on a written script. When the band was inducted into the Canadian Songwriters Hall of Fame a few years ago, I volunteered to say a few words—and only found out later that they expected the speech to be "as bilingual as possible." Yikes! My French reading skills were up to, say, the comic-book level (*Tintin* books a favorite), but I was very unpracticed at speaking the language.

The day before the event, in Toronto, I spent several hours with a local French teacher, polishing up my phrasing and pronunciation, and on the night, I also had the benefit of a teleprompter at the back of the room. It came off okay, but it was *hard*. The same was true at Freddie's event, but I hope I was able to share a few insights into why Freddie truly was a legendary teacher, to those of us fortunate enough to have been "cultivated" by him.

After Freddie's passing, his longtime friend and trustee Edythe Bronston was clearing out his safety deposit box and found this letter from me to him. I had written it during my "exile" in England in January 1998, with my late wife, Jackie, after the death of our daughter, Selena, in August 1997. The letter was written at the darkest point of my life—though I didn't know then that just a week or two later, we would get the diagnosis about Jackie's terminal cancer. So I was between deaths, as it were. (The gate of that year opened on a *prison cell*—what seemed to be an eternal sentence of grief, confusion, and emptiness. There was no light.)

I am especially touched that Freddie valued this letter enough to keep it carefully locked away all those years.

Another loss to the world in 2011 was the Anglo-American writer Christopher Hitchens. He died young, at sixty-two, of esophageal cancer—which also claimed my friend Ian Wallace a few years ago. Though I didn't know Mr. Hitchens, I greatly admired his powerful mind and graceful writing. A quote of his reflects on some of the same topics we have been discussing here: of faith, *using* one's time, and facing life's blessings and tragedies with grace and gratitude.

The only position that leaves me with no cognitive dissonance is atheism. It is not a creed. Death is certain, replacing both the siren-song of Paradise and the dread of Hell. Life on this earth, with all its mystery and beauty and pain, is then to be lived far more intensely: we stumble and get up, we are sad, confident, insecure, feel loneliness and joy and love. There is nothing more; but I want nothing more.

Even writing close to his own end, as he did for *Vanity Fair* magazine, where so many of his trenchant essays were published over the years (their obituary described him as "incomparable critic, masterful rhetorician, fiery wit, and fearless bon vivant"), Christopher Hitchens maintained that integrity.

If the highest gift art can offer is inspiration, then encouragement is not far behind. Mr. Hitchens has made me braver—for good or ill—about speaking my own mind. No one expects to change anyone's *beliefs*, though as Hitchens also said: "What can be asserted without evidence can be dismissed without evidence."

The inspiration comes from encouraging others to hold up the flag of reason—not just against the "believers," but against those who use that faith for power. The earlier-described religious zealots like to claim that Thomas Jefferson and the other founding fathers intended to establish a *Christian* nation. Here's what the great man actually said.

**47 PARK STREET**
WESTIN DEMEURE HOTELS · LONDON

47 Park Street, Mayfair, London W1Y 4EB
Telephone: 0171-491 7282, Facsimile: 0171-491 7281

JANUARY 7, 98

Dear Freddie,

Thank you so much for your heartfelt message last week. You have a rare grasp of the scale of the darkness that continues to surround us, and expressed it in such a beautiful fashion that I found myself wanting to give you a call, but I can't help but feel that right now it would be too emotional for either of us to handle.

However, know that I am deeply touched by the quality of your feelings, and of your friendship. You're a good man, and I miss you.

Hell, I miss everything. Not only Selena, but ourselves, our friends, and our lives together. It's all been blasted into such a howling chaos of sorrow and meaninglessness, and we're only now beginning to grope for a path ahead.

It sure won't be easy, but I hope we'll find some kind of peace—if never the joy we knew before.

I'll call when I'm able,

Neil

Shake off all the fears of servile prejudices, under which weak minds are servilely crouched. Fix reason firmly in her seat, and call on her tribunal for every fact, every opinion. Question with boldness even the existence of a God; because, if there be one, he must more approve of the homage of reason than that of blindfolded fear.

To "question with boldness" is not the same as to preach or deny. Likewise, to number one's accomplishments is not the same as bragging. (Baseball player and commentator Dizzy Dean: "It ain't braggin' if you can back it up.") I once heard some popstar diva asked about something to do with the "price of fame," and she paused and said carefully, "Well . . . I mustn't seem to be *complaining*."

In the same breath, neither must one seem to be *bragging* (unless you're a rapper, I suppose). So in reference to the actions I feel good about this year, I'll only cite my adherence to another piece of worthwhile advice: "If you do well, try to do good."

I have done well, and I have tried to do good. I know that a few

times I have improved the lives of both strangers and loved ones—and by deliberate acts, not just being "cool by example," or anything effortless like that.

So . . . thus have I arrived at my sixtieth year, more or less gracefully and gratefully, feeling healthy and strong, and feeling that I am putting words together and hitting things with sticks better than ever. (Though it's worth noting that I trained for two months to be in good drumming shape for those sessions. The passing years do demand more attention to fitness and stamina.) Now I have the reward of listening to the drum parts I have performed for this album and recognizing with quiet satisfaction that I am working at a whole new level of both funky, dirty, greasy *groove* and fancy show-off technique—a combination I have been seeking my entire drumming life.

And if I have shone a little light into the lives of others this year, often enough I have felt that light reflected back, in gratitude and goodwill.

"I said to the man who stood at the Gate of the Year, 'Give me a light that I may tread safely into the unknown.'"

Seems to me you have to bring that light yourself.

# WHERE WORDS FAIL, MUSIC SPEAKS

**My first principle of art is** "Art is the telling of stories." What might be called the First Amendment is "Art must transcend its subject." However, sometimes art's natural subject—*life*—transcends even the mightiest attempt at conveying it.

Despite the love and respect I have for words, I know too well that there are occasions for which words are, alas, hopelessly inadequate. Even the combination of words and pictures, as I have worked into these stories for some years, has its limits. There are depths and heights of experience and emotion that the most accomplished arts of man only rarely capture.

Grief is one; joy is another.

But it doesn't mean you shouldn't try. And a moment like the one above must be one more example—in two senses: in the surreality of the circumstances, and in my own failure to speak as eloquently as I wished I could. I tried, but . . . words failed.

It was the evening of April 11, 2012, at the Club Nokia in downtown Los Angeles. The occasion was the *Revolver* magazine Golden

Gods Awards, at which Rush was presented with the Ronnie James Dio Lifetime Achievement Award.

Earlier in the year, we were asked about attending the ceremony in Los Angeles in April. The admirable Jack Black and his Tenacious D bandmate, Kyle Gass, said they would present the award, if at least one of us showed up to accept it. Geddy said he couldn't be there because he would be in Japan, and I said I couldn't be there . . . *because I'm me*.

Never comfortable amid crowds of people, especially if they're making a fuss about *me*—plus facing up to public speaking and public praise—I just feel tense and embarrassed. Anyone acquainted with me knows I try to avoid such situations whenever I can. (Of course it's different when I am drumming—that is a more or less *natural* environment for me.)

So Alex manfully volunteered to appear on our behalf and accept the award. However, just days before, Alex had a personal situation at home in Toronto that wouldn't allow him to travel to Los Angeles for the event. Discussing it all on the phone with our manager, Ray, he started to say, "I don't suppose you would consider—"

I cut him off. "No possible way—are you serious? You know I don't do that kind of thing. And it's my *moving day!*"

That was true, but in the same breath that was saying "no," my mind echoed with the true answer, "yes."

Clearly I would have to do it, that's all there was to it—it was the right thing to do. The *only* thing to do. Obstacles would have to be surmounted. Or ignored.

Alex felt terrible about disappointing everyone, and I felt a loyal obligation to bail him out. And besides, it would be too rude for *none* of us to show up. We are Canadians, after all.

So . . . the day my family moved from one overcrowded house where we had lived—and collected junk—for eight years, to another house that was soon overcrowded with boxes to be unpacked and organized, I had to duck into a shower that worked, find some decent clothes to wear (a leather crew jacket from our *Snakes and Arrows* tour—the closest I have to "rock clothes"), and go say a few words that I hoped would be courteous, appreciative, and gracious.

My longtime riding partner and security chief, Michael, picked me up at home and distracted me with vicious banter on the way. (A friend once commented to Michael and me that she couldn't believe how nastily we talked to each other. The two of us shared a look of

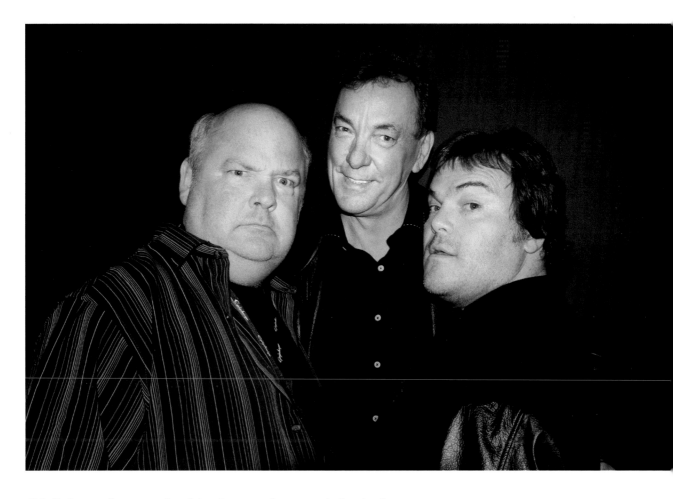

Me 'n' D

disbelief. Nasty? We were insulting, base, crude, sarcastic, ironic, the-atrical, gay, obscene, vicious, disgusting, and funny—but never *nasty*!)

We left the backstage parking lot and walked into a dark, crowded theater, and my senses were brutally assaulted. Strobing lights slashed and flashed in the darkness, and the air throbbed with noise from grinding guitars and double-bass pedals triggering samples (an insult upon the ears and sensibility of an old-school drummer). Flamboyant (an errant finger just coined a neologism: "glamboyant") rock people filled the hallways, and with head down to avoid being "noticed," I glanced around in disbelief at a phantasmagoria of wild rock costumes, spiky black hair, and tribal makeup.

My brief presence did not include witnessing what must have been bizarre duets combining Johnny Depp and Marilyn Manson, or Dee Snider and the Black Veil Brides, but I saw and heard plenty. As my handlers and I shouldered our way through the backstage crowds, bright video lights illuminated rock veterans being interviewed in front of cameras—Gene Simmons here, Slash over there, and Alice

Cooper that way. They were posed, arrayed, and lighted like figures in a wax museum.

I noticed their elaborate rock costumes—Alice in black leather pants with silver conchos, Gene in black leather pants and boots with intricate metal tooling—and I asked Michael, "Where do they get those clothes?"

Michael answered, "I hope you never find out."

I suggested that there must be a store for them in Hollywood, and adopted a radio commercial voice: "Rock Clothes for the Mature Male."

He laughed and said, "There probably is a store like that."

Standing amid all that with an almost dizzying sense of surreality, the stage manager told me which way to go up, and which way to come down. Jack Black inducted the band with his signature high-voltage *School of Rock* oration, then I was up there and holding a miniature Stonehenge (the award—shades of *Spïnal Tap*) in front of blinding spotlights and a sea of youthful faces that seemed to be saying, "Who?"

I did my best to explain my presence and express my feelings, but alas, I fear words failed.

Later, for the magazine, I offered a more considered, written attempt:

I will start with raw honesty. (And why not?) It is the kind of thing that is "hard to know what to do with." (No, ha ha, I don't mean the actual award—Alex, Geddy, and I have long had a rule that all awards go *straight* to the office of our manager, Ray Danniels.)

Of course, I mean the honor.

On the one hand, it is wonderful to be appreciated, naturally. But on the other hand, you mustn't let such appreciation *affect* you—mustn't take it too seriously. Yet on the third hand (hey—I'm a drummer!), basic courtesy demands that you take it seriously enough to express proper gratitude for the respect and tribute it represents.

See what I mean? It's complicated . . .

Such issues have never been a big problem for the three of us—simply because not much of that kind of thing came our way. For our nearly thirty-eight years together, we have been fortunate enough to have had our loyal and enthusiastic audience (perhaps *they* should receive the lifetime achievement award), while the rest of the world was mostly oblivious—with a minor, if apoplectic, gallery of raging haters. So whenever an honor was offered to us, we would be surprised, and even a little suspicious:

*"Are you sure?"*

One quality that Alex, Geddy, and I share (among enough other points of agreement and humor to have kept us together for almost thirty-eight years) is that we are always looking forward—in life, and in music. It is said that nostalgia isn't what it used to be, though I would say that these days it is rather *more* than it used to be. But not for us. Even on our *Time Machine* tour, in 2010-11, when part of the show included performing our 1980 *Moving Pictures* album in its entirety, there was no feeling of "going back" for us. Choosing that music, and performing it every night, was all about what that music meant to us *now*.

Sure, the old songs we continue to play in live shows are a part of our musical autobiography, but they are also simply a part of *us*. We liked them when we wrote them, and we like playing them now.

The Rush "mission statement" has always been clear: we make music we like, and hope other people will like it, too.

It also seems natural that we always feel strongest about our newest music—like the soon-to-be released *Clockwork Angels* album. Yet people will keep asking me, "What is your favorite Rush album?"

How terrible it would be if you had to answer with anything *but* your most recent work. To confess that your best work was past? Face *that* music?

Oh no.

The three of us, and the friends and collaborators around us, are very excited about *Clockwork Angels*. We modestly believe that it represents our best work on every level of our craft, and we sincerely (earnestly) hope other people will agree.

So, as I mentioned in my speech at the award presentation, our lifetimes aren't over yet, and we hope our achievements aren't either.

Now, in early 2012, we are poised to begin preparing to launch a major tour later this year, continuing into 2013. So we've got a lot of work to do.

We have to keep trying to deserve this award.

A few weeks later, the feelings that overwhelmed me at the *Revolver* event were amplified tenfold. The three of us met in Ottawa to be presented with the Governor General's Performing Arts Award for Lifetime Achievement. We shared the honor with several "*real* artists"—concert pianist Janina Fialkowska, dancer and choreographer Paul-André Fortier, theater director and stage designer Denis Marleau, filmmaker Deepa Mehta, political satirist and broadcaster Mary Walsh, theater director Des McAnuff, and a highly influential fundraiser for the arts, Earlaine Collins.

Earlier in the year, when the award was first offered to us, the stipulation was that all of us (yes, they stressed, *all* of us) would have to attend three days of celebratory events (two "black tie" and two "business attire") and cooperate in the making of a short film in advance that would accompany the "gala night" finale.

Pegi in our office laughed at our very different replies to her first email on the subject—Geddy saying he would be glad to have another medal; Alex writing, "I accept, Your Majesty"; and yours truly wailing, "Three days of hoopla? No-o-o-o!"

However, as I almost always do, I acquiesced to the wishes of my bandmates, the Guys at Work. As I have said before in other circumstances—like to reluctant fathers with determinedly maternal wives—"When someone you love wants something really badly, you have to help them get it if you can."

So I basically surrendered. When asked for a statement for the Canadian press, I offered this, with a similar ending trope:

> As we put the finishing touches to what will be our twentieth studio album, *Clockwork Angels*, followed by a tour behind it this fall, we especially appreciate the presentation of this lifetime achievement award now—while we are still active. (Too active, our families might say!) Since our performance "lifetimes" aren't quite over yet, this high honour is not just a reward; it is an inspiration. We will continue to try to earn it.

The celebration of the surreal began at Canada's Parliament Buildings. With the other inductees, we were welcomed to the private office of the Speaker of the House, Andrew Scheer. He acts as an arbitrator in the House of Commons, and at a boyish thirty-two, he is the youngest Speaker in Canadian history. Moving down the hall to his dining room, we enjoyed a pleasant lunch, getting to know the others a little bit. Then we were all ushered to the House of Commons, for a Canadian Parliamentary ritual called Question Period.

We listened in on the astonishingly wide range of topics introduced—from the cost overruns on a new fighter jet (for the Canadian Air Force—so perhaps literally *one* fighter jet!), to the Newfoundland seal hunt, to an oil slick in the Pacific off British Columbia, to charges among the parties of corruption and slander.

Amid all that withering controversy, and sometimes heated tempers, we heard gratuitous references to Rush songs woven into the arguments, and one angry peroration on the city's political machinations concluded with, "This is indeed . . . a *villa strangiato*."

Another MP who seemed to be getting the worst of an argument suddenly spread his arms and looked up to the Speaker's Gallery and shouted, "I would just like to say that Rush is here today! Welcome to our . . . parliamentary limelight!"

Later, our friend the Speaker (a *child!*) read each of the laureates' names into the Parliamentary Record, and the Members rose and applauded us.

One disconcerting observation we shared was that it seemed the entire government of Canada was younger than us. Sure enough—

the *average* age of Canadian Members of Parliament is fifty—nearly ten years younger. Many of them were in their *twenties*. Seriously, I ask you—how is it possible for politicians to be younger than rock musicians? (Though perhaps the better question is "How can rock musicians be older than politicians?")

(I think of P.J. O'Rourke's quip, "Giving money and power to politicians is like giving whisky and car keys to teenage boys.")

With Governor General
David Johnston

The second day centered on a ceremony at Rideau Hall, the palatial residence of Canada's Governors General. Traditionally, they were representatives of the British Crown, but the role today is largely ceremonial—though they still act as worthy, non-political ambassadors to Canadians and world leaders. (The day after our visit, Israeli president Shimon Peres was arriving to stay at Rideau Hall.)

Part of my attitude of "surrender" to those three days was that I hadn't examined the program too carefully—I figured I would just go where and when I was told. Remembering back to when the three of us were given the Order of Canada in 1996 at Rideau Hall, there were no speeches, and I presumed anything we had to say would be part of the next night's "gala" at the National Arts Centre.

Earlier that day I kept myself distracted by walking around Ottawa with my daughter, Olivia, who, at two-and-a-half, was impressed by our capital city's modest grandeur. It was a warm spring day, sky washed blue, trees and grass in fresh spring green, and beds of red and yellow tulips in full bloom. Olivia liked seeing the squirrels chasing each other; the Rideau Canal; the Château Laurier, a castle-like hotel; the glass-paneled National Gallery; and the Houses of Parliament—dubbed by Olivia "The Castle of Canada."

While enjoying that time with her, and carrying her back to the hotel on my shoulders when she got tired, I felt edgy inside, like on a show day, a feeling that increased as the afternoon departure neared. In the time leading up to those days, our women had made frequent comments about how "easy" it was for us guys, just having to wear a tuxedo or a suit. Maybe so, but they have never had to struggle with nervous fingers on tuxedo shirt studs and tiny buttonholes.

It was only when we met in the lobby that afternoon to depart that I learned the speeches were to be presented *that day*! Earlier we had agreed that instead of one of us taking on the responsibility, as I have done a few times, each of us would speak a short piece. Alex and Geddy had exchanged emails that afternoon about what each of us might say, but I had missed them all.

Words fail again!

I had thought I might spend some time the following day preparing a few remarks, and try to make them a little bilingual. The previous year, at a songwriters award show in Toronto, I had been very impressed by how smoothly nearly everyone had moved between English and French—not translating, but alternating remarks in our two official languages. It was very admirable, and seemed to represent Canada at its best, so I had been glad to face the challenge (*faire face au défi*) of doing that myself.

However, there was no way I could improvise in French, so I limited myself to remembering the proper formal greeting, "Your Excellencies, honored guests, ladies and gentlemen," then I said something about none of us laureates having arrived at that place *alone*. Or, spreading my arms back toward my bandmates, even just with a band.

I managed the opening okay, which seemed most important—and most likely to *fail*—and only vaguely remember what else I said. I mentioned how it had all started for me with my parents giving me drum lessons for my thirteenth birthday, and how they were "here today." I talked about the contribution of those around us, like our office people and our road crews, and how our families were subjected to long and frequent absences. I closed with something about my bandmates of almost thirty-eight years, and passed the podium to Alex, then Geddy. They read briefly from their prepared notes (cheaters!), adding our thanks to our fans and to the Canadian arts community. Later they both told me how nervous they had been, and it was nice to know I was not the only one.

At this moment on the following night, we were standing at the front of the mezzanine balcony of Ottawa's National Arts Centre, in

a row of the laureates and the Governor General and his wife. We were looking and gesturing toward the stage, responding to a funny induction speech by another good friend, Matt Stone. Matt had generously traveled to Ottawa for the occasion, and the segment devoted to Rush included the *South Park* clip Matt and his partner Trey Parker had created for our *Snakes and Arrows* tour—the kids from the show performing "Tom Sawyer" as L'il Rush.

A short documentary had been put together for each laureate, shot by edgy young directors for Canada's National Film Board. Ours mixed interviews with the three of us and a band of dedicated teenagers from Waterdown, Ontario, called Inner Volition. In the film's final scene, Geddy said something about us still trying to improve in everything we do, and I laughed and added, "We are *still* trying to get better!"

After a perfect beat, Alex, sitting between Geddy and me, smiled and angled his thumbs outward at us, and said, "Well . . . *they* are."

Genius.

As Matt talked about Rush and what we had meant to him in his youth, he circled back to that joke. "And they're still trying to get better . . . except Alex!," which got a good laugh.

Then the curtains drew wide to reveal a children's choir, who sang "The Spirit of Radio" a capella. They were followed by a full symphony orchestra playing "Tom Sawyer."

Once or twice Alex, Geddy, and I caught each other's eye and just *looked* at each other. Delighted, of course, but . . . bemused might be the word. If words didn't fail so epically.

The final performance in the gala was by Des McAnuff, a theater director and—evidently—would-be rock star. Backed by his Red Dirt

Band, his film was a rock-video style performance of a lilting song with the refrain, "The Rain It Raineth Every Day" (a quote from *King Lear*, appropriately, as Des was director of the Stratford Shakespeare Festival in Ontario).

Then Des and the band took the stage to play live, launching into a medley of songs from the Who's *Tommy*. To the audience's surprise and delight (though we knew about it before, confidentially), they were joined by the composer himself, Pete Townshend, the Godfather of Rock. Des and Pete had worked together for some years on staging a musical version of *Tommy*, and Pete had accepted his invitation to perform. It made the perfect finale to an astonishing evening.

With Matt Stone (Pete and Des in background)

More than anything, it made me proud of *Canada*—that an event like that could embrace the country's artists across such a broad spectrum, from high-falutin' artsy types to rock bums like us, and represent them with international luminaries like Matt Stone, Pete Townshend, and Salman Rushdie. It must have taken a great deal of time, energy, and money to put together all of those events, and I couldn't imagine it happening in any other country.

We were ushered backstage to meet up with Matt and thank him warmly for doing us that honor, then into Pete Townshend's dressing room. Usually I don't care much about meeting celebrities, like the actors or athletes who come to Rush shows, but this was one meeting and photo op I was more than glad to attend.

To briefly recap a long history, the Who were my first favorite band. In my mid-teens, my bedroom was papered in magazine photographs and posters of the Who, hung with pop-art mobiles I made from photos of them, and my dresser had a Union Jack painted across its top (a triumph of clumsy masking and brushwork). In the middle of one wall I had painted the bass-drum logo from Keith Moon's famous "Pictures of Lily" kit. (Another challenge for my mediocre artistry with paints.) I possessed every one of their singles, albums, and compilations, and every magazine that mentioned them. On the "drumset" I made across my bed from old magazines, in the layout of Keith's drums, I could play along with all of their songs.

Around that time I had a high-school science teacher who was exasperated by my constant finger-tapping on my desk. When I said I couldn't help it, he said, "What are you—some kind of *retard?*"

Seriously.

He sentenced me to a detention in which I would have to sit and tap on a desk for one hour. I played *Tommy* from memory; the teacher had to leave the room.

To the teenage me, Pete Townshend set the example for what a rock musician should be: "He smashes guitars—and reads books!"

So . . . meeting him now, forty-odd years later, I remained full of admiration, respect, and gratitude—for his *example.*

As we shook hands, I was pleased to tell him that my first concert, at age fifteen, had been the Who, with the Troggs and the MC5 opening. He smiled at the notion of losing my concert virginity to *that* mix!

The conversation among the four of us was a little halting, necessarily, but when we told Pete we had just finished making an album, he scoffed, "Waste of time, making albums these days." We said we knew, but had to do it anyway.

Pete told us about some volunteer work he had been doing in a British prison, trying to encourage the inmates to explore music. He said, "All they want is *decks*"—meaning they wanted to be DJs, not musicians.

As we turned to leave, I made one last comment to Pete. "I also really enjoyed your prose writing—are you doing any more of that?"

He told me he was just finishing writing his life—which I took to mean "life," like Keith Richards' autobiography.

He went on, in his soft, sonorous voice, the accent melodic and pitched perfectly between cockney and Oxbridge, "A lot of people thought *Horse's Neck* was about me, but it wasn't, really."

I nodded agreement with that observation. I had learned from my own attempts at fiction that if you invent a story about an entirely imaginary musician, say, naturally people smell thinly disguised autobiography. That is partly why my own prose writing shifted to non-fiction. If you follow the dictum, "Write what you know," it is difficult, and unnatural, to stay away from the characters and settings of your own life.

If those characters and settings happened to be drawn from other youthful experiences, like sailing—Melville, Conrad, London—or war—Hemingway, Mailer, O'Brien—then you had the makings of fine fiction.

Backstage, not so much.

In any case, for me non-fiction was and is *liberating*—I can write about being a musician, a birdwatcher, a motorcyclist, a reader, a cross-country skier, a cook, or an opinionated faith-basher. The broadest possible canvas in which to fail.

A quote from Hans Christian Andersen gave me my title, "Where words fail, music speaks."

Here Matt Scannell and I are speaking that language. On April 16, at Henson Studios

in Hollywood (across the hall from where Rush had just been working on the final mixes of *Clockwork Angels*), we recorded a drum track for a Vertical Horizon song called "Instamatic." Our method was pioneered by Nick "Booujzhe" Raskulinecz and me earlier this year, for that Rush album. (See "At the Gate of the Year.")

The basic theme of that method is minimal preparation—just listen to the song a couple of times to get a "sense" of it, then start recording. My conductor, Nick or Matt, guides me through the arrangement with a drumstick, counting me into the various changes, and giving me suggestions and encouragement between takes.

I have described before what a *huge* breakthrough this is for me in my approach to recording, and—I think—in the character of my playing. Where I have always painstakingly worked up carefully orchestrated and detailed drum parts and then delivered them from memory, now I improvise my way through from the get-go. A month or so before the Henson session, Matt and I had worked on a demo for the song and explored a few ideas that seemed to work. But even then, I had been careful not to listen to that demo more than a few times, because I wanted the final recording to capture a performance as fresh, and uncertain, as possible. Wild flights can happen in the heat of recording, in the course of shaping a part that is faithful to the song, but remains necessarily edgy, fresh, a little dangerous, and hopefully exciting for the listener.

It was certainly exciting (and fun) for the drummer and producer! At the end of each take Matt and I would share smiles, laughter, and excited chatter. (My wife, Carrie, says that when the two of us get together, we are "like a couple of puppies." That's kind of nice.)

While I was playing, Matt's dancing was . . . enthusiastic.

Coincidentally, thinking about Pete Townshend and the Who, and the enduring influence of Keith Moon's drumming on my own, it occurs to me now that certain parts of my performance on "Instamatic" suggest what Keith Moon *might* have sounded like if he too had lived to be almost sixty—instead of dying from an overdose of anti-alcoholism medication at age thirty-two. Too soon, and too sad.

I have much to be grateful for in my working life, but perhaps paramount to me is the opportunity to collaborate at a level of mutual delight with a circle of *friends*—musicians, artists, writers, producers, designers, editors (brother Danny this time), drum makers, cymbal makers, and . . . all the way around.

"Six Degrees of Bubba," as a friend once described it.

Outside of music's language, there is the language of *friendship*, and Matt is one of my dearest friends and collaborators. We have combined music and lyrics for a rock ballad, "Even Now," and I played drums on that and two other songs on Vertical Horizon's *Burning the Days* album. We also composed what we thought was a very fine country-pop song (just to prove it was possible!) called "A Promise or a Threat." It will be a *huge* hit one day, when the right male "hat" singer discovers it. We have also written a fun theme for a cartoon show, which remains unproduced—but never mind, we had fun making it.

And, famously, there are our grand conceptions for the Broadway stage, like "Snowdance" (see "The Best February Ever" in *Far and Away*) and "Supernatural Lover" ("A Winter's Tale of Summers Past," also in *Far and Away*).

In our classic ironic, arch tone, Matt and I modestly assert that, "When we are together, magic happens."

Certainly it is true that when we get together, music speaks.

Another example of music's incomparable "speaking voice" was seeing the Jack DeJohnette Trio perform at Catalina's Jazz Club in Hollywood in mid-May. The other—oh, let's say "iconic" just this once—members of Jack's trio were Chick Corea and Stanley Clarke. Together they created sublime, wordless music, with the classic palette of grand piano, upright bass, and sweet-sounding drumkit.

Jack's playing was supremely delicate and subtle, yet interspersed with deceptively complex rhythms and cymbal shadings, and a constant, yet seemingly effortless pulse. Driving home after with my friend Chris Stankee (also Jack's representative from the Sabian cymbal company), we talked about the rhythmic lilt that lingered, echoing in our minds' ears. It was a Latin kind of syncopation, but the astonishing thing was that it was a rhythmic statement they had never actually *played*, but only *implied* in the inner clockwork of their music.

(A note about this photo of Jack and me: in the background is a poster of "A GREAT DAY IN L.A.: A Celebration of Jazz," which features my late teacher Freddie Gruber in the front row. Freddie was very proud to have been part of that, as it replicates a famous photo from 1958 called *A Great Day in Harlem*, which Freddie always had in his house. Also, this was the same green room in which the photo of

Freddie, Roy Haynes, Jim Keltner, Ian Wallace, Ndugu Chancler, and myself was taken—see "At the Gate of the Year.")

Jack DeJohnette's career has been wide-ranging, and always at the highest elevations of modern jazz—from Miles Davis to a stellar recording called *Parallel Realities* with Pat Metheny and Herbie Hancock, to an entrancing duet called *Music from the Hearts of the Masters*, with Foday Musa Suso, a West African who plays the kora (a stringed instrument resembling the guitar and harp). I believe Jack DeJohnette bridges the traditional and modern styles of drumming more than any living player. His boundless virtuosity and improvisational eloquence are truly inspiring.

There's a quote by Bob Dylan I have repeated from time to time in interviews for years.

The highest purpose of art is to inspire. What else can you do? What else can you do for anyone but inspire them?

Where words fail, music speaks.

Sometimes pictures fail, too—and need words to clarify them.

If "Art is the telling of stories," then some stories require more than one art. Words and music, say, or words and pictures.

One good example is a print by an artist named Julianna Swaney that was given to me by my friend and fellow bird-lover Craiggie. It is a pen-and-ink drawing of a Victorian gentleman setting free a flock of birds from a wire cage. Craiggie found it through a serendipitous thrift-shop connection and knew I would like it. The description might seem like a happy and blameless image, and a pretty metaphor. But alas, Craiggie and I knew that the reality was far from happy, blameless, or pretty.

In the late nineteenth century, a British drug manufacturer named Eugene Schieffelin got it into his belfry that all of the birds mentioned in Shakespeare's plays should be introduced to the United States.

Let us just pause on that notion for a moment . . . while we consider the artist.

I admired the skill as well as the irony of the drawing, and wanted to know who the artist was. All I had to go on were the initials "J.S." penciled on the print (17 of 40), and I feared the work might represent one of the many unrecognized hobbyists whose art appears only at flea markets, yard sales, and thrift shops.

By a stroke of Interluck, I searched Schieffelin's name plus "drawing," and stumbled on an oblique connection (as you do). A friend of the artist wrote something about her—Julianna Swaney—on her own site, where I also learned that Ms. Swaney had titled the drawing *Oh My Cavalier*. (It's a nice twist on the adjectival form: "offhand and often disdainful dismissal of important matters.") About it she said, "I always liked the strangeness of this story and the image of a fancy nineteenth-century man releasing cages of birds in a snowy landscape."

Schieffelin's plan to introduce all of the birds mentioned in Shakespeare's plays began with skylarks and thrushes, but they did not thrive. Where skylarks failed, starlings succeeded—all too well. In 1890–91, our cavalier released 100 British starlings in New York's Central Park, and thus launched an avian plague. Despite the starling's pretty name, and a plumage speckled with flashy iridescence, they breed prolifically, nest and feed opportunistically, and bully weaker birds out of their way. Within about fifty years, starlings had spread across the continent. The shadow of their inexorable path westward was the displacement of native woodpeckers, flycatchers, swallows, and bluebirds, and today scientists at Columbia University estimate the North American starling population at 200 million—all descended from Schieffelin's 100 birds.

Flocks of up to a million starlings, called "murmurations," can be dazzling as they perform synchronized aerial ballets across the evening sky, like schooling fish with telepathic motion. But those same flocks can devour twenty tons of potatoes in a day, and choke jet engines to death—mechanical and human. In 1960, an airplane taking off from Boston flew into a flock estimated at 10,000 starlings—strangling the engines and ultimately killing sixty-two people.

Attempts at eradication included broadcasting starling distress signals, placing artificial owls, spraying detergents and poison, firing roman candles, and stringing electric wires around the Capitol columns in Washington, D.C. In 1931, the U.S. Department of Agriculture even released a recipe for "starling pie"—presumably at least a *little* tempting during the Great Depression—but nothing availed. Like other invasive species such as kudzu, zebra mussels, killer bees, the Russian thistle (better known as tumbleweed, a symbol of the American West as potent as the saguaro cactus), and fire ants, starlings are here to stay—no matter how much I would prefer bluebirds.

Here is another deceptive image of birds in flight. The scene is Malibu Lagoon, nearing sunset on a Sunday afternoon in December 2011. The beach was tranquil, only a few small groups of people here and there, silhouetted on an isthmus of sand between the surfer-dotted Pacific and the waterbird-dotted lagoon.

In the background is the Pacific Coast Highway, a justly famous Sunday cruising ground for cars and motorcycles, and just at this moment a battalion of open-piped V-twins shattered the evening peace. (You know the kind.) If those Sunday-afternoon outlaws took any notice at all, perhaps they laughed to see the frightened birds panic and circle into the sky.

Words fail, pictures fail, people fail.

What hope, then?

Well, great art never fails. And we can always try again—try to do better next time. There is always hope in the spirits of those who *do* try, in words, pictures, music, and everyday living.

"Lifetime achievement" is all about trying, really. The proper reward for any success is love and respect, and perhaps the only award for failure is the opportunity to try once more.

Even if it takes a desperate flight of 5,951 words and twelve photographs—only to fail again.

As Samuel Beckett said, "Try again. Fail again. Fail better."

There will be another time, another place, another story.

And there is always music.

# 7

# THE BETTER ANGELS

OCTOBER 2012

**This classic archetype** of the American West—lone rider traversing badlands, bison, cottonwoods, and sage—was captured in Theodore Roosevelt National Park, in Western North Dakota, early on the morning of Tuesday, September 25, 2012.

The notion of "West Dakota" has humorous resonance for frequent co-adventurer Brutus and me. In our collaborative building of Bubba's Bar 'n' Grill, the cooking department on my website, we wanted a quirky name for the location of Brutus's branch of Bubba's test kitchens. We combined a disparaging nickname for his hometown of Calgary and an invented Western state to create "Cowfart, West Dakota."

Later we actually received a few grumbling messages from people demanding to know the *exact* location of Bubba's Bar 'n' Grill, so they could visit it. Given the place's "virtuality," the only possible answer is that Bubba's Bar 'n' Grill is *everywhere* (which perhaps explains the person who wrote to thank us for a great time there). At least one couple wanted to be married at Bubba's, and another frustrated

Deep in West Dakota

seeker claimed, "I found West Dakota, but I can't find Cowfart." To which the only possible response is "?"

This particular morning began for me and my American riding partner Michael in a cold, sunny Walmart parking lot in Bismarck, North Dakota. On show nights we sleep on the bus while driver Dave delivers us to my chosen drop-off point, and in these days of budget-shuttered rest areas and crowded truck stops, he often parks us at a Walmart. (Their company policy welcomes RVs and travel trailers—overnight guests are potential morning customers.) After the previous night's show in Minneapolis, we had a day off before the next one in Winnipeg.

Among my duties on a show-day afternoon is planning our rides for the next couple of days. The relevant paper maps are spread around me on the floor of the bus's front lounge, and after a period of high-concept scanning, I highlight a meandering route along the smallest roads and through the tiniest dots of communities (preferably of the one-stop-sign variety). Hunched at his computer station in the corner, likewise on the floor, Michael transfers that route to the GPS program, Mother, then to our onboard units, Doofus and Dingus. Early the following morning, after breakfast on the bus, we roll the bikes off the trailer and load up our supplies for the overnight journey. Finally pulling away and raising my feet to the pegs always combines a feeling of relief at having the morning's pre-travel chores done at last, and anticipation for the coming ride. The maps displayed on the bike-mounted Doofus and Dingus guide us more or less unerringly along an intricate chain of tiny backroads and secondary highways.

As I have remarked before, "The best roads are the ones no one travels unless they live on them, and there's one even rarer category—roads no one even *lives* on."

Because our travels this tour began in the heavily populated East (more about the actual *shows* later—some people have the crazy notion that these tours are about something more than the motor-cycle rides between), designing routes like that could be a challenge. As an example, consider just the first puzzle: getting from the opening show in Manchester, New Hampshire, to the second in the D.C. area.

As a rule, after the shows I try to "stage" the bus somewhere along the direct interstate route to the next city, for Dave's sake—it's no fun navigating a forty-five-foot bus and a twenty-foot trailer along roads no one travels unless they live on them. Because I sleep much better when the bus is stationary, I usually try to keep those drives to two or three hours. (I have remarked before how pleasant it is to feel the bus

being maneuvered into a parking spot, and the main engine shudder and die into the steady drone of the generator. Now my bed is not going to move anymore.)

Before the Manchester show, I sat on the bus floor and spread out the maps of the intervening states—New York, Pennsylvania, Maryland, West Virginia, and Virginia. With much furrowing of brow, I tried to string together enough of the little roads and small towns to make an enjoyable two-day ride.

However, it was a real head-strainer. Whichever way I looked, so many cities and densely populated areas blocked the way, with interstates the only through routes. As a card-carrying shunpiker, I

First show day, Mount Washington Auto Road, New Hampshire

conscientiously avoid major roads except into and out of major cities. Especially on days off, I make every effort not to travel even one mile on a four-lane road. But in this impossible situation, I finally settled on a "hybrid" route—choosing some more desirable areas and connecting them by a couple of interstate links. Thus I would use the big roads for their intended purpose—as mileage-disposal units and relatively speedy ways through or around cities.

From the "Cliché Busters" series– New Jersey.

The next morning, from a Walmart parking lot in Newburgh, New York, Michael and I unloaded and packed the bikes. We followed sweet little roads through the Delaware Water Gap area of New Jersey, quiet and densely forested, across a tiny toll bridge over the Delaware River to the Pennsylvania side. (Right around there I once saw a black bear cub.) We had another remarkably long stretch of serene riding, narrow roads winding through woods and around small lakes dotted with rustic cabins.

Then, at the strategic point where things were about to get congested, we jumped on the superslab—just in time for a monsoon rainstorm. In heavy rain, I would much rather be on a backroad, because the trucks on the interstate throw up such a cloud of spray that you can't even see the road's surface.

To a motorcycle rider, nothing is more important than the road's surface.

But, it was what it was, so we slowed down and kept things smooth and careful.

On the other side of that urban and suburban nexus of Harrisburg-Reading, we made our escape to the little roads again, down through Southern Pennsylvania into Maryland.

Among many changes leading into this tour, onstage and off (patient reader, in the fullness of time, I will try to address them all), Michael decided to get serious about photography. Even in principle, I was all for that—he would be taking better pictures of *me*!

He bought a professional-grade SLR body with a big fancy lens and got some instruction from a knowledgeable friend on how to use it. On our earliest rides, even his first experiments demonstrated the remarkable difference in what he could capture compared to my little hand-held model. We could pick a scenic backdrop and set up a shot, and I would do a couple of passes for Michael while he fired off a machine-gun-like series of images. (He called it the "spray and pray" approach.)

At least one of them was bound to be good—and they were. But now I had a new job every show day—edit-

ing the dozens of photographs that Michael would download and pass over to me. That job added another hour's work to that always-busy time, and choosing from all the "sprays" was sometimes as head-breaking as the mapping—but the rewards of both should be clear in this story.

Getting back to the route-mapping, other early rides this time didn't require such desperate mea-sures. For example, we had a couple of days of absolutely sublime riding in West Virginia—all in all, after long and careful evaluation, the best motor-cycling in the East. The state weaves a wonderful variety of twisty paved roads, usually lightly trav-eled, and among its leafy mountains, it also hides the largest number of what I have come to consider a kind of shunpiker's Holy Grail, for their rarity and pleasure—one-lane paved roads. We also try to toss in some off-pavement riding every day when we can, and in that cat-egory, West Virginia never fails to throw some adventure back at us.

(Speaking of those leafy mountains, I couldn't help thinking of the strip mines, clear-cuts, and chemical plants that also scar West Virginia, and noted, "So much beauty hiding so much ugliness.")

This time, just before we were about to start a long unpaved sec-tion, we paused for a minute at the roadside. A pickup truck stopped beside us, and the driver said, "Do you fellas know where you're going?"

I said I *thought* we did, and walked over with my paper map. I showed him the dotted line that led between a nearby town, Webster Springs, toward another dot called Pickens. He shook his head, puz-zled, and said, "I don't know what that road might be, and I've lived here all my life."

He pointed up the way we were going. "This road is gated—you can't get through."

However, in the course of a leisurely, West Virginia–style conversation, it turned out that our man worked for a logging company that controlled about 360,000 acres in the area, and his boss planned an inspection of this particular section soon. Our man was just about to drive up and unlock the two gates, and he invited us to follow him through.

Now here was a road that took shunpiking *all* the way: no one lived on it, no one traveled it, and no one was even *allowed* on it.

After a long stretch of linked gravel trails and tracks, often running along high ridges on logging roads at around 3,000 feet—high for the East—we emerged at the time-capsule community of Pickens. Deep in the heart of West Virginia, Pickens (population sixty-six) might be the most remote settlement in the East. It certainly felt that way to us—like entering a *Twilight Zone* episode—as we emerged from gravel roads through deep woods to see its quaint little post office, freshly painted railroad depot (though the tracks were long gone), and a couple of hand-carved wooden signs, one reading "School" and the other "Leper Grave." (Whoa!)

This "attraction" evokes some curious history and a local hero, Dr. James Cunningham (1863–1965), who practiced in Pickens for over sixty years. He delivered 3,600 babies without losing a mother, and treated one of West Virginia's three known cases of leprosy. A Syrian railroad worker named Rashid was exiled by company officials to Pickens—even then "the most remote terminal on the line"—where he died soon after.

Southeastern Ohio

On the day of my sixtieth birthday, September 12 (yay, I'm a sexagenarian!), I was able to plot 332 miles from a Walmart in Columbus down through Southwestern Ohio, across Northern Kentucky, then up through Southeastern Indiana to Bloomington.

In all that seven hours of riding, most of it as good as it gets, we did not experience one *minute* of congestion. Think about that for a moment—a whole day of moving through the world at a velocity determined solely by your own energy and whims. Just winding little roads, rural countryside, crossroads towns, and glorious weather and scenery.

"Roads no one travels unless they live on them."

It was a fine birthday present.

As often seems to happen in my seemingly random explorations of rural America, those early rides also introduced some unexpected themes that would echo in other days. At the bottom of the Mount Washington Auto Road, on the day of the first show in Manchester, we noticed an encampment of primitive-looking canvas tents, open fires, and people wandering around in costumes from centuries past. My first thought was "Civil War reenactment," which I knew to be a popular hobby for some Americans, but Michael pointed out that we were too far north for that war. The tricorn hats worn by some of the campers were another clue—they were Revolutionary War reenactors. Who knew?

But it was the Civil War that haunted our travels for the next few days. In Pennsylvania, we passed Gettysburg, where President Lincoln's famous "Four score and seven years ago" address was delivered after a terrible battle, then south to Maryland and past Antietam—the site of one of the deadliest single battles in American history, leaving over 26,000 dead. Such slaughter is sad to contemplate.

In searching for hotels in that region, I wanted to stay at the nearby State Line Motel, on Mason-Dixon Road (named after the eighteenth-century surveyors who drew a symbolic line between the North and South), just for the name and place, really. But once we arrived for a look-over, the property appeared neglected.

After years of surveying motels in smaller towns and deciding "yea" or "nay" by purely visual, external clues, lately, for my ongoing study of Roadcraft, I have been trying to define the details that give me the feeling that a place just isn't being *cared* for. The paint, for one, and the landscaping, but perhaps the best indicator of neglect is weeds and grass growing up through the asphalt. That may well represent the care given to other aspects of the property. Like the sheets and towels. In any case, the restaurant beside the State Line Motel was closed, a dealbreaker for us. Onward to the Best Western in Hagerstown, Maryland, and a gigantic buffet, full of gigantic people, with a wine list offering a choice of soda pops.

The next show's venue was near Manassas, Virginia, where two horrific battles were fought near the creek called Bull Run. In Philippi, West Virginia, a sign announced the town as the site of "the first land battle of the Civil War." Beside what must be a uniquely large covered bridge, a sign described its use by both Union and Confederate armies.

On a previous tour we had ridden right beside the courthouse at Appomattox, where the surrender documents were signed by generals Ulysses S. Grant and Robert E. Lee. Driver Dave, an American history enthusiast, always left a selection of his magazines by my bedside, often about cowboys and the Old West, and among them this time was a *U.S. News & World Report* special edition on the Civil War. The stories and pictures came alive as I traveled among the places where those events had happened so long ago.

That war, and others like it, were also forward in my thoughts because of the book I was reading early in this run: *The Better Angels of Our Nature: Why Violence Has Declined* by Steven Pinker. (In a nice coincidence, the title is a quote from Abraham Lincoln.) A Canadian-born cognitive scientist and professor of psychology at Harvard, Steven Pinker is one of those rare and precious academics who is able to convey his deep knowledge and extensive research in a form that

is both understandable and thought-provoking to what is called in publishing "the general reader." I definitely consider myself a general reader, in that sense, and had much appreciated an earlier book of his, *How the Mind Works* (1997), a Pulitzer Prize finalist, and reviews of *The Better Angels of Our Nature* had seemed intriguing.

On the morning of the first show, I carried that weighty volume with me for a stroll down the main street of Littleton, New Hampshire, from the quintessential motel to the quintessential diner, delightfully named Topic of the Town. These were both small-town delights I had discovered and written about on our last tour, while a new discovery in Littleton was Bishop's Ice Cream. Riding in the previous afternoon, I was tempted by its location in an old house on the edge of town. (Later Michael observed that in a town like Littleton, every business from plumbers to doctors to banks seemed to be in an old house.) I had a wonderful blueberry milkshake, which was locally called a "frappe," I learned when I asked the owner why I didn't see milkshakes listed on his menu board.

At the Topic of the Town, over my orange juice and coffee, I waited for my oatmeal and eggs, recreated a self-portrait from that previous visit, then started reading . . .

One of these days I will push aside the cobwebs over at Bubba's Book Club and write up the growing list of great titles I have read in the past year or so. (Before the tour, in the last of my "free time," I was carrying around a box full of about fifteen books that I wanted to start writing about—but it was not to be.) A full report on this book will surely find its way onto that list.

Meanwhile, here is a quote from the *New York Times* review by Peter Singer that piqued my interest: "[It] is a supremely important book. To have command of so much research, spread across so many different fields, is a masterly achievement. Pinker convincingly demonstrates that there has been a dramatic decline in violence, and he is persuasive about the causes of that decline."

I will have more to say about the reflections the book inspired during my travels around the eastern United States, as Steven Pinker's revelations and reflections evoked and clarified some of my own.

Another semi-related theme emerged on the way to a show in

Fallingwater

Pittsburgh, when I routed us up from West Virginia through Maryland and onto a Pennsylvania backroad I had traveled with Brutus back on the first concert tour I did by motorcycle, *Test for Echo*, in 1996. That time, only by chance did we ride near a settlement named Bear Run, where I saw a sign for an attraction called Fallingwater. I recognized the name of a legendary masterpiece by revered architect Frank Lloyd Wright. Quickly computing that we had time for a visit, Brutus and I strolled down the path through the woods to encounter this exquisite structure set directly over a stream, just above a waterfall. Then and now, it was breathtaking and unforgettable to see. A home not only *in* its place, but *of* its place, and surely an expression of our better angels.

Allowing this narrative to spin out according to theme rather than chronology, about ten days later I was on the bus floor with my maps trying to plot an interesting route between St. Louis and Minneapolis. The obvious way would have been up through Wisconsin, with fine little roads for motorcycling among its humped green farmland. But it would be a Sunday, when every other two-wheeler in the state would be clogging the roads and little towns. (Michael once made me laugh by referring to summer Sundays in the Midwest as "Trike Day," but perhaps that's too esoteric an observation for the "general reader.")

On a Wisconsin Sunday in good weather, you were likely to come up behind long "processions" of cruisers doing what they do—cruising—but in tremendous numbers of staggered pairs, and very slowly. They actually get huffy if you try to pass your way through them, growling over as you try to cut in, "Don't break up our procession!" (Really.)

So, Wisconsin on a Tuesday? Absolutely.

On a sunny Sunday, not so much.

So, I thought, "Go West, old man," and pulled out the map of Iowa. I had chosen a similar diversion on our way from Indianapolis to Chicago, and on a previous tour, Iowa City had been a pleasant discovery—a small city enlivened by its university, the proverbial "college town." Both times we traced some lovely country roads through Western Illinois and Southern Iowa, paved and gravel, cornfields on one side and soybeans on the other (don't know why, but it always seemed to be that way), up to Iowa City. Despite its population of only about 67,000 people, the vitality and sociability of the students combines with the worldliness of the faculty members to create a vibrant energy. It was the kind of place where we could stay in a sophisticated boutique hotel and stroll down a pedestrian-only street offering plenty of choices for eclectic dining—a rare combination in America's smaller communities. Other college towns, like Bloomington, Indiana, also shine that way.

Banking through Iowa
(Cliché Busters 2)

The Wikipedia entry for Iowa City offers a couple of telling factoids. "Iowa City is tied with Stamford, Connecticut, for the U.S. metropolitan area with the highest percentage of the adult population holding a bachelor's degree or higher; forty-four percent of adults hold a degree." And, "Iowa City was ranked as the tenth best city in America for singles in 2012 by Kiplinger." (Michael was excited by that prospect, but during his visit, he remained among those singles. Now he wants to visit the other nine.)

One more worthy detail I noticed on the way into Iowa City was that my GPS showed us to be only 2.5 miles from the midtown hotel, yet I was still passing farms and open fields, with few other vehicles.

Same on the way out—within minutes of leaving the hotel you are on a peaceful country road.

So Iowa City was already on our "favorites" list, but Mason City was pretty much an unknown to me. I had passed through and stopped for gas there on my *Ghost Rider* travels back in the spring of 1999, but you don't learn much about a place that way. Crouched over the Iowa map and scanning for likely routes and an overnight destination, I

Park Inn, Mason City, Iowa

called over to Michael, sitting at his customary perch in front of his computer, online and likely up to no good.

"Yo, Mackel—do me a favor. Look up lodgings in Mason City, Iowa—see what they got."

A minute later he announced, "They have a historic hotel designed by Frank Lloyd Wright."

My disbelief must have been manifest, as he added, "Seriously."

So, of course, off to Mason City we went . . .

Built in 1910 to house a bank to the left and a hotel to the right, the building had been restored at great expense, and in elegant detail, down to the furnishings in the lobby and the twenty-seven guest rooms. (Mine was the entire front of the pagoda-like turret to the far right, beautifully proportioned, windowed, and appointed.) Framed photographs in the rooms showed a couple of Wright-designed private homes in Mason City that were also splendidly envisioned and uniquely executed.

We found a good restaurant nearby, even on a Sunday evening, so our approval of the town was complete. The night music of Mason City (good title) was numerous train horns—the long mournful chord sounding frequently through the night.

Staying with that theme of memorable accommodations (among our usual Walmarts and chain motels), while I was figuring out how best to spend two days off between Chicago and Detroit, I had hoped to visit Isle Royale National Park, in Lake Superior. However, research showed not only how hard it was to get to—four hours by boat from the Upper Michigan side—but the only accommodations on the island closed on September 8, one week too early for my plans.

Since childhood I remembered hearing from time to time about an island in upper Lake Huron that had banned automobiles long ago, and everyone traveled by horse-drawn vehicles. Mackinac Island, it was called, near Mackinaw City (both pronounced the same, just French and English spellings of the Native name). By having Dave drive us to Green Bay, Wisconsin, after the Chicago show, Michael and I could get across the Upper Peninsula of Michigan to St. Ignace by mid-afternoon. We parked our bikes in the ferry company's shed and boarded the passenger ferry for the short ride to the island. We would have two nights and a day there. On the way over, our accommodations came into view . . .

At the ferry dock, among other horse-drawn vehicles, we found an elegant carriage in shiny dark red lacquer with "Grand Hotel" gold-leafed on its sides. It was pulled by two dapple-gray draft horses in ornate harnesses. Climbing in knee-to-knee with a few other tourists (once school opens, most travelers seem to be about eighty—which suits me fine, as I am anonymous among them), we were carried up the hill. The hotel's porch is advertised as the longest in the world, 900 feet—almost a football field. Automobiles were outlawed in 1898,

Grand Hotel,
Mackinac Island,
Michigan

THE BETTER ANGELS

119

and the horse-drawn carriages are not just for tourists—only emergency vehicles and construction machines are allowed.

During that long, *easeful* day off, Michael and I took a private carriage tour of the island. ("No Michael, it was *not* romantic!") Our guide, Rebecca, told us what it was like to live there year-round. The winter population was around 600 people, and when we asked what they did, she said, "We drink a lot of beer."

The island was actually the second designated national park in the United States, in 1875, after Yellowstone, and was looked after by the soldiers from Fort Mackinac. After twenty years, the military abandoned their fort, and with no one to take care of the preserve, it reverted to the state of Michigan, which still holds eighty percent of the island as a state park.

Again, such a place surely represents "the better angels of our nature," as I continued to read Steven Pinker's book during that restful day.

Interestingly, as Pinker sets out to show that people are not only dramatically less violent than past generations and cultures, but even measurably smarter, his list of factors—reason, education, democracy—does not include religion. As befits a serious scholar, he is carefully even-handed and gives credit to the influence of the Quakers in abolishing the slave trade and to the African-American churches for helping to keep the Civil Rights struggles from becoming violent (though noting that Martin Luther King Jr. was more influenced by secular philosophers and Gandhi than by his Divinity studies). But at the same time he is unable to avoid showing that the religious wars of the past millennium were the cruelest and most murderous times in history and that, overall, religion has *not* been an "improving" force in human behavior.

Reason, education, and democracy have been the *real* faith, hope, and charity in that elevation.

It bothers me a little to have gained a reputation as a "faith-basher." Though I get how some of my lyrics and other writings inspire that tag, in an everyday way I don't feel like I stand against anything that strongly. I feel more like a *positive* audience for the world I move through. (As Paul Theroux said, "It takes a lot of optimism to be a traveler.")

For me, such reactions always result from direct *observation*. Or in this case, confrontation.

Two quotes apply. The first I have tried to keep in mind for many years, after watching a foreign correspondent speaking to camera on location in some troubled place. In telling what he had seen, he said something like, "I only report this, I do not comment."

The second is one of the deepest thoughts ever attributed to Ronald Reagan: "Don't be afraid to see what you see."

I have been thinking about that one for years.

When I am anywhere in my native Canada, or Europe, or in California, or around the East Coast, religion is not a subject I think about very often. Recognizing its controversial nature and not wanting to be vilified for something that doesn't mean much to me, I frequently resolve not to bother writing about the subject again.

Until . . . my travels push me south and force me to confront a shocking fortress, a walled kingdom buttressed by church signs and billboards, all shouting at me, assaulting me, with breathtaking arrogance and ignorance. It can be funny at first, but soon becomes appalling—such a backwards drag on the country and the world.

As described in *Roadshow*, it was the American Mid-South with its smack-you-in-the-face-right-to-hell kind of old-time religion that inspired the reactions I wove into that book, then into the lyrics for *Snakes and Arrows*. The same unavoidable reaction seeped into many of the stories I have written since—based on personal exposure to those benighted regions.

You know what it's like? It's like when I find myself riding in a state with no helmet law. Helmet-wearing is another issue I don't think much about in most places in North America or Europe, where people wear helmets, whether by law or by choice. When I suddenly start seeing bare-headed riders looking all pea-headed (in both senses), it gets my attention, and my thoughts, and begs to be reported.

Pinker's research also shows that *everyone* thinks they are above average—in intelligence, driving ability, and morality. (Psychologists call it the "Lake Wobegon Effect," after Garrison Keillor's fictional Minnesota community "where all the children are above average.") Pinker also points out the even more absurd belief that almost everyone considers themselves to be "lucky." So basically people figure they're too smart to be fooled by anything and too lucky for anything bad to happen to them.

With protective clothing for motorcyclists, as with religion, there's no point harping on it—you're not going to change anyone's stubborn convictions. But you have to speak out for the young people—you might just plant a seed of sense or rebellion in a young mind.

At the beginning of this tour, the modest churches in New England didn't faze me at all—just decorative centerpieces for the villages. But as we rode into Southern Pennsylvania, then West Virginia and Kentucky and so on, our eyes and brains were assaulted by a constant barrage of scolding church signs and lurid billboards.

"GOD ONLY WROTE ONE BOOK. DON'T U THINK U SHOULD READ IT?"

(So wrong, on so many levels. Even theologically.)

"SERVING GOD IS LIKE LEARNING TO PLAY GOLF. KEEP YOUR KNEES BENT AND YOUR ARMS EXTENDED."

(Seriously?)

Or how about riding past a "Christian riding stable" with a sign advertising their mission statement: "TEACHING THE LORD'S TRUTHS THROUGH HORSEMANSHIP."

I only report this, I do not comment.

Whistlin' past the graveyard

Mid-South meander

In a small Kentucky city, the sheriff's car was one of those retro-mobster Chrysler models blacked-out and armored like dystopian battle-wagons that are so popular with LEOs (law enforcement officers) in small towns and certain state patrols. Apart from the usual insignia, its trunk was decorated with gold-leaf letters reading "IN GOD WE TRUST," plus the chrome "fish" emblem devout Christians often sport on their vehicles (without considering the unfortunate metaphor—like the sheep one they also favor), and also a painted scripture reference, "PSALM 118." (A particularly rapturous hymn of praise, it also contains the scary line, "All nations compassed me about: but in the name of the LORD will I destroy them.")

Just seeing what I see, and sharing it. You gotta testify.

Because . . . I love these roads and little places I ramble through, and believe these people are good at heart—just brainwashed from childhood. I dislike the elitist coastal notion of Middle America as "flyover country"—for me it is "ride-through country." I would rather fly over New York City and Los Angeles and ride through the rest!

In *Deer Hunting With Jesus*, the author Joe Bageant writes about growing up in Northwestern Virginia, near the West Virginia line, then moving out into the "wider world." In an affectionate lament, he shakes his head over the fates of his former neighbors, seeing how they defiantly stand in their own way and stubbornly vote against their own best interests. If you care about the well-being of your fellow humans, such a plight is bound to bother you.

Ozark water crossing

Steven Pinker convincingly illustrates how Southerners have retained from their Scots-Irish ancestors an outdated "honor code"— a thin-skinned pugnacity that leads to a culture of violence. (He also shows that the distinction is *not* racial—Yankees of all races are less violent.) I only repeat this, but it does seem as though that "oh yeah?" response is reflected even in the belligerence of their *faith*.

*The Better Angels of Our Nature* also cites clinical tests showing that people everywhere will pretend to believe what those around them profess, as a simple human desire to "fit in." We all know that people who are pretending something get *very* angry if mocked—because

Theodore Roosevelt
National Park

they are *embarrassed*, a tiny step from resentful rage—and as for guilty doubters of a faith, they may well be the fiercest voices in the choir.

One giant billboard a hundred feet above the road asserted, "HELL IS REAL."

At a stoplight, Michael said, in a world-weary tone, "Oh, I know. I'm *in* it." He didn't mean the place—he meant my company. (Bitter, hateful man.) But let us ride away from these unrewarding subjects. ("Bye, Michael!")

I would merely point out that such fanatics hold themselves back, and the rest of us, too. Radical Islam is a worrisome barrier to the world's upward motion, but there are others eager to impede reason ("Lean not on your own understanding"), education (ancient myths taught as "science"), and democracy (medieval beliefs become national policy). Such throwbacks only impede the progress of our better angels.

The theme of great beauty hiding terrible ugliness brings us, at last, all the way back to Western North Dakota and Theodore Roosevelt National Park. Winding toward that segue, we also carry along some other themes, like a traveler's natural wonder about what is really best for the world around him.

This one's a tough nut—people will have to judge for themselves.

Clues appeared as Michael and I rode west from Bismarck, beginning our day off with something over a hundred miles on Interstate 94. (A necessary sacrifice to get us to Theodore Roosevelt National Park, where I could collect a new passport stamp—all meaningless to Michael—and get us close enough to the next show in Winnipeg to make it on the show day.) On that bright, chilly morning, we passed many semis carrying unusual loads—clearly marked modules of oil wells, for example, portable construction offices, and long, wide structures of unidentifiable hardware.

It was when we left the park that things became bad. I had looped through Eastern North Dakota on a previous tour and thought I knew what the state was like. Wheat and ranchland dotted with bird-friendly wetlands, occasional small towns with water towers and cottonwoods, and many abandoned farmhouses (describing those at the time as the "state symbol"). This time, highlighting my route from the national park up toward Minot for the night had seemed easy—long, straight backroads north through the Fort Berthold Indian Reservation (another fascinating history), a couple of small dots and town names among the likely wheat and ranchland, then over the Little Missouri River and a casual northeast zigzag.

The reality was harshly different.

Backtracking a few miles east on the interstate, we turned north on little Highway 85 and were immediately surrounded by trucks. Looming ahead of us, and thundering toward us, were road construction vehicles, side-loading semi dump trucks, and dozens of tankers—not the shiny mirror ones you see on the interstate, but crude, trellis frames around muddy gray iron cylinders.

I had routed us through Killdeer, thinking it looked big enough on the map that it should have a gas station, and because it is named after a bird I like (a grasslands plover that fakes a broken wing and distress call—its namesake "kill-deer, kill-deer"—to lead predators away from its nest). At its crossroads, we approached a scene of raw devastation on a huge scale, a vast construction site of mud and gravel where the intersection was being enlarged from two lanes in each direction to what looked like it would be *six*. We had to weave through the muddy gravel and semis to the gas station, and through what *used* to be a typical prairie town. As we traveled north, the construction sites increased, and we were shunted on makeshift detours where miles of road were torn up and diverted onto dirt and gravel lanes. If it had been raining, we would have been in big trouble on a surface like that (as I knew from experience on such "roads" in the Arctic when it rained). In one case, a long stretch of highway was simply barricaded off while they blasted and widened it, sending us about a hundred miles out of our way. Anywhere else in America, that would never stand. (My paper map still showed that road as a dotted-line "scenic route," so I knew whatever was going on around there, it had changed fast.)

Theodore Roosevelt
National Park

Encampments at the roadside were scattered with hundreds of small travel-trailers, dormitories for the workers and drivers, and water was being pumped out of roadside sloughs to fill the tankers that sprinkle the detours to keep the dust down. Ranchers and farmers posted homemade signs offering patches of open land for truck parking. I couldn't figure out what was going on around us, but I thought, "Whatever it is, it's *awful*."

All of that construction and traffic slowed us down a lot, as did the long detour, and it was late in the day before we reached Minot. We almost never have trouble finding rooms in whatever little town we roll into, and I had explored Minot's meager offerings before, so I knew the Holiday Inn was about the best to be had. But as we rode past the fairgrounds and saw parking lots full of trucks and RVs, and the hotel parking lot jammed with pickups, I began to worry.

Sure enough, it was state fair time, and not a room to be had in the whole town.

Remarkably, there was no grumbling—we just faced our fates, fueled up, and kept riding, another hour east to Rugby, North Dakota. Rugby bills itself as "The Geographical Center of North America," and on that theme, we had the Hub motel (big metal sign showing a map of North America with a starred dot in the middle) and an attached restaurant. After an eleven-hour day and almost 500 miles, we would not begrudge its basic comforts.

Nor would there be any complaining the next morning, when we rose early, scraped the frost off our saddles (it was exactly freezing— 0°C), and rode another 300 miles to Winnipeg. Michael was really having fun now, and said, "Why is it that when I'm traveling with you, I'm always either sweltering or shivering?"

I said, "Because you always have the wrong clothes!"

But that evening in Rugby, after a simple dinner at the Hub of North America (once again, with a wine list of soda pops), I leafed through the newsletter we had been given at the national park. There I found the story behind my impression of "awful," under the headline "What's going on around here?!"

Surprised by the amount of truck traffic in the area? Unable to get a hotel reservation? Can't find the sleepy cowboy towns you remember? The reason for the incredible changes this area is experiencing lies two miles below the surface of western North Dakota—a formation called the Bakken. The Bakken formation is a rock layer rich with oil reserves. Until recently, the oil was not extractable. A new and controversial technique—hydraulic fracturing or "fracking"—has allowed oil companies to more than quadruple their daily oil production in the last five years. The huge influx of activity has brought tens of thousands of new jobs to the area. In a national economy where jobs are scarce, North Dakota has become the "land of opportunity" for many.

All three North Dakota National Parks are experiencing serious issues due to the oil boom. New wells are going in every month; many can be seen from inside park boundaries. Each new well means another drill rig, well pad, pumpjack, debris pit, flare pit, storage tanks, and access road on the landscape. Each new well requires 2,000 "trucking events" to complete its setup and to begin pumping oil. Noise and dust from heavy truck traffic and pumping equipment is constant. Numerous flares can be seen in the formerly dark night sky as excess natural gas is burned off. Socioeconomic impacts are altering local communities. A multifaceted topic to be sure, the oil boom begs a difficult question: how can we develop our resources while still protecting our parks and communities?

That is another very even-handed appraisal, it seems to me, for a national park publication. And the question they raise about balancing development and protection is "difficult" indeed. This oil boom in Western North Dakota has only been underway for about three years, and the pace of it is frenetic, rapacious. The only similarly careless extraction of resources regardless of consequences I have witnessed are in Northern Canada, China, and West Africa. The only such devastation disguised as road construction I have witnessed is in the Arctic, and in Argentina. These are not good examples.

Theodore Roosevelt
National Park

Now, having learned a fair amount about what's going on "Deep in West Dakota," especially from first-hand accounts of people living and working there, I am fairly horrified—but trying very hard not to go off into an environmental rant. In the spirit of "Don't be afraid to see what you see," though, and wanting to share it, for the above article to say that extracting fossil fuels by hydraulic fracturing, or fracking, is "controversial" is wildly diplomatic. (And that must be a unique oxymoron.) Groundwater is poisoned, often permanently; farmland is destroyed, often for decades, by leaks of the poisonous "brine" used in the process (and, unbelievably, the oil companies alone are responsible for reporting their own spills, with almost no oversight). Surface water from the prairie wetlands that serve as migration oases for millions of birds is pumped away to dampen the dusty roads. Tens of thousands of workers—not to mention tens of thousands of semis—have a far-reaching effect on the environment. Just for one small example, those encampments of house trailers—where does their sewage go?

So it's a big mess.

My first response was accurate: "Whatever it is, it's *awful*."

And yet . . . in a few brief years North Dakota has shot from being a state in population decline, in a time of economic recession, to having the lowest unemployment rate in the United States, workers flocking in from everywhere, and a billion-dollar state surplus. All of a sudden, North Dakota is the second-largest oil producer in the United States, after Texas. This is indeed a boom.

One can easily parrot the justification—"to reduce our dependence on foreign oil," and if we add another hot political keyword, "jobs," the sum of that equation is "votes."

It adds up to the same equation that strips the mountaintops of West Virginia for coal (I saw the same thing happening on a remote backroad in Alberta, just west of Edmonton), and—indeed—that keeps the coal industry going at all. But I've ranted about that before. This is about what is happening two miles deep in West Dakota.

And the thing is, in all of these places, I *want* people to have jobs. But not these dirty, nasty jobs, and a life that answers the dark premonitions of Thomas Hobbes (who is frequently referenced in *The Better Angels of Our Nature*): "No arts; no letters; no society; and which is worst of all, continual fear, and danger of violent death: and the life of man, solitary, poor, nasty, brutish and short."

That surely describes how life can be in coal towns and oilfields, and I don't wish an existence like that for anyone. Even if it will "reduce our dependence on foreign oil" and produce jobs. Or votes.

A further metaphor about "roads no one travels unless they live on them" says something about integrity. The roads I travel are the ones I *live* on—in every sense. In the largest abstraction, the work I do and the way I live has to reflect that direct engagement with the world around me.

Not everyone lives on the roads they travel—especially, say, politicians and financiers. They talk the necessary talk to get the votes or the deals, and console themselves that they are doing the right thing, and the lies are just a means. So they aren't riding that road—but they don't care. The rest of us should.

Perhaps the saddest roads in America are the ones that people *used* to live on, but don't anymore. Some stretches of Old 66, little towns in the Midwest whose Main Street stores are boarded up, with maybe a few optimistically repurposed as antique shops or local museums (in a formulation I have expressed before, the closed shops, restaurants, and gas stations represent the death of someone's

Ozark mountain
roller coaster

dream), and—aptly—the abandoned farmhouses of North Dakota. Places where people don't live anymore.

For myself, I plan to keep exploring these roads and seeing what I see.

And I plan to keep making Michael's life as much of a living hell as I can.

Because he knows what the billboard preaches: "HELL IS REAL."

Oh yes.

My journal notes from the first few days of this tour mention the idea of the "rolling stage." In our professional life, arenas sometimes have a portable stage on wheels, and at the beginning of the day it is positioned toward the center of the "rink." Thus the overhead work on P.A., lights, and video screens can go on while our band crew assembles the instruments on the rolling stage, away from that aerial activity. Once the overhead stuff is ready, the stage is pushed into place, at the end of the rink under the lights, by a team of stage-hands. (Drum tech Gump *very* much appreciates those stages, as he has more time to put up the kit than if our band crew doesn't get onstage until the overhead stuff is done.)

A rolling stage also stands as a decent metaphor for a concert tour and, stretched a little farther, for what Michael and I (and sometimes Brutus) do.

From the interior vantage point, onstage or on the bike, I am performing—"operating the machine." Mind and body are fully engaged in the mechanics and art of executing, adapting, and being as smooth and accurate as I can. But at the same time, I am observing the "rolling stage" in front of me—whether a pageant of scenery or an appreciative audience.

Just before band rehearsals, I wrote a piece for Drum Workshop's *Edge* magazine about my long preparations, physically and musically, and each of the band members brought that dedication to the rehearsal hall from the beginning. Over the course of many months, we built up the most musically adventurous and visually "active" show we have ever presented. Deciding to do two different shows on alternate nights, with a number of songs changing, and even a few "one-off" songs for special occasions, has been uplifting for us.

Iowa morning

Perhaps most uplifting of all has been adding "guest musicians" to our show for the first time in our lengthy career. Having the Clockwork Angels String Ensemble join us makes the second set really special. The eight string players were chosen by arranger David Campbell, who wrote the scores for the *Clockwork Angels* album as well as for a number of older songs in the set.

The string arrangement for "YYZ" was an afterthought. That instrumental was originally planned to be played as a trio, after we said "A Farewell to Strings." But when we noticed that it began with Geddy playing string *samples* on his foot pedals, after the real thing, it just seemed wrong. David wrote an arrangement for the strings to accompany us, and that song came to represent the climax of the show, I think—at least on our side of the barricade.

I am not able to watch the string players perform, as they are on a riser behind me, and I can't listen to them much. (Needing to lay down a strong foundation for all those players, as in a big band, I have to concentrate on the accuracy and smoothness of my own part.) But I can certainly feel the *energy* they bring to their performance, add to our show, and contribute to the interplay my more mobile bandmates are able to have with them.

As my young (well, mid-thirties) nephew Sean said about an early show, "Those string players sound amazing—and they *rock!*"

Live in Edmonton

On both my rolling stages, it is good to feel that we are exploring new territory, with unflinching determination, youthful energy, and great satisfaction in doing it.

And even with this story's prodigious length, I am skipping so many wonderful images and tempting stories from our 7,000 miles of motorcycling—the Lafayette Hotel in Marietta, Ohio; riding the Ozarks with Tom Marinelli or the backroads of Saskatchewan and Alberta with Brutus—and how each of the twelve shows kept getting better and more energized as we went.

But at this late hour, I must sacrifice the perfect for the good, because soon enough my stages will be rolling again. There will be more stories and more photos, as I lead Michael on the never-ending roller-coaster ride to hell.

He knows, and Brutus knows, and the Clockwork Angels String Ensemble is beginning to learn—everybody behind me is going to burn.

Oh yes . . .

# 8

# WITNESS TO THE FALL

**NOVEMBER 2012**

**It was a chilly, rainy day** in mid-October, amid the radiant fall colors of Ontario's Muskoka region, the lower belt of the boreal forest. Boreal means "northern," as aurora borealis means northern lights, and true boreal forest stretches only across Canada, Scandinavia, and Russia. Other northerly regions offer spectacular displays in this season, like the brilliant yellow aspens and larches in the mountains of the West, or the more muted but still colorful palette down through the Appalachians, but nowhere else does the mix of tree species create this splendid autumn variety of yellow, gold, orange, and crimson.

To capture this image, your intrepid reporter had to park his motorcycle at the roadside and climb high through wet underbrush and slippery mud to the rocks in the foreground, the Canadian Shield, sculpted by glaciers and erosion. Standing above the rain-shiny road as it curved around Lake Windermere, I waved down to the waiting Brutus to ride through the shot a couple of times.

A few days before, Michael and I had been wandering up and down the backcountry of Pennsylvania and New York, but even on bright, sunny days, the treescapes didn't seem as vivid as my memories of the season from Ontario and Quebec. I was guessing that during our short tour break in early October, we must have missed what can be the briefest season—full-on autumn. I wondered if there had been some wind and rain around there, because that kind of weather will bring down the colorful leaves prematurely. But locals I spoke with didn't recall strong winds or rains in recent weeks, so I figured we had simply missed it.

Then, on the day off between the two Toronto shows, Brutus and I rode north, and there it was, all around us. Even in the flat light of a dull and rainy day, the trees seemed luminous.

Any time the rain let up long enough to allow us to get the cameras out, we stopped and photographed each other riding through it.

Between the Toronto shows and Montreal, Brutus and I explored the backroads of Eastern Ontario and Quebec, and once again we were kind of "in our own backyards." We had both lived in those cities and areas at different times in our lives. The idea of backyards—as in the "NIMBY" principle, "Not In My Back Yard"—had been on my mind lately, in New York State and Pennsylvia, and now in Ontario. Along the country roads and in small towns I saw signs in people's front yards, some protesting the "fracking" I wrote about last time, with the word "FRACK" in a red circle with a slash through it, while others apparently worried about the local drilling of oil ("NO DRILL/ NO SPILL"), and some even spoke against wind turbines. In an area of Upstate New York where there were hundreds of them, a sign showed a drawing of a turbine above the caption: "IT'S A S**WIND**LE."

In Central Ontario, I saw signs against a proposed hydroelectric station, too. So it appeared people didn't want oil, natural gas, wind, or hydro power, at least in their own backyards.

Further south, though, in the coal-mining areas of Pennsylvania, West Virginia, and Southeastern Ohio, the message was different— billboards and signs spoke in *support* of the coal industry. They wanted to *keep* it in their backyards. As discussed in my previous story, you can't blame them, because it's a livelihood for their families and communities. But on reflection, I was pretty sure it was the *bosses*, not the workers, who had posted those messages . . .

Southeastern Ohio is a region I have come to greatly appreciate for

its hilly countryside, winding little roads, pretty farmland and woods, modest churches, and crossroads villages. In that area, a more complicated story was playing out. I hadn't traveled around the United States in October during an election year since 1996 (Clinton vs. Dole), and this time, in 2012, I was equally fascinated to watch the vast mechanism of democracy in action. Placards and staked signs at every intersection, and many front lawns, exhorted Americans to turn out and vote for everyone from local tax commissioners and school board officials to Obama-Biden or Romney-Ryan. As Michael and I wound our way through chilly rain across the rural counties of Southeastern Ohio, many lawns were decorated with signs reading, "STOP THE WAR ON COAL—FIRE OBAMA."

I could only guess we were in a strongly Republican region, but the opposite was true—many local voters were traditionally Democratic and were being blitzed by an invented issue that pretended to threaten them. (As Michael scoffed, "There is no 'war on coal!'") Because Ohio was an important "swing state" on the federal level, it seemed to be an effort to scare them into voting Republican. (Results in those counties did swing that way.)

Muskoka trail

A story I saw about coal miners complaining that their employers had ordered them to show up at a rally for Mitt Romney, without pay, took place in that same corner of Southeastern Ohio.

One sign spoke from a different, harsher perspective: "PROSPER AMERICA—FRACK, BABY, FRACK."

That slogan was patterned after "Drill, Baby, Drill," a 2008 Republican rallying cry in support of the indiscriminate drilling of oil wells—as mouthed by the likes of Sarah Palin. After the disastrous oil spill in the Gulf of Mexico in 2010, the slogan became less politically acceptable and was ridiculed with variations like "Spill, Baby, Spill," and "Kill, Baby, Kill."

One friendly feature in small-town Ohio is the great number of picnic pavilions—very welcome for a motorcyclist on a rainy day. Elsewhere, shelter for a rest and a smoke can be hard to find—unless you come across a spray-wash—but every little village in Ohio seems to have a covered picnic pavilion. This particular setting tells a few other stories. Apart from the somewhat jarring "no handguns" sign on the post, across the road is an old square-log farmhouse, rambling barns (one painted with the venerable "CHEW MAIL POUCH TOBACCO" advertisement), and a tree in autumn flame in front of the wooded hillsides of late fall.

I also notice now that the overhead lightbulbs in the pavilion have been removed, presumably only installed when they are needed. Probably that gesture is more against "unauthorized illumination" in a place like that, rather than vandals—though it's hard to know, given that "no handguns" sign.

That day Michael and I were on our way to Marietta, Ohio, for the second time this tour. Typically, our day-off destinations are not chosen for themselves, but for the roads that lead to and from them—the most scenic and serene ride we can have, leading to a place just big enough to have a motel and a restaurant, and not too far from the next concert venue.

Back in September, we had rolled into Marietta from the southwest and found ourselves at the small city's main intersection, right on the bank of the wide Ohio River. We paused in front of an old hotel on the corner, the Lafayette, and gave it a look-over. Such places are a gamble. For a start, they are not as convenient as the classic (and disappearing, alas) motels where you park in front of your door. Your luggage has to be carted inside, upstairs, and often down long narrow hallways, and often the bikes have to be parked in a garage that might be several blocks away. Also, an old hotel can be . . . an old hotel.

I asked Michael to have a look inside and see what he thought. He came out with a thumbs-up, so I started unloading my bike while he checked us in.

Here I am standing on the New Orleans–style wrought-iron balcony holding my post-ride glass of Macallan. Inside, my room's ornate dark wood furniture and richly patterned fabrics reflected the "historic riverboat era" the hotel dates from, being almost 100 years old. Marietta was named after Marie Antoinette, in tribute to France's help to the United States during the Revolutionary War. The hotel is named after the French Marquis de Lafayette who served as an American general in that war and who visited Marietta during an American tour in 1824–25. Now, 180-some years later, Michael and I were visiting Marietta on *our* American tour.

Marietta is sited at the confluence of the Ohio and Muskingum rivers, and like many of America's river towns, it is frequently troubled by spring floods. The most notorious flooding rose over ten feet in the Lafayette Hotel's lobby during the 1930s, but every few years the overflowing rivers reach at least the lower lobby level. The hotel's solution is ingenious—the carpeting and wall panels of the ground floor are removable and are taken upstairs when the waters rise, then easily reinstalled when the flood recedes.

Lafayette Hotel, Marietta, Ohio

The parking lot across the street had a "Motorcycles Only" space, which is always endearing to us Scooter Trash (or West Side Beemer Boyz), and the Gun Room restaurant in the hotel offered good plain food. The previous photo was taken on our September visit, on a bright sunny day, while a rainy October day gave this view of Front Street—a seemingly thriving example of small-town America's traditional Main Street.

In the rainy twilight, migrating Canada geese and snow geese rested on the riverbank, while rafts of ducks floated downstream. Behind them, a massive train of barges pushed by a low-riding tug appeared out of the dusk and moved slowly up the river. I was reminded of John McPhee's book *Uncommon Carriers*, in which he wrote about riding with a river barge crew in Illinois. Such river traffic was an important part of early American history, before and alongside the railroads, and is still surprisingly active today.

Marietta's history began at least 2,000 years ago, with the so-called Hopewell culture that constructed massive earthworks, of which some remnants are still preserved in the area. In 1770, George Washington, then a British colonial surveyor, visited the Ohio Valley

and encouraged its suitability for settlement. The first soldiers and settlers arrived in 1788, building forts against the indigenous people, like the Shawnee, who did not welcome them.

Despite that hostility, George Washington said at the time, "No colony in America was ever settled under such favorable auspices as that which has just commenced at the Muskingum . . . If I was a young man, just preparing to begin the world, or if advanced in life and had a family to make provision for, I know of no country where I should rather fix my habitation . . ."

From the Lafayette balcony, we look down at the "Motorcycles Only" parking spot, and across the Ohio River to West Virginia (with a strikingly modern house on its bank). A sign in the left corner reads "Restroom Facilities Available in Lafayette Hotel." Again, an example of Ohio neighborliness that is not always found elsewhere. A running/cycling path along the riverbank actually seemed to be used by the citizens—which again is not typical.

Just behind the bikes is a large marker stone with the following inscription:

**SOUTHERN BOUNDARY**
**PICKETED POINT**
THIS STONE IS PLACED TO KEEP
IN REMEMBRANCE THE HISTORIC
POINT WHERE DWELT DURING FOUR
YEARS OF INDIAN WAR 1791-1795
EARLY SETTLERS OF OHIO
ERECTED BY THE WOMANS CENTENNIAL
ASSOCIATION 1903

In the early 1800s, Marietta College was used as a station on the Underground Railroad, helping slaves to escape north. Industry, railroads, and steamships all played a part in Marietta's development, as did oil booms around the turn of the twentieth century. Today its population is about 15,000 people, and to me, it is simply . . . a nice little town.

In October, the weekend before Halloween, the Lafayette was hosting a "Murder Mystery Weekend," with costumed characters appearing around the hotel, and that seemed kind of quaint and fun. A bar across the street was having a costume contest (I told Michael, "You should go—disguised as a human being!") and it raged until very late, loud voices waking me in the small hours.

To us, Marietta's most important quality is that like Williamsport, Pennsylvania (which I was delighted to learn is locally called "Billtown"—that's cute—and where twice we have enjoyed an unexpectedly sophisticated restaurant, 33 East), or Iowa City, it is just big enough to be "accommodating" and strategically located among nice country roads between big-city showdates.

Speaking of riverboat towns, let us now take a quick trip down the Ohio to the Mississippi, and all the way south to its terminus at New Orleans.

En route to
Billtown, Pennsylvania

In *Roadshow*, I recalled how many years ago the band was playing in the gymnasium of Louisiana State University in New Orleans, and on a locker in our dressing room I saw a typewritten list entitled "How to Stay Young."

It was attributed to Leroy "Satchel" Paige (1906–1982), a legendary pitcher from the so-called Negro Leagues. (Bandmate Geddy has been a major contributor to that heritage, donating memorabilia from his collection to the museum in Kansas City.) Satchel Paige's life and career spanned an incredible metamorphosis in American sporting and cultural history, and here are his words of wisdom:

1) Avoid fried meats which angry up the blood.
2) If your stomach disputes you, lie down and pacify it with cool thoughts.
3) Keep the juices flowing by jangling around gently as you move.
4) Go very light on the vices, such as carrying on in society. The social ramble ain't restful.
5) Avoid running at all times.
6) Don't look back. Something might be gaining on you.

Obviously, there is much good advice there, and after a series of hometown shows in Toronto and Montreal, the one that resonated for me was "The social ramble ain't restful."

Extroverts gain energy in social situations, while introverts are drained by it. I always remember a question in a psychological handbook called *Please Understand Me* (1984) in which a variation of Jungian archetypes was used to help define what kind of person you, or your friends, might be. The key question for me was "Do you find social interaction energizing or draining?"

How people answer that question says an awful lot about them.

The book was given to me by a professional psychologist, who was later somewhat horrified to hear that I had been using it as a "party game"—having friends answer the questions and define their personality types just for *fun*.

But it *was* fun—and enlightening.

Some friends were mortified by what it revealed about them and denied its truth—but to the rest of us, the resulting descriptions were both amusing and undeniably real.

The observation that "the social ramble ain't restful" is especially clear to me on show days. Because I almost never stay after a show, but bolt straight from the stage to my bus, the only time I can entertain local friends or family is in the afternoon before sound-check. Over time I have learned that I can sustain a maximum of two social encounters at that time. Three or more such meet and greets start to drain me to the extent that I feel it during the performance, in a way that rattles my concentration.

So . . . before the first hometown show in Toronto, I planned to host my mother and father for dinner in the Bubba-Gump room

and to meet with my first drum teacher, Don George—for the first time in over forty-five years. In 1965, at the age of thirteen, I started drum lessons with Don at the Peninsula Conservatory of Music in St. Catharines, Ontario. When he stopped teaching there a year or so later, I didn't see him again until the day of that first show in Toronto, on October 14, 2012.

In recent years, Don and I had been in touch by mail and email, and he sent me videos of his current teaching ideas and methods.

I was pleased to see that he was obviously still a gifted and dedicated teacher. For his part, when talking about this long-ago student, Don was once quoted as saying, "Neil didn't have another teacher for thirty years, so I must have done *something* right."

And he did—Don guided me toward what I needed to know well enough that I could follow his direction through those decades. Most of all, he gave me the encouragement that I could *be* a drummer, if I worked at it. Essentially, Don kept me climbing that mountain for three decades, until I needed Freddie Gruber and Peter Erskine to guide me to higher elevations.

Unfortunately, while I was struggling up the mountain that night (every night a mountain, and me always Sisyphus), I had a painful attack of tendinitis in my left elbow. The previous morning, after a show in Philadelphia, I had awakened on the bus lying on that arm and feeling a sharp pain. It didn't bother me on the motorcycle that day, riding through the Catskills and Adirondacks of upstate New York to Cape Vincent for the night. (A couple of signs I noted that day—a small-town bar offering "WARM BEER, LOUSY FOOD," and a sign in front of an old church reading, "FOR SALE BY OWNER." I had to think about that for a few miles—"Who owns a church?") The next morning my elbow felt tender, but tolerable, as we crossed into Canada on a cold, rainy morning via a pair of ferries through Wolfe Island to Kingston, and a long, wet slog along Highway 401 to Toronto.

Michael astonished me that morning. Leaving Cape Vincent early, before breakfast or even coffee, we loaded the bikes in the rain and caught the little ferry to Wolfe Island. There we passed through the tiny open-air (open *rain*) border crossing with minimal fuss, then rounded the island through steady rain and fog. At the dock in Marysville, where we had caught the Kingston ferry a couple of times before, a sign announced that the ferry dock had been moved a few kilometers up the road. (Later I learned it was the "winter dock.") We arrived at a raw-looking installation of concrete and steel, but there were no signs giving ferry times. It was a Sunday morning, the weather was bad—maybe there *wasn't* one. We stood in the cold rain, undecided and a little anxious. My brain was busily planning alternatives—figuring where the nearest bridge to Canada was, if we had to backtrack. Out of nowhere, Michael said, in apparent seriousness, "I love it when we do stuff like this."

I turned and just stared at him, with a look that spoke volumes, and said, "Oh, shut up." Or possibly something stronger.

But he continued to play it all earnest, and insisted, "No, I really do—it's an *adventure*!"

Maybe he really was serious, at least at that moment, but trust me, dear reader, Michael does not often express enthusiasm for my little "excursions." Especially in bad weather. Maybe it was a feeble attempt at a joke. (Or manliness.)

See, there I go again. It is obvious that I often use Michael as the butt of cheap humor (did that come out right?), but I swear I never stray far from the truth. With that pledge in mind, as this story spins out, the reader will see how the scales fall . . .

In any case, it was *me* who was "unmanned" during that night's show, as the pain in my elbow grew steadily worse. Toward the end it hurt so badly that I simply couldn't hit as hard as I usually do with my left hand. Before the second Toronto show, I consulted a local doctor, who prescribed some anti-inflammatories and an elbow brace, and that helped me enough that at least I could play properly. It still hurt quite a lot, but as I had learned during a similar attack on my other arm, back on the *Test for Echo* tour in 1997, I didn't mind the pain as long as it didn't interfere with "the job."

This tour Michael has been encouraging me to share occasional brief messages or photographs on social networks, under the banner of the West Side Beemer Boyz (Michael, Brutus, and me). One of the first such messages (I call them "twits") I authorized Michael to launch was a wry observation about the "gems" he told me he was sharing with his own "followers." (And isn't that word choice an interesting reflection on how such public oversharing is growing into something like a religion?)

When I sneered the following accusation at Michael, he insisted we had to twit it. So I double-dog-dared him. "All you do is text meaningless nonsense to people you don't even like."

For our collective audience for the West Side Beemer Boyz, I started out tentatively, as I had years ago when we launched the website. Every few days I approved a scenic motorcycling photo or offered a few pithy remarks that I hoped were fun or provocative. Each of those was introduced with "Bubba sez," for authenticity.

For example, "Bubba sez, 'Vengeance is for losers'" (as it must be), and "Bubba sez, 'What doth it profit a man to ride 450 miles, of which 50 are nice?'" That existential question referred to the North Dakota ride that made up a good part of the previous story, and a few commenters nailed the correct answer: the profit is 50 miles.

Sometimes on the bus after the show, when Michael and I were liberally refreshed and feeling highly amusing, we discussed ideas for twits that were . . . let's say, controversial. So I established the "Atatürk rule."

See, Mustafa Kemal Atatürk (meaning "father of the Turks") was an enlightened, cosmopolitan leader of Turkey in the 1920s and '30s. He was determined to build a Westernized, secular state, and early on outlawed the fez and the burqa. However, Atatürk was a drinking man, and late at night, in his cups, he was given to issuing wild commands—like, say, "Napalm Ankara!" So, his attendants learned to postpone taking any action until the morning, when they could ask their president if he had *really* meant those orders. Often enough he would cringe and say something like, "Oh dear, no, no."

Clearly, the "Atatürk rule" on late-night, over-refreshed communications of any kind is something many people would be wise to adopt.

After some painful nights onstage, my after-show suffering inspired a couple of cryptic messages that I did have to allow Michael to send. By way of explanation, motorcyclists who adopt the old-school "biker" pose refer misogynistically to riding on the pillion, or passenger seat, as "riding bitch." Thus I offered the defiant stoicism, "Bubba sez, 'Pain rides bitch.'"

Later, we sent out another expression of will conquering pain, which turned out to have biblical roots: "Bubba sez, 'The body is a good servant, but a terrible master.'"

Matt Scannell's childhood friend Doctor James (or "Bro-Doc," as I have dubbed him), gave me reams of information and recommendations for treating the condition. He informed me that it was properly called "lateral epicondylitis," which I much preferred to the frivolous-sounding "tennis elbow." Along with the brace I wore while drumming, Bro-Doc James recommended icing the area immediately after the show and wearing a splint at night that would immobilize the wrist from overextending that tendon in my elbow. The only real treatment was rest, and that wasn't possible. Back in '97, I had played with pain and an elbow brace until the end of the tour, and then it didn't really get better until a month or two after.

So . . . for now, "pain rides bitch."

A big story along the East Coast in late October was "Frankenstorm." (I prefer the Germanic, heavy-metal Frankenstürm.) Hurricane Sandy was predicted to merge with other weather patterns and create an unstable and dangerous vortex. In the days before, for the first time all tour, I had the television on in my hotel room, tuned to the Weather Channel, as it was on the bus. As we moved south from shows in Buffalo and Cleveland to Charlotte and Atlanta, I began navigating not by the maps or through my usual favorite areas, but by the weather patterns.

Even then, staying inland and at lower elevations down through Ohio and Kentucky, we endured steady rain, wind, and cold temperatures—42°F. All day. That morning, with heavy rains predicted, Michael had argued that we should just stay on the bus and not ride in that weather. "It's not safe, it's not smart, and it's not fun."

Kentucky rain

Michael doesn't like riding in the rain, but I don't mind it. (I did mention to him later that day that we hadn't seen a single other motorcycle on the road for three days. He grumbled sarcastically, "Yeah—all those *other* riders must be crazy to miss out on this.") There are only two weather conditions that will make me call off a ride: lightning and snow. One summer morning a few tours ago we woke up on the bus around Jefferson City, Missouri, with thunder and

lightning all around, and the satellite pictures showed those conditions prevailing all the way to the show in St. Louis. For many years I hadn't known that lightning could kill you on a motorcycle, but once I learned that, I feared it. So we stayed on the bus that day.

One morning last April, we woke up at a motel in Sarnia, Ontario, to see the ground—and bikes—covered with snow. It was a day off anyway, so we just took a "snow day" and were able to ride to the show in Hamilton the next day.

This time, Frankenstürm was predicted to drop two feet of snow in the higher elevations of West Virginia, so although those mountains were the way I would have preferred to travel south, we stayed away from that area. (They got that snow, too—even while Sandy was pounding New Jersey and New York City.) I figured I could route us down through the backroads of Kentucky to Knoxville, Tennessee, safely, with only the minor inconveniences of cold and rain. (And Michael's melodramatic fake shivering and teeth-chattering at every stop.)

In a Roadcraft aside on riding gear, here is what it takes to withstand that kind of weather. (Even at 50 mph, the wind-chill factor at 42°F is well below freezing.) Waterproof leathers, boots, and thick insulated gloves, and a plastic rain jacket to cut the wind. The wiring visible above my leg is for the heated vest, which is like an electric blanket around my torso, worn between two cotton turtlenecks which are further cinched around the neck by the rain jacket's hook-and-loop. One's neck can be particularly vulnerable to cold and wet, but the Schuberth helmet is well designed in that area. The handgrips are electrically heated, which also makes a huge difference. Long underwear, sock liners, and—in the most extreme cold—a thin balaclava under the helmet. (We even have electrically heated socks and gloves, which saved us in the cold spring of 2011—see "Eastern Resurrection"—but didn't resort to those this time.) The riding pace has to be relaxed and smooth, lean angles minimized, braking and acceleration gentle.

Getting from Knoxville to Charlotte, though, would be a problem. The forecast over the Smoky Mountains to Asheville was for 33°F and snow, so I arranged with bus driver Dave to meet us the next morning at the hotel in Knoxville (another old-time, downtown property we took a chance on, the Oliver Hotel, and it was nice). We loaded the bikes into the trailer and rode the bus to Charlotte and, sure enough, looked out at heavy snow on the trees beside the interstate, and it was 33°F.

I was gratified to see my judgment vindicated, and as Michael, Dave, and I looked out the bus windshield at the snow-covered trees and rocks, I sneered to Michael, "See? I know when 'It's not safe, it's not smart, and it's not fun.' I might be crazy, but I'm not *stupid!*"

He said bad words and turned back to his computer.

Charlotte was the night before Halloween, and lately we had been seeing plenty of decorations around the Midwest. I read once that Halloween was the second-most widely celebrated holiday in America. (The first might be a toss-up between the Fourth of July and Superbowl. But no, I kid—I'm sure it was holiday *spending* they were talking about. So of course, Christmas.) Pumpkins, witches, skeletons, and cornshocks decorated housefronts, and white-sheeted ghosts hung from cobwebbed trees. Some yards were decorated with little cemeteries of cardboard headstones celebrating the death of "Cancer," "War," and—wait—did that one say *"Democrats"*?

Our two female string players, cellist Adele and violinist Audrey, appeared onstage in wildly elaborate face makeup that night, from David Bowie's *Aladdin Sane* to rhinestone arabesques. The Guys at Work and I always appreciate it when those around us go out of their way to entertain not just the audience, but us.

On the day off after Charlotte, I would like to have routed us through the mountains of North Georgia toward Atlanta, but even there the temperatures were in the thirties, so I kept us to the Piedmont and Low Country of Eastern Georgia and South Carolina. There we finally felt a bit of relief, seeing the bike's thermometer rise into the fifties and low sixties, as we rode under a canopy of oaks and Spanish moss to a night of rare luxury at the Palmetto Bluff Resort along the May River in South Carolina.

In fact, Spanish moss is neither "Spanish" nor "moss," but a so-called "air plant," or "bromeliad" (pretty word), which takes nourishment directly from the air. Thus it is not a parasite on the trees,

Spanish moss

though too much of it can block the light necessary for the tree's photosynthesis. And the weight of all those hanging plants, especially after rain, can cause branches to break. The graceful gray beards hanging from oak and cypress trees are a romantic symbol of the Old South and a staple of the Southern Gothic atmosphere. One interesting bit of trivia is that the seats for the Ford Model T and other cars and carriages of the era were stuffed with Spanish moss.

Riding across Georgia and Northern Florida, I noticed that Spanish moss most often appeared around houses and in towns, apparently cultivated for its decorative appeal. Easy enough to do—you just hang it on a tree and it grows—but I was sure I remembered something about that symbolic plant almost dying out years ago. The story was hard to find but turned out to be true; in the 1970s, a blight attacked Spanish moss across the South and almost wiped it out, but a blight-resistant strain of the plant rebounded. It is certainly widespread once again.

These trees with their long gray beards have a melancholy, even mournful look, like the weeping willows I grew up with in Southern Ontario. (The first home I owned, a farmhouse near Beamsville, Ontario, had a big willow in front, and I used to like climbing its thick branches to a high perch.) Another sad-looking tree is the weeping yew, which I had planted around the memorial to my first wife, Jackie, and daughter Selena.

Those thoughts about sad trees converge because we have been visited by another family tragedy—manager Ray's twenty-three-year-old son Shane was struck down by a brain tumor, succumbing on November 1, only nine weeks after the terrible diagnosis.

It was the day of our show in Atlanta, and that night Geddy gave a subtle reference to Shane in his introduction to "The Garden," which had been one of Shane's favorite songs.

Two nights later, after the final show in that leg, in Tampa, I flew to Toronto with the other Guys at Work in their "bus" (Challenger 605) and spent some time with Ray. I knew how it felt to lose a child. After fifteen years, I think of Selena every single day, and from time to time (birthdays, black anniversaries), I am still rendered helpless with grief at that unbearable loss.

Before heading for the airport to get back to my own (second) family in Los Angeles, I attended the memorial gathering, and it was achingly sad and hard for me to bear. My sorrow must have been obvious, because it seemed like Ray was comforting and support- ing *me*. And in the following days I received messages from several friends asking if *I* was okay.

The gathering was held in the same "Visitation Centre" at Toronto's Mount Pleasant Cemetery where we had mourned Andrew MacNaughtan earlier this year—and from where you could just about see my first family's memorial. (I do not visit it, though I know others do and are comforted by it.)

I think of the lines from "My Way" about living, laughing and cry- ing, and having your fill of losing.

Witness to fall after fall—and I'll keep riding on. With pain riding bitch.

But enough darkness. It just seems right to share a little of the

shadows as well as the light. Many people cling to the fantasy that an elusive phantom called "success" or "wealth" would bring them freedom from pain.

Let me tell you, it does not.

To strike up a brighter memory, when Brutus and I were rambling around Muskoka north of Toronto, I saw a sign for a place called Windermere. The sign pointed left, away from our route, but on a whim I led us on a brief detour. In the winter of 1982, the band spent a few weeks at a resort on Lake Windermere, working on the songs for our *Signals* album. I had never been back since, and thought it might be fun to see the place again. We had worked there in late winter, with four feet of snow quilting the ground, trees, and buildings to create a surreal white world. The resort hotel itself was closed and shuttered for the season, and looked like a scene from *The Shining*, its massive bulk mostly buried under a deep shroud of snow. I went snowshoeing for the first time in my life there, across the frozen lake under a full moon.

We stayed in some small condos nearby, and our gear was set up on the second floor of one of the resort's outbuildings. As Brutus and I rode up to the compound, I saw the huge white hotel of Windermere House looking well tended and prosperous. The lakefront condos where the band and crew had stayed had been replaced by more upscale accommodations, but when we rode behind the hotel, I saw the very building we had worked in, looking remarkably unchanged after thirty years.

I had Brutus snap my picture in front of it and emailed the photo to Alex and Geddy under the title "Pop quiz," with the caption, "Where am I?" Alex nailed it right away, and at dinner together before the next show, we shared a good laugh about our memories of that time. On the *Clockwork Angels* tour, we have been playing two songs from the *Signals* album, "Subdivisions" and "The Analog Kid." In another coincidence, our friend Ben Mink was guest violin soloist on "Losing It," and one of the members of our Clockwork Angels String Ensemble, Jonathan Dinklage, told us he had been inspired to learn to play the violin by that performance.

And we continue to be inspired by that rockin' string section—more and more it feels like when we are onstage with them our little trio grows into an eleven-piece band. The Atlanta show was outdoors, and with the crazy weather afflicting the East (I always liked how one climate scientist explained that "global warming" was too simplistic a description of these times of climate change—he said it was more accurate to call it "global weirding"), the temperature around

showtime was predicted to be in the *forties*. My sympathy went to the people in the audience, mainly, because we would have the stage-lights, and with the activity of drumming, I would be creating my own heat. (The only difference would be that I wouldn't turn on the little fans that cool my hands and back—usually needed by the second or third song, but not that night.) However, my bandmates and the poor string players would also suffer. For once the "string-ers" wouldn't mind the "wall of fire" pyro effects behind them—which are usually both uncomfortable and a menace to their delicate and precious instruments. Cellist Adele had told me that she and Jacob hunched over their cellos during that part of the show—not to "rock out," but to protect their instruments from the heat.

In Atlanta we also had visits from Peter Collins, coproducer of *Power Windows*, *Hold Your Fire*, and *Counterparts*, and Nick Raskulinecz, "The Mighty Booujzhe," coproducer of *Snakes and Arrows* and *Clockwork Angels*. From the start of the second set, the *Clockwork Angels* songs, Booujzhe stood in the pit in front of us, conducting and miming along with every note, beat, and word. I couldn't help laughing, then had to look away because it was making me weak.

Finally, perhaps the biggest news of all in the fall of 2012 was the American presidential election. The night I flew from Toronto for a few brief days at home, still reeling with sorrow for Ray's family, I received a text from Michael saying, "We won!!!! No magic underwear!!!"

(Like many of Michael's utterances, that one might require an explanation to some "normal" people. See, devout Mormons are required to wear at all times what they call "temple garments," or simply "garments." These resemble a two-piece set of underwear, decorated with symbols chosen by church officers to protect the wearer from harm. So, in effect, they are indeed something like "magic underwear"—in the minds of derisive gentiles like Michael. Wouldn't think of it myself . . . )

But look at me—I have managed to come all this way (over 6,000 words about almost 4,000 miles of motorcycling across the American East) without even mentioning religion, let alone ragging on it. But it was bound to become inescapable—just as it seemed to become for American voters.

Mormon readers have sometimes written to thank me for being respectful of their history and their struggles—and I am. But that doesn't mean I would be comfortable with one of the self-styled "saints" (or the one Michael suspects is their "anointed prophet") in the White House. Neither would I welcome a Scientologist, fundamentalist Christian, Hasidic Jew, or Wiccan. It's not prejudice or "profiling"—only that to your average rational person (or to each *other*—think about how a Mormon looks at a Scientologist and vice versa!), such beliefs are so far *out there*. Worse, the fanatical defensiveness about those beliefs is frightening.

Likewise, I have only commented "observationally" about politics. But it has to be said that this was an anxious election for those of us who worry about true individual rights (key question, perhaps: "Does a woman own her body?"), compassionate government, and the separation of church and state.

I define myself as a "bleeding-heart libertarian," unwilling to let people suffer unnecessarily (even if it's "their own fault"), so I am repelled by the cold-hearted and crypto-racist attitudes of the so-called "Christian" right. Michael is what Republicans call a "RINO," or "Republican in name only," which can probably be defined as "right-wing liberal"—politically conservative, socially liberal, and not sympathetic to religious influence on society at large. As he clarifies it, "I'm a registered diehard Republican. I only seem liberal because I believe hurricanes are caused by low barometric pressure and not by gay marriage. My party left me!"

Generally, while believing in individual rights and responsibilities, we favor the classic liberal values of generosity and tolerance, and fear the religious oppression that has wormed its way into modern Republican platforms. (And that is a *good* metaphor.)

A huge billboard in Florida asked, "SICK AND TIRED OF HOPE AND CHANGE?" followed, of course, by "VOTE ROMNEY." Were it not for the snowbirds and retirees, Florida would likely be the reddest state in the Union. On a Saturday afternoon, as Michael, guest rider (and Florida native) John Wesley, and I rode through Florida towns to the Tampa show, Tea Party activists stood on many street corners railing like Old Testament prophets, waving signs and flags, while passing drivers honked in support. Church signs urged us to "PRAY—THEN VOTE WISELY." One announced a "PRAYER VIGIL NOV. 5," and we could imagine what they wanted to pray for. (Or against.) At the Tampa venue, Michael called me outside to see what a skywriter had printed across the sky: "LOVE GOD VOTE."

Michael, me, and Wes

In the fall of 2012, I was witness to all that and feared its Frankenstürm of fear and sanctimony would overwhelm the country. However, like many, I was relieved that the radical fringes could not prevent the Fall of the Prophet or hold back the forward motion of hope and change (see "The Better Angels"). Still, the people of the United States remain divided almost exactly in half—like so much of our sad and beautiful world.

Once again, I can only hold up the compassionate wisdom of Philo of Alexandria, who said 2,000 years ago, "Be kind, for everyone you meet is fighting a hard battle."

Because we are, aren't we?

# 9

# ADVENTURES IN THE WILD WEST

DECEMBER 2012

**We began the third leg** of the *Clockwork Angels* tour, in mid-November 2012, with a computer crash. Such a mundane event fostering an adventure would have seemed unlikely to me, but perhaps not to Michael. I am sure he has those kind of techno-geek dreams all the time. ("I was reformatting a hard drive and writing code for a killer app—when suddenly I opened a portal in the space-time continuum!")

After an all-too-brief break at home, Michael and I flew to Portland, and Dave picked us up with the bus and trailer. He drove us north toward the first show, in Seattle, but following my request, parked us south of there, in Chehalis, for the night. I planned a short "warm-up" ride for the show day, and in the morning Michael and I unloaded the bikes and set out into the inevitable rain.

Later that day, on the bus outside the old arena in Seattle, I looked over the paper maps of Southern Oregon and Northern California. I needed to work out a route to the next show, in San Jose, but knew that, unfortunately, I would have to stay away from the higher mountains, like the Cascades and Sierras. They would already be snow-covered. So, sticking near the coast, I highlighted some tiny roads through Oregon and into California, including one I remembered traveling with Brutus back in 1996. When I told Michael about that, he acted incredulous—shaking his head and saying, "How can you *remember* that?"

The only reply ought to be, "How could I forget?"

Certain roads etch themselves into my mind like a good song, and are remembered the same way—the melody, background, cadence, changes, and overall mood. It is also similar to how I might remember a person once encountered—how they looked, how they behaved, and how we . . . "got along."

Also, one settlement on that Northern California backroad was called Happy Camp, and that would tend to stick in one's memory. (Who wouldn't want to go to Happy Camp?) But more than that— I recalled how the road followed a river (the Klamath) in long, uninterrupted stretches of fast, sweeping bends. I would

be glad to revisit such a road, especially in the opposite direction (for every road is really *two* roads—maybe more, if you add in weather and seasons). From there, I thought we would work our way over to the Pacific coast at Cape Mendocino ("The Lost Coast"), and maybe down to the town of Mendocino for the night. (I always have to put that "maybe" in any riding plans, and this day would be a prime example of why. My all-time favorite church sign: "WANT TO MAKE GOD LAUGH? TELL HIM YOUR PLANS!")

After Michael translated that route from my paper map to his computer's navigation program, Mother, he tried to copy it to our onboard units, Doofus and Dingus. It was an operation that he typically did every show day, but this time, it just wouldn't work. Time after time, the cyber-minds failed to communicate. Michael is a trained computer forensics investigator, and he eventually determined that the problem was in his machine. It wasn't a conventional catastrophic crash, a sudden collapse into chaos (what a flight of accidental alliteration—there goes another one!), but a more gradual loss of its faculties—like Hal in *2001: A Space Odyssey*. (And it would soon be singing the equivalent of "Daisy Bell"—"*On a bicycle built for two*." A good story hangs on that reference, for techno-geeks. It was the first song sung by a computer, in 1961.)

Later that day, or night, after many attempts at patches and fixes, Michael thought he had found a workaround. He copied the outline of the route, like a digital stencil, and pasted it onto the maps in Doofus and Dingus. The route and the map were joined at last, but we would learn that they interpreted that design *very* loosely.

The following morning was cool and misty as we set out early from a Walmart in Grants Pass, Oregon. The paper map showed a tiny gray line leading down into Northern California, and although it was marked as paved, I wasn't too alarmed to find us on a gravel road, winding through deep conifers. But as Doofus and Dingus kept making turns onto ever-smaller routes, mere gravel tracks and abandoned logging roads, I began to wonder. I tried to keep an eye on the compass, to make sure we were tending south. Then I began to see patches of snow here and there, and started worrying.

Further episodes in this story will show that we can get through most obstacles—eventually—but not deep snow. Still "the Boys" kept leading us onward, the purple lines on our screens turning this way and that. It seemed like they were just plotting a more or less random route, with Michael's applied "stencil" serving as a rough guide to its shape and direction. The riding wasn't unpleasant, but its aim was worrisome, and when I eventually saw a small brown-and-white sign, a marker for a National Forest road, with a number, I felt a sense of relief. "At least we're on a road that has a *number*." By that point, after rambling through endless evergreens on logging roads with no sign of recent tire tracks, it seemed like civilization.

Then came the "false dawn" of a glimpse of paved road. It might have been the one we were *supposed* to be on the whole time—though

at least two hours earlier, without all that meandering around the rainforest—and it led in the proper direction, toward the southwest. The problem was that it took us *higher*, and more snow was appearing. Eventually, as shown in the opening photograph, we were threading narrow lines of pavement between streaks of packed snow and ice. Worse was the fear, after previous episodes in Oregon, New Mexico, and Washington State, that we could soon be marooned in a snowpack.

This time the fates were with us, and the road turned downhill, away from the snow, and we emerged just where we (and our route) had hoped to be: Happy Camp, California. As I had remembered from fifteen years ago, the road from there along the Klamath River was a winding delight. After forty miles of that, we paused at the roadside for a break, and Michael declared it his favorite ride of the tour.

However, technology wasn't finished messing with us yet. The transplanted route-map worked fine once we were back on major roads, and we made our way over to the main highway, California 101, and a few miles south to the turnoff for Cape Mendocino—the Lost Coast. Brutus and I had explored that area back in 1996, on the *Test for*

The Lost Coast

*Echo* tour, and I had passed through on my *Ghost Rider* travels, in 1998. A few years later I returned by car, taking a long scenic route home from a track day at Thunderhill in my Aston Martin DB9.

The road around Cape Mendocino is a narrow, twisting strip of pavement (sometimes quite "technical" for riding or driving) that leads from the picturesque Victorian town of Ferndale through dense, mossy woods out to a grand vista of the blue Pacific. This was Michael's first visit to the area, and later he told me he had been dazzled to emerge from the dim forest to this fantastic expanse of sea and sky.

When we turned inland again, my route was to take us through the giant redwoods of Humboldt Redwoods State Park, then down through the big trees on a scenic route called Avenue of the Giants. However, the Boys had other ideas and led us away from all that, southward into a complicated network of narrow paved roads, little more than one lane wide, twisting through forested hills. The going was slow and difficult, and I was pretty sure those roads had not been on my highlighted route.

The air was often fragrant with the slightly skunky perfume of growing marijuana, as we were in a remote part of Humboldt County, famous for growing California's medicinal (and recreational) weed. Passing through one remnant grove of redwoods (so few of the big trees were left after the wholesale logging of the nineteenth and early twentieth centuries that each grove has a name), we were suddenly in a dark twilight, our headlights a pale spray on the pavement.

By the time we emerged at the main road again, the light everywhere was fading into evening, and it was time for a rethink. I knew that if we continued on to Mendocino, we would face a two-hour ride along a dark coast, on a tortuous little road, with fog another possible hazard. (To quote Michael from a previous story, "It's not safe, it's not smart, and it's not fun.")

Pausing at the intersection (always wanting to be safe, smart, and fun), I went through the buttons on Dingus to scan the list of local lodgings and saw there was a Best Western just two miles away. I decided we would take shelter there and revise our plans for the following day. Finding ourselves in Garberville, California, willy-nilly, we decided we liked it fine. With our bikes parked in front of our rooms at the classic Best Western, we unpacked and enjoyed our post-ride plastic cups of Macallan. I made up a little song for Michael:

*Get up early, and ride all day*
*But when it gets dark, find a place to stay.*

He just sniffed, but I'm sure he thought it was a pretty good song. I'll bet he was singing it in his helmet for days . . .

The town offered a selection of motels and restaurants (including a Chinese one with the groan-worthy name of "Cadillac Wok").

Michael and I strolled a few blocks to a New Orleans–style place and noticed the local "plantocracy" all around. Young people in a variety of hairstyles from dreadlocks to "man-buns" wore colorful clothes that appeared homespun. One guy's outfit I could only describe as "snowboarding pants made by an Incan grandmother." Another young man in blond dreads wore a hoodie decorated with a Grateful Dead

album cover. They all looked prosperous but freaky, and we decided that Garberville was definitely "Growerville."

The next morning I led Michael on a backtrack north through part of the Avenue of the Giants, so he could see the majestic redwoods for himself. He thought he had seen them before, on a ride in the Sierras, but I informed him that those had been sequoias—a related species that can also grow to be thousands of years old. The sequoias are actually larger in girth, but the coastal redwoods are taller (the world's tallest tree is a redwood, at almost 380 feet).

With a sarcastic tone, Michael said, "How did I manage to live so long without needing to know things like that?"

I snapped back, "There's obviously so *much* you've managed to stumble past without thinking you needed to know. Pretty sad, really."

He said a bad word.

(Michael says a *lot* of bad words.)

But you know, it occurs to me that an episode like that might be a good example of why Michael and I get along pretty well—despite traveling together day after day, night after night, and mile after mile. (Ten years now, and something over 100,000 miles.) Our attitude toward each other tends to be constantly nasty, but in a funny way. In contrast, as the 2012 part of the *Clockwork Angels* tour was grinding to an end, after three months, we had both noticed an atmosphere of tension during the workdays. With sixty-five people living and working together in tight quarters in our traveling circus (carried this time by six buses and nine trucks), sometimes individuals get weary, tempers fray, patience fails, and there are altercations. The daily good humor and morale-raising jokes continued (for example, we and

Mojave Joshua trees

our audiences would often be surprised by costumed characters capering about during the shows), but during the day, I would catch the backstage gossip and hear about certain crew members or drivers getting into verbal scraps. After many (many) tours, you learn that it always seems to happen like that toward the end.

But Michael and I talk so awful to each other all the time that nothing has to be held back—no tension or resentments build up inside. Petty issues are spewed out in a constant stream of gay banter, acid remarks, vicious insults, and gutter profanity that doesn't allow any grudges or annoyances to linger. It's like a pressure-release valve that's *always* on, just a little. Or a lot.

Michael still laughs over my comment from a few tours ago, "I love that you feel you can talk to me like that—but I really wish you wouldn't."

Many relationships might benefit from such "loose tongues."

After a week of working "from home," commuting to shows in Southern California by car (those freeways are no fun on a motorcycle), we were on the bikes once again, riding out early across the

Mojave Desert to Vegas. On previous tours we always seemed to do that ride in mid-summer, with the temperature well over 100, so it was pleasant to experience that well-loved landscape in cool November weather. The next day, though, the desert would not be so gentle with us.

After the Vegas show, Dave drove us to a truck stop in Kingman, Arizona. Michael's computer had been replaced by then, and Mother and the Boys were once more playing nice together. After unloading the bikes in the morning, we followed my chosen route down through Western Arizona, on long stretches shown on the map as unpaved. We call those the "mystery roads," because we truly never know what we're going to get. On the previous tour I had chosen a road just east of this one—up through the Vulture Mountains toward Prescott— that was shown on the map with the same dotted line, and it turned out to be a nice paved two-lane through undulating cactus desert.

This one started out as graded gravel, through the middle of what we would come to know is called the Arizona Outback.

And we would come to know *why* . . .

At one point, I stopped and straddled the bike and waited for Michael, who was hanging well back out of my dust. (For that reason, a crosswind is welcome when riding in the dirt.) I put on my four-way flashers and held up my hand—the understood signal for a photo stop—and asked him to photograph me riding through that background. Because, I told him, "It's the only place in the world where you will see both saguaro cactus and Joshua trees. And I believe the Arizona Joshuas are a slightly different species from the California ones."

He shook his head and repeated, in a weary, acid tone, "I don't know how I've managed to live all this time without needing to know that."

I suggested he perform an anatomically impossible act.

The signs that welcomed us to a couple of *long* stretches of gravel, and an eventual rather desperate plight, were only mildly daunting. Most of the time, these "primitive roads" were decently graded gravel, and the riding was fairly easy, through vast, rugged panoramas of saguaro, mesquite, and Joshua trees. After thirty or forty miles, we came out to pavement again and paused for gas around Wickieup. From there we turned west once more, into the Outback, on Chicken Springs Road. (You pretty much know a road with a name like that is going to lead you into desert desolation.) For a couple of hours everything was fine, more graded gravel and fetching cactus desert scenery. The temperature climbed into the eighties—the first time we had been truly *warm* on the bikes for about two months—and it felt just fine while we were moving.

It was November 24, 2012—the Saturday of Thanksgiving weekend—so there were more people about than we would usually encounter on such a remote track. Ahead of us, long clouds of dust announced the approach of small all-terrain vehicles, "quads," and we kept well right on the track to avoid them—or let them avoid *us*.

At one crossroads, Doofus and Dingus pointed us forward, but a large yellow sign announced, "NO THROUGH ROAD." A few big pickups with flatbed trailers were parked in a clearing, and people were loading and unloading their quads. One rider had a shotgun mounted across his handlebar, and I asked him what he was hunting. "Quail," he said.

I pointed up to the sign and told him we were trying to make our way to Alamo Lake, then south to Wenden. My paper map and the GPS said the roads connected. He nodded, seemingly knowingly, and said offhandedly, "Oh, you can make your way around."

Those words would come to haunt us, as we discovered what it meant to "make your way around" that lake.

Alamo Lake is a reservoir on the Bill Williams River, and its deep blue expanse came into view among the folds of green-dotted brown hills ahead of us. Somewhere across that lake was the road we needed to get to—to get gas, to get water, to get anywhere.

The road continued to be fairly firm gravel, with only a few deeper stretches where our wheels sank in and threatened to "upset" us.

Those tended to be in the lower dips—so-called washes—where flash floods leave loose debris that is later simply graded over. Sometimes we had our feet down as outriggers, ready for a dab to steady our balance, but there was nothing too dramatic. Just a normal "primitive road." However, as we neared the lake, that road became something *less* than primitive—either unborn, or long dead. We circled around a few small, rough tracks that meandered into dead ends, and it truly seemed to be a "no through road" situation, despite what the hunter had said. Trying one last loop, we encountered a couple sitting in their quad, and I pulled up beside them.

With a self-deprecating smile, I asked, "Do you know where *you* are?"

The woman laughed and nodded, and when I explained our situation and our quest, she said that one of the tracks *looked* like a dead end, but wasn't. She said they were headed back that way to their camp across the lake, and we could follow them if we liked. The man said there was some silt—"like talcum powder," the woman added—and a stretch of sand, but they seemed to think we could manage it.

It is a truism of adventure travel that when things get *really* bad, you seldom stop to take photographs—you're busy trying to survive, and nothing seems more important than to keep moving forward. The trail they led us down was narrow and very rough, just wide enough for a quad to negotiate, with tight, winding switchbacks up and down through close-set ravines. The surface was rutted, eroded, and studded with rocks of all sizes and troughs of sandy gravel—fine for an all-wheel-drive quad, but more difficult for heavy motorcycles. As my bike bucked under me and I fought for control over boulders and skidded in gravel, I was thinking, "I am going to get hurt." I knew I was going to fall over, it was only a question of *when*—and there were so many hard things to land on.

Michael got stuck first, his rear wheel spinning into gravel and sand on an uphill hairpin. I parked my bike and walked back around the corner to help. His rear wheel was buried so deep that the best fix was to lay the bike right over on its side, slide it sideways a bit, then stand it up on firmer ground. We set off again, but minutes later, I was down. However, the bike lay against a rut that kept it upright enough for me to raise it myself. Then, trying to tiptoe down a steep, narrow, rutted incline, I went over *hard*, jumping clear as the bike landed far down on its side. Switching off the engine, I said some bad words. Another group of quad riders was waiting at the bottom for me to get out of the way, and a couple of them helped me get the bike upright again.

The next time it went down, and we got it up and started again, a middle-aged guy with a Harley T-shirt said, "If my bike fell over that many times, it would never start again." By then I had lost count of how many times we had been over. Several times I got mired in deep, loose gravel, and smelled burning clutch as I tried to power out. This was all getting a bit . . . *serious*.

Finally we reached the "landmark" the first couple had told us about—the rusted carcass of an old-style, rounded school bus, about half of it buried under sand and gravel. (Perhaps a clue to a flood that had destroyed what *used* to be a road around there?) We had made it through the silt, a few inches of light powder over a hard surface, so not too bad. But now came the sand, and the other quad riders gave us the impression there was quite a stretch of it.

The exertion and the high-eighties temperature were getting to Michael, who does not tolerate heat well. He rested in the shade, grateful for a bottle of water and a can of Sprite offered by our "guides," Stephen and Karen. (I was carrying a little water, but Michael was not. I had asked him back at Wikieup, just before we turned onto Chicken Springs Road, when there was a store across the road, if he wanted to stop. He had said, "No—I'm all right." Now he wasn't. Some kids never learn . . . )

I rode ahead to have a recon. Almost immediately I bumped down a steep bank into a deep expanse of sand. Down went the bike, and with it my heart. I saw that the expanse of bare, rippled sand stretched ahead a long way, and we were *never* going to make it across that. Yet going back was out of the question. We were getting low on gas, and even the spare gallon on my bike's rear rack might not be enough.

And then, out of nowhere—a miracle of humanity occurred. All of those quad drivers gathered around to help us. Three couples in their fifties spent a good two hours of their holiday afternoon to help these two stranded motorcyclists.

One couple had their dog with them on their quad, a black spaniel named Mandy, and I joked that I was going to remember this rescue as "Operation Mandy." The man called John brought over a length of heavy yellow rope—saying that his friends always kidded him about carrying it—and we tied it around the forks of Michael's bike. Tom, with the Harley shirt, and I held it upright while his wife, Cathy, pulled with the quad. It was still tough going, just keeping the bike

on its wheels in that deep sand. Holding onto the handlebar and the luggage case, my boots scrabbling for traction, I was leaning so hard into it that it felt like I was supporting most of its weight. After a while I said to Tom, "I'm about to lose it." He said, "Me, too," and called ahead for his wife to stop. (I liked how he always called her "Baby.")

Behind us, another strategy was being attempted. Michael, Stephen, and John lifted the front wheel of my bike into the rear box of Stephen and Karen's larger quad, and that proved to be the best solution. Michael and Stephen crouched in the back to steady the bike, while Karen pulled slowly along. Their little caravan soon caught up to our noble but less effective effort, and a group decision seemed to favor waiting for the larger quad to get my bike to "solid gravel," then come back for Michael's. Tom and I were left alone with Michael's bike, and things were quiet for a long time. We stood beside the stranded motorcycle in the shade of cottonwoods, tamarisk, and dwarf willow in the dry riverbed. This belt of green looked better watered than the surrounding desert, and I felt a distinct coolness seeping from them. I asked Tom if the river flowed underground in that area, as desert rivers sometimes do, and he said he thought it did.

Tom and I made some small talk—he had lived in Arizona for over thirty years, because his wife was from there, and I told him that was why I lived in California, too. He scouted ahead a short distance and thought the next stretch of the trail looked firmer—perhaps if we pushed the bike that far, it would be rideable. I said, "I like the way you think," and he replied, "I'm not the kind to just stand around and wait." I said, "Yeah—I'm that way, too. I'll try pushing while you ride, if you like."

It seemed right that I, as one of the "strandees," should do the heavy work, while my rescuer should ride—if he could, anyway. And it turned out that Tom's Harley T-shirt represented a *real* rider (not always the case, as even non-riders probably know). Just by the motion of his left hand on the clutch lever—smooth and easy—I could tell he was good. He sat astride the bike and got the rear wheel spinning, while I leaned into the rear rack and started pushing. Dust and sand sprayed up over me, but it worked. Our progress was slow, but steady, and when we reached the firmer area, Tom rode a long distance. I followed on foot—happy just to be moving *forward*. Eventually Tom got mired in soft sand again, and when I caught up with him I pushed for another stretch, until we reached a worse obstacle—a steep, rutted bank of sand up to higher ground. John came along in his little quad, and directed his wife, Pam, to drive it through the scrub up in front of the motorcycle. (These men and women were all so *competent*.) There he tied on his yellow rope and towed the bike up and over that last hump. The trail seemed ridable

from there, so I offered to take over from Tom. He snickered and said, "Sure—let me do all the riding, then take all the glory!"

The whole group of us, rescuers and rescued, gathered where my bike had been delivered to the end of the gravel road. Earlier, after taking a few shots during a pause in pushing Michael's bike, I had passed my camera to John on his quad, asking him to take any photos he could. As we posed for a group shot at the end, with Pam holding my camera, someone pointed to it and said, "That is one *dusty* lens."

Sure enough, the photo was a bit blurry, but—historical.

It was at this point that I astonished Michael by introducing myself—by name *and* by profession—to our rescuers. I started by asking Tom, "Are you a fan of rock music?" He nodded tentatively, not knowing what I was getting at. Turning to face all of them, I said, "Well, I play for the band Rush. If any of you are going to be in Phoenix tomorrow night, I would like to invite you to our show."

Tom shook his head and said, "Whoa—I used to listen to Rush all

the time." Then he made a wry face, "I just wasn't sure if you meant that *modern* kind of rock."

The rest of them seemed excited about the idea, so I brought out my little Montblanc notepad (always properly accessorized, even in the Outback), and they wrote down their names. Michael gave them his cell number in case they had any trouble picking up their tickets.

(Later he said to me, "Wow—after traveling with you all these years, I've never seen you 'come out' before."

I fixed him with an ironic glare, "Someday you'll learn that there's always a *proper* time to come out.")

Our new friends looked at me with a little more interest now (I suppose to them, it was as if some kind of *alien* had dropped into their midst), but in a nice, easy, Western way. To me the important thing was that they had devoted all that time and effort to helping us—just *because*. I have learned from traveling in many inhospitable areas, from Africa to the Arctic to the American deserts, that people in such places band together. When you have a problem, if you are fortunate enough to find any people around, they are going to help.

(In this case, they even invited us back to their camp for steaks! We were certainly hungry—but we needed to move on.)

The sun was just setting as we fueled up at the Wayside—a funky desert oasis in the middle of the Outback, offering food, fuel, and RV spaces. With darkness coming on, we decided against the thirty miles of gravel that would bring us to the highway near Wickenburg—the nearest town where we might expect to find a motel and a meal. Instead we rode a few miles of gravel to a paved road, then down and around eighty miles. (Longer, but wiser.) The moon was nearly full, which cast a comforting light over the utter darkness of landscape and road, and the air was still warm. I rarely choose to ride at night, for reasons of safety and (lack of) scenery, but this was one enjoyable night ride, to a very welcome Best Western in Wickenburg, Arizona.

When Michael walked out of the lobby after checking us in, he was carrying two small lunch-size paper bags, and handed me one. "A present just for bikers," he said. The brown bag was decorated with the above artwork, by Kenzie, the owner's seven-year-old daughter— "because she likes motorcycles," the front desk clerk told us. (You have to love the "ya-hoo!"—and the "harley-davidson" on the tanks.)

When little Kenzie suggested to her parents that their motel should give motorcyclists a "special present," it was decided to offer these little bags—containing a couple of washcloths for bike-cleaning (the darker reason for those being that too many riders use their room towels for that purpose), a Tootsie Roll, and a couple of hard candies. It was a sweet ending to a long journey.

As Michael remarked, "This has been the kind of day that raises your faith in humanity."

I agreed. The "better angels" had definitely been on our side, and it could have ended *much* worse.

But as I sat in the plastic chair outside the motel room with my Macallan, and tried to put down some notes about the day, different shades seemed to complicate the story. Not taking anything away from our rescuers (indeed, I will forever remember them with affection and gratitude), a reconstruction of events took me back to the hunter who told us, despite the "NO THROUGH ROAD" sign, that we could "make our way around." Maybe he was the kind of man who can never say "I don't know" (we've all met them) and felt compelled to offer that casual misinformation. Or maybe it was because he was sitting on a four-wheeler instead of a two-wheeler and didn't know the difference in what we could "make our way around."

Either way, if that Thanksgiving Saturday had been nearly any other day of the year in that remote corner of the Arizona Outback, there would have been no one to ask. Our choice would have been between what the map and GPS said, and what the sign said. I am sure we would still have gone forward, but less confidently, and when the road petered out into nothing, we would have turned back—while we still could have.

Then at that very juncture, that very point-of-no-return, we met Stephen and Karen, and they, too, had encouraged us, offering to lead us down a trail we would never have found and which they couldn't know we wouldn't be able to ride.

So, I summed up the day with this little metaphor:

People get you into trouble,
People get you out.

Talking to the friendly front-desk guy, he told us the Rancho Grande Best Western in Wickenburg was one of the original five charter members of that association. That impressed me, because for many years that blue and yellow sign was my default choice in my random travels around North America. Up through the '90s, each property under the Best Western sign was independent and unique, and many of them were classics of the old-school motel—where you park in front of your room and walk to the attached restaurant.

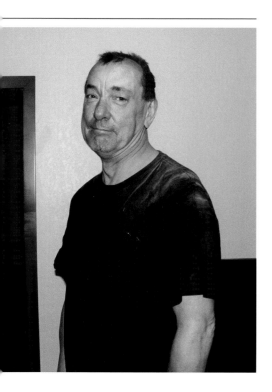

Desert rat

However, lately I had been disappointed to see the brand betray that heritage by devolving into an increasingly watered-down chain of corporate outlets. It seemed they were even buying up big-box joints from budget chains and calling them "Plus," when they were *minus*—the room-front parking, the restaurant, and the character.

Asking about restaurants for dinner, our front-desk friend highly recommended a nearby barbecue place, but they closed early. Michael and I were not ready to go anywhere—not even out of our riding clothes yet—so we opted for take-out. (Another key to a successful partnership: I think up good ideas, Michael executes them.) Still covered in the dust of the day's journey, we sat at the little table in Michael's room and tore into deliciously smoky racks and brisket and beans.

Back in January, when manager Ray first sent me the proposed itinerary for the tour, there were two features that immediately stood out to me. They were not the cities where I would be playing shows, because where I work doesn't matter much to me—not as much as how I get there. So my eyes tend to be drawn to the days off, and especially if I see two of them in a row. Those rarely come along (not "economically sound") but can allow me to stretch my travel range between shows to some amazing journeys. One perfect example from a couple of tours ago: two days off between Phoenix and Albuquerque—the first day spent riding through Arizona to Monument Valley for the night, then through Colorado to Taos, New Mexico, for the second night. In this Bubba's touring life, it doesn't get much better than that.

This time, I was looking at two days off between Chicago and Detroit, which suggested interesting possibilities around the Upper Peninsula of Michigan. (That eventually became our sublime day off on Mackinac Island—see "The Better Angels.") The second pair of free days lay between Phoenix and Dallas, setting me up in the heart of the Southwest. My first inclination was to aim for Southern Utah, with its unparalleled national parks—Bryce Canyon, Zion, Capitol Reef, Canyonlands, Arches—and one of my favorite destination towns, Moab. (Not least because it's in the middle of *all that*.)

But . . . it was *November*, and all of those places were cold and potentially snowy. Another always-welcome candidate would be Grand Canyon National Park, but its low temperature at the time was 16°. Oh, no. I would need to think "South."

That spin of the compass needle directed me right to Big Bend National Park, way down deep in Texas.

For those two days we would be joined by a guest rider, Brian Catterson, longtime friend and veteran moto-journalist. (Like a number of my friends, we began as a "mutual appreciation society": I liked his work; he liked mine.) As a traveler, Brian is a calm, competent companion (there goes that alliteration again) and has made an appearance on every tour since *Vapor Trails*, in 2002. Now just past fifty years of age, he spent his professional life immersed in the sport and documentation of motorcycling. He is experienced in every kind of two-wheeled action, from extreme race machines to the light and agile motocross bikes of his youth. (We could have used bikes like that in the Arizona Outback!) Lately, after retiring as editor-in-chief at *Motorcyclist* magazine, he returned to motocross bikes, as a hobby—or maybe a career. (My invented diner placemat of ads on Bubba's Bar 'n' Grill listed "Catterson's Small Engines," and we joked that it was coming true.)

I would find it impossible to name my favorite national park, among so many splendid places (truly America's crown jewels), like Death Valley, Yellowstone, or Bryce Canyon, but if I did try, Big Bend would be a contender. Other than Death Valley, it is also the national park I have most frequently visited.

Brutus and I first passed that way back on the *Test for Echo* tour,

Brian and Michael, Big Bend National Park

the first concert tour I did by motorcycle, in 1996–97. In March 2003, it was the destination on the car trip that became the centerpiece of my "musical autobiography," *Traveling Music*. Since then I had led Michael there two or three times, often staying in nearby Lajitas at the same fine resort where Brutus and I had stopped for breakfast that first time.

It was Brian's first visit to Big Bend, and his first time seeing much of West Texas—our three-day journey would cover a thousand miles of Texan backroads between Van Horn and Dallas. Brian was usually content to ride behind Michael and me, and being on my spare bike (red, like every motorcycle I have owned), he called himself "the little red caboose."

When I led Michael and Brian up to the Chisos Basin area of the park, with its monumental rock formations and winding switchbacks, Brian said, "Mountains in Texas! Who knew?"

I pointed over to Emory Peak, which I had hiked up during the *Traveling Music* journey in 2003, and told him it was almost 8,000 feet. Yet the Guadalupe Mountains to the north had a few peaks that rose even higher. Texas most assuredly has mountains. It's got pretty much everything.

Writing about Texas reminds me of trying to write about Africa— hard to describe to people who have never been there, or even to those who live there and haven't seen much of their homeland. The Big Bend area may be the most spectacular, but I also love the vast expanses of West Texas, the Gulf Coast around Corpus Christi and Padre Island, and east toward Louisiana, with bayous and cypress trees, the Piney Woods north of there, and the Hill Country west of Austin.

Texas truly is a country unto itself, beyond all the clichés, and its people are equally varied and unique. For example, it still remains true that rural Texans are the most courteous drivers in the country, perhaps in the world. Riding the two-lanes (which Brian was also delighted to see posted at 70 mph), cars, pickups, and larger trucks will pull right onto the shoulder as you overtake them. Sometimes you're not even thinking about passing them yet, willing to cruise behind them for a bit, but when they pull over like that, you feel you *have* to go by—always with a big wave.

Some readers might be surprised to learn that law enforcement is equally relaxed in Texas—especially compared to police states like, say, Ohio. In maybe 20,000 miles of riding in Texas over the years (over 2,000 just that *week*), I remember being pulled over only once—

back in '97 with Brutus. Even then, the officer was friendly and let us go with a warning. Generally, if you respect the towns and villages, as we always do, you're not going to have a problem on the open roads. I have *never* encountered a speed trap in Texas, except on the interstate—and those speed limits are so high (80 on the long rural stretches), you've got to be pushing pretty hard to get into trouble even there.

Another part of Texas Brutus and I explored on that first tour was its most southerly region, south and west of Corpus Christi. That time we rode down from San Marcos and stopped for breakfast at a tiny crossroads town called Tilden. I believe that was in November, too— sixteen years ago. I want to retell that story here, as recounted in *Traveling Music*, because now it has a different ending . . .

Chisos Basin,
Big Bend

Hill country byway

Somehow the open spaces on the map of South Texas had led us to expect a desolate land, but it was obviously fertile, and artfully cultivated. Plow and disk harrow had combed the brown soil into neat contours and swirls, like a Chinese garden, and the fields lay in elegant fallow. With my farming heritage and farm-equipment background, I had to admire this example of deft tractor-handling, and "excellence on earth."

The farms gave way to arid, rolling ranchland, and dark herds of cattle hunched under the dull sky. A pair of hawks flew between the few bare trees, their plumage dramatically patterned in dark and light, like magpies. The scrubby ground-cover was green with the recent rain, and occasionally dotted with small oil wells, a prehistoric-looking "dipper" rising and falling in slow-motion rhythm . . .

Thoughts of breakfast were beginning to gnaw, and I was tempted by signs pointing toward towns a few miles off our route, where we might find a diner. Many of the towns in that part of South Texas had names like Peggy, Nell, Rosita, Alice, Christine, Charlotte, Marion, Helena, and Bebe, and I imagined lonesome cowboys pinin' for the girls they left behind. (The female population of frontier Texas, like all the West, was probably half wives and daughters, and half prostitutes.)

Brutus and I rode on, pinin' for the diners we'd left behind. Finally we came to another little crossroads town, called Tilden, the seat of McMullen County. A new brick courthouse with a tiled roof stood on one side of the road, and opposite it, the Cowboy Cafe.

The walls inside were lined with rows of well-worn cowboy hats, each tagged with a name and year, and a poster for a '50s Western movie starring Rex Allen, the "Oklahoma Cowboy." A framed black-and-white glossy of Rex himself was autographed with folksy good humor, testifying that the Cowboy Cafe "filled us up real good."

Brutus and I peeled off a few more layers of clothing as Willie Nelson played on the radio, then sat down to the strains of "Don't Come Home A-Drinkin' With Lovin' on Your Mind." This late in the morning, the Cowboy Cafe had only one other customer, a silent man in a straw cowboy hat hunched over his plate. A tiny Mexican woman shuffled to our table, her crippled body barely as tall as we were—sitting down. She wore a large, shapeless T-shirt reading "Always a Lady," and her toothy smile and good-natured banter soon had us laughing with her. We looked at each other and smiled; this place was the real thing.

Former Cowboy Cafe, June 2010

A tall, lean man came in, dressed in neat denim jeans and jacket, and a collared work shirt. He sat at the table beside us, saying "Morning, Gloria," and after a bit of banter with her, he leaned over to us. He looked to be in his fifties, his smooth-shaven face refined-looking, only mildly weathered by an outdoor life.

"I see by your license plates that one of you fellows is from Ontario."

I raised a hand, "That's me."

He stood and introduced himself, shaking our hands. "I'm Johnny Nichols, and I run a ranch just down the road here. The man who first settled it was John Fitzpatrick, who come down from a place called St. Catharines. You know it?"

I laughed, "Sure do—I grew up there!"

"Right near Niagara Falls, right?"

I nodded, smiling.

"See, I've looked into it *all*."

Johnny Nichols sat down again as Gloria brought his coffee, then continued. "Uncle John, we called him, he come over to Canada from Ireland in the 1860s. He wanted to come down here then, but the Civil War was on, so he started farmin' up there. Then once the war was over, he worked his way down the Mississippi on the log booms, all the way to New Orleans, then made his way over here, and started runnin' sheep. A couple-a years later, his younger brother Jim followed him down, but one cold morning his horse was kinda skittish, and it reared up on him. Jim was tryin' to hold on, and his hand come down on the hammer of his gun and he shot himself in the leg. Died of blood poisoning."

We made the appropriate grimaces of sympathy and shook our heads.

"Then old Uncle John, he'd been battlin' with this neighbor of his for a long time over water rights, and things started gettin' bad. They all used to stay out on the range in tents, you know, and one day this neighbor come ridin' into Uncle John's camp, shootin' and hollerin', and Uncle John shot him out of the saddle, dead."

He paused for effect, then added, "But he got off for self-defense."

. . . Then Gloria brought his breakfast, and a couple of other ranchers came in and joined Johnny Nichols at his table. All of them looked the part of ranchers and cowboys in their denim jeans and jackets, high-heeled boots, and hats. . . .

Their conversation was sprinkled with the relative merits of petroleum, its color, pressure in pounds-per-square-inch, and the percentage of water they were pumping. Johnny Nichols shook our hands again as we left, and just south of Tilden we saw the sign arching above a sideroad, "Nichols Ranch, Est. 1879 by John and Maggie Fitzpatrick."

Their ranch had been established by "Uncle John" Fitzpatrick, who had made his way down to Texas from St. Catharines, Ontario, my hometown, way back in 1866. From then on that little crossroads town and county seat of Tilden, Texas, took its place on our "mental maps" for good, and we would never forget the Cowboy Cafe, or Johnny Nichols, or Gloria, or even Rex Allen, the "Oklahoma Cowboy."

The reason for that long digression (apart from correcting the spelling of "Nichols," and the wording on the sign) is because it describes a place and people that are now completely *gone*.

In the years since that first visit, I have often routed Michael and myself through Tilden. It made part of a nice ride toward Padre Island, where I liked to stay between shows in East Texas. (Even just for the music of the surf through my open door all night.) On my second ride through Tilden, early in the 2000s, I was sad to see the Cowboy Cafe closed (replaced briefly by a barbecue place, which was also closed on my next visit a couple of years later). But the little town and the surrounding landscape of mesquite ranchland remained pleasant to travel through, on long, straight two-lanes with little other traffic. As recently as June 2010, I had passed through and found it unchanged.

This time, it was all different, and after what I had witnessed in Western North Dakota back in September (see "The Better Angels"), I knew *immediately* what was going on. It was those frackin' frackers. What Johnny and his fellow ranchers had been doing the old-fashioned way, pumping up a little oil more or less as a sideline, was now a vast industrial complex pumping chemicals two miles down to smash the oil out of the rock.

The West Dakota boom, on what was called geologically the Bakken formation, had been going for three years, while this South Texas operation, on what was called the Eagle Ford formation, had to be less than two. Doing some online research, the only date I found was 2011, so maybe only one. The machinery of modern fossil-fuel extraction moves swiftly, and massively. Hundreds of semis, crude-looking tankers and construction gondolas crowded the little highways, warping the pavement into lumpy black dough that pounded us on the bikes. The mesquite scrub was lined with new fences of white steel pipe,

pierced with dozens of gateways and raw gravel roads. Travel trailers stood at the gates with security guards in Hi-Viz vests, checking trucks in and out. Plumes of flame belched from high steel stacks, burning off natural gas, and vast construction sites for processing and storage works—enormous tanks, pumps, and pipes—were scraped out of acres and acres of mesquite. A huge truck stop was under construction near Tilden, and the ramshackle buildings that had housed the Cowboy Cafe were gone—completely obliterated.

The next town south, Freer, seemed to be the center of the boom, as it was of the region. Freer was surrounded by improvised RV parks spread out on acres of bare gravel, offering electricity, water, and—one hopes—septic tanks. Multiple signs advertised for truck drivers, and a brand-new Best Western glared with fresh paint in its unfinished gravel lot. Other construction sites rose up like broken teeth.

How it was in June 2010–calm and timeless–before the approaching storm . . .

As I observed earlier about not taking pictures when things get too hairy, that is also true when things get too *ugly*. I hadn't taken any photographs of the devastation in West Dakota that time, and the only one I took around Tilden this time was the Nichols Ranch gate.

Comparing it with a similar photo I took in 2010, the fence of barbed wire and wooden posts had been replaced with the white steel pipes, but the most telling difference was the mailbox—gone now. Sad symbolism. No doubt before long the sign will be gone, too. Johnny and his family, like all the rest of the ranchers who once ran their cattle and pumped their watery oil above the Eagle Ford formation, don't live there anymore. (Echoes back to something I wrote in "The Better Angels": "The saddest roads in America are the ones that people used to live on but don't anymore.")

As I rode south from the old Nichols ranch on that pounded (and pounding) road, I felt sick to my stomach, and even a little prickly around the eyes. A place I loved like an old song, like an old friend, had been devastated. Nothing more than a sleepy little cowboy town, and some lonely two-lane roads between hardscrabble ranches in the mesquite scrub—but it had meant something to me. The mess in West Dakota had been shocking and appalling enough, but now it was *personal*.

Modulating to a more positive key, Michael and I ended the day with this view of the beach on Padre Island. (Yes, Texans drive trucks on their beaches—but I'm sure they still pull over to let you pass!) In late November, the beach chairs were piled by the concrete boardwalk and drifted around with sand. The offshore oil rigs were a further reminder of what I had seen that day, and the pipeline running across the beach seemed ominous—but apparently it only carried sand and water, to replenish the beaches after storms. And in the warm night, the waves murmured their steady, rhythmic music.

Getting back to music, as I would have to do the next day in San Antonio, the three shows in Texas marked the end of this year's part of the *Clockwork Angels* tour. For a few months we would be saying goodbye to our touring world—which, for me, centers on the bus, the Bubba-Gump room, the daily motorcycling, the backroads and motels, and, of course, the stage.

Before soundcheck at the final show, in Houston on December 2, the three of us gathered in front of the string players, which had become a daily custom. After they had tested their instruments and monitors, and before we all played together, I would sit cross-legged on the subwoofer behind my drums, while Alex and Geddy came in from their sides of the stage and we talked and joked for a few minutes with the "stringers."

By now the soundcheck routine was well established. Together we played the first half of "Clockwork Angels" and the first half of "Red Sector A," which checked out everybody's various "systems." Then the three of us gave sound engineer Brad the beginning of the opening song, "Subdivisions," so he was set for the start of the show. When Brad had heard enough, he would shoot up his hand for us to stop, and that became a game among us—watching for that upraised hand, and stopping *immediately*, laughing as we all froze on the same beat.

After soundcheck, dinner, and my warm-up in the Bubba-Gump room, I changed into my "stage costume" and walked with Michael down the hallway to stage left. It was showtime—one more time.

One fun feature I have added to my performance this tour is the T-shirt gun. For many years, at the beginning of our encore, Alex and Geddy have carried out baskets of bundled T-shirts and tossed them out to the crowd. That never appealed to me—not feeling comfortable in *front* of my drums—but somewhere I must have seen one of the air-powered guns that are used at sporting events to shoot souvenir T-shirts into stadium crowds. That, I thought, might be fun.

Michael soon took over as my weapons handler, while John "Boom-Boom" Arrowsmith, our pyrotechnician and daily-events photographer, prepared the "ordnance" (T-shirts tightly bundled in fluorescent tape—so people can see them coming!). I run out for the encore, and Gump hands me the loaded gun. I climb up on the strings riser and wait for the lights to come up on the audience (again, I want people to *see* the flying shirts—don't want anyone getting hurt). I fire the first two rounds, then bend down to let Michael reload while I turn the dial to prime the pressure. Soon we had it down to a tight routine and were getting off four separate shots. Then I would lay down the gun and scramble across the subwoofer to the drums, ready to start "Tom Sawyer."

At first I was shooting T-shirts with my "yearbook" photo from the tourbook—created by Geddy for all three of us on an app called Oldbooth—then one with my "g'nome" character on the front, and finally a West Side Beemer Boyz version, with a riding shot on the front, and on the back my phrase about "the best roads."

Here is a great shot by Boom-Boom, showing the first shirt in flight, and the second just leaving the muzzle. Michael waits to load the last two shirts.

One aspect of my "distribution system" that particularly pleases me is that my T-shirts go high into the crowd—"far and away"—into the less-expensive seats. Consequently, I have never seen anyone down front wearing one of them at another show, as I regularly see the ones Alex and Geddy toss into the front rows.

After thirty-five shows, and 13,632 motorcycle miles, we finished the Houston show on a very high note, so to speak. The performance itself felt triumphant, and after, we gathered with the stringers for a champagne celebration. It was the first time I stayed after a show on the whole tour, and a couple of the stringers joked that they were used to seeing me as a blur on my sprint to the bus.

A few nights earlier, when we were filming some shows for an eventual concert DVD, director Dale had a cameraman trying to capture my flight. He caught a comment from a security guard, an older lady with a broad New York City accent. She turned in amazement as I ran past, and gasped, *"Oh my god! He runs faster than Britney Spears! And she was running full out!"*

But on this night I stayed behind and raised a glass to my bandmates—all ten of them! Geddy proposed a toast to the stringers and said that not only did we love their contributions musically, and the energy they brought to their performance, but they were fun to hang out with, too.

He nodded toward me and said, "I've never seen *him* so happy on a tour! He's been . . . Mr. Goodvibe!"

Nothing wrong with that, obviously, but I was a little mystified. I hadn't actually *felt* any different. Maybe the "deeper currents" of my being were calmer; my inner compass steadier—I don't know. Fundamentally, I liked the way I was playing, and felt strong and consistent from night to night. I was beginning to master the improvisational mode I had been pursuing for several years—and in three different solo contexts throughout this show. (Michael calls the third one, on the electronic drums, the "Binary Love Theme." He says that's where I play the "love notes," as opposed to the "hate notes" on the acoustic drums.)

"Love Notes"

Just before soundcheck at the Seattle show, I recorded a radio interview with Michael Shrieve (veteran drummer with Santana, Go, Automatic Man, and more). In my early drumming years, Michael was a strong influence on me—his legendary solo with Santana in the

Woodstock movie a formative paradigm. All these years later, drums were a kind of *religion* that the two of us shared—we could easily have talked for hours. During our conversation, Michael mentioned the resonance for him of a quote I had used in Bubba's Book Club.

"The most valuable of all education is the ability to make yourself do the thing you have to do, when it has to be done, whether you like it or not."

(I didn't remember the source, until Michael told me it was Aldous Huxley, from my review of his novel, *After Many a Summer Dies the Swan*.)

Classic arena backstage scene—bus, trailer, bikes, dumpster

So, considering my recent life in those terms, for all those months I had been doing what I had to do—my job. But I had also been doing what I *wanted* to do: making that job as interesting, challenging, and rewarding as I possibly could. (Everyone knows it doesn't always go that way.)

Musically and visually, I was proud of the show we were presenting—the overall production and aspects like the alternating sets, with a few different songs from night to night. After thirty-eight years together, I was confident that *Clockwork Angels* was our masterpiece, and I felt that the string section during those songs elevated our whole presence. Drum tech Gump had been keeping our elaborate setup perfect, and any glitches had been few and minor. With regular treatment and a brace when I played, my aching elbow had held out for the duration, without inhibiting my playing. (I think I wrote once before, "If I'm not happy on the drums, I'm not happy *anywhere*.") On my bus, Dave and Michael and I had a comfortable routine, and my motorcycle explorations had been entertaining and rewarding.

And now I was going home to my family for a nice long rest, before starting up again next spring and summer. Soon three-year-old Olivia and I would be walking down the streets of our neighborhood, singing a new song we made up together:

> *I'm so happy–*
> *I'm so happy–*
> *I'm so happy–to be with you!*

Somehow I know that when Michael rides behind me again, in a Midwest monsoon, a snowy Oregon road, or a cloud of Wild West dust, he will sing that same song. But with some bad words added . . .

# WINTER LATITUDES

MARCH 2013

**It was mid-afternoon** in early February 2013, in the Laurentian Mountains of Quebec. The temperature was near 0°F, further embittered by the driving wind and my passage on cross-country skis. Snow lay three feet deep on the ground and filled the air with icy slashes. After two and a half hours of that kind of abuse, and that kind of exertion, I was glad to be on the trail's home stretch.

Like the Action Self-Portraits I take on my motorcycle, this opening photo was captured in motion. While gliding downhill, my left hand held the camera out to the side and snapped away. At this moment, my eyes were obviously glancing over to check the camera angle, but I like how the expression seems to say, "Are you serious?"

That long, gradual downhill for my photo opportunity came near the end of a fifteen-mile loop (it had been a long, gradual *uphill* at the beginning). All that time I had been striding over the gentle ups and downs and occasional flats, struggling up the steepest inclines or nervously careering downhill between the trees. Despite the cold, my inner layers were wet with sweat, and I was tired and pleasantly sore. Like after a three-hour concert, or an all-day motorcycle ride, I was hurting all over—but that was fine. If I drive myself hard, and properly use every muscle, they should all feel it. Just no individual aches in knees, shoulders, elbows, and so on, thank you.

My area of the Southern Laurentians offers an extensive network of cross-country ski trails, but I have always favored one particular loop. I once compared it to a yoga practice, dynamically, for the way it builds gradually in intensity, sustains that pace for a long period of varying terrain and technique, then eases down gently toward rest. It begins with an easy kick-and-glide cruise along an old railway alignment, then turns uphill for about twenty minutes, through alternating degrees of steepness. On a gentle grade, the wax will hold against the snow as I press down before the kick, if conditions are right (and the wax well chosen). Then I continue my rhythmic stride, even sometimes gliding upward a little between kicks, if previous skiers have glazed the surface of any new snow. A few more degrees of rise might require a firmly planted ski with each stride to hold against the backward-slipping gravity. The next level of gradient needs the skis stepped out and edged in at the back, and the steepest of all demand the full splayed-out herringbone, leaving the namesake pattern in the snow.

I always consider that extended climb as my personal "Test Hill." Every year when I come back to it, it represents a measure of my fitness level. As long as I can do that relentless climb in one go, without pausing, then I figure I'm okay. I do not look forward to the day when I discover I cannot.

Here, through the magic of my personal invention, the SkiCam™ (I lean down over the tips and snap the trail ahead), we see the woods covered with new snow. I was breaking trail through a few inches of powder that had fallen overnight and during the morning. It was mid-afternoon, and nobody had been on that trail before me that day. On a weekday, I sometimes ski that whole two-and-a-half-hour loop without seeing another skier. At most, two or three.

That is part of the reason why if the temperature is below about 0°F, I don't go out alone. In fact, that is around –18°C, the temperature at which long cross-country ski races will be canceled. The cold itself is not uncomfortable, because cross-country skiing generates a good deal of heat. But if anything should go wrong—injury or equipment

failure—and you *stop* generating that heat, you could be in bad trouble pretty quickly. It has to be admitted that I am not the most graceful or coordinated of skiers, and I fall quite often, especially on tricky down-hills with narrow curves. Trees, with their unyielding hardness, are always too close and available to be crashed into. More than once in an out-of-control tumble, my skis have clattered into a tree, or I have felt my backpack brush against something hard as I go head over heels. A broken collarbone, or even a twisted ankle, could leave me helpless in unforgiving cold.

Yet of course that very solitude is part of what I like about cross-country skiing, so it can't be avoided. Just as I face up to the risks of motorcycling while trying to minimize them, I try to be prudent in the winter woods, too. On colder days, or on weekends when more people visit the ski trails, I'll go out on snowshoes instead. You don't need a trail with those—you can walk anywhere you want, just head out the door and into the woods, following old logging roads or survey lines. And there's little danger of a bad fall.

Another rule I maintain in the winter woods (a subcategory of Roadcraft called Trailcraft) is that I won't cross frozen lakes or ponds

alone. More than one neighbor of mine has fallen through a beaver hole, or a place where moving water thins the ice, and clearly that can also mean serious trouble, especially if you are alone.

And that kind of cold bites *fast*. On that same bitter, blizzardy February afternoon, I got back to my snow-covered car at the trailhead. That is always a welcome moment of combined weariness and relief, now free of urgency or the need of *will* to drive me onward. I took off my gloves to fiddle with my camera, and looked through some of the Action Self-Portraits I had attempted that day, then took a few of the car (Audi S4 wagon—ideal winter machine) half-buried in the driving snow.

My hands had been warm coming out of the gloves, but they were wet with sweat, and before I knew it—not more than two minutes—my fingers were suddenly numb. I tried putting the gloves back on, but they were wet inside and icy cold already. Reaching into my backpack for the car keys, I couldn't feel them. I had to look in and find the ring of keys, then claw them out with lifeless fingers. Even to hold the key fob and thumb the button to unlock the car was a struggle. Opening the rear hatch and loading the snow-covered skis and poles inside chilled my fingers even more. The numbness was now tinged with pain, so that I dreaded curving my fingers under the cold door handle to raise it. Behind the wheel, it took both frozen hands to clutch the key between them, guide it to the ignition, then turn it to start the engine. I was more than usually glad to hear the V8 rumble to life and settle into a steady throb. One curved claw pulled the shifter back to neutral, and the handbrake upward. I rubbed my hands and waited for the car to produce heat.

After a long bout of outdoor exercise, it is a traditional ritual for certain louche and contrarian Canadians (okay, me) to light up a smoke—but at that moment, I couldn't manage that to "save my life!" (Ha ha.) With thumbs paralyzed and nerveless, there was no way I could operate my LRL (little red lighter). I could push in the car's lighter, but my dead fingers could not grasp the knob to pull it out. I had to laugh a little at that predicament, and at myself. Safe in my car and headed home, I was not in any danger, but that sudden helplessness was still a little scary.

It reminded me of Jack London's classic story "To Build a Fire," set in the Klondike Gold Rush in the Yukon in the late 1890s. A *chechaquo*, newcomer, sets out in the dark midwinter to hike to his remote camp, accompanied only by a "wolf-dog." The temperature falls to a scarcely imaginable –75°F—Alaska and the Yukon have both reported

−80°F, while the coldest temperature ever recorded was in Antarctica, at −128°F. (We wouldn't go out skiing alone in *that*!)

London illustrates the severity with a telling detail—the man's spit crackles and freezes before it reaches the ground. His destiny combines bad judgment with bad luck, as tragedy so often does, when he falls through the ice over a hidden spring. He needs to start a fire—*fast*, while his fingers can still manipulate the matches. The conditions are extreme, man and nature at its most elemental, and so is the man's fate, vividly described in Jack London's muscular prose. (Friend Craiggie shared a link to a pretty good filmed version of the story by the BBC from 1969, narrated by Orson Welles.)

In a brief but significant tangent, there is one tiny detail—one word—in "To Build a Fire" (published 1908) that damns it to present-day readers. This sentence appears in an early descriptive passage: "He held on through the level stretch of woods for several miles, crossed a wide flat of niggerheads, and dropped down a bank to the frozen bed of a small stream."

You see the problem. It seems a shame that one word might cause a classic masterpiece to be put aside in school curricula. Perhaps another story, less likely to delight a young boy but less apt to offend his parents, would be selected instead. The tale is set in the late nineteenth century, and the word commonly described tussocks of Alaskan sedge grasses—the *meaning* isn't racially insensitive, just the consonants. It clearly will not sit well with people nowadays, yet the prospect of censoring the literature of the past, or "bowdlerizing" such words with acceptable euphemisms, is problematic, too. That example could be changed to "crossed a wide flat of sedge tussocks" without any loss—and maybe publishers should take it upon themselves to do that. But it would be a big, controversial task.

Among many other writers of the period, Kipling, Twain, Conrad, and Hemingway used the root of that word "comfortably," and Harper Lee and Ian Fleming even later. Many black writers employed it in "realistic" fashion, which gets a pass—while these days television networks censor even its deliberately absurd use in the classic Mel Brooks comedy *Blazing Saddles* (co-written with Richard Pryor). I would like to think the future will bring a racial calmness, when words won't carry forward such prickly burrs from the past.

Anyway . . . Jack London (1876–1916) had been on my mind in other ways around that time. I was thinking about his brave credo:

> *I would rather be ashes than dust.*
> *I would rather that my spark should burn out in a brilliant blaze,*
> *Than that it should be stifled by dry-rot.*
> *I would rather be a superb meteor, every atom of me in*
>     *magnificent glow,*
> *Than a sleepy and permanent planet.*
> *The proper function of man is to LIVE.*
> *I shall not waste my days trying to prolong them.*
> *I shall use my time.*

That is an inspiring vision, all right, and I especially resonate with the thought, "I shall not waste my days trying to prolong them. I shall use my time."

However, in Jack London's case, the dates tell the ironic tale. He did not waste his days in prolonging them, it's true, but the way he lived probably shortened his time. He was addicted to opium and alcohol, and had multiple health problems—some stemming from his hardships in the Klondike, others perhaps from a quirky

diet favoring oddities like nearly raw duck. He was only forty when he died at his Northern California estate, Beauty Ranch, of kidney failure and a suspected accidental morphine overdose. During my *Ghost Rider* travels in the late '90s, I visited Beauty Ranch and walked around the ruins of Wolf House, the home he had been building with his wife, Charmian. It burned down just before his death, symbolizing a dream future that he did not live to inhabit. Nearby, a simple boulder marks his grave.

We may contrast Jack London's credo with one espoused by Ernest Hemingway, who quoted a motto from a statue of one of Napoleon's generals, *"Il faut d'abord durer"*—"First one must last." Or, the shorter version I prefer, "At first, to last." (That was one inspiration for the Rush song "Marathon.")

For myself, I figure I have already "lasted." As I begin my seventh decade, one frequent realization is the number of people I have *out-lasted*—not only did Jack London die so young, but Ernest Hemingway

Heron nests

Redpolls flock to Bubba's

was just sixty-one when he ended his torments with a shotgun. And how many musicians—how many *drummers?* Why, it's the stuff of punch lines. (See *This Is Spiñal Tap, Good Night Keith Moon*, etc.)

Such thoughts always give me pause—but not in the conventional way. The notion doesn't make me *fear* time or aging. To the contrary, I feel like I've already won. The rest is all bonus . . .

One Sunday afternoon, I was joined on snowshoes by my neighbor Charles (silent "s"), who had been my partner on the "Quest for the Phantom Tower" a few years back. From my door we headed into the woods, following paths we knew well, commenting on the number of trees that had been snapped off by a recent heavy snowfall. Feeling secure with a companion, we traversed frozen lakes and ponds, and passed a few nests left by the summer residents, great blue herons. All the while we discussed the animal tracks we encountered—the stories in the snow. Deer, fox, hare, weasel (ermine, in its white winter coat), grouse, and squirrels. We were especially delighted to see where a moose had been "nesting" in the shelter of some evergreens. Moose are rare in our neighborhood, and still hunted every year, so we are always glad to learn they are still around.

Even from indoors, I had been watching the stories in the snow every day. My birdfeeder, Bubba's Seeds 'n' Suet, was busy most of the time, with chickadees, common redpolls, red-breasted nuthatches, and hairy woodpeckers. Below it, tracks had been left by squirrels, rummaging in the snow under the feeder for seeds or bounding across the white surface from one tree to another.

Pretty well every day I saw a line of prints, straight and purposeful, left by a fox. No matter how often I looked out, even during the night, I never saw the animal itself. Charles told me he saw it all the time, but my single sighting had been the winter before, and that was only for a few seconds, as the reddish body and long tail darted across my yard.

So I was pleasantly surprised one morning to look out and see a fox poking around the feeder, sticking its nose into the snow here and there—probably sniffing for mice. Slowly I backed away from the window and picked up my camera, amazed to have time to snap a dozen shots of it, before it stepped lightly across the snow back to its den in the hill by the road.

A few days later, I looked out the window at another story in the snow, starring my neighborhood fox. (I knew she was a female, having seen her squatting in the snow to . . . micturate. Or as I put it less delicately but more poetically in letters to friends, "I know she's a she/ 'Cause I saw her pee!") A line of her tracks led away from the house, at the bottom left, then suddenly stopped, turned left in three swift bounds that left deep depressions in the snow, then trotted away in a straight line over its surface again. A mousie for brunch, I guess.

I once described the perfect life as a working vacation that never ends. Well, in those terms, at least I had a perfect two weeks. Waking early, with the first hint of light, I looked up through wide-open curtains to greet the day. Sometimes a ballet of snowflakes filled the air, which always makes me happy; other mornings were crystalline, icy hard and frigid-looking. Several nights the temperature plunged to −30°C (−22°F), which is pretty darn cold. The chill emanated from the windows by my bed, like icy fingers creeping through the double glazing. No matter how good your house's heating, insulation, and window and door seals are, that kind of cold seeps through and gives an edge to the air. An *electric* edge, even, when you touch something and the super-dry air sparks with static electricity.

Looking out on a severely cold morning, under a sky that seems infinitely blue, the bare trees sway stiffly, like rigid skeletons. The natural suppleness of their trunks, branches, and twigs is paralyzed by frost, and they move in unison like a single frozen sculpture. Seeing those trees, and feeling the chill on my nose, is fine to experience from a warm bed—but there is a day to begin. With a surge of will, I roll out and dash into the main room (which sensibly combines kitchen, dining area, and sitting room), quickly sparking up the fireplace with paper and kindling. Then I crawl back under the covers for a while, maybe read a few pages, until the fire starts to spread its spiritual warmth through the house.

Story in the snow

Get dressed, make the coffee, squeeze the juice, then settle at the counter to look over the previous day's writing and start adding to it. After a year of neglecting Bubba's Book Club, I had collected a list of twenty-one titles that I wanted to write about. I had thought I would choose a few that most inspired me, but when I noticed they were nearly all novels, all but one from the previous decade, and all by living writers, I recognized a theme. I can never resist a theme—

whether it's Action Self-Portraits, Ghost Rider photographs, or national park passport stamps. I had to try to write about all of those books.

It was hard work, but rewarding in sometimes unexpected ways. It has occurred to me that writing book reviews can be like writing letters—trying to put impressions and reactions into words, you sometimes discover things you didn't know you knew. I like to paraphrase something E.M. Forster said, "How do I know what I think until I see what I write?"

So I spent my mornings adding pieces to that massive, brain-straining mosaic of words. (See Bubba's Book Club—Issue 17.) Somewhere along the way I would fix some breakfast—soft-boiled eggs with raisin toast, Shreddies cereal (a Canada-only favorite), or blueberry waffles with Quebec maple syrup—then carry on writing until just before noon. Then I would close the laptop and change into my long underwear, fleecy top, windbreaker, boots, and gaiters, and gather up the scarf, balaclava, and gloves that had been drying from the previous day's outing.

Every few days, my property manager and majordomo Keith would drive out from town to bring me some groceries, then stay around to tidy up and load in more firewood. (I burn a lot.) In two weeks, I never drove farther from home than a few miles to the ski trails, out only once at night to visit neighbors Paul and Judy for a welcome dinner-not-cooked-by-me. I visited the nearest village just one time, to get gas for the car. I liked being a recluse like that—it suited me. At least for a while.

I stow a sandwich and some drinks and snacks in my old backpack, and drive to the trailhead. Cold days with fresh snow are easy to wax for—Special Green most of the time, crayoned along each ski's "wax pocket," under the binding, where you press down for grip to kick forward. Then lay the skis flat on the snow, step into the bind-ings, strap the poles around each wrist, and—shove off.

In "The Best February Ever," back in 2008 (can it really be five years?), I described that state of mind: "Many times I have noticed that as soon as I plant my skis in those parallel tracks in the snow and push off, it seems as though my mind is suddenly *transported*."

With all those books to think about, I had no lack of raw material. And even better, none of that was *pressing*—yet it was rich with possible insights, connections, and revela-tions. Another quality I observed in that story: "On the ski trails, while I'm kicking and gliding across the snowy landscape, thoughts parade through my mind in a somehow *stately* fashion, without urgency."

So it remains for me, and my thoughts ranged from postmodernism to what I might eat for dinner (simple comfort-food basics in my solitary retreat—pasta with shrimp sauce, ribeye steak fried in butter and garlic with boiled potatoes and broccoli, pork chops with apple sauce and jasmine rice). As always, my mind gathered what I saw and felt and played the game of trying to put it into words, into sen-tences, that might be shared with others.

Home by late afternoon for a hot shower and maybe a nap, I would stoke up the fire again and pour myself a large Macallan on ice. That was one of the day's rewards—but only one of a *series* of prizes, on a day like that had been. The day itself was an unfor-gettable treasure. My body felt heavy as I sank into the armchair, feet up on the ottoman, and relaxed into the satisfying bone-weariness and the mental emptiness from having exercised my brain, too. Now I would soothe my body with ease and whisky, and reading over the morning's work, red pen in hand, was a reward for the mind. (As was the whisky.)

I was careful to glance over at the windows regularly, not wanting to miss any of the phases of changing light as evening came on. Sometimes I would stand up and walk around from one view to another, maybe catching a brief, evanescent light effect that lasted less than a minute. The line of treetops far across the white lake turned pinky gold in the last rays of the lowering sun. Before the snowy ground faded into blue shadows, it seemed to pause and radiate its whiteness even stronger than in sunshine—briefly holding onto the light, like, say, the walls of Grand Canyon. But this radiance was soft and gently rounded, like cake frosting, while the trees were dusted with light snow. Through the hemlocks to the west, an orange spark glinted and faded, and above, the sky turned white, then pale blue, fading to pink around the rim.

So that was one latitude of my experience with winter solitude, winter sports, and winter's blessings—up around forty-five degrees North. However, most of my winter season was spent a little more than ten degrees of latitude closer to the Equator, in Southern California.

At the risk of understatement, winter is different there.

Still, it should be remembered that Westside Los Angeles, at thirty-four degrees North, sits only halfway between Canada and the true Tropics, north of the Tropic of Cancer by another ten degrees plus. So Southern California is not tropical, but has a temperate, "Mediterranean" climate. It is sometimes moderated by the Pacific Ocean, other times chilled by Alaskan currents and weather patterns. The seasons retain a subtle rhythm, and in winter, it can get chilly. Driving or bicycling on the wider east-west boulevards on clear days, the snow-capped San Gabriels make a postcard backdrop behind the columns of towering fan palms. Once every decade or so, snow will dust the Santa Monica Mountains above Malibu.

One January morning, I rode my motorcycle over the Santa Monicas to the other side of the San Fernando Valley, to go for a hike with Greg Russell (Master of All Things Creative—graphic arts, music, animation, my website, visuals for the band's live show). We call our hybrid sport "motohiking," where you ride some twisty canyon roads to get to a hiking trailhead. Those mountains feature a wonderful network of "sporting" roads, just minutes from my home.

While riding over Malibu Canyon at about 8:00 that morning, my bike's thermometer showed 36°F. (Good thing I'm Canadian, and know how to dress for that. That's why my American motorcycle-touring partner Michael, with his characteristic cultural insensitivity, calls us "Icechuckers.") Twice that January, Greg and I started our hikes at 41°F—but Greg grew up on Long Island, New York, so he knows from cold. And when you're marching in the Santa Monica Mountains, with plenty of uphill work under a radiant sun, cool weather is a benefit rather than a hardship.

That is not the case on a motorcycle, or in an open car. In my early twenties, my first car was a purple MGB roadster, and growing up Canadian also taught me how to drive with the top down in chilly weather. You wear a hooded jacket for your ears and neck, leather gloves for your hands—and turn up the heater and defroster full blast!

The right music can heat things up, too. On a recent afternoon drive up the Pacific Coast Highway, temperature in the forties, I was blasting not only the heater, but a gorgeous-sounding album (*Eyes Open*, 1992) by the great Senegalese artist Youssou N'Dour. (One singer not noted for humility, Bono, once described Youssou N'Dour as "the best singer in the world.") His music's blend of African, Western, and Latin influences (Latin rhythms having blossomed somewhere between the pulses of African and Western music, it occurs to me for the first time) cannot help but warm the day.

Around that time, music was also on my mind, and working on my body—or at least, my body was working on music. Getting ready for it, that is—it would soon be touring time again. Even before I became very, very old, I was fairly disciplined about tour preparations. The band had only finished part one of the *Clockwork Angels* tour in early December, so I hadn't really got *out* of shape yet. For me, the performance edge starts to dull after about three weeks, but my general fitness had stayed strong—hiking

Before the cave

in January, cross-country skiing and snowshoeing in early February, and later that month, back to the gym and the pool three times a week.

Hiking in the mountains is always a worthy alternative to a workout session—great exercise in a much more attractive environment—and I was happy to play hooky from the Y to join Greg for some good marches in beautiful settings. Winter is by far the best season for hiking in our area, when the landscape is greener from the rains, and the temperatures are cooler. Not as cool as the above extremes, generally, but better than summer days, which can often be triple digits. The same goes for motorcycling and top-down driving. Winter is also the time of year when I am most likely to be at home, as the band does not tour in snowy climes. (Because, um . . . *motorcycling?*)

Every winter in recent years, Greg and I have been getting together now and again to enjoy the scenic and challenging trails we've hiked before, and to explore new ones.

This seemingly wild and remote scene is actually a suburban park in the San Fernando Valley, near an area known as Ahmanson Ranch (now the Upper Las Virgenes Canyon Open Space Preserve). Its area of 3,000 acres may not sound like all that much of an "open space," but

the landscape is intricately folded to create a maze of narrow valleys and ridges. They are upholstered in a similar variety of grasslands and California live-oaks, so one area can look much like another, and the trails are not well marked.

Greg and I hope to volunteer to help correct that someday, as others have done in the older parks and usually well-posted trails in the Santa Monica Mountains. On our first visit to Las Virgenes, we had maps and a planned route, even Greg's handheld device with GPS, but there were too many game trails and old ranch roads branching off everywhere. We kept our sense of direction and bushwhacked a little to get to the trail we wanted, but maybe we were lucky. Just a few years ago, a father and son got lost in that seemingly enclosed and limited space—got off the trail and couldn't find it again. With dark coming on, one of them became dangerously hypothermic, and they had to call for rescue. Even a small slice of "the wild" has to be taken seriously.

This preserve is a modern miracle. Surrounded by endless miles of tract houses on three sides, with the Simi Hills behind, the park was set aside as recently as 2003. Under sustained public pressure, a bank abandoned its plan to build 3,000 homes on the site, and sold the land to the state as a park.

Eyes of the eagle

Outsiders might not think of "hiking" and "Los Angeles" in the same breath, but a map of the city shows a crazy quilt (apt metaphor!) of built-up areas and many green patches—natural sanctuaries. Hikers, dog walkers, nature lovers, mountain bikers, and equestrians appreciate them. Wildlife is plentiful, too—mule deer, coyotes, bobcats, raptors, roadrunners, rattlesnakes, even a few mountain lions. The remnant big cats that roam the Santa Monica Mountains are all numbered and radio-collared, and sadly do not amount to a "viable population," but they still occasionally make the local news by somehow managing to cross a ten-lane freeway into a different park. It is not the kind of Tinseltown story that titillates the tabloids or makes the entertainment news, but we should remember how hard people fought—regular people and elected representatives, even celebrities—for some of these preserves.

When I am out on the trails in Quebec, if I encounter one of the ski patrol people (not that often, but still), or start out from their parking area and booth in the village, I like to buy the trail pass. For generations, volunteers and low-paid seasonal workers have maintained those trails, marked them clearly, secured permission to cross private lands, and these days even groom the trails with snowmobile-drawn track-setting machines. (We used to break our own trails, and that was fine—but now is better.)

Down in my other "winter latitude," Temescal Gateway Park, just off Sunset Boulevard, is a narrow canyon of mixed woodland and scrub around an intermittent creek. At the top is a waterfall, varying from a trickle in dry weather to a torrent after winter rains. The name Temescal, brought north by the Spaniards, comes from a word in Nahuatl—the language of the Aztecs—meaning "sweatlodge." Perhaps native dwellers in this canyon built similar structures—but that is among the many things we will never know about those people. Even what they called themselves is lost to history—they are known only as the Gabrieleños, after the San Gabriel Mission that "civilized" them so fast they didn't even know who they were anymore.

Into the cave

From the Temescal parking area, trails loop upstream through sycamores and mudstone formations to high chaparral ridges looking out over the glittering blue Pacific. In the distance lay the silhouettes of Santa Catalina and some of the other Channel Islands. The park charges a modest parking fee, to contribute to the maintenance of the trails (they take a beating in winter's monsoon rains). However, on weekends I see many people parking their cars up and down nearby streets, then hiking on into the park—as if they are getting away with something. And I guess they are—but not what they think.

Before our second visit to the Las Virgenes Preserve, Greg sent me a note: "Do you want to start in the same spot or try the Cheeseboro entrance? I just went to Cheeseboro for the first time on the bike and it was beautiful. Happy to start from there, or at Vanowen and Valley Circle, where I can show you some badass caves."

I wrote back, "You had me at badass caves."

In the earlier photo titled *Before the Cave*, we are climbing from little El Escorpión Park (named after a nearby mountain, now called Castle Peak, and a Spanish-era *rancho*) toward the gash in the rock at center. You enter the cave there and climb high, and steep, through

water-sculpted passageways to the top, below the notch in the central ridge. It was a hand-over-hand, scrabble-for-toeholds kind of climb —mild considered as rock climbing, but fairly extreme for hiking.

When we emerged from the chimney and clambered over the boulders to the top of that ridge, we looked down over a stunning view. The hills and valleys were draped in velvety green, dotted with darker live-oak trees, and traced with brown trails and fire roads. Only in the far distance could I see a flat and unnaturally geometric arrangement of streets and houses.

For me, the view is the keystone feature to every favorite hiking trail—it should lead upward to some high place with a spectacular vista. Ideally, that point should come about midway through the hike, to make a lunch stop—like on the Eagle Rock loop in Topanga State Park, where Greg and I have often hiked. I took another friend, Matt Scannell, around that trail for the first time, and as we packed up after lunch to head down, Matt said, "This restaurant has a *great* view."

Add all the clichés about food tasting great outdoors, and after exertion—because it's true. Much depends upon lunch.

One of the pleasures of hiking with a friend is talking. That is also true of snowshoeing, for the same reason—because you can walk side by side, or close behind, and carry on a conversation as you go. I have done a great deal of hiking and snowshoeing alone, and solitude is fine on a motorcycle or while cross-country skiing—where you wouldn't really be able to talk to a companion anyway. Just as snowshoeing with Charles is a friendly encounter between neighbors and nature lovers, hiking with my friends encourages companionship and talk, and the time and distance pass easily.

While Greg and I hike, we share thoughts about our children, our friends, our work, music, motorcycling, stories from our pasts, and bad jokes. We tend to laugh a lot. In his early forties, Greg is a generation younger than me, and one time he told me he gets tired of hanging out with guys who complain about their wives all the time.

We don't do that. It seems disloyal, disrespectful, and . . . almost always boring for anyone else to have to listen to.

Another reward of time spent at home is—well, time spent at home. When you travel a lot, for work and for Icechucker sports, then participating in the smallest details of everyday life can seem like luxury. Being a good husband or father is not attainable without the basic element of one's *presence*, but I try to make up for it when I am home—making Carrie less of an abandoned wife and single parent, and three-year-old Olivia less of a fatherless child.

Getting up early with Olivia, making her breakfast, shopping and cooking, and *important* tasks like drawing and coloring—it all signifies. When Olivia was a baby and I went away on tour, she didn't miss

Greg at Ahmanson Ranch

me so much—there were others to take care of her needs. These days, as her awareness grows along with our closeness, Daddy's absences can be upsetting for her.

When I was away on tour in 2012, Olivia and I communicated best by drawing pictures together over computer video link. Whether on a motel notepad, or the back of a postcard, Olivia "directed" me in creating immensely complicated sketches. I showed them to her as I went, and she suggested ever more intricate details.

This one, for example, was drawn on the back of a postcard from the Ritz-Carlton in Toronto, while Olivia guided my black and red marker pens.

I asked Olivia, "What should I draw?"

"You should draw Olivia—she should be *flying*."

"What should she be wearing?"

"Red and white striped pajamas. She should have bare feet."

"What kind of wings should she have?"

"She should have feather wings."

Then the ideas came more quickly, "She should have a crown, with stars on it. She should be holding a wand."

I asked her, "What shape should the wand be?"

"It should be shaped like a guitar."

(*Brilliant* ideas she comes up with, all the time.)

"She should be holding a spiral lollipop." (A particularly symbolic object to Olivia, especially after our visit to FAO Schwarz in Manhattan, where their candy department's huge display of spiral lollipops amazed her.)

"She should be singing." When I asked what song, Olivia went into a verse from *Dora the Explorer*.

She told me the tower should have a "normal weathervane" (like in *The Old Red Barn*), while the barn should have a weathervane "shaped like a fairy."

(Of course.)

And the ducks, "They should be quacking *loud*." (She knows we show things that are loud or bright with little lines radiating out from them.)

"There should be a dog—he should be panting."

"There should be a cat, licking its paw."

And so on. I just drew what she said . . .

Another project I have undertaken in this winter latitude is assembling a book called *Art With Olivia*. I gathered all the little sketches I did for her while I was away, and photographs of many of our large-scale works, done at home on her work table—sometimes over two or three days.

I wrote down what I could remember of the "narrative" behind all that art, and also included a number of the songs we have composed together. That kind of magic often happens while I push Olivia on the swings. Something about the rhythm of swinging brings out the music in us.

Sometimes we are in the backyard, or at one of the local parks, or where people in the neighborhood have hung swings under the big trees along the street in front of their homes. (Very neighborly, that.)

Olivia is a cowgirl, a mermaid (here wearing a T-shirt from Uncle Craiggie that reads, "I'm Really a Mermaid"), a firefighter, a ballerina, a gymnast, and a fantastic art director and songwriter. Some

Coda: My ski hat this winter, knitted and given to me by a fan on our *Clockwork Angels* tour. Now that's cool. And warm!

of our songs are extended ballads, built up verse by verse over many swinging sessions, while others are riffs on standards like "Swinging on a Star."

Because I do not share such experiences every day, they are all the more precious to me. And so are the memories. One time when Greg and I were hiking, we were talking about Native American names, and I decided mine would be "Brave Manywinters."

I am pleased and proud to add this winter to my ever-growing collection, and I hope to gather a few more yet. Especially for Olivia's sake. However, not my decision to make, of course. So, like Jack London, "I shall not waste my days trying to prolong them. I shall use my time."

Perhaps not wisely, but as well as I can—in every season, at every latitude.

# THE SWEET SCIENCE

MAY 2013

**The phrase was coined** a couple of hundred years ago by an English sportswriter, referring to . . . boxing.

This reporter has never sensed anything "sweet" or "scientific" about a couple of guys punching each other's lights out, but some people feel it. Among the many superb non-fiction writers to have appeared serially in the *New Yorker* over the years (Joseph Mitchell, Dorothy Parker, Truman Capote, John McPhee, etc.), A.J. Liebling revived the theme for a series of articles about boxing in the 1930s and '40s that were later collected in a book titled *The Sweet Science* (1956).

Personally, I can think of human activities that seem infinitely sweeter than pugilism (though the Greek word is fun—*pygmachia*—but perhaps not as fun as *eros*), and others that are more truly scientific. Even, dare I say, more *artful*. And without causing facial mutilation and irreversible brain damage.

One late April day on my motorcycle, railing through the forested mountains of North Carolina on a relentless sequence of curves in every possible geometry, I thought, "*This* is the sweet science."

Threading a series of corners like this with sporting intent (i.e., swiftly and smoothly), a great many decisions are made and executed. You choose your entry speed and gear early, get the bike settled before you bank it in, and keep to the outside of the lane as long as you can,

to see through the corner as far as possible and into the next one—and *be* seen by any oncoming traffic. Turn in early toward the apex, always allowing a little leeway to adjust your line, speed, or banking angle to dodge a pothole, a spray of gravel, an oncoming vehicle wandering into your lane, or—on blind rural corners—a tractor or a cow. With everything in balance, once you're committed to the turn and in a steady state, a few degrees more or less throttle should be all the steering you need. To adjust the lean angle is to adjust the radius of the arc.

Exiting the turn, you run out wide again, head turned to look through the next corner (a counterintuitive technique that has to be *learned*—"Don't look where you are, look where you're *going*").

The science of physics rules everything here, perhaps most of all where the rubber meets the road—the so-called coefficient of friction (COF, or $\mu$)—where your tires roll on pavement, gravel, dirt, wet leaves, manure, or puddles. On a motorcycle, you experience no "lateral Gs"—the rider always feels ninety degrees of gravitational pull, never thrown from side to side as one would be in a car.

Follow the eyes

However, the corollary is that a motorcycle has a very small contact patch—virtually two hand-prints gripping the road—and it is a "singletrack" vehicle. It has been said that, "A motorcycle is so stupid it can't even stand up by itself." That is a mantra to be kept in mind at all times. (My friend Rick Foster adds another groaner: "A motorcycle can't stand up by itself—because it's two-tired.")

At its best, the rider's rhythm through a series of corners is like a slalom course on skis, or a hot lap on a racetrack—linking the turns gracefully, smoothly, and safely. No doubt the experience is sharpened by constant awareness of the *consequences*.

Getting it right is very satisfying; getting it wrong could be very painful.

Tour itineraries vary almost infinitely in the way showdates are connected and ordered—and thus in the areas between I am able to explore on days off. The early dates on this run of the tour happened to fall such that I was able to route us through North Carolina on several consecutive days off, commuting among shows in Orlando, Nashville, Raleigh, and Virginia Beach. Thus, by lucky happenstance, North Carolina became my "new discovery." (A few tours ago I told Geddy that my latest discovery was Pennsylvania, and he said, "I'm pretty sure it's already been discovered—people live there and that.")

Previously I have rhapsodized about riding in other East Coast regions such as Virginia, West Virginia, and upstate New York, but this time the mountain backroads of North Carolina greatly impressed me. They gave Michael and me a rich and varied playground—I mean *scientific laboratory*.

One theme I have been pursuing in our photo setups is seeing how many corners we can get into one scene. Extreme settings, like

a series of steep switchbacks in the Alps or Andes (see *Far and Away*'s "The Power of Magical Thinking"), make it easy, but "regular" mountain roads are more of a challenge.

One of those North Carolina byways made our highest score so far—five curves in one shot. It will be hard to beat—not just numerically, but for the road's lack of shoulders, power lines, guardrails, or other unsightly distractions. As I ride along with an eye out for photo settings, countless possibilities are rejected simply for having ugly power lines in them—a dealbreaker for me. (Yes, I know there are easy ways to "fix it in the mix," as musicians used to say, and that's fine for "decorative" photos. But not for "scientific" ones. We have our standards.)

Another science of paramount importance to a motorcyclist is meteorology—the *weather*. (As a "weather enthusiast," I confess that seems like a sweet science, too.)

Virginia byway

Unlike passengers in a car, a motorcycle rider is exposed to every degree of temperature, every drop of precipitation, and every unsettling crosswind. I have noted before that on the motorcycle, I can feel a rise or fall of only two degrees, and of course the difference between riding on a wet or dry road surface changes *everything*. Temperature and moisture have a direct effect not only on one's comfort level, but on that all-important physical relationship with the road.

Traction, control, margin of error, not falling down.

Then there is the "vision" thing, to see and be seen. Clearly (or not), the weather has much to do with that, as well . . .

This first leg of the second part of the *Clockwork Angels* tour, in spring 2013, had been designed to be an East Coast run. However, late last year the band was informed that our presence might be required at some little awards show on the West Coast, in mid-April.

At the time, the odds of us being inducted into the Rock and Roll Hall of Fame seemed unlikely-to-absurd, after something like fourteen years of rejection, but apparently we were "on the ballot." So manager Ray insisted we had to factor it into our plans, and adjustments had to be made.

"Fogline" drive, Shenandoah National Park, Virginia

One change that suited me was that instead of band rehearsals taking place in Toronto, as usual, they would be in Los Angeles. So I would have a few extra weeks at home. In December, I got a message from Ray asking me to call him. Fearing bad news (we get our share of that, like anyone else), I called him with a little trepidation. When Ray told me we were "in," it took awhile to process the mix of feelings: disbelief, delight, and a little *more* trepidation. There would be . . . challenges . . . (See "Where Words Fail, Music Speaks.")

2013 meets 1976
(or 2013 meets "2112")

Following my own pre-tour preparations at the local Y, and at Drum Channel's studio (two and a half weeks of playing along with the recorded versions of the show, tuning up my technique and stamina), I joined the Guys at Work (Alex, Geddy, and our crew) at a warehouse in the San Fernando Valley.

That was when things started to become surreal.

On our last day in the warehouse, we were joined by Dave Grohl and Taylor Hawkins from the Foo Fighters, and our mutual coproducer Nick "Booujzhe" Raskulinecz. They wanted to rehearse their spoof of us from . . . thirty-six years ago.

By now, the televised show in all its glory (I have faith it will retain the essence of what it was like to experience the real-time event—truly larger than life) will be widely shared. The performances, the speeches, the humor, and the overwhelming gathering of the Great and the Good are part of some kind of history now. However, the inner experience of *living* all that was something else again. Not larger than life, but exactly life-size.

The only way to portray even the ghost of what that few days felt like from the inside might be to jump ahead to when it was over—to a "reflective" moment.

The day following the event, I was able to bring my family with me to Austin, Texas, for a few days, for two production rehearsals and a day off before the first show there. Late on the night of the travel day, I found a moment of peace and reflection, and the next day I started writing a report to a group of friends called the "Breakfast Club for Cuties." Brutus came up with that name for an informal email circle of four scattered Canadians (Icechuckers)—Brutus in Cowfart, Alberta, me in Westside L.A., friend Craiggie in Pasadena, and brother Danny in Vancouver, British Columbia.

All early risers, and in similar time zones, we gradually fell into the habit of exchanging notes early in the day—jokes, comments, thoughts, insults—almost daily for a while. They tapered off when one of the members had to go away on tour, but we still continued to communicate from time to time, as touring life allowed (for me, more likely late at night on the bus after a show than early in the morning).

After that night's solitary reflections, I played the entire show the following night and arrived home on my motorcycle feeling stimulated by both the performance and the dark ride home.

(I rarely choose to ride at night, especially in a region with so many deer, but it is certainly exciting. A milder version of Sir Winston Churchill's great quote, "Nothing in life is so exhilarating as to be shot at without result.")

So, tired and sore and yet all abuzz, I lounged outside on the balcony of the family condo with a large glass of the Macallan, and continued trying to put down some reflections to share with the Q-Tees™.

Subject: Aftermath
Austin, TX
Gentlemen:
Some story notes I will share with my fellow Cuties.

Last night, I was sitting out late on the balcony of our family condo on the shore of Lake Travis, near Austin. B [Brutus] will remember it as a dam-widened stretch of the Colorado River (the Texas one, not the Grand Canyon one) near where the Pedernales (a much more "Tex-Mex" kind of name) flows in.

For the flight here with the Guys at Work on their Falcon (nice—like the one B 'n' me shared with them in Germany one time), with Carrie and Olivia, I dressed in Cowgirl Olivia's honor—in my "cowboy clothes." Hat, shirt, and the boots I bought here in Austin last December (my first cowboy boots EVER!).

So, settlin' back on the comfy outdoor sofa, I had my boots up on the table. The night was a little chilly, so I had a blanket around my shoulders.

Rehearsal—serious face

From what must have been a bar at the marina across the water, a pretty good blues-rock band was playing (Friday night).

So, I was settin' there, looking out at the dark water dotted with pretty colored lights, digging the band's groove, and treating myself to a little extra ration of The Macallan. It was then I finally had a chance to reflect a little on the past night.

That thought flashed into my head, thinking—that was only LAST NIGHT!

The contrast between that frenetic state of mind and my present peaceful equilibrium was a complete polarity.

It's going to take a week or so of reflection to sift through that entire overwhelming experience—just processing the data, as it were, slowing down the replay to remember moments in isolation and string them together into some kind of . . . narrative. Even my own *interior* narrative.

However, for me, the all-important part of last night's reflections was the mood that colored all my scattered memories—bathed in a glow of *satisfaction*.

Not for the honor and glory—but basically just because I had "done my job" properly. The key elements of that satisfaction were simple: I had spoken and played well.

Not only on our songs and the "Crossroads" jam, but even laying down a (hopefully) funky groove behind a pair of full-on master rappers. (Michael witnessed the "rehearsal" for that, just an hour before showtime, and he wished he could have filmed it. Geddy and I met in a backstage room with Chuck D from Public Enemy ["*911 is a joke in your town*"] and the "DMC" of Run-DMC. They described the rhythmic feel, and where we should come in, and on what line we should stop. We nodded.)

There was also the star- (guitar-) studded "Crossroads" jam, for which I was also responsible for laying down the foundation of tempo and feel. So . . . my state of mind leading up to "all that" might best be expressed by "yikes!"

Just moments after it was over, as Geddy and I met in the quick-change tent at stage left (just like Madonna!), he said, "We laid it DOWN."

And, shockingly, we did.

During the previous night's rehearsal (our hip-hop brethren did not attend), after the "Crossroads" jam (do you believe that lineup of guitarists? Whoa!), one of the "presiding geniuses," some rumpled-looking guy in a suit and tie, came up to me onstage and suggested that the tempo should be slower. I knew I was playing it the way we had recorded it, modeled on Cream's version, but—I am a professional.

So I pulled it back a notch, and we played it again. It felt fine to me either way, but the boge [our slang for "square"] said it felt heavier and better for the soloists to breathe. I could see that. Then he suggested even a notch slower yet, and I said, "Okay." There was no time to rehearse that, but I fingered out [how Brutus always says "figured"] a proper "feel" for a slightly slower tempo in my brain ('cause it ain't just *math*, eh?). I also asked the geniuses to pass around to all the other players that I would be playing it slower.

(If nothing else, I wanted them to know it was on *purpose*!)

Well . . . Geddy wrote back in response to that report with, "That boge was Jann Wenner!" [Founder of *Rolling Stone*, and co-director of the Hall of Fame.]

Ha ha! Perfect!

The world's most powerful Rush-hater, rumored to have personally kept us out of the HOF all these years!

[Taylor Hawkins told me later that at that moment he had to walk away so he wouldn't hit him—and when I wrote about it to another mutual friend and fellow drummer, Stewart Copeland, he wrote back that he wished he had been there, so he could head-butt the guy!

Rehearsal night

Nice to have the support of my drum-brothers, but I didn't see it as an *insult*, but a challenge. I am Canadian, and "We aim to please."

The only problem was . . . doing it.]

But on the night, once again, I delivered just what I had wanted to, nailing exactly the tempo I imagined and holding it there—playing by the KISS technique ["Keep It Simple Stupid"]—with what felt to me like a good solid groove.

The speech thing also got complicated. We had planned to be brief and improvised, with some remarks about our families, our office people, and our fans—but then we were told "Rash" needed time between the induction and their performance to change into their . . . kimonos . . .

They needed at least five minutes—yikes again!

So . . . I made some "point form" notes. Then heard that we couldn't use the teleprompter for OUR speeches. (I *loves* me some teleprompter.) All the presenters used it, and even the rappers, but I guess the geniuses had some idea about keeping those of the inductees "natural."

(And oh—wait until you guys up Nord see the Flavor Flav show. Oh my, eh, Craiggie?)

So I wrote out my speech in full, and printed it out LARGE—hoping I wouldn't have to use my glasses.

Then midway through the show, we heard that our speeches *would* be on the teleprompter. So . . . good.

That worked!

Praise Allah, it *all* worked.

[I began my speech with an improvised remark about how for years we had been saying this was no big deal—then followed with a turn of phrase typical of my friend Matt Scannell, "Turns out, it kind of IS!"]

Now—back to business-as-usual for us Rushians. First full-production rehearsal tonight, then again tomorrow night, then a day off, then the first show.

Then some more shows . . .

On that subject, one photo that reached me by chance seemed to tell a nice story—because it is a true fan's-eye-view, a random moment from a random place in the crowd. Typically, it was captured on one of the thousands of cellphone cameras we see out there every night. (Some people seem to spend half the show looking through, or at, their handheld devices.) Matt Scannell asked me to arrange a pair of tickets for a friend of his at one of our shows, and later, the friend sent Matt his thanks, and a photo, taken by his guest. I like to leave it anonymous, as a symbol of something that seems important. I am always playing for somebody named "A. Fan." Perhaps an ideal listener I consider The Fan.

It also captures a moment I wrote about in a previous story—the cello players hunched over their instruments to protect them from the heat of the pyrotechnics. (I told Jacob he is rocking a Chuck Berry pose.)

The show this time out is the same musically and visually as the one we performed last fall—thirty-five times—so you could say we "have it down." While that's true, the performance is never easy, and

because of that, it remains rewarding to get it right—to feel that I'm getting the sweet science of drumming smooth and strong.

And even after all those shows, before starting certain especially complicated songs, like "Grand Designs" or "Headlong Flight," for example, or before one of my solo spots, I pause to engage a "higher gear" of concentration. Some songs I can just count in and "launch," but those examples demand just a little more attention to detail.

Some roads are like that, too. Sometimes you have a relaxed cruise, an easy flow down a straight open road. In the mountain roads of North Carolina, you need a little more attention to detail, a higher gear of concentration . . .

If motorcycling is science, traveling is art. Getting from one place to another independently, with a sense of adventure and appreciation, requires a creative vision, technical experience, and, perhaps most of all, adaptability.

The high concept is "What is the most excellent thing I can do today?" but it must sometimes yield to realities like time and distance, weather

Blue Ridge Parkway

and traffic, or even just getting to work on time. Because sometimes work is the most excellent thing I can do today, and I can only try to embellish the work with some recreation and exploration.

In artistic terms, adaptability is improvisation, a pursuit to which I have been dedicated musically for several years. Sometimes traveling has to be equally improvised—like when I draw a route on the map that appears "excellent" to me, but when Michael and I are "on the ground" that day, real-world elements like bad weather, rough roads, heavy traffic, or fading daylight may bring us to a point of decision. We pause and make other choices—on a day off maybe stop for the night sooner than I had planned, on a show day take a faster route to get to work earlier.

With the first show in Austin, and the second in Fort Lauderdale—a mere 1,300 miles apart—I had two days off and the show day to get there, but still faced difficult choices. Between those two points, the most excellent overnight destination is certainly New Orleans, so I designed the first day as the "reward." Dave parked us in Lake Charles, Louisiana (in what we have come to call "Château Walmart"), and in

**FAR AND NEAR**

the morning we set out to meander around the southernmost back-roads in the Louisiana bayous, Cajun country. (A sign I saw along the coast, "THE CAJUN RIVIERA.")

The landscape was mainly flat grasslands, half-drowned and cut with manmade channels, most of the buildings built on high stilts. The surrounding area had been destroyed repeatedly by hurricanes, but kept springing up again, however reduced. Several shrimp and crab companies had processing plants, while large compounds housed service facilities for the offshore oil rigs, with ranks of helicopters lined up outside, and rugged-looked workboats and tugs tied along waterways. The sky was gray, the light flat, and we took no photographs that day. But there was one encounter I remember with pleasure—a small ferry across the Calcasieu Channel, near Cameron, Louisiana.

As the ferry pulled away on its short crossing, one of the workers offered me a "World's Finest" chocolate bar—the kind often sold for local fundraisers. He had just bought them from a garbage truck driver crossing the other way, who was selling them for his daughter's school. As I accepted with a smile, "Why, thank you!," he said, "I bought five dollars' worth," then pointed to his coworker, a round-faced young man with glasses, bangs, and a friendly expression. "He bought *fifteen* dollars worth, and he's already eaten three—in about five minutes!"

The young man smiled and nodded, while the first one continued, "When he finishes a cup of coffee," he held up a thumb and forefinger two inches apart, "there's still *this much* sugar in the bottom!"

The other smiled and nodded again.

"He likes his sugar with a little coffee in it!" We all laughed at the old joke.

Somehow being included in this friendly raillery between coworkers made me feel good—you know, "normal." That is always a precious feeling in my highly abnormal life. And that very week two friends had remarked on how "normal" I was. I don't get called *that* very often.

I loved this little excerpt from a note Dave Grohl sent to the three of us after the Hall of Fame show: "Just when I thought life couldn't get any weirder, I wind up in blond bangs and white platform boots, playing my all-time favorite jam in front of my heroes. I would pitch a reality show, if I only lived in reality . . ."

After the reward of that day's scenic ride, and arriving in New Orleans to a nice hotel and a fantastic dinner, we would pay the price—merging from downtown New Orleans onto Interstate 10 to ride over 800 miles of freeway, across Louisiana, Mississippi, Alabama, and down through Florida. It was worth it (barely), and spending two days living on "Planet Interstate" was good scientific research. The self-contained network of highways, gas stations, motels, and restaurants ends at the offramp—Cracker Barrel, Chili's, Shell, Exxon, Motel 6, and Red Roof Inn—a closed world with everything the "express traveler" requires.

Other days off were much more suited to the pursuit of excellence, adventure, and the art of travel.

Deep in the Everglades

After sleeping on the bus after the Fort Lauderdale show at another Château Walmart, Michael and I rode as deep as you can go into the Everglades, down to Flamingo, the remotest tip of the continental U.S. From there, we rode back up to the Tamiami Trail, the old east-west highway across Florida's southern tip, before "Alligator Alley," Interstate 75, was built.

Heading west to Sanibel Island for the night, we explored every sideroad, including a long, unpaved loop through the most emblematic part, the watery cypress swamp. After about four such explorations (*scientific* explorations) over the years, I have observed every part of the Everglades reachable by any kind of road. (Someday I will make time for one of the airboat tours.)

Crossing the vast sweeps of grassy savanna (the name Everglades derives from "river of grass"), the scrub forest of palmettos and pines, and those deepest, prettiest stretches of true swampland, cypresses, and mangroves, the thought occurred to me, "Nothing is ever just one thing." That seems a crude and slippery notion at the moment, I know, but I have hopes it will grow up into a Deep Thought.

I was thinking of people who hold only one impression of what these places mean: a mental picture of bayou country, the Everglades, the Great Plains, any desert, or any range of mountains. Even a forest—a coral reef. "Nothing is ever just one thing."

Every time I visit an area like, say, Death Valley, or the mountains of North Carolina, I add pixels to the resolution and scope of my mental portrait of the world. (Reminds me of a geek T-shirt Michael loves, "I SEE DEAD PIXELS.")

While riding slowly on a dusty track through watery swampland, I

glimpsed a pair of eyes and a snout poking up from the brown water. I waved Michael to circle around and have a look and, sure enough, it was a "gator," five or six feet long. Michael pointed out another one nearby, about the same size, and sighed dramatically, "I wish we had some kittens!"

After Orlando, we had two days off before Nashville, and I started surveying the "Book of Dreams," the road atlas, for possible areas of exploration. (Like interpreting dreams, maps can present confusing ciphers and vague symbols that require some "divination.") As my eyes traced the red and gray lines, and considered the topography—gazing into the crystal ball of knowledge, curiosity, hope—I didn't decide upon a route so much as a design was *revealed* to me.

Hard to explain—without years of experience at the sweet science of the art of travel—but the vision developed like this . . .

Run to the bus after the show, Michael pours me a drink, and Dave drives all night north to Atlanta. Unload the bikes and wind

A rare dusty day in the 'Glades

our way through the mountains of North Georgia (praised in *Far and Away*'s "A Winter's Tale of Summers Past"), into North Carolina and overnight at the Biltmore Estate near Asheville. A morning meander around the Blue Ridge Mountains, and the obligatory transit of Deals Gap—a legendary stretch of U.S. Highway 129 in the corner of North Carolina and Tennessee which some promoter dubbed "The Tail of the Dragon," boasting "318 turns in eleven miles."

(A motorcycle journalist living in Florida described his state as having "eleven turns in 318 miles." And most of those would be onramps! Yet Michael and I discovered what must be the curviest road in Florida, a little country lane west of Sebring that zigged and zagged merrily in ninety-degree turns—around old property lines, no doubt—and even included a stretch of gravel for variety. Like certain country roads in Iowa or Illinois, it had never been deemed "important" enough to be straightened by the bulldozers of "eminent domain." On a warm Sunday morning, I was puzzled that we didn't see one other rider, yet later on Florida's Turnpike—certainly one of the *least* entertaining roads in the nation—long parades of cruisers, dozens together in glittering processions, rode toward us on their loud chrome chariots.)

That same "Winter's Tale" story described the sideshow-like atmosphere of Deals Gap in the summer of 2008, and I had hoped a weekday in late April might be "calmer." But no. The parking lot around the little motel was *jammed* with cruisers in long shining rows, and a rally for Mini drivers (the BMW generation) drew hundreds of cars to the area, passing us in the other direction for hours.

Winding through its eleven miles that day, my main concern was the riders coming toward me losing it, crossing the line, and taking *me* out. Typically Deals Gap sees many crashes and several fatalities every year. A few sportbike riders on their race-replica machines were making crazy passes, going around slower bikes on blind curves, and we passed two fresh crash sites, where damaged bikes were being loaded onto flatbeds. The riders seemed okay (no ambulances)— probably just overcooked one of those 318 turns and slid off the road in what is called a "low side." (A "high side," where an out-of-control bike spits you off, is much more dangerous.) So I kept the pace conservative, with lots of space and time to maneuver.

Three separate photography companies were set up on different stretches, aiming cameras into the turns at each rider, with their internet addresses prominently displayed—you were expected to go online and purchase photos of yourself riding the Tail of the Dragon.

Trying to decide which was the most ill-suited vehicle on the road that day, I was torn between a Harley "trike" (you would need the shoulders of Hercules to muscle around those corners), a step-through scooter (a "maxi-scooter," but still), and the Harley in front of us with ape-hanger bars, the slow and wobbly rider wavering even more when he had to lower his left hand to wave by every following rider.

Deals Gap

It was a circus, and its absurdity has only grown.

Thing is, though, that stretch of U.S. 129 is a *beautiful* piece of road, perfectly engineered in banking, immaculately paved, and combining a pleasing rhythm of tight turns. Having been mythologized, "fetishized," by a certain subculture has been its ruin. (You might say the same about Sedona, Arizona, or Pigeon Forge, Tennessee.)

But never mind—even just in North Carolina, devotees of this sweet science can find many other roads that offer delights without de crowds.

From there we rounded the Great Smoky Mountains to stop for the night in downtown Knoxville, Tennessee. Last fall we took a chance on a small old hotel there, the Oliver, and were impressed. It had been restored in a modern way that respected its past and was part of the charming character of downtown Knoxville.

Which brings me to another area of scientific research that never ends: lodgings.

A capsule history of American hotels might begin with the railroads, then change abruptly with automobiles. Independent travelers did not need to stay in big cities, and gave rise to "motor courts," "motor hotels," and eventually motels.

Blue Ridge backdrop

The archetype must be the grouping of small cabins with parking places, often nestled in trees or along a shore, but their disappearance was lamented as early as the 1950s by recent immigrant Vladimir Nabokov, in his unlikely classic, *Lolita*.

More space-efficient rows of rooms, with parking out front, became the classic motel. Now those in turn are disappearing, because people seem to prefer the "big box" variety of chain outlets. So these days, full circle, I am back to exploring downtown hotels—at least in small cities—that seem to be having a resurgence. The restaurants are definitely superior to the fare in Planet Interstate.

Littleton, New Hampshire; Knoxville, Tennessee; Bloomington, Indiana; Iowa City, Iowa—all worthy hubs for my travels.

Looking for interesting territory to explore between shows in Nashville and Raleigh, North Carolina, I wanted to cross Great Smoky Mountains National Park, and check out some more of those great North Carolina mountain roads. I picked a new destination for the night: Mount Airy, North Carolina. The birthplace of Andy Griffith, it was said to be the model for the fictional town of Mayberry—a connection that allows Mount Airy to thrive with nostalgic baby boomers. *The Andy Griffith Show* was hugely popular in the early to mid-'60s and continued in frequent reruns for years after.

The Mayberry Motor Inn was the quintessential clean, comfortable, convenient family motel, right across the road from Goober's restaurant and Aunt Bea's diner. (Should be "Aunt Bee's," of course—must be a copyright issue.) Out front was a mid-'60s Ford police car, with license plate "BARNEYF," and a '50s pickup painted with Emmett's Fix-It Shop, the "filling station" where Gomer and Goober Pyle worked.

It was all like going back in time sixty years, and Michael and I both declared that stay the most *relaxing* night off we'd had all tour. In the morning, we cruised the main street, passing large stores selling Mayberry and *Andy Griffith Show* memorabilia and—inevitably—Floyd's Barber Shop.

After Raleigh, heading up to Virginia Beach, we explored another side of North Carolina—the Outer Banks. Overnighting at the Château Walmart in Greenville, we rode down to catch the ferry from Cedar Island out to Ocracoke Island.

We pulled up at the ferry's ticket booth, side by side on the bikes, and the attendant leaned out—an older, prim-looking lady with tightly permed gray hair and rimless glasses. She said, "Are you traveling together?"

It should have been obvious, but it gave Michael an irresistible opportunity. "Oh yes—we're on our *honeymoon*!"

"Them that died was lucky"

Without a smile, she said, "O-o-okay," and turned away. Not impressed.

Boarding the ferry, the crew told us it was pretty rough out there and advised us to stay with the bikes—for the entire two-and-a-half-hour crossing.

At least we had shelter from the wind and rain on the covered deck, and we were dressed warmly against the chill. I had been carrying around the previous Sunday's *New York Times* magazine, hoping for an opportunity to do the crossword puzzle—and here it was. I sat on the steel deck and worked on that, while Michael raised his hoodie and plugged in his iPod, grooving to the Moody Blues, *To Our Children's Children's Children*. (Michael is a generation younger than me, at least numerically, and I always laugh to see him "discovering" music I grew up with—recorded before he was *born*.) The sea was heaving steadily, especially when the ferry changed course, but the bikes remained stable.

Laughing about our encounter with the ticket lady, Michael scrawled "Just Married" in the dirt on the back of his luggage cases. I added a heart to dot the "i."

That graffiti wouldn't last long, however, as the rain would be with us for most of the next week, and soon dirtied up our bikes again. As rainy days followed one another in a damp parade, soon I was thinking of the quote from *King Lear*, "The rain it raineth every day."

Early the following morning, we had to make another fairly long ferry crossing, and only later did I reflect that our morning exemplified another facet of the art of travel. The journey comes first, not comfort or convenience, and you just keep going, whatever it takes. Without comment or complaint, without breakfast or even coffee, Michael and I got up early, loaded the bikes, and set off into the rain. Fully three hours later, we parked at a nice roadside diner around the delightfully named Kill Devil Hills, near famed Kitty Hawk. We shed some of our wet gear on the chairs around us and didn't just enjoy, but very much *appreciated* a hot breakfast.

The show that night in Virginia Beach was outdoors, with the temperature in the fifties and a gusty, chilly wind. My bandmates, the crew, the string players, and the audience were all bundled up, and I hope they didn't suffer too much. A drummer never needs to worry about generating his own heat. The wind affected me, though—several times when I tossed a stick in the air it was blown off course and out of reach—but that was a minor concern.

Looking over the map that afternoon for the upcoming rides, I was considering all the historical sites in Virginia—presidential residences and such. I asked Michael a fun question: "Who is your favorite founding father?"

I was thinking about Thomas Jefferson's home in Monticello, which I had always wanted to visit. A few tours ago, Michael and I had even stopped there, but it was a weekend morning in summer, and the jammed parking lot was enough to scare us off.

Michael agreed that Jefferson was pretty great, but also favored John Adams—his friend, enemy, then friend again. "Frenemies," I said, "like you and me!"

Rain on Cape Hatteras, North Carolina

He put on a wounded expression, his lower lip trembling. "But we're supposed to be on our *honeymoon!* I *hate* you!"

Then he lashed out with some pathetic profanity.

Bus driver Dave is an American history enthusiast, so he was glad to join us, and we had a guest rider, Richard Moore, a Toronto classical percussionist, versatile drummer, and fellow BMW GS rider. We slept on the bus at the Château Walmart in Charlottesville, then drove over to Monticello for a morning tour.

I had long admired Thomas Jefferson's reverence for reading and reason, science and nature, and his quote, "I cannot live without books." However, during the tour, as we stood in his library (I was surprised to see how *small* all the rooms were—but of course in the eighteenth century, heating was primitive), the guide informed us that although the great man had been devoted to books and reading, he did not like novels.

Well. Outside, I had to have a few words with the man about the power of fiction . . .

The rain held off during our Monticello tour, but poured down again as Michael, Richard, and I rode onward through the pretty Virginia countryside. Stopping overnight at the wonderful Homestead Inn, dating back to 1766, with portraits of all the American presidents who have visited—most of them, it seemed—we enjoyed a night of luxury and fine dining.

The next morning, Michael needed to get some service work done on his motorcycle, so he took the "express route" toward the next show in Baltimore. Richard and I would also later face about 200 miles of rainy, miserable interstate, but first we were treated to a sublime morning ride—seventy miles of backroads in Virginia and West Virginia, in which we did not overtake *one* other vehicle, and only put our feet down for maybe three crossroads stop signs. That's pretty spectacular "freedom of the road."

"The rain it raineth every day"

Oh sure, it was raining—the steep West Virginia byways completely awash—but it was still beautiful. And sweetly scientific. Excellent practice for smooth technique.

Another sweet science would certainly have to be *botany*. A rose by any other name, et cetera. Down in the Everglades, I had been determined to get a shot of me riding by some mangroves. I pulled us over to the roadside and pointed to the scene I wanted Michael to capture, stressing the mangroves, and he said, "Um—what? The 'manscapes'?"

Oh, he makes me laugh, but really doesn't care about the names of things like I do. Same in the Blue Ridge and Great Smoky Mountains—I noticed that the "leaf line" was about 4,000 feet, and above that the trees were bare. The only green at higher elevations was the roadside grass and the evergreen rhododendrons in the understory. (Catawba rhododendrons, at that elevation, I learned later.) Michael gave me the same blank look when I told him to make sure he was getting the rhododendrons in the shot.

Throughout our northward progress up the East Coast, people's yards were aglow with vivid pink and purple blossoms, fruit trees and lilacs. In the woods, I noticed sprays of white flowers on small trees among the greenery, and I wanted to know what they were. Like the redbuds in the spring of 2011 (see "Eastern Resurrection"), the more I noticed these flowering trees, the more curious I was to know their name. Eventually I stopped at the side of the road, walked over to one low-hanging branch, picked a few of the flowers, and finally identified them for sure—dogwoods. Michael was *fascinated* to learn that they were actually made up of white *leaves*, rather than petals.

(But no—he only sneered derisively and cast aspersions upon my masculinity. I fear our Michael is no natural scientist. And he's certainly not sweet.)

This sublime curve of empty road and surrounding woodland scenery were part of a day and a series of riding photographs that would astonish many Americans. Waking at the Château Walmart in Newburgh, New York, we rode south into New Jersey in the Delaware Water Gap area and spent all day on scenic, lightly traveled backroads. It was the only day without rain we had all week, and I think we collected more "keeper" photographs that day than any other—not least because I kept looking at different combinations of winding roads and early summer woods and thinking, "People wouldn't believe this is New Jersey."

It was all very far from the "Joysey" clichés of pop culture—*The Sopranos*, Springsteen, unscripted lowlifes, and a century of cheap jokes from New Yorkers. Our route meandered around for almost 200 miles of pleasant riding, varying from rural two-lane highway with actual hills and curves to narrow strips of paving without painted lines, and even a stretch of rough dirt. I had tried to hit every dotted

Dogwoods in Western Jersey

line on the map, which usually means unpaved (thinking of the theme "Every Dirt Road in Jersey"), but most of these were just *badly* paved—patchy and bumpy.

We ended the day in Princeton—another addition to our list of favored smaller cities, often "college towns," like Iowa City and Bloomington, Indiana, with quaint downtown hotels, plenty of restaurants of all kinds, and easy-in, easy-out convenience.

One more show to go—Atlantic City—and one more rainy day. I had mapped a ride down through the Pine Barrens region, a long stretch of dotted line through the Wharton State Forest in the Pinelands National Reserve. We had ridden that way before and knew it had some fairly challenging stretches of sandy gravel. So when the gray heavens opened once more and heavy rain pattered on our helmets and churned up the dirt road, I turned us around: "Know when to fold 'em."

In deepest New Jersey

The dominant science that day was certainly meteorology, and its effect on physics, optics, and natural history ruled our day. The night, though, was ruled by the sweet science of music, and by *people*—our audience.

For our Hall of Fame speeches, the three of us chose "themes" that each of us would focus on—families for me, fans for Geddy, and for Alex, well . . . blah-blah-blah. (What a moment *that* was, when he hadn't warned us what he was going to do. Geddy and I couldn't see him "acting," and thought he was going all Flavor Flav. [No doubt that poor soul's rambling, embarrassing, endless blather, under Chuck D's stern, arms-folded scowl, will be trimmed for the broadcast.] Geddy muttered to me, "How can we make him *stop?*" and I raised my heavy "trophy" behind Alex's head as if to brain him. The two of us have long declared Our Lerxst to be "The Funniest Man Alive," and of course his performance was a huge comedic success. But he should have warned us.)

Another special facet of the event (perfect jewel analogy) was to meet some artists I had long admired and to feel I *knew* them, right away. Taylor Hawkins had been a friend for a few years (my bandmates appeared onstage with the Foo Fighters in Toronto, playing one of our songs with Taylor), but I had never met Dave Grohl, Tom Morello, or Chris Cornell.

When I traveled in China many years ago on a bicycle tour, I met another cyclist who had visited Tibet, and he told me about the greeting *namaste*. He defined it as "I recognize the spirit within you." It was like that with Dave, Tom, and Chris, appreciating and respecting their work, and them as artists of *integrity*. Meeting face to face for the first time, I felt I *knew* them—felt openness and trust, and saw it in their faces.

Perhaps less expectedly, I felt the same communion with Chuck D. Our music couldn't be more different, but it seemed the spirit of it was the same. After the show, the three of us stood in a back hallway with him for a few minutes, and he told us a story.

"I grew up in Roosevelt, Long Island, near Nassau Coliseum. I had a friend who worked there, and one time I went to visit him, and you guys happened to be playing. I looked out through the doors at the audience and saw like 20,000 people completely *focused* on what you were doing. You were playing something quiet, and I said something about that dedication to my friend—and people in your audience 'shushed' me. That's when I thought, I want to be part of something like that."

Again, it comes back to appreciation not of us, but of our *fans*. (Whether we earn that or not is something else—but I know we *try*.) One reality that impressed me greatly that night was that not only had our fans clamored for *years* to get us inducted into that Hall of Fame (one of the directors joked that he didn't know what he was going to do with all his free time now that he didn't have to field the constant protests from Rush fans), but they took the time, trouble, and expense to *be there*. Right from the beginning of the show, everybody in the house knew that our fans ruled that place. That was pretty sweet. They were proud of us, and we were proud of them.

But, in "normal" life (there's that word again), people can always keep you *grounded*, too.

In my pre-tour preparations in February and March, going to the Y three times a week for my fitness regime, one day I was on the

cross-trainer, pumping through the endless cardio routine with grim determination. Exercise, for me, is an exercise of *will*. It may be science, but it is not sweet.

On the neighboring machine was a middle-aged lady, maybe a few years younger than me, with earbuds in. At one point, she pulled out one of her earbuds and leaned over to say, "I've got a couple of male friends who are, like, total *groupies* for you!"

As usual, I was a little embarrassed to be suddenly "public," jolted out of a far-off state of mind, so I just looked over, gave her a little smile and a nod, and kept pumping.

Then she said, confidingly, "But I won't tell them!"

I nodded and smiled again, and said, "Thank you."

A few more minutes passed, my arms and legs working in a rhythmic cycle, breathing deep and measured, mind wandering off on its own. I concentrated on my pace and heart rate, and watched the crawling timer.

Then she popped her earbud out again, and said, "So—do you still drum at all?"

# DRUMMER WITH
# A SINGLETRACK MIND

MAY 2013

This story was written during our *Clockwork Angels* European tour in May 2013, for a British motorcycling weekly. They asked for about 700 words and a photo or two, and I gave them 1,700 words and eight photos. They said they would run it like that, but took a few liberties—not so much with the text, but perhaps because the story was part of an "adventure touring" issue, they replaced Brutus's and my iconic U.K. photos with more exotic images from a previous tour in South America.

That's fine, for their purposes, but not for mine—trying to *share* an experience as deeply as I can. So I decided to present it here in its original form, which would also fill a gap in the tour's documentation.

I will retract the British spellings, for consistency (and personal taste), but keep the "cultural references," for fun.

**Since 1996,** I have been traveling on Rush tours by motorcycle, riding to virtually every concert in the United States, Canada, South America, and Europe. Hundreds of shows, tens of thousands of miles, and a million memories—almost all good, and many spectacular, like the American West, the Brazilian rainforest, the Stelvio Pass, and the Yorkshire Dales.

A more or less typical example of my touring life would be the

U.K. part of our *Clockwork Angels* tour in May 2013. Here's how it works . . .

On a show night, after I have pounded and sweated for about three and a half hours, we reach the last song in the encore—a version of our "Grand Finale" from the *2112* album.

While the final echo of our burnout ending rings in the arena, and Geddy is still saying a grateful good night to the audience, I bow and wave and run offstage. Through the dark backstage labyrinth, I follow the bobbing blue flashlight beam waved in my direction by the running shadow ahead—Michael, my American riding partner and road manager. He leads me to the bus, and I run onboard. While I change out of my sweaty drumming clothes in the back, driver Malcolm gets underway. My riding partner in Europe (and anywhere outside the U.S.—long story), Brutus, pours me a refreshing measure of The Macallan, and I sit down in T-shirt and towel at the front lounge table, usually browsing through the photos Brutus and I have taken, editing, cropping, and refining my "three star" selection—what I liked to call the "money shots." After a long day of motorcycling and drumming (some days it's difficult to say which activity was *harder*), it is an unspectacular, but rewarding time.

After an hour or so, Brutus and I wander off to our berths, while Malcolm pilots the bus through the night, then parks at an agreed-upon dropoff point. After sleeping in a *non-moving* bus for another few hours, Brutus and I rise painfully early. Ahead of us is always what Brutus calls "a full day."

On a show day, my mental and physical energies necessarily have to peak at about 11:00 at night, so coming down takes awhile. I won't get to sleep before about 1:00 a.m., and that means the alarm at 7:00 is not always a welcome sound. Still, I raise my tired and aching body (drumming is a serious athletic workout for me, especially as I begin my seventh decade, so it causes some pain), and—here's an important distinction—I don't get up *against* my will, but *because* of it. Stumbling up to the front lounge, I greet Brutus and Malcolm, cut and squeeze some oranges, fix a little cereal with bananas and blueberries, and draw a cup of good, strong coffee from the bus's excellent grinding-and-pouring machine.

All cleaned up after a dirty day

That will, that *resignation*, is only possible because I am powerfully motivated by the "full day" ahead.

I define my approach to each day I am given as, "What is the most excellent thing I can do today?" Sometimes, like nearly everyone, the most excellent thing I can do today is go to work, and that is fine. I do love most everything about my job, but it requires being away from home a great deal, and that is not the fantasy it sometimes seems to others. However, the silver lining is that I am free to choose an excellent way to get to work.

That's where motorcycling comes in. Our bus tows a small trailer holding two BMW 1200 GS motorcycles, and after breakfast, Brutus and I suit up (ATGATT—"all the gear, all the time"), layering according to the weather. (We follow the ancient Canadian wisdom, "There's no such thing as bad weather, only the wrong clothes.") Malcolm helps us unload the bikes, and we arrange our luggage (dress-up suits for fancier destinations carefully folded in a suit bag and packed alone in one side-case so we can look good after arrival—helpful Roadcraft technique for upscale bikers).

Mounted up, I lead Brutus away into the morning, following his route, carefully researched and designed, on the GPS screen in front of me. Its motorcycle-shaped cursor traces the purple line that squiggles along the smallest roads Brutus can find, through the most scenic parts of Britain.

To our sportier natures, the lightly traveled B roads of Wales and Scotland are endlessly entertaining, inspiring us to rail through a series of sweeping bends with controlled aggression and technique. That is certainly exciting and fun, but our favorite roads are the little singletracks.

Devon Lane

Creeping along between the dense hedges and stone walls of Devon or the Cotswolds in first or second gear, dodging sheep and tractors (I call us "hedge-huggers" in country like that), or on a narrow, winding ribbon of pavement laid across the barren Welsh and Scottish mountains (with more sheep), or threading the fells and narrow valleys of the Lake District (dotted ditto), the riding is relaxing, even serene, yet technically demanding. There is definitely an art to riding slowly over dynamic terrain.

By nature, Brutus and I are both radical shunpikers and stay well away from motorways (literally one percent of our riding, at most), and even A roads—the crowded and potentially deadly hunting grounds of White Van Man, Mondeo Woman, Yellow Vest Man, and marauding gangs of the dreaded Kneepuck Man. (Knee sliders on the public roads? Seriously?)

"The Struggle"

On the singletracks, other than the sheep, we may encounter an occasional rare specimen of Welly Man, or Landy Man.

Yorkshire Dales

In four tours of the U.K. by motorcycle over the past decade or so, Brutus and I have explored hundreds of miles of singletracks, stopping often for photographs. A "full day" does not mean a great distance, because rambling around like that we might average twenty miles per hour—then fetch up at some splendid country hotel Brutus has booked.

Post-ride refreshments mark that most pleasurable time (inspiring one of my stories in *Far and Away*, "The Hour of Arriving"), then a fine meal (Lord Byron was right: "Much depends upon dinner") with good wine. We retire early—to catch up on the previous night's missed sleep, and ready to rise as soon as breakfast is served and get back on the road.

Early one rainy morning in the tiny Yorkshire village of Ramsgill-in-Nidderdale, I looked out the window of our hotel ("a restaurant with rooms") at the soggy gray sky, the deep green trees and grass, our dripping-wet motorcycles in the forecourt and, leading away between the ancient stone buildings, a narrow strip of shiny wet pavement. I smiled to realize that despite the unpromising weather, and the need to get to Sheffield and perform a show, I was actually looking forward to the day's ride across Yorkshire's lanes. (And did I mention the sheep?)

The Trossachs,
Scotland

After all these years, all those miles, all those rainy days, and all those sheep—obviously I still love to ride those sweet little single-tracks.

Back in the mid-'90s, Brutus and I took up serious motorcycling at the same time, and soon discovered we shared a preference for a style of travel that didn't have a name then, but soon became fetishized as "adventure touring." (See ADV Man.) After thrashing our way to Arctic Canada and around Mexico in our first, more sport-touring BMW models, we each bought the first "oilhead" GSs, the R1100 GS, and promptly shipped them to Europe and made our way down through Austria, Italy, and Sicily to the Sahara in Tunisia, then back through Sardinia and Switzerland.

"Oh yes," we thought, "this is the way *we* roll."

Around that time, I began to consider the notion of using my motorcycle not just for adventures, but for "business travel"—riding it between shows on the band's tours. My bandmates were happy to fly, and I had my own bus with a trailer and a riding partner (in case a mechanical or tire problem interrupted my commute to work, I could commandeer the other bike and get there—but in tribute to

the GS's reliability, careful maintenance, and good fortune, that has never happened).

[Fateful words—see "It's Not Over When It's Over."]

Since then, with Brutus or Michael, and sometimes both, I have ridden tens of thousands of miles of backroads, adopting the motto, "The best roads are the ones no one travels unless they live on them."

Better yet, and infinitely more rare, are the roads no one even lives on (except millions of sheep)—like around Britain's fantastic national parks.

However, one thing that puzzles Brutus and me while we're riding these wiggly singletracks and serene country lanes is that we never— but *never*—encounter other motorcyclists.

We agree that, all things considered, that is for the best. Those little lanes are messy and unpleasant, often rainy, and quite possibly dangerous. Terrible, really. Not scenic or anything. And there are all those sheep.

We strongly advise other riders to keep far, far away from those nasty little British singletracks. Trust us, they are not at all fun, and we're sure you wouldn't like them.

# SHUNPIKERS IN THE SHADOWLANDS

JUNE 2013

Bavarian waltz

**Before our first few motorcycle rides** on the *Clockwork Angels* tour of Britain, in May 2013, I would ask Brutus about the next day, maybe how far the ride was. As usual, outside the U.S., he had done all the route planning and booked the destinations. It would all be a surprise to me, and that was fine—we had traveled together like that for about seventeen years, so there were no doubts. I would simply follow the route he had programmed on my GPS—Brutus the navigator, me the helmsman.

But just as I like to have some notion of the next day's weather, to know how to dress (of critical importance on a motorcycle), it is good to have some idea of the shape of the ride, to know how to prepare myself mentally and guide our pace.

However, in answer to my query, Brutus would just nod his head thoughtfully, and say, "It will be . . . a full day."

Soon that became a joke between us, understanding that the day's journey had nothing to do with distance. On many rides, in the mountains of Wales, Scotland, or the Yorkshire Dales, say, we could easily spend seven hours puttering around little singletrack lanes, yet with the necessarily slow pace, and frequent photo stops, we typically covered less than 200 miles in that "full day."

That was all very well, naturally, and at the end of those long rides, several in the rain (always making a long day longer), we would settle into some luxurious country hotel and clink our glasses with a laugh, saying, "To another full day." Still, after ten of those full days, and five shows (at least equally "full"), I decided I would like to have an *empty* day.

Brutus and I were discussing what to do after the overnight ferry from Newcastle to Amsterdam. We had a rare, second day off before the show, so—where should we ride? Holland has some pretty countryside, Belgium some good riding in the Ardennes Mountains and along its rivers, and twice before Bruges had been an enjoyable destination. However, my answer was "You know what? Let's go . . . *nowhere*."

After the ferry's morning arrival, we checked into a stylish little hotel in Amsterdam, overlooking a postcard-perfect canal, and just *stayed* there.

I am also pleased to be able to begin this story in Amsterdam, after the British run, because on that previous attempt to write about Europe, "Singletrack Minds in the Sceptered Isle," I had stopped at the end of the British travels, promising to pick up the Continental European part later. I never did—but I guess I am now.

Looking back to a theme from a previous story, "Nothing is ever just one thing," there are infinite degrees of shunpiking. Muddy, lumpy trails through the forest, narrow lanes pinched between hedges or stone walls, and sweeping ribbons of pavement that lay sinuously over hills and valleys—all are a shunpiker's delight.

Shunpiking in Germany

Roads no one travels . . .

Shunpiking in Europe is generally more extreme than in North America, mainly because of the greater number of singletrack roads

Der zigzags

available. (Though North America has far more unpaved roads.) The other big difference shunpikers enjoy in Europe is the *destinations*. In North America, it is unusual for a fabulous ride to lead to a fantastic destination, save perhaps in the national parks, but in the Old World, luxurious accommodations with fine restaurants are an attraction in themselves.

So planning ahead is important, and Brutus is a master at it—because he understands that when you are plotting a route, you are tracing your future *life* across that map. You are truly sowing what you will reap, and those squiggles and dots represent the environment that on a given day you will inhabit, move through, and savor—that you will *live*.

After a full day's travel through northern Bavaria that we later agreed was Germany's best motorcycling (as illustrated in all the previous riding photos), second only to the Alps, Brutus's researches led him—and thus *us*—to Rothenburg, a picturesque town in Bavaria. Rothenburg is regarded as the best-preserved medieval walled city in Europe, and it is very much a tourist showplace. During World War II, Rothenburg escaped the worst of the bombs and artillery that devastated other German cities only because of one of history's quirks. A high-ranking American general was aware of the city's history and beauty, and he ordered it spared. (A similar sentiment saved Kyoto, the ancient capital of Japan, an equally historic and picturesque city. Before the war, an American general had spent his honeymoon in Kyoto, and so aimed the bombers at places like Hiroshima and Nagasaki instead. In a further historical twist, Brutus and I saw busloads of Japanese tour groups in Rothenburg, drawn there because it was the setting for a popular animated series, *Sugar: A Little Snow Fairy*.)

In these times, it seems pointless to expend words and images on a celebrated attraction—interested readers can go see for themselves with a few keystrokes—but the countryside and villages remain the province of the real-time traveler, and so too does what I might call "living history."

With that in mind, I wish I could simply report that Brutus and I had some "interesting" rides across Germany and Poland, and that the weather was fine.

However, when you travel in places with long and tragic, even brutal, histories, it is impossible not to feel something—a perceived darkness that evokes the "Shadowlands" of the title. Apposite to George Santayana's chestnut "Those who cannot remember the past are condemned to repeat it" is the reality that those who *do* remember the past are condemned to *relive* it. Traveling in parts of the world with dark histories, you tend to see shadows everywhere—in this case, shadows of the swastika and hammer and sickle.

In my childhood of the '50s and early '60s, World War II was fresh in the world's memory, and we saw it dramatized constantly, in prime-time shows like *Combat!* and *Twelve O'Clock High*, and even more so in dozens of war movies seen at the Saturday afternoon matinees and on the weekend double-feature late shows on TV.

As for the Cold War, it was *now*—the all-pervasive background to my childhood, and fairly terrifying to live through. During the anxious and potentially apocalyptic days of the Cuban Missile Crisis in October 1962, I was ten, so not much aware of global politics. However, I watched my father prepare an emergency shelter in the basement of our suburban split-level—a pathetic-but-telling attempt at preparation for the nuclear attack everyone feared. In our kitchen, I overheard the neighboring dads discussing the Russians and how

Rothenburg, Germany

Thuringia, former
East Germany

they would surely bomb Niagara Falls because of the hydroelectric generators. Niagara Falls was fifteen miles away.

In the early '90s, just after the Berlin Wall came down, followed by the dominoes of all Eastern Europe, I wrote the lyrics for a song called "Heresy," about the bittersweet end to all that. I hadn't even heard the song for maybe twenty years, and I don't think we ever played it live, but the lyrics and vocal lines were echoing in my helmet all through those rides. One verse particularly addressed the weight under which the whole world had lived—nuclear annihilation, or "Mutually Assured Destruction" (apt acronym).

It seemed—and seems—outrageous that the entire planet endured decades of anxiety, not to mention all the stunted lives in these Shadowlands, under the totalitarian boot-heel, for the sake of some misguided ideology. (Someday, I trust, the same will be said about religion.)

*All around this great big world*
*All the crap we had to take*
*Bombs and basement fallout shelters*
*All our lives at stake*
*The bloody revolution*
*All the warheads in its wake*
*All the fear and suffering*
*All a big mistake?*
*All those wasted years*
*All those precious, wasted years*
*Who will pay?*

George Santayana offered another quote that still resonates loudly in our world today: "Only the dead have seen the end of war."

From Rothenburg, Brutus and I started out on the "Romantische Strasse"—Romantic Road—which connects some picturesque towns and castles in Southern Germany, ending at Mad King Ludwig's ultimate fantasy castle, Neuschwanstein. Riding north toward the show in Cologne (German spelling Köln), we enjoyed a few hours of shunpiking, following winding little roads past dark green forests and swollen brown rivers. But, with far to go to work that day, we eventually had to surrender to a lengthy stretch of autobahn. We did not love it.

The inside lane was a solid freight train of trucks traveling at about 60 mph, while the outside lane was much faster, even sometimes "unlimited." So big Mercedes, BMWs, Audis, and Porsches came racing up from behind at well over 100. Our motorcycles, and especially our tires, were oriented toward sport and adventure riding, and were not comfortable above 90 mph. We were caught between the traffic's natural flow—pulling out to pass a truck through its turbulent wake, wrestling for control, and at the same time keeping an eye on our mirrors at all times. The road was straight and dull, yet the mood was tense and loud—not our kind of thing at all. But as with American interstates, sometimes it was a price worth paying.

The next morning we awoke on the bus at what appeared to be the usual "motorway services" (truck stop) on an autobahn. However, when I opened the blinds to check out the day's weather, I noticed unusual details. All around us stood tall metal watchtowers, and the modern Shell gas pumps were sheltered under a vast canopy of much greater age and less sleek design. Old, dowdy-looking gray buildings of poured concrete were painted with large, weathered letters reading "ZOLL." (Customs.)

With a chill, I realized we were looking at another kind of "walled city" from the past—from another kind of hyper-medieval era, the Cold War. We were on the former East German autobahn near Eisenach, for many years one of only three crossing points by road between the savagely divided parts of the country.

Writing about a time that is nearly unimaginable now, the venerable travel writer Jan Morris observed, "Traveling from west to east through [the inner German border] was like entering a drab and disturbing dream, peopled by all the ogres of totalitarianism, a half-lit world of shabby resentments, where anything could be done to you, I used to feel, without anybody ever hearing of it, and your every step was dogged by watchful eyes and mechanisms."

Over the next few days, as Brutus and I traveled through the former East Germany and then into Poland, everything I saw was colored with the lenses of that shadowy history—what those places had endured, and what the people who lived there had done, what had been done to them, and what they had been denied.

Again, verses from "Heresy" kept playing in my helmet, as once more I felt the emotions stirred by the sudden fall of Eastern Europe.

(At least three things I never thought would happen in my lifetime: peace in Northern Ireland, the end of apartheid, and the tearing down of the Berlin Wall.)

*All around that dull gray world*
*From Moscow to Berlin*
*People storm the barricades*
*Walls go tumbling in*
*The counter-revolution*
*People smiling through their tears*
*Who can give them back their lives*
*And all those wasted years*
*All those precious wasted years—Who will pay?*

Twenty years later, I still felt that sense of injustice and anger. Because these people are *still* paying, literally with their lives, while the villains and ideologues who laid them all low were allowed to play hero while secretly committing unspeakably horrible crimes against humanity—against so many individual *humans*.

"Everyone is equal," they insisted—but those few were obviously much more equal than the masses.

Like Prohibition, the rise and fall of communism is sometimes written off as a "Noble Experiment," but any way you look at it, collectivism is precisely the *opposite* of noble. (Once I wondered about the fanatics behind both communism and fascism, "Were they evil psychopaths or just misguided morons?" I decided it was a mix of both—the deadliest combination in history.)

Riding through so many backroads and villages in the former East Germany, and spending the night in Dresden, there is no doubt things are better now—yet they still lag behind their compatriots in the former West Germany.

River in flood,
Southern Germany

And if the former Karl-Marx-Stadt is now back to Chemnitz, I was still genuinely surprised—even appalled—to ride into the former East Berlin along Karl-Marx-Strasse. Likewise on a previous tour, when Brutus and I crossed out of a ride through Poland at Frankfurt (the secondary one, on the Oder), my eyes widened to see their main street still named after Karl Marx. These days you don't see any Hitler or Stalin streets, and Leningrad is back to St. Petersburg, yet it's a safe bet that no individual in history has been the cause of so much slaughter and suffering as Karl Marx.

(His only competition might be the *imaginary* ones, the Deities—referred to by Marx and his buddy Friedrich Engels as "the opiate of the masses." If you ask me, it's more like the crystal meth of the masses.)

In the spring of 2013, the international media were reporting about the severe floods in Southern Germany, and friend Craiggie wrote to Brutus and me from South Pasadena, California, to warn us about the situation. We were fortunate that our routes were not affected, but riding into Dresden, we witnessed another kind of human unification against a common enemy—great numbers of citizens joining together not to fight against another group of people, but against Nature and "global weirding."

Through Dresden's *zentrum*, along the banks of the Elbe River, we rode past many thousands of people—mostly students, it seemed—working in relays to unload, pass, and stack sandbags, from army trucks and even regular delivery vans, to build temporary levees above the pavement. Other people in the streets pushed carts filled with large bottles of drinking water and other emergency supplies. With the river level so high, the bridge arches were far too shallow for the rivercraft to pass beneath them, so the tourboats and barges were trapped between, tied to drowned quays and wharves.

At our hotel, we were told that the city's flood wall was nine meters (thirty feet) high, and the waters were currently at eight and a half meters (twenty-eight feet). We would not be able to park our motorcycles in the hotel's underground garage, but would have to leave them on the street. (We didn't mind that convenience—one disadvantage of riding into older European cities is that the parking can often be distant; in Rothenburg, the lot for the Herrnschlösschen Hotel was many blocks away, and we had to have a car pick us up, then take us there again in the morning.)

After dressing up for dinner at the hotel's fine restaurant, Brutus and I took an evening stroll in the city's vast central area, which was in the process of being redeveloped into something like its former glory. Dresden's heart seemed less baroque and "stagy" than Munich or Vienna, and less frenetic and edgy than Berlin—more like a plaza in a Southern European city. Sidewalk cafés overlooked a vast cobbled pedestrian area, the surrounding buildings splendidly illuminated, all centered on an enormous cathedral, the Frauenkirche. (It had lain in ruins, as a monument, from 1945 through the Soviet era, until its restoration in the early 2000s.)

We sat at one of the outdoor cafés, enjoyed a cognac, and marveled at how the city had rebounded not only from the Soviet doldrums, but from total annihilation in the infamous firebombing of Dresden. Near the end of World War II, in February 1945, British and American aircraft dropped thousands of tons of explosive and incendiary bombs on Dresden. The entire central city was destroyed, and 25,000 civilians were killed.

Once again, interested readers are invited to look further into that story, which is not without controversy (as usual, victors write the history), and especially to view some of the harrowing photographs taken after the bombing. Kurt Vonnegut's novel *Slaughterhouse-Five*

(1969) evokes his experience in Dresden then, as a prisoner of war, and in the introduction to a later edition of the book, he wrote, "The Dresden atrocity, tremendously expensive and meticulously planned, was so meaningless, finally, that only one person on the entire planet got any benefit from it. I am that person. I wrote this book, which earned a lot of money for me and made my reputation, such as it is. One way or another, I got two or three dollars for every person killed. Some business I'm in."

The second verse of "Heresy" describes the rise of Eastern Europe, and especially places like Dresden, from both the ashes of war and the Soviet concrete and rust.

> *All around that dull gray world*
> *Of ideology*
> *People storm the marketplace*
> *And buy up fantasy*
> *The counter-revolution*
> *At the counter of a store*
> *People buy the things they want*
> *And borrow for a little more*
> *All those wasted years*
> *All those precious, wasted years*
> *Who will pay?*

The third man

In 1991, just a year or so after Reunification, I traveled through a good bit of the former East Germany, with eyes wide open. It absolutely *was* that "dull gray world" I described in the first verse of "Heresy," and the hints of returning color stood out almost garishly—cheap plastic articles in shop windows, fresh coats of paint on scattered houses in the villages, and brightly colored older Volkswagens and smaller BMWs in used-car lots among the homely, smoky Trabants. (An East German make universally acknowledged as one of the worst cars ever made: with its two-stroke engine and body panels of "Duroplast"—not much stronger than cardboard—Trabants are absent from the roads now, and will soon exist only in museums. As artifacts—not art!)

By 2013, over twenty years later, the transformation of East Germany was all but complete. They still lagged slightly behind the West in development and prosperity, but the gap is closing, and most clearly the *flair* is back in life again.

But how awful to reflect that fully two generations of people

Eastern German byway

there—the people, middle-aged and older, that I saw on the roads all day, and often waved to in passing—had to endure that repression, had to have their lives so impeded, and for the young, such a limited prospect for their futures.

The chorus of "Heresy" offers what is perhaps the necessary resignation:

> *Do we have to be forgiving at last?*
> *What else can we do?*
> *Do we have to say goodbye to the past?*
> *Yes, I guess we do*

If East Germany has regained much of its prosperity and *joie de vivre* in the past twenty years, Poland, alas, has not been so fortunate. On a previous tour, Brutus and I had ridden through a small part of Poland and hadn't been impressed, but figured that taste was too limited a sample to form any worthwhile impressions. This time we covered quite a lot more territory, riding all day through the villages and countryside, and even along some seaside resorts in the direction of the port of Gdynia, where we would catch an overnight ferry to Sweden.

We viewed the country the way we experience everywhere we visit, by the backroads, farmlands, villages, and small towns, and at the end of that day, the best Brutus and I could say was . . . the weather was nice.

Polish byway

We passed through miles of rather scruffy farmland and pulp-wood tree plantations, all in ordered rows of a single species. Those vast tree farms had been planted about fifty or sixty years ago, so during the communist era—maybe to keep the soldiers busy enough not to be launching coups d'état.

As in much of Northern Europe, wind turbines were sprouting everywhere, and that could be considered an admirable sign of modernization. To the eye of this beholder, those gigantic white propellers do not add to a landscape's beauty—but that is why they are most often placed where the landscape does not *possess* much beauty. The farms and villages were charmless, drably painted, and without much in the way of parks, gardens, or decorations—save for the signature stork nests, great bundles of sticks built on platforms erected by the community, because a nesting stork is considered to be good luck.

And the roads—the all-important roads—were just terrible. Not only when they were *supposed* to be terrible, understanding that as shunpikers we often seek out the roughest and most remote roads (and we weren't disappointed there)—but even the major secondary roads, what would be called A roads in Britain or state highways in the U.S., were bone-jarringly rough.

Some of the country lanes that obviously dated from the communist era were literally handmade—concrete blocks laid in parallel

Shunpiker in Poland

tracks across the countryside. No doubt another make-work program for a sluggish economy, like the pulpwood tree plantations. (I always remember bicycling through China in the mid-'80s, and seeing nine workers in the middle of the road on their hands and knees, painting the white lines, with different size brushes for outlining and filling them in. At least those nine people had jobs, I guess.)

And talk about Shadowlands . . . oh, Poland, poor Poland—tragically sited between the warlike pincers of Russia and Germany. (Something like a Mexican president said about his country: "Poor Mexico—so far from God, and so close to the United States.")

My bandmate Geddy's parents met as youngsters at Auschwitz, and he told me once how his mother recalled that when they were finally freed—after ninety percent of Poland's Jews had been exterminated—they were certain they must be the last people alive on Earth. Because if they had endured so much horror, and the world had allowed that to happen, how could anyone else have survived?

That notion inspired our song "Red Sector A," with the lines, "Are we the last ones left alive?/ Are we the only human beings to survive?" The title gives the song a whiff of science fiction, which perhaps makes it seem less grim than the true history it relates, and that is fine with me. (In a now delicious irony, "Red Sector A" was the name of our viewing area as guests at the launch of the first Space Shuttle, *Columbia*, in 1981.)

A memoir by another female survivor of Auschwitz filled in more details, like how if anyone appeared too ill or feeble to work, they would be sent straight to the gas chambers. So even in that dehumanized nightmare, people showed "grace under pressure" and tried to help each other appear "healthy." ("For my father and my brother, it's too late/ But I must help my mother stand up straight.")

Gdynia, Poland

So as I rode through those Polish villages, I imagined those horrific times, the Jews being rounded up—or willingly surrendered by the local authorities—to be sent to their deaths in the Final Solution. Like the time Brutus and I spent a day visiting several of the World War I battlefields of France and Belgium, the stories that haunted us during our travels in Eastern Germany and Poland felt increasingly dark and heavy, and we were glad to board the overnight ferry to Sweden.

And at last we can move on to happier, brighter subjects—like overnight ferry rides. Brutus and I just *love* those! Like the boat from Newcastle to Amsterdam, the Baltic ferries usually run overnight, so we could have "a full day" on the motorcycles and get to the port by mid-afternoon. I never mind the waiting time, catching up on journal notes and the Sunday *New York Times* crossword saved from the previous Saturday's *International Herald Tribune*, but you never know when Yellow Vest Man is going to appear and signal you to move—when you will have to quickly rearrange your belongings and riding gear, fire up the bike, and get moving to keep your place in line and not hold up others. Maybe you'll ride a few hundred yards to where another Yellow Vest Man signals you to stop. That often happened three separate times, and even then you wouldn't know if the motorcycles would be loaded first or last. So the boarding process reminded me of one definition of soldiering—"long hours of boredom punctuated by moments of sheer panic." (Only without the bombs, bullets, and bayonets, of course.)

Once the bikes were safely tied down in the hold, though, we could check into our cabins and enjoy a pleasant dinner and the *deepest* sleep I have ever known—something about the low-frequency vibrations, or the sea air, I don't know, but it's certainly an effective soporific for this traveler.

For the price of a cheap flight and an average hotel, we traveled in luxury and pleasure—and for a few Euros more, Brutus booked us cabins in "Commodore" or "Panorama" class, with views over the bow of the ship. The word "posh" derives from British people traveling by ship, preferring "port out, starboard home" for cabins with the best views, so we were *better* than posh. And the restaurants were usually pretty good, too.

Waiting to debark

After breakfast (one ship waking its passengers one hour before arrival with Louis Armstrong's "What a Wonderful World" playing over the ship's PA—that was kind of nice), we hauled our luggage to the car decks (sometimes waiting a little too long there—though the camaraderie, and anonymity, among fellow riders could be sweet), then rode out into another "full day."

Being off the boat and away on the shunpikers' roads of Sweden and Finland brings me to a delicate subject—European driving standards versus their lack in North America. See, in four European tours now, Brutus and I have ridden thousands of miles of all kinds of roads, and not once—not one single time—have we encountered a driver who cut us off, flipped us off, ran us off, or did anything unexpected. No one has *ever* failed to use his or her turn indicators. (A bumper sticker I saw in California said, "JESUS WOULD HAVE USED TURN SIGNALS.") And I seriously mean not a single exception—not one discourteous or unsafe move ever menaced our well-being on the road.

You could not survive a single day on the roads of Canada or the United States without having *something* ugly happen. Often many things.

Of course, Americans hate to hear that *anything* European might be at all superior, and Europeans are the same, in other ways. They may admire American blue jeans, rock and roll, jazz, action movies, and Route 66, but tend to generalize American people as morbidly obese, gun-toting religious fanatics. (A stereotype that's only maybe fifty percent true!)

That same half of the American population views Europeans as snooty, suspicious, snail-eating socialists. (Again, only half right!)

Swedish backroad

But for all these people on both sides of the Atlantic who have never seen the places or people they disparage, there's a worthy quote from St. Augustine: "The world is a book and those who do not travel read only one page."

I have also long admired a West African saying: "The one who does not travel knows only his mother's cooking."

On the theme of road manners, that wisdom might be amended to, "The one who does not travel knows only his father's driving."

One theory I consider likely is that Europeans lived communally for thousands of years, in which almost everyone was born, lived, and died among the same small group of people. So courtesy and responsibility were *necessary*. No one could get along without their neighbors, except aristocrats (who still sometimes simply chose courteous behavior as being more, well, aristocratic). Perhaps such social habits survived into modern times, when those medieval peasants and merchants began driving cars.

North America's peoples came together in a much different way, arriving in small groups from widely varying cultures, to places that were transitory and crude. Other individuals they encountered were all strangers—to be judged with suspicion, prickly hostility, and hair-trigger retaliation. And that is how they *drive*.

Apart from the occasional quaint scene, and the area around the pretty island of Öland we visited on the *Time Machine* tour, the countryside of Southern Sweden is much like that of Southern Ontario, where I grew up, so maybe a little too *familiar* looking. We had some pleasant rides there, especially on the unpaved logging roads (much of Scandinavia, like large parts of Canada, is covered in vast stands of single-species pulpwood—though on an infinitely larger scale than Poland) and some paved backroads that were enjoyable enough, but straight and scenically . . . familiar. We didn't stop too often for photographs.

Not having mentioned any of the actual *shows* yet, the one in Sweden provides an exceptional example. The arena concerts in the

U.K., Amsterdam, and Germany had gone very well, the audiences enthusiastic, and we thought we were playing okay. The string section continued to be an uplifting presence, musically and socially. However, this was something far outside our usual performance routine— headlining one night of a huge three-day festival called Sweden Rocks. Bands were playing all day on three or four different stages, more or less continuously, so there would be no soundcheck. Our show would start a couple of hours later than usual, and instead of our two sets with intermission, we would play one *long* set, about two hours—and we would play to 35,000 *people*. That was a little overwhelming to contemplate, but I didn't really have a sense of that crowd from the stage—with all the barricades and photo pits, even the closest people were farther away than usual. I really like to see people's faces—to see them smiling, singing along, getting excited—but still, it was an impressive sea of humanity.

After another pleasant morning of shunpiking around Sweden, Brutus and I caught our third overnight ferry, from Stockholm to Turku, Finland. The ride through the city, certainly one of Europe's prettiest, was gorgeous on that warm sunny day, and while waiting at the ferry dock, I had a transcendent experience. Because of the ten-hour time difference between Central Europe and Southern California, I had been able to have fairly regular video chats with three-and-a-half-year-old Olivia in late afternoons, when it was early morning at home. That day, sitting on my bike on its centerstand and working on the previous weekend's crossword, I received a text from Carrie saying that Olivia wanted to see Daddy. I texted back that we were waiting for a ferry and didn't have Wi-Fi. She replied, "Aren't you *always* waiting for a ferry?"

Ha ha. It was really only the third time, but I felt bad that Olivia wanted to see me and I couldn't make it happen. I was determined to try to connect with her. The Wi-Fi hotspot on Brutus's phone didn't work, but we picked up a signal from a nearby hotel's free network. I gave it a try, and it worked!

Usually my comment about modern gadgetry is "Technology is never as smart as it thinks it is," but when I saw Olivia's smiling face on the little iPad screen perched on the tankbag of my motorcycle on a ferry dock in Sweden, I said to Brutus, "Now this is the way technology is *supposed* to work!"

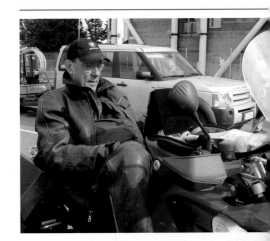

I could show Olivia all around the harbor and the other boats, and even had Brutus take a photo of the scene on my cell phone, so I could send it to her and give her "the whole picture."

Other passengers standing around were also delighted to hear Olivia belt out "I've Been Working on the Railroad" at full volume.

Brutus and I had ridden in Finland twice before, but both encounters were brief and rainy. This time we had a dry and mostly bright day, plus a masterpiece of a route by Brutus that included all the good kinds of shunpikers' roads—from logging tracks to lightly traveled, nicely winding backroads through the rural countryside and mixed woodlands. (Forests cover three-quarters of Finland, though what we saw were second or third growth—but still, the trees were mixed somewhat "naturally" as opposed to the single-species plantations of Central Planning.) Among the familiar spruce, pine, and birch trees, I occasionally noticed a different kind of conifer, dark and drooping with graceful, gestural branches. As best I can deduce (just try to learn the name of one tree in the forests of Finland!), they were Finnish spruce, a variant of the Siberian species. In any case, just that one unfamiliar and attractive tree gave the woodlands of Finland a more exotic atmosphere.

Finnish backroad

Wildflowers were plentiful along the roadsides, seemingly scattered deliberately, as country people do. Yellow and white blossoms were most common, which seems typical everywhere, but there were bright splashes of red, like poppies. I was especially attracted to the multicolored lupins, in pink, lavender, and

Brutus among the lupins

purple spears, and I asked Brutus to ride through one scene for me a couple of times. (Michael would have called me *terrible* names for that.)

At such a northerly latitude, the growing season is brief but intense—summers are short, but the days are long, essentially giving twenty-four hours of light. The trees, pastures, and wildflowers around us seemed positively swollen with burgeoning life and color. It was now early June, and even at midnight, the sky was not completely dark. As in Northern Canada, only in winter do those people dwell in the Shadowlands.

But it's a place we all pass through, some of us more than once, and Brutus and I have both survived some seriously dark times and trials. Often—like our journeys—we had shared them. Over the past year or two, Brutus had been through a particularly bad time, health-

wise—cancer (*stupid* cancer, I insist it should always be prefaced), perhaps life's ultimate Shadowlands. (Though grief would be close.) After multiple surgeries, therapies, and a dodgy prognosis, this European tour was Brutus's first big motorcycle journey—so it represented a crucial "test" for him, a test of his future Quality of Life.

Without saying anything, I was a little anxious about his ability to handle it (serious traveling is *hard work*—like what Paul Theroux said, "When I come back from a journey, I haven't *had* a vacation; I *need* a vacation"), and of course Brutus's concern, and perhaps fear, ran deeper—all the way down.

A lot was riding on this tour, spoken and not, and as the days went by, I was happy and relieved to see Brutus making it—keeping up with me and enjoying the ride. Out of all our darkness, he and I had emerged purified, ennobled, and enlightened—we knew how to *appreciate* life.

Riding into Helsinki for the final European show, after 5,314 kilometers (3,321 miles), Brutus and I were a couple of happy shunpikers, riding out of the Shadowlands and into the light.

# 14

# ON DAYS LIKE THESE

JULY 2013

**Some stories just want to begin** where they end. Like songs, days, journeys, lifetimes, and even love affairs, everything is colored by how things turn out. If any of those stories ends badly, the rest of it probably won't shine too brightly in memory. For example, if this pillar of basalt on the northwestern shore of Nova Scotia had responded to my little joke by falling on me, it wouldn't be just a metaphor. It

Balancing Rock

would be a variation on the classic definition of comedy and tragedy: if the rock falls on Michael, it's comedy. If it falls on me, it's tragedy.

The date was July 13, 2013, a day off before our second show in Halifax, the last one on the penultimate run of our *Clockwork Angels* tour. The formation is called Balancing Rock, and in retrospect, it has come to seem like a multifaceted symbol—both universal and personal. Everyone knows what it's like to have days like these—when you're standing in a hard place and pushing against an unyielding wall of stone. Also, for this reporter, nothing could be more representative of the dynamics of my life than "balancing rock." Thirdly, the actual moment, as opposed to the symbol, echoes a time and place in a previous life that ended badly, and thus does not include any bright memories.

In September 1996, on the occasion of my forty-fourth birthday ("Ah, were we ever so young?"), my late wife, Jackie, gave me a birthday card in which she wrote her gift to me: "Seven days of freedom."

Brutus and I, living with our families in Toronto then, and in the second year of our infatuation with adventure touring on motorized two-wheelers, discussed where we might be able to ride to and from in that seven days. It happened that around that time I was watching Canada's Weather Network (as you do), and as part of a series of "Canadian Postcards," Balancing Rock, near Tiverton, Nova Scotia, was pictured. Brutus and I could get to Nova Scotia and back in seven days, and I thought, "Well—let's ride to Tiverton. Make sure that rock is still balancing."

So, way back in 1996, Brutus planned a typically circuitous route to lead us up to Lac Saint Jean in Quebec, down across the Gaspé Peninisula to New Brunswick's Grand Manan Island, then onto the ferry from Saint John to Digby, Nova Scotia. Following the narrow peninsula at Nova Scotia's northwestern tip to a small ferry over to Tiverton, we hiked through the boggy woods of black spruce and tamarack to Balancing Rock, and saw that it was good.

Seventeen years later, Brutus and I—taking Michael along with us this time—were drawn there by the same spurious quest, to see that the legendary rock was still balancing.

Because other people might not bother to check on things like that.

They might think they have something more important to do "On Days Like These."

Which brings us back to our title. For me, that song title is a perfect fit for pretty much every day—evoking many stories, and many memories. Few songs have haunted my helmet the way that one

has—maybe only Jeff Buckley's masterly rendition of "Hallelujah" (especially on rainy days) and Sinatra's versions of "Gentle on My Mind" and "Everything Happens to Me" come close.

The song itself is a recent discovery, and only because I saw it mentioned in two different British classic car magazines. The journalists were test-driving Lamborghinis from the '60s, and both of them happened to remark that they felt like they should be hearing "On Days Like These" by Matt Monro.

Matt Monro, I knew, was a British singer in the Sinatra style. In the '60s, he had a few hits in North America, like "Portrait of My Love" and "Born Free," and I remember riding in my father's pickup truck with the radio on (as always), and hearing Matt Monro described by the DJ as "the English Frank Sinatra." My father, a lifelong Sinatra fan, as I have since become, scoffed out loud at that. But these days, Dad and I agree that Matt Monro was actually very good and is a story in himself—discovered by George Martin, the Beatles' producer, he had a successful career internationally, until at the age of just fifty-four, he was struck down by stupid cancer.

At that time, Frank Sinatra himself said, "His pitch was right on the nose, his word enunciations letter perfect, his understanding of a song thorough. He will be missed very much not only by myself, but by his fans all over the world."

Upper Peninsula, Michigan

I hadn't heard of the song "On Days Like These," but in context of the car magazine stories, my guess was that the lyrics must express some joyous feeling of in-the-moment existence—like driving a classic Lamborghini through the English countryside. However, the connection was both more esoteric and more dramatic. In the opening scene of the original version of *The Italian Job* (1969), actor Rossano Brazzi is pictured driving a bright orange Lamborghini Miura (considered the original "supercar," with its low, swoopy bodywork and mid-mounted V12) in the Swiss Alps, near the old Saint Bernard Pass. On-car cameras captured the Miura's perfect handling of the winding, narrow pavement, twisting through the snow-streaked mountains. The high-pitched howl of the V12 blipping down the gears segues into the opening bars of the song.

Iowa—"When skies are blue, and fields are green"

With a melancholy air over a minor chordal soundscape and a lilting tempo, Matt Monro sings one line in Italian to set the romantic mood, "*Questi giorni quando vieni il bel sole.*"

(These days when the beautiful sun comes up.)

Then into the first verse:

*On days like these, when skies are blue, and fields are green*
*I look around and think of all that might have been*
*Then I hear sweet music float around my head*
*As I recall the many things we left unsaid*

So, it's the classic "lament for lost love," wistful and nostalgic. (The music is by the great Quincy Jones, and the lyrics by Matt Monro's *manager*, if you can imagine that, Don Black, who also set words to memorable movie themes like "To Sir, With Love" and "The World Is Not Enough.") In the song's next part, the voice and orchestration step up with more emotion.

*It's on days like these, that I remember*
*Singing songs and drinking wine*
*While your eyes played games with mine*

The second verse falls back to the lower register, dynamically and emotionally, once again quietly sentimental about a memory that he likes to wish might be shared.

*On days like these, I wonder what became of you*
*Maybe today you're singing songs with someone new*
*I'd like to think you're walking by those willow trees*
*Remembering the love we knew—on days like these*

In the movie, the song fades out just as the Miura enters a dark tunnel. To describe what follows would be a "spoiler," but in any case, apart from the artful driving footage, in one of the world's most spectacular landscapes, it was the *song* that captivated me.

L'Isle-aux-Coudres, Quebec

Every riding day during this run of the tour, through New York, Pennsylvania, Ohio, Indiana, Iowa, Illinois, Wisconsin, Michigan's Upper Peninsula, and across Ontario, Quebec, New Brunswick, and Nova Scotia, that song played in my helmet. (Talking about that phenomenon with other riders, we agree that a song can be mentally playing while you're cruising along, then when you need to concentrate on more demanding traffic or road conditions, the music goes into "pause." When mental space allows, the song of the day will resume at exactly the same place. That would be one advantage of listening to that "analog" playback as opposed to digital earbuds—it cannot distract you at the wrong time.)

"On Days Like These" was not like what is called an "earworm," some annoying old song that you can't get out of your head, but a combination of words and music that always rang true. Every day seemed like "that day"—perfectly appropriate for that song, playing over and over in my inner jukebox.

*"On days like these . . ."*

And here is another story that begins at the end. Your correspondent rests on a plastic chair in Newberry, Michigan, comfortably settled in front of a motel room and enjoying a post-ride plastic cup of The Macallan. Following what had been a very "full," adventurous, and dramatic day in Michigan's Upper Peninsula, the drink—and the moment—tasted especially delicious.

After the previous night's show in Milwaukee, I asked bus driver Dave to carry us north to Green Bay, where he parked at our usual

show-night accommodations, the Château Walmart. That would set us up for a good ride across the Upper Peninsula, then down to the next show in Grand Rapids.

Michael and I had crossed the U.P. several times, as recently as the previous fall (see "The Better Angels"), so in Milwaukee I had scanned the Michigan state map looking for some different routes. I highlighted a section of unpaved road leading toward Pictured Rocks National Lakeshore, but as happens to us fairly often, when Michael tried to translate that route into his computer, the mapping program, Mother, did not totally agree with the paper map, and interpreted its own version.

Such "interpretations" have led Michael and me on many an unexpected adventure . . .

We always call those parts of an upcoming ride the "mystery roads." Michael would inform me that Mother didn't seem to agree with the line I had traced, and we couldn't know if we would get a "normal" unpaved road of graded gravel or a bumpy trail through any kind of obstacles—mud, loose gravel, deep ruts and puddles, studded boulders, washed-out bridges, or long stretches of sand (a serious hazard on our heavy bikes—see "Adventures in the Wild West"). So we always had to be prepared to improvise.

Our mystery road on that day in the Upper Peninsula began pleasantly enough, as a gravel logging road winding through the scrubby forest of mixed second-growth pines, tamaracks, and leafy hard-

woods. It gradually degenerated to a narrow little track, with grass in the middle and both sides overgrown to where we sometimes had both elbows in the leaves and needles. ATVs had left occasional deep ruts on damper ground, though not recently—maybe during the previous fall's hunting season. But we kept moving without difficulty and weren't yet concerned.

When people ask about the off-pavement abilities of our BMW GS motorcycles, I always say, "We can handle a bad road or a good trail." And indeed, occasional signs seemed to indicate that we were now on snowmobile trails. We encountered a few water crossings, which are always dramatic photo opportunities, and once I had made it through, I would wave Michael to a stop behind me so I could get out my camera.

Around this point, things started to get a little rougher, and for a while we didn't take any photographs. I have pointed out before that when things get *really* bad, the last thing you want to do is stop for pictures—you just keep going and try to get out of there. And all the while, the farther you go, you know that if you have to turn back, every obstacle you have overcome becomes one you will have to face again. It is not a fun feeling.

We encountered some stretches of slimy mud and deep sand that sent the bikes slewing around, forcing us to put our feet down for balance. Always keeping an eye on my mirrors, and even stopping to look back after particularly bad stretches, I saw Michael go down in a mud hole, his out-of-control bike plunging sideways into the trailside brush. Parking my bike on its sidestand and dashing back to help, I saw his gray machine lying on its side in the green underbrush, and heard the engine still running. Then it suddenly died, and I heard only silence. That was not what I wanted to hear just then, and I couldn't see Michael at all. Clambering around the fallen bike, I saw his upper body and helmet. He was on his back among the saplings, thrashing around a little on his elbows.

That was also an alarming sight, and I said, "Are you all right?"

"Yes," he said doubtfully, "I *think* so. But I can't get up because the bike is on my leg."

At moments like that, your brain races with adrenaline and imagination—me picturing his leg being burned by the muffler, or broken by the weight of the bike, and us stranded in that *very* isolated place. However, moments like that also give you superhuman strength, and I quickly lifted the rear of the bike away from Michael.

He struggled slowly to his feet, testing out his arms and legs, and giving his helmeted head a quick shake. "Just doing a systems check," he said.

After I had seen each of Michael's limbs move at least once, we turned to his fallen motorcycle. In the tangled undergrowth and slippery mud, it was hard to get it on its wheels again, and to work it back over toward the trail. Both of us were nervous about whether it would start again—but it fired right up, ready to face the next challenge.

The next time it was my turn—my front wheel plowing into deep sand while the rear caught a rut, and just like that, the bike was down. I was necessarily riding slowly and fell clear of the bike, without injury. Once again, we got my bike back on its wheels and carried on.

(Both of our GSes were fairly new at that time—mine just past its first major service—so they were receiving their true "baptism by fire" as West Side Beemer Boyz mounts.)

At one water crossing, my bike plunged into the deepest water I had ever tried to cross, a brown flood that reached up over the cylinder heads. I just managed to power through, then parked on the other side to shoot Michael's passage—warning him about the depth.

With that in mind, Michael decided to take the center line, between the ruts left by ATVs, figuring the water would be shallower there. While that was true, the flaw in that plan was that when Michael *did* start to skid and needed to put a foot down, he had only deeper water on either side. Even a non-rider can guess what is about to happen here . . .

At least Michael was able to steer the out-of-control machine to the side again, into the underbrush rather than the deep water—which might well have been terminal for the engine. I waded into the brown pond, ignoring the water flooding into my boots, and once again we wrestled his bike out of the bush and onto its wheels and got it restarted.

Every time we stopped like that, black-flies and mosquitoes swarmed around us in ever-thickening clouds. As I had experienced in the Canadian Arctic and Alaska, we had to keep our helmet faceshields down whenever we were stationary. (I had laughed to notice a dot on the Michigan map named Slapneck—I knew what they were talking about.) It would be a terrible place to be stranded for any length of time.

And still, we couldn't know if this snowmobile trail would get worse—become truly impassable in some way, sending us back on an ever-longer and more inhospitable route. One trailside sign read, "OHV AND SNOWMOBILE TRAIL, NOT MAINTAINED FOR PASSENGER VEHICLE TRAFFIC." Another warned snowmobilers about the "WINDING TRAIL." Finally, we had to laugh out loud at seeing a sign that represented the end of our trials: "CAUTION: HIGHWAY."

That warning was for the wintertime snowmobilers, of course— because we two-wheelers were pretty glad to meet that highway. It led us first to a gas station, which we needed by that time, then eastward on some winding pavement around Pictured Rocks toward the town of Grand Marais—the best motorcycle roads in Michigan, I would venture.

We had stayed in the village of Newberry before—a typical northern hamlet that was a seasonal destination for hunters, snowmobilers, fishermen, and summer vacationers. I couldn't find the motel we had stayed at before (sad to report, the mom-and-pop places are steadily disappearing, year by year), but we settled at the similar Knollwood Inn. It was the first proper park-outside-your-door motel we had stayed at since the Mayberry Motor Inn, back in May. (See "The Sweet Science.") After an hour or two of sitting outside and watching the cars, trucks, and occasional packs of loud motorcycles (you know the kind) pass on the highway, and sharing our photos from the day, we dined

at the attached restaurant on T-bone steaks and corner-store wine. We were exhausted and sore, but supremely content—I was still hearing "On Days Like These."

Here is another story that begins at the ending, historically speaking. The setting is Put-in-Bay, Ohio, in the Bass Islands, a short ferry ride out in Lake Erie. The monument is called Perry's Victory and International Peace Memorial, and is one of the tallest in the United States (higher than the Statue of Liberty, for example—that's little old me on my motorcycle in the middle). The column, along with three enormous flagpoles nearby that display huge American, Canadian, and British flags, commemorates a great naval battle that took place just offshore (won by the Americans, led by Commodore Oliver Hazard Perry) in a war that is largely forgotten except by Canadians, the War of 1812.

I grew up on the other side of that lake, in the Niagara Peninsula between Lake Erie and Lake Ontario. That area was the scene of several of the land battles in that war—Queenston Heights and Lundy's Lane, for example—so the War of 1812 is perhaps more familiar to me than even to most other Canadians. The history is long and complicated, but briefly, the Americans declared war on Great Britain because of trade restrictions brought about by the Napoleonic Wars, American merchant sailors being brutally kidnapped into the Royal Navy (the notorious "press gangs"), British support of Native tribes against American expansion, and a possible (though hotly debated to this day) American interest in annexing Canada. (There was no "Canada" then, only a British colony until 1867, but Canadians still like to think "they" beat back the Americans. The truth seems to be that the Americans hoped to hold Canada temporarily, as a kind of "hostage," to reinforce their *other* demands. The war was settled in 1814 by the Treaty of Ghent,

Put-in-Bay, Ohio

which left all borders as they were, so the Americans did not seem very interested in annexing Canada.)

Historical highlights of the War of 1812 that *are* better remembered by Americans include the Battle of New Orleans (hit song by Johnny Horton in 1959), the burning of the White House and Capitol, the Battle of Baltimore (which inspired "The Star-Spangled Banner"), and the Battle of Lake Erie. That naval encounter alone is quite a story, for interested readers. (In tangents that might not be of general interest, I have learned to be content to plant a seed of curiosity, and let it grow where it will.)

Our travels between shows in early summer 2013 also took Michael and me through parts of Indiana and Iowa on "days like these" that were mostly sunny, or at least *dry*—though we passed many swollen brown rivers and signs of recent flooding. Even in such relatively flat states, the true backroads remain surprisingly twisty,

Rounding the corn in Indiana

because they trace around old property lines between corn and soybean fields in ninety-degree angles, rather than blasting straight through them in the modern fashion.

And speaking of modern fashions, Michael and I also traveled through a lot of Amish country, especially in Ohio and Indiana. I have been fascinated by the "plain people" since my first encounter with them, on the Fourth of July, 1984. On that day off between shows in

Indianapolis and Cleveland, I was riding through Ohio on my bicycle, on my first ever "Century" (100-mile day), and I noticed that the Amish farmers driving horse-drawn plows waved to me, as a fellow "non-mechanized" person.

In my motorcycle travels since then, I have observed the various enclaves of Amish and old-order Mennonites with a mix of curiosity and amazement—that they can live that way in today's world, and that

they *choose* to. Like the Mennonites, Mormons, and Scientologists, the Amish grew out of the vision of a single charismatic individual—Jakob Amman, in this case—and in all these out-of-the-mainstream faiths, and some similarly restrictive societies like Ultra-Orthodox Judaism, it is truly astonishing to see such complete adherence to principles (often *inconvenient* principles, if not downright nutty) laid down centuries ago by one man who claimed to know God's will, and convinced others that he did.

One fun fact is that Amish men wear beards but not mustaches because those are associated with European military officers and militarism in general. The Amish do not fight in wars or take part in any violence, even in self-defense. But if they do not make war, they certainly make love. The Amish are among the fastest-growing populations in the world, with an average of seven children per family.

A few years ago in Pennsylvania, Michael and I came up behind an Amish buggy, and while we waited to pass, we returned waves from two young boys in the back wearing flat-brimmed straw hats, plain blue shirts, and suspenders. Michael said later that he wanted to buy those two boys BMW GS motorcycles, but what I have always wanted is a photograph of me passing an Amish carriage.

Michael wants to change the world—I just want to capture it. With me *in* it.

Ahead of us on an Ohio country road, I saw the dark shape of a horse-drawn buggy (with its government-mandated Slow-Moving Vehicle triangle, which the Amish communities resisted strongly, and some sects still do—though these days you see more "progressive" buggies with reflective tape and even battery-powered flashing lights). I stopped Michael and sent him ahead to set up with his camera, then waited until he was ready before passing the buggy.

In retrospect, now that I see it was a young woman with her baby,

I feel a little guilty. She was not in any danger from us, but she might have *felt* she was, and that's bad enough. (In Roadcraft, as in life, the Three Deadly Sins against others are: 1) Causing Pain, 2) Causing Fear, and 3) Causing Worry.)

Two louts on motorcycles buzzing around would have made her nervous, because it is sadly true that the "plain people" are sometimes tormented by the outsiders they group together as "the English," and I

am sorry about that. (But I guess she'll probably never read my apology—too bad, in more ways than one.)

(Incidentally, I'm sure the plastic baby-seat must also be an unwilling concession to state law—the Amish don't do plastic—but what about her tinted glasses?)

I did know that the rumored Amish aversion to photography is not about *being* photographed—stealing their souls or anything like that. They are only forbidden to *pose* for photographs, which would be considered vain.

I kind of feel the same way about posing for photographs (especially with strangers)—but I know when to make an exception. On the night of our show at an amphitheater outside Chicago, some players from the Chicago Blackhawks, who had recently won the National Hockey League's Stanley Cup, brought the actual Cup out onstage in "YYZ," toward the end of our show.

I knew in advance about the event, so during the second set I wore one of the hats I had made for the "Hockey Theme" project (see "Fire on Ice" in *Far and Away* for more context on the momentousness of this occasion), with the logos of the "Original Six" NHL teams. I turned the Chicago logo to face prominently front and center and, during the show, had to smile for John "Boom-Boom" Arrowsmith's close-up.

The last five shows of this run were in Eastern Canada, and after crossing the border on the bus in Sarnia, Ontario, and parking in the local Château Walmart, Michael and I unloaded the bikes from the trailer and rode north to catch a ferry to Manitoulin Island. Brutus had been riding east from Alberta and would meet us there that night—the West Side Beemer Boyz reunited again, and riding

together for a few days—as only happens in Canada. During the following days off between shows in Hamilton, Ottawa, Quebec City, and two in Halifax, the three of us had some fantastic rides, with weather varying from rainy in Ontario to hot and sunny in Nova Scotia, and we stayed in the kind of pleasurable, treasurable accommodations only Brutus can discover.

The only dark spot was the Quebec City show. It was held outdoors in a vast open area—another famous battleground, the Plains of Abraham, from a battle between the French and English in 1759. It was just one theater of the Seven Years War—perhaps the *real* World War I, as it involved most of the Western Powers. (In Voltaire's satirical novel *Candide*, published in 1758, he described the North American part of this war by saying they were fighting over *"quelques arpents de neige"*—some acres of snow.) That war's effect on Canada's history will come into this story again, when we finally "return" to the ending, Balancing Rock in Nova Scotia.

With something like 40,000 people in front of us—making more of a *landscape* than an audience—the first set went very well. During intermission, Geddy remarked how much he enjoyed playing these

The scenic route
to Quebec City

festival-style shows. (We had recently played similar events in Ottawa and Sweden.) He liked how the younger fans were able to make their way up front, instead of the older (and wealthier) people buying up the front rows, and the overall energy and excitement in such a setting.

I agreed, but said, "The weather always makes me nervous."

During the second set, just before we began "The Garden," I started to see flurries of raindrops in the spotlight beams over the crowd. As we launched into the song, the wind gusted up, swirling rain all through the colored lightbeams flashing around the stage. Behind the vast crowd in front of me, lightning flickered in the distant darkness. Raindrops covered my cymbals enough to dampen their sound (literally and figuratively), and striking a crash cymbal sent a colorful fountain into the air. Of greatest concern were the exposed electronics—keyboards and foot pedals—and the delicate violins and cellos. (Later cellist Jacob told us, "If it had been anyone but you guys, I would have been *off* that stage.") Just as we finished the song, monitor engineer Brent's voice came over our ear monitors, "The show is *over*. A storm is right on us. Make an announcement, and get off the stage."

In front of the stage,
pre-show, Quebec City

Hard to believe that in almost forty years, we had never had to stop a show in the middle like that. Only once, a couple of tours ago in Chicago, had an outdoor show been called just minutes before we were supposed to go onstage. (We made that one up later.) But never once in all those years had we stopped a show in the middle—so we had no *policy.*

I ran offstage, following the usual series of backstage flashlights from Donovan, Tony, and Michael, climbed onto my bus, and started to change out of my sweaty clothes. Dave aimed the bus toward the next show's dropoff point, while Alex and Geddy, in their cars, drove off to the airport to fly home for the night. The three of us took Brent's words at face value, "The show is *over*," and although it was extremely strange for us, and we regretted the *coitus interruptus*, we didn't feel we had cheated anyone. We had played at least three-quarters of the show, close to three hours—more than many performers give. And I must admit it felt nice to have "The Garden" reverberating in my brain after the show for a change, instead of the chaotic burnout at the end of 2112.

But unfortunately, there was some unpleasant fallout the next day. Geddy had made a quick announcement before we ran, but it must be remembered that Quebec in general is ninety percent francophone, and Quebec City closer to one hundred percent—and no one came out to explain the situation in French.

It turned out that the storm veered away, and the rain stopped after fifteen or twenty minutes. Some bands on other stages resumed their performances, as we might have done if we were there. The Quebec City press spread the impression that it had been Geddy *personally* who had stopped the show, which was wrong and misleading.

So . . . the next day we issued a public apology, and even went so far as to record the six songs we had missed playing that night at the next show in Halifax, then gave them free to a Quebec City rock station. Nothing more we could do.

Early the following morning, Brutus, Michael, and I stopped for gas, as we do every 200 miles or so, and were captured in a rare photograph (because riders like us just wouldn't think of snapping a photo at a gas stop).

Fuel stop

(Brutus, incidentally, was riding the fourth of my GS bikes, Geezer IV, which made its debut on the R-30 tour, then was sold to him a few years ago. I am on my newest bike, Geezer VII, with Geezer VI in the trailer for backup. Geezer V, with just over 50,000 miles, was just sold to one of our truck drivers, Don Johnson, and Geezer III belongs to our artist liaison man, Kevin Ripa. Because I look after my motorcycles so carefully, I am always glad to pass them down through the family when it's time to upgrade.)

Having lost an hour passing into Atlantic time, and with a ferry to catch, we had set off obscenely early from the bus in Woodstock, New Brunswick. An hour or so later—still only about 8:00—we pulled off the Trans-Canada Highway for gas and saw two of the crew buses pulling in behind us. One of the drivers, Lashawn, snapped this little portrait. We joked that we wanted her to wake up the crew for an inspection by the boss, and she said, "They just went to bed about an hour ago."

It was strange to contemplate, but we had been getting up when they were going to sleep. However, their hours were different—on show days, a few hours longer than mine on both sides of the night. Lashawn also remarked that it was the first time she'd seen me since the beginning of the tour. Some of us in the touring vortex (sixty-five of us, this time) were on such different schedules that we *never* saw each other—except at our end-of-tour bowling parties.

Over the years, both Brutus and Michael, as my riding partners, had encountered the perception from other crew members that they were just "joyriders"—looked down upon because all they did was follow me around on motorcycles. They didn't have *real* jobs, like the techs and drivers. I understood how it might appear that way, from a distance, but the reality was different—typically seven hours a day on the road, plus the shows, and no days off. Michael, Brutus, and I certainly knew, as I wrote in a previous story, "Serious traveling is hard work."

The coast of Acadie

Or as the great American journalist Ernie Pyle used to say when describing someone's difficult job, "Try it sometime."

That day would offer its own little drama, too. After waiting in line for the ferry to board in Saint John, I started up my motorcycle and saw the tire-pressure warning light flashing, showing that I was down from 42 pounds to 30 in the rear tire. I knew what that meant—a nail or a screw in the tire causing a slow leak. But how slow? For the entire two-hour crossing, I was mentally prepared to return to the car deck and find a flat tire. I would have to push the bike off the boat, then try to find the puncture (seldom easy) and plug it, and we still had far to go.

Riding off the ferry, the indicator showed 20 pounds remaining. Better than none, but too low for safety. I rode delicately to the nearest gas station and pumped it up again. Within a half-hour, it was back down into the twenties, and I stopped again for a refill. From then on, there were no more gas stations all the way to our remote lodge in the Nova Scotia outback, part of it on a road called the Evangeline Trail.

Another big story . . . but briefly stated, when the British defeated the French in that Seven Years War, they gave the French settlers in Canada a choice: swear allegiance to the British king, or get out. Those that departed were called the Acadians (after a French village called La Cady, apparently), and they settled in Louisiana—where they became the Cajuns.

West Side Beemer Boyz,
Trout Point, Nova Scotia

*Evangeline: A Tale of Acadie* is an epic poem by Longfellow, set during and after the Acadians' expulsion. So we were in Acadia, which clung to its dwindling French heritage in music, a regional flag, and even language. On a previous journey Brutus and I had stopped in nearby villages where even young people spoke a unique, antiquated French.

All through that ninety-minute ride, my eyes were glancing at the number on the tire pressure indicator, watching it fall. However, I was relieved to see that lower pressure seemed to escape more slowly, and it held at a safe level (for cautious riding) until we arrived. Once we were parked in front of our cabin, Michael and I found the nail, pulled it out, and plugged the hole. It would hold temporarily, but only until we could get the tire replaced. When you only have two tires under you, you don't take chances. And that's when it's good to have a backup bike in the trailer—Geezer VI.

The two shows in Nova Scotia separated by a day off gave us a rare chance to stay in one place for more than one night. The cabin at Trout Point was a few hours away from Halifax, on roads that I wouldn't advise for a bus and trailer, so after the first show we slept on the bus at the Château Walmart in Digby. In the morning, we rode out on the pilgrimage to Balancing Rock, and back early to Trout Point in time for a swim.

The little lake was exactly the color of The Macallan eighteen-year-old single malt whisky, in this case tinted by peat rather than sherry casks. It reminded me of the lines from the great hobo classic by Harry McClintock, "Big Rock Candy Mountains," which defines a hobo's paradise, with such attractions as "cigarette trees" and "lemonade springs."

*There's a lake of stew,*
*And of whisky too.*
*You can paddle all around 'em*
*In a big canoe,*
*In the big Rock Candy Mountains.*

So I floated in the whisky lake, feeling muscle-sore and bone-weary. (An observation about this tour that made me smile: Show-day mornings start with a multivitamin, while post-show mornings start with Advil.) It had been a difficult few weeks, with twelve demanding shows and 4,235 miles of motorcycling, on all kinds of roads and in all kinds of weather.

Not for the first time, I allowed myself the brief fantasy that I could just stay in a place like that, soaking in the whisky (inside and out), hiding out from the world, and from work, and not feeling any more pain.

*Oh, I'm bound to stay*
*Where you sleep all day*
*Where they hung the jerk*
*That invented work*
*In the Big Rock Candy Mountains*

(Love that line, "Where they hung the jerk/ that invented work." And from the 1920s!)

There were other sources of pain stirring in me, too. Not to put too fine a point on it, but I tend to forget that much of Ontario is haunted for me. Shadowlands. I can face memories from a story that ended badly when I'm *prepared* for them—but in Ontario it was always too easy to be struck out of nowhere. Between the Hamilton and Ottawa shows, riding into our lakeside resort in Algonquin Park, I saw a sign

The Macallan 18 lake

for the summer camp that Selena had gone to in her teens, and where we had visited her. It didn't hit me immediately, but later, sitting alone by Little Joe Lake, it beat me up pretty bad.

The band had recently been overseeing a remixed version of our *Vapor Trails* album, from 2002, as we had never been happy with how it turned out. I found that trying to listen to those songs again was too upsetting, taking me back to a mindset and emotional state that hadn't been good to live through then, or to relive now. I had to "recuse" myself from those judgments, and the Guys at Work understood, of course.

Floating in the lake of Mac 18, I looked around at the wooded shore of pines, tamaracks, and black spruce—perhaps the signature tree of Canada's Atlantic Provinces, with a uniquely pungent smell from rural chimneys. I thought about trees and their growth rings—how botanists can retrace the annual history of what a given tree has experienced and endured in its entire lifetime. Dry years, wet years, insect infestations, maybe the scattered wildfire or lightning strike, all printed in the growth rings.

Quebec scenic route

It occurs to me that we humans have our growth rings, too, and like even the mightiest old tree, the heartwood retains the memory of being a fragile little sapling.

But we don't dwell in those times, or in those Shadowlands.

We live on days like these . . .

# 15

# IT'S NOT OVER WHEN IT'S OVER

AUGUST 2013

**Once again I find myself** beginning a story at the end. Maybe it's my new style. Maybe it's just my age—laying things out according to *freshness* rather than chronology.

Here Michael and I are riding into the rainy load-in area behind the arena in Kansas City, before the final show of the *Clockwork Angels* tour, on August 4, 2013. (Photo by Mac McLear, our lead truck driver since . . . 1977!) Later that day, when I added up my mileages for the tour, I learned that with Michael, Brutus, and occasional guest riders, I had ridden my motorcycle over 28,000 miles between those seventy-two shows.

Last day at work,
Kansas City

Flaming Gorge,
Wyoming

As always, completing the final ride was a stirring moment. I swung my leg over the saddle for the last time with a palpable sense of . . . complicated emotions. Something like a sandwich of whole-grain pride and satisfaction, around a thick wedge of weariness, and a side of relief. A phrase I came up with years ago rings ever more true: "When I am riding my motorcycle, I am glad to be alive. When I *stop* riding my motorcycle, I am glad to be alive."

That afternoon I asked bus driver Dave about his mileage for the tour, taking direct routes between the shows. Even discounting the 3,000 miles Brutus and I rode in Europe, with a different bus, my two-wheeled traveler had covered 5,000 miles more than the buses and trucks.

And oh, the places I had gone . . .

(My motorcycle and I are a tiny dot in the middle of this "far and away" photograph, a majestic panorama hazed by a forest fire Michael and I had ridden through a few days before.)

Lately the phrase "It's not over when it's over" has become another one of those endlessly resonant and applicable mantras—like "On Days Like These" in the previous story. The twist, and possible addendum, to Yogi Berra's famous quote "It ain't over till it's over" applies to many of the situations in my touring life—and perhaps beyond. Like the end of a show, the end of a day's motorcycle ride, or the end of a long, hard tour.

In the early summer of 2013, as we approached the end of the tour, friends outside the touring vortex were saying things like, "It's almost over now," "Only six more to go," or "I bet you can't wait for that last show."

Well, yes—but in reality, it's not like you play the last note of the last show and suddenly feel perfectly wonderful. Oh no. And even one show is a serious barrier between "being" and "nothingness" (in a good way!). Sustaining that performance edge, giving everything you have every night (or every second night), is a "constant loss" system. You can't possibly replenish the expended energy, so the reserves just gradually deplete.

"Hi, Craiggie!"

Same after each show—I don't suddenly feel good just because it's over. There are wet clothes to peel out of and hang up (hat on one closet handle, shirt on another, pants on another, socks draped over my riding boots), all on a moving bus that's often jostling out of a parking lot onto bumpy city streets, with sudden stops and turns. Bad words are sometimes spoken.

Towel off the sweat, dig out a dry T-shirt, and gather the towels to bring to the front lounge to sit on (bus-surfing all the way against swaying and bouncing), and to continue drying the still-oozing sweat on my forehead. Then sit and put my feet up on the opposite bench for that precious first drink and smoke, as the previously ignored pain starts to blossom all over my body.

When the tour is over, for real, I will be so drained and strained that it will be many weeks before mind and body start to return to some kind of "equilibrium"—when the pain subsides and the mental tension begins to ease. My drumming is an athletic activity, no question, which requires months of preparation. The process of relaxing means letting that go—getting *out* of shape. That can be nearly as painful as getting *into* shape. Day after day, each muscle group takes its turn to release its tension and fatigue, and I will feel it all unwind.

But what a truly *triumphant* tour it was!

The emotional resonance of the final show, in Kansas City, inside us and around us, could only compare to the first show of our *Vapor Trails* tour, in Hartford, Connecticut, on June 28, 2002. That "new beginning" came after five intensely difficult years since our last performance on July 4, 1997. When that Hartford show was over, I said to our manager, Ray, "It would have been a shame if *that* had never happened again." He smiled and nodded, and we raised our glasses of champagne.

Eleven years later, that August night in Kansas City was the ultimate tour-ending show in all our thirty-nine years of "roadwork."

The Clockwork Angels
String Ensemble,
"As if to Fly"

It affected us in ways we could never have expected, and most of that emotion was centered on the Clockwork Angels String Ensemble. Usually the Guys at Work, band and crew, finish a tour believing it's just a break—that it will all start up again at some point, and we'll all see each other again. All seven of the "stringers" knew that this time it truly was, like the lovely title of a Hemingway story, "The End of Something."

Mario, Adele, Jacob, Audrey, Gerry, Jonny, and Entcho had traveled together, played together, and *lived* together for the better part of a year. In their own words, they had become "a family"—sharing buses, dressing rooms, and stages for all those shows, and the days off between them.

So the final show, in Kansas City, was both triumphant and bittersweet.

The ten musicians on that stage knew that, no matter what, there would never be another performance like that. We gave it everything, and the audience gave it right back. There were tears, all right (I warned Adele, "Don't you start crying, or I will, too. I cry *very* easily!"), but they were happy tears.

At the start of "The Garden," certainly the most emotional song in our set this tour, tiny sparks appeared in the darkness, people holding up hundreds of small electric lights, like fireflies. That added to the magic of the moment, and somehow to its depth of feeling. In Olden Times (the '70s), audiences used to do that with lighters during particularly "intimate" parts of a rock concert, and here was an attractive and touching revival.

Coincidentally, the beginning of "Closer to the Heart" used to be a moment like that in our shows, back in the day, and that song brings another wonderful connection. Just before that Kansas City show, the stringers visited our dressing room and presented the three of us with a CD they had recorded on their own—"Closer to Our Hearts," an intricate string arrangement of our song by cellist Jacob. The disc was packaged with style and detail, accompanied by a signed copy of the score and, of course, an eight-by-ten glossy. They had also collaborated on a framed "award" for each of us, to commemorate the selling of "three copies"—a humorous echo of the Canadian gold records for *Clockwork Angels* we had given to the stringers at an earlier show. Jonny gave a little speech that was heartfelt and funny, and when some of them told us this tour had been the greatest musical experience of their lives, the three of us could only agree. For all of us, after long careers, that was saying something.

At the previous night's end-of-tour bowling party, a tradition going back many tours (and *much* more fun than golf, some of us think), we all had a joyous, even riotous good time. I am not skilled at bowling—or any sports—but at least I *looked* the part, in my Bubba's Bar 'n' Grill bowling shirt. (I received many inquiries about it from crew members, as did truck driver Steve in his matching number. I told them we were sold out of the "normal" sizes, but suggested they *all* be sure to mention it to merch guy Patrick. Later Patrick stopped by my lane and gave me a wry face. I responded with surprised innocence, as he told me we would soon be restocked.)

Actor Paul Rudd spent much of his youth around Kansas City and was visiting at the time of our show—so he joined us for the bowling party. We had kept in touch since our scene together in *I Love You, Man* (2009) and Paul's appearance with Jason Segel in the show-ending movie for our *Time Machine* tour. The bowling alley kicked us out at 9:00, because it was time for the all-important, perhaps even *sacred* "Leagues" to have their turn, and Paul took us to a private room in a friend's bar—with Kansas City truly *rocking* in the streets all around us. What a party town on an uptown Saturday night!

I think it was as late as midnight when Michael and I were heading back to our hotel. (I smiled to pass a huge mural of native son Count Basie, who launched his fiery, stomping big-band sound in Kansas City.) That witching hour was fairly shocking for us West Side Beemer Boyz, who were usually asleep by about 9:30 on nights off— especially lately, with all the long rides in the Intermountain West. With the absurd distances to travel every day, I had been dragging my riding partners (a couple guest riders for those "Big Sky" rides) out of their beds at 6 a.m. to get in a hundred miles or so before breakfast.

(A worthy title: "A Hundred Miles Before Breakfast.")

The bowling party was a crowning event for the sixty-five of us who had worked together on that tour. The camaraderie among band and crew had never been greater, and morale had never been higher. Such happy spirits were not shared among certain other groups of people we encountered on that same night . . .

It happened that the bowling alley was across the street from the arena where we would play the following night, which that night hosted Taylor Swift. Driving up to the bowling alley, we encountered a street thronged with Taylor Swift lookalikes ("Swifties") and many of their less-excited-looking parents. In the middle of all that, a demonstration was being staged (apt word) by the "Christian" group called Westboro Baptist Church. Two prominent signs were "GOD HATES FAGS" and "GOD HATES SLUTS." Not sure under what category they hated Ms. Swift. Comment seems superfluous, but it struck me that their free speech, however hateful and demented, was protected by a cordon of police, on foot and motorcycles.

Oh yes, right—*motorcycles*!

Look at me going on all this time, and I haven't even mentioned the motorcycling!

My travels with Michael, and occasional guest riders, between those shows had their own elements of triumph and physical and emotional strain. This image appears to be a glorious moment—a pre-Raphaelite painting in the forest dawn, as a leather-armored knight manfully negotiates a wilderness path, bathed in "ecclesiastical" light. And it happened to be Sunday morning, too.

Bubba in hallowed light

However, the cause of that "halo effect," which might be the envy of the band's lighting director, Howard, was not the dust of our passage, but smoke from a major forest fire. We were about to ride straight into it, with no idea.

At 6:00 that morning, we pulled out of the motel in Wenatchee, Washington, knowing we had a long way to travel to the show near Portland. Also, an early part of the day's route was one of our "mystery roads"—a long, unpaved stretch I had highlighted on the paper map. Michael's mapping program, Mother, had balked at it, but pro-

duced some kind of route for us to follow. However, we knew from much experience that Mother's interpretation might lead us into abandoned logging roads that were no longer passable, or *barely* so (see "On Days Like These"), or even steel barricades or fallen bridges that would send us back the way we had come.

At least the previous day's mystery road had been a success. Leaving the bus at the Château Walmart in Burlington, Washington, we rode east through North Cascades National Park to the drier side of those mountains. (The word "rainshadow" sounds gloomy, but it means the side that *doesn't* get rain—where it's bright and sunny!)

The weather was superb, the scenery majestic, and the roads winding and entertaining. In early afternoon, we rounded the shore of Lake Chelan, and I saw the GPS route was leading us away on a paved highway. I knew that wasn't right and kept going—my memory of the paper map overruling Mother, both GPS units, Doofus and Dingus, and even Michael. (He is often fooled by Mother that way, when he clicks on two points on my route and expects her to draw the desired line between them. She very well may not. After every episode like that, I wag my finger and scold Michael like a third-grade teacher, "Check your work!") When he didn't appear behind me for a while, I rode back and found him stopped at the side of the road, waiting for me to ride back to him—like he was *sulking*.

North Cascades
National Park

All urgent and confident, he said, "This isn't the right way—I remember from Mother. We were supposed to turn left back at that highway. We have to turn around."

At first I could only look at him. Then I said, "Why do you always get like this near the end of a tour?"

"Like *what?*"

"All argumentative, all stroppy, all negative, all . . . insubordinate. All your 'cognitive dissonance.'"

(One prime example of that psychological mechanism that Michael and I always refer to is when someone is about to be separated from a loved one and picks a fight—so they can go away *mad* instead of sad.)

I impugned his masculinity and said, "We have lots of time and lots of gas—just man up for a few minutes and let's check it out."

That prompted Michael to laugh and add one (actually *two*) more items to the list: "We have time. We have gas. And we have . . ."

Let's say "fortitude." (Michael is so often unprintable, while I strive to keep my contribution to our discourse to the highest standards of decency.)

Climbing Shady Pass, Washington

Where the pavement ended, Michael stopped to talk to a local on an ATV, and the man told him it would take us four hours to get through that way, and that we should backtrack to the highway.

I don't know, I must have been feeling "determined" or something, but it didn't seem that way to me. Right at that point, where the road turned to gravel, a sign read "PRIMITIVE ROAD—NO WARNING SIGNS" (which was warning enough, in its way). More useful was a final sign listing distances and destinations. I recognized Entiat Valley from a town of that name on our route and thought that was a good omen. It was 26 miles away—but 26 miles of *what?*

I switched to the compass screen for navigation and noticed that sometimes we were heading northwest instead of roughly southeast. I too became doubtful, but then the track would swing around again through the pines—vast stretches of them bare gray columns from a forest fire, just greening again in the ground cover.

I also kept an eye on the elevation and saw us climb to about 7,500 feet—the delicious thinness of mountain air and the evergreen fragrance a sensory delight. Here was a fitting answer to Michael's doubt, an antidote to any negativity. Worth turning around after, if necessary.

But despite Michael's trepidation, and the unhelpful Mother (Doofus and Dingus did okay, under the circumstances), Shady Pass proved to be everything it ought to have been—remote and challenging, yet delivering us to our destination.

Shadeless Shady Pass

The next morning was an entirely different definition of "everything it ought to have been." Heading for Portland at 6 a.m. (which always seems like a "nice round number" for this rider), at first we were back on a "PRIMITIVE ROAD," through dense second-growth forest. When we climbed into more open landscapes of sage and juniper, the scenery was magnificent. A few obstacles appeared—like a herd of cows that refused to leave the road, but just galumphed gracelessly ahead of us until we could ease past each one. The route led us down into areas where fresh logging was underway, and the track had been covered with a bed of large, softball-sized stones—a good surface for the massive tires of heavy logging equipment, but not for our little two-wheelers. When we hit an uphill stretch like that, the stones were too big and deep, and we started to have trouble moving forward. My back wheel became trapped between stones that acted like chocks, very hard to power over without losing the front wheel.

Colockum Pass, Washington

Behind me, Michael straddled his bike and circled his hand in the air, the "turnaround" sign. On a day off, I would have followed my hunch that if we could just work our way up that one slope, even if we had to push each other, we'd probably make it through.

But turning back proved to be a wiser decision than I knew.

(Once again, the rider is far and away, a minute dot in the vastness of the Intermountain West.)

We had to circle all the way back to Wenatchee to be able to cross the Columbia River, and programmed Doofus and Dingus to lead us there— glad at least to be following a different road, instead of turning back. Retreating down the same road feels more like defeat. We began to see wisps of smoke ahead—nothing too severe, maybe like small grassfires that had been deliberately set to fertilize the earth. But then I was seeing scattered patches of flaming brown grass right beside our road, the dry flicker almost invisible in the bright sunlight, but the rippling heat-haze and smoke unmistakable. In just another mile, we rode through a scene of blackened desolation, a charred wasteland, and obviously recent. Both sides of the road were completely black with burned vegetation, smoke still wafting here and there. Half-burned utility poles lay across the road, still smoldering, while the wires lay along the shoulder. (Fortunately not *across* the pavement, or we wouldn't have dared to cross them.)

Where transformers had exploded in the heat, the toxic fluids were being absorbed by scatterings of a kitty-litter-like substance—another riding hazard. We passed a couple of destroyed buildings—a mobile home burned to its cross-braced chassis, and a wooden structure left in ashes. Drifts of smoke rose everywhere, resembling the geothermic vents we would soon be seeing in Yellowstone National Park. Later we learned that the fire had started right there, only the previous morning, and had now moved on to . . . where we were heading.

A couple of police SUVs with flashing lights approached, and I pulled to the side. A hefty sheriff with a smoke-yellowed mustache asked me where we were coming from. I explained as best I could, with much pointing in different directions.

He got all gruff with me. "You head straight down this road, but *very slowly*, watching for utility and firefighter vehicles. And you find somewhere *else* to ride."

We started passing firefighting personnel carriers from all over Washington State, even Seattle and little Vashon Island, and the firefighters in their yellow "work clothes." Amid the devastation, a couple of houses had been saved—oases of green lawns around them. One detachment was guarding a roadblock to stop all traffic from entering the area—the very region through which we had just blithely ridden.

Here is the scene of the *real* fire, as seen from across the Columbia River—very near a remote amphitheater called The Gorge that we had played a few times. (The last show on our *Time Machine* tour, for one, on July 4, 2011.)

Good thing we weren't booked there that night, because that show would have been canceled for sure. Apart from the venue being downwind of the massive fire, with the sky filling with dense smoke, the deep, rugged river gorge was also clouded with thick, roiling banks of white smoke. To the right in this photograph are the blackened sides of the Columbia Gorge, exactly where we emerged, and clearly burned over the previous day (the fire had first been reported that morning) in the inferno's inexorable passage. The so-called Colockum Tarps fire became big news in subsequent days, eventually destroying over 80,000 acres. As we circled around to the south on the interstate, the visibility was reduced to riding through a thick fog.

And talk about "not over when it's over," think about forest fires, their effects often calamitous and enduring.

And what about *floods*? Which brings this story right back to the beginning. (Love it when that happens.) The first show of this final run had been scheduled for July 24 in Calgary, but just a few weeks earlier that city endured a massive flood. The arena we were sup-posed to play in was underwater up to the tenth row.

It was fairly certain we would not be playing *that* building, but rather than cancel our show, I suggested to the Guys at Work and manager Ray that we move it somewhere else, to higher ground—maybe outdoors—and play a benefit for those people who had lost so much. Everybody readily agreed, and Ray set about making it happen. It turned out that nowhere in Calgary itself was going to work, and the considered alternatives of Lethbridge, Alberta, and Kelowna, British Columbia, were rejected in favor of . . . Red Deer, Alberta.

Dead Rear, Red Deer

(I love bringing up place names like these to American readers. I know they're all, like, "What?" Incidentally, to locals, or perhaps typically competitive neighboring towns, Red Deer is "Dead Rear," as Calgary is "Cowfart.")

At least the arena in Red Deer could accommodate our production—the whole superstructure of sound, lighting, and rear-screen technology that surrounds the stage. That is no small concern, or limitation—what usually happens is that the rear screen gets squashed very low behind us. These days some historic stages like Red Rocks in Colorado and the legendary Hollywood Bowl can no longer fit our show. (A touching sign I saw held up in the arena audience in Denver: "I'M PRETENDING I'M AT RED ROCKS.") Maybe sometime we'll bring a smaller one. (Doubt it—"Can't stop thinking big" and all that.)

However noble our motives, even what should have been our golden karma could not prevent that show from throwing up a unique challenge just before showtime. In "On Days Like These," I wrote about leaving the stage mid-show in Quebec City because of a looming storm, and how in thirty-nine years we had never once stopped a show like that. Well, this would be the first time in thirty-nine years we ever played without *monitors*!

Just before showtime, we were informed that the monitor board was down and being worked on feverishly. There would certainly be a delay in starting the show. The possibility of having to cancel *this* show, out of any of them—a benefit for many worthy causes that would eventually raise over half a million dollars to help them—seemed a particularly cruel twist of fate. I tried to think how we might possibly work around it. Half-joking, I said, "Oh never mind—we'll just play to the house mix."

A little later, Geddy said, "It looks like you might get your wish."

Not exactly my *wish*!

Yikes!

Talk about a juggling act! To explain what that actually *meant*, each of our pairs of in-ear monitors receives a unique mix of "information." For myself, I have an ever-changing blend that always includes drums and vocals, and usually bass and guitar, but sometimes eliminates those so I can concentrate on a sequence of keyboard patterns or vocal effects that I need to play in sync with—and set up the tempo for in advance, perhaps the biggest challenge of all.

Changes like that might be programmed not just for every song, but maybe a dozen different *sections* of each song. I had a *lot* to hold together—especially when the strings were onstage with us. I had to lay down a foundation for nine other musicians.

The other guys might need to hear more high-hat in a particular passage, or more bass drum, or vocals—not to mention countless hours spent refining the perfect balance and stereo placement of each of Alex's 4,000 effects. In the "house mix," these elements are all blended, with lead vocals and guitars to the fore. The things I need to be in sync with are just background textures, barely audible.

But . . . we did it! For the first set, anyway, because the audio crew was able to get the mixing board fixed in time for the second set. (Much relief there, on my part—and others' too, I'm sure.) But that first set was quite an "adventure" all right, more an exercise in *imagination*—trying to aurally picture what I was supposed to be hearing. As I said to the Guys at Work during intermission, "My poor brain! I think we got through it okay—but I wouldn't want to hear a *recording* of it!"

And once again I have let *musical* adventures distract us from our motorcycle travels. They sure weren't any less dramatic.

In the early weeks of 2013, I first received Ray's plan for the upcoming shows. Right away I saw a rare two days off in a row, and in the West!—between Portland and Salt Lake City. Ooh, that would set me up for any number of possible landscapes in the Intermountain West. Picturing the area on my mental map, I fixed on two touchstones—Glacier National Park in Montana, and Yellowstone National Park in Wyoming.

A little preliminary figuring showed that hitting those destinations over two days ought to be "possible"—but that would depend on how you define "possible." It began with a five-hour bus ride from Portland to La Grande, Oregon. After sleeping in the Château Walmart, we unloaded the bikes (with guest rider Chris Stankee from Sabian on my backup bike, Geezer VI) and set off painfully early to ride 523 miles. That would be a long day on any road, but not one of those miles was interstate. It was all challenging two-lanes, mostly through mountainous terrain, with lots of technically demanding riding.

Flathead Lake,
Montana

Crossing the ranching and haymaking country in Idaho and Montana, I observed the people living that life and considered the similarities and contrasts between them and their southern counterparts in Texas. On both sides of that divide, everything was "big"—country, sky, hats, boots, belt-buckles, and pickups—but there were differences. A double portrait would be worth researching, but one generality is that the Northern "costumes" were less fancy, especially for townspeople—fewer of the kind of Westernized city-folk that Texans themselves refer to as "all hat and no cattle."

And, for the past twenty years I have noticed that little "espresso huts" are common all around the Northwest (not just Seattle—but all the way east to rural Idaho and Montana), with pickups lined up for their morning "jolt." You don't see that in Texas.

All around us that day, I noticed the usually pin-sharp, super-high-resolution landscapes were hazy, from the smoke spreading downwind from that Washington fire we had "experienced."

It was a punishing day, but a necessary price for a worthwhile goal. That evening found our three motorcycles parked in front of a delightful row of cabins along a blue-green river, on the western side of Glacier National Park. (Earlier in the tour, knowing of my plans to hit more national parks, Michael had bought us each annual passes—how proud I was to stop at the gate and display that, to be the kind of person who has an annual pass to America's national parks.)

Those cabins had been booked about three months in advance. Usually I like to ramble around for the day, and just pick someplace to settle down when it gets to be near cocktail time. However, that carefree approach would not be possible in midsummer, in some of the most popular national parks in the country. Every motel and campground we passed in those parts was marked "FULL."

I do believe in magic, but know that often it requires some *planning*.

Years ago I tried to ride through Colorado's Rocky Mountain National Park with Brian Catterson on a midsummer afternoon, and it was a big . . . no.

Like being in a freeway traffic jam, with nicer scenery.

Glacier National Park, Montana

My plan was to stage us just outside the parks, then ride through them at 6 a.m., before the freight trains of RVs and plodding "processions" of motorcycle cruisers could clog the roads. Glad to say, it was a sound plan, and we were able to experience the magic of those parks with all the space and time the season could allow.

If magic can be prepared for, so too can its opposite—at least to some degree. The red containers of gasoline on the back of my and Chris's bikes came in handy that day, in the wide-open country of Montana. We crossed Glacier on the famous Going-to-the-Sun Highway, one of a very few roads in all North America (and the world) that were built just to carry people to scenery. The Columbia Gorge

Parkway in Oregon, Pikes Peak and Mount Evans in Colorado, the Blue Ridge Parkway in the Appalachians, the Natchez Trace in the Mid-South, and the Mount Washington Auto Road in New Hampshire are a few other examples. Nearly all roads follow a simple formula I came up with years ago, wondering about a remote road in Idaho that ended at a mountaintop. In that case, there had once been a mine at that summit, and it suggested a relation that proves generally true, "Every road has money at one end, and a bank at the other." (Come to think of it, most of those "scenic" roads have tolls—so there's still money at one end and a bank at the other.) Road numbers in rural parts of Texas are prefaced with "FM," for "Farm to Market"—a plain example of that principle.

(Ah—but which is the "bank," the farm or the market?)

From Glacier down to Yellowstone was another long, two-lane day—440 miles, much of it across a prairie landscape, with even a decent stretch of gravel. The Canadian side of Glacier National Park, in Alberta, is called Waterton Lakes National Park (together forming an "International Peace Park"). Waterton's slogan is "Where the Mountains Meet the Prairie," and the same was true heading south through Montana to Wyoming. Rugged gray mountains on one side, brown-grass prairie on the other—the skies, alas, still hazy from "our" forest fire. They were blue above, but white and fuzzy around the horizon.

At a gas stop, Michael was excited to tell us how he had seen bears crossing the road, a mother with two cubs, and in the park we had all seen moose, bighorn sheep, and deer. Always nice to see big animals, but that day, the wildest part was going to be the *weather*.

Late in the day, as we neared our destination of Gardiner, Montana, dark mountains rose up to blockade the southern horizon, and looming above the peaks were even darker curtains of rain. For the last hour or so, we would surrender to a slower "rain pace" down the valley to Gardiner, just on the edge of Yellowstone National Park. Like the previous night, it was a carefully planned destination, and proved to be a great one—a tour favorite. Our cozy little cabins were a short walk from the small town's selection of restaurants, which is a rare and much-appreciated treat in such mountain towns, like Gunnison, Colorado (which we would also revisit in days to come); Littleton, New Hampshire; or Logan, Utah.

The following day would be the longest distance I think I have ever tried to cover on a show day—440 miles. Thinking of the adage, "He travels fastest who travels alone," I suggested to Michael that I

Montana hayfields

head out on my own, early, with him and Chris behind me in case of any trouble. They could linger over the tourist attractions, like Old Faithful, that I had seen before, but would cost me too much time on this journey. I told them, "You've probably known about Old Faithful since you were about eight—and when will you get another chance?"

And anyway—I enjoy riding alone (though the *end* of the ride is more fun with others). Maybe by that point in the tour, I pined just to be *alone* for a while.

But Michael wasn't having that, especially on a show day. We agreed to get up at 6:00 and start riding, and see about breakfast later. However, when I met Chris in the twilit parking area, Michael had already set out, riding straight for Salt Lake City. That didn't make sense to me, but I presumed he had his "reasons."

In any case, I soon forgot about that, because as soon as I started rolling, the tire-pressure warning light flashed yellow, then red, show-ing that my rear tire was dangerously low. "Not again!" I thought, after going through the same thing in Nova Scotia a few weeks ago. Punctured tires just aren't that common these days. I waved to Chris and pointed to the gas station across the

1,000 hard miles in two days . . .

street, where we filled the tire and our tanks. Many times in the past, I had been able to limp through a day with a slow leak, sometimes—like in Mexico—having to carry on like that for a couple of days until I could get the tire replaced. (Screws, for example, hold pretty well—big nails, not so much.) Plugging is possible, and I carried the kit for it, but it's sometimes troublesome, and not always effective. I would save that option for if it became unavoidable.

I kept to the intended route, riding south through Yellowstone's dense pinewoods, on a chilly morning (just above freezing) and often foggy. The pace was slow anyway, as we always had to be ready for unexpected obstacles on the road—like large animals. Unlike my pre-vious visit (see "A Little Yellow Cabin on Yellowstone Lake" in *Far and Away*), we did not see any bison, but occasionally I could *smell* their funky pungence. (Think "sweaty horse" times ten.) We arrived at Old Faithful (not that "faithful" these days—an eruption can only be pre-dicted by the time and intensity of the previous one), too early for the Visitor Center to be open, so no passport stamp—I had to get one at the ranger station on the way out of the park.

We carried on south past Grand Teton National Park, my rear tire still holding its air pretty well. In Jackson, Wyoming—one of those gold-plated Western towns like Sun Valley, Idaho, or Aspen, Colorado, where the streets are lined with Swarovski crystals—I filled up with air one more time.

We had made it almost 300 miles when the road started to descend, and the temperature rose into the nineties. The heat seemed to accelerate the leak, and in the vast, treeless Great Basin country of sage and juniper shrubs, with just a solitary cow here and there (the kind of rangeland that needs an average of forty acres to feed one cow), gas stations were long distances apart. The day's tension kept mounting, and I hoped the tire wasn't about to fail utterly and force me to commandeer Geezer VI from Chris and leave him in the scorched sage to await a flatbed. The GPS listings showed a Sinclair gas station in nearby Randolph, Utah, and we headed for it. This was it—we would have to try to plug the tire, then hope to carry on.

Grand Tetons

At least the big shiny nail wasn't hard to find, embedded in the black treads. Unlike the thin one I had saved from Nova Scotia, this Montana specimen was a monster—about four inches long, and an eighth thick. When I grasped its crushed head with the Leatherman pliers and pulled it out, the remaining air escaped in one quick sigh. It was a big hole. Chris and I wrestled the plug in, but when we put a quarter in the air compressor (really?), it wouldn't hold air.

Chris said, "You want to try another plug?"

I shook my head. "No—I'm afraid we're done." I had faced this situation before, and knew two plugs were not going to help.

Chris, "a good man in a storm," understood what had to happen. While I shifted my belongings to Geezer VI, he was on the phone to Michael, who was already waiting for us at the BMW dealer in Salt Lake City. They would send out a truck and trailer to pick up Geezer VII—and Chris. I gave him a hug and said, "I'm sorry."

He said, "Hey—we know about 'nails in the road.'"

Well said! Yes we did, literally and metaphorically.

Leaving Gardiner to ride through Yellowstone that morning, I was hoping to stop for breakfast somewhere later. As things progressed, so to speak, it was almost ten hours later before I sat in the front lounge of the bus, still in most of my riding gear, and devoured a delicious omelette, courtesy of band chef Frenchie.

For a show day, it had truly been "the longest day." As for Chris, after his long day, with plenty of waiting around, he arrived with my repaired bike around showtime, then flew home that night. The Salt Lake City BMW dealer came through big time, working late to replace my rear tire, which was a good thing, because we would have another guest rider for the next couple of days, John Wesley—"Wes"—guitarist and vocalist with Porcupine Tree, and on his own solo work.

Flaming Gorge, Wyoming

Truth to tell, I was really about ready for a rest from riding—from everything—but there was only one more "big" ride, and I couldn't imagine missing it. With a day off between Salt Lake City and Denver, and those landscapes and roads—the most excellent thing I could do that day was not sleep on the bus and hang out in a hotel room.

From a truck stop in Green River, Wyoming (what—no Château Walmart?), Wes, Michael, and I set off south through the Flaming Gorge country—named for the late-afternoon sun reddening the cliffs, by another John Wesley, Powell, a one-armed Civil War veteran who explored much of the Southwest. Powell and his party were good place-namers, too. Making the first known descent of the Colorado River in 1869, through the Grand Canyon, they named one waterway Dirty Devil Creek, after a companion with dubious hygiene. Farther along, to atone for their possible blasphemy, they called another creek the Bright Angel. (Still the name of a lodge on the South Rim.)

Down through a corner of Utah, we crossed into Colorado, occasionally slowed by rain and wet pavement. Late in the day we found ourselves on a truly wonderful road, Colorado 92, high, winding, and lightly traveled, traversing the interior flank of Black Canyon of the Gunnison National Park.

Later, we dodged or endured occasional rain showers down and around to the town of Gunnison. From a stay there with Brian Catterson five years previously, I remembered a charming motel, the Swiss Inn. That day Michael had tried to call it a few times, but the

Colorado 92

phone just rang. When we got there, the business was obviously shut down. Tell-tale weeds were creeping up through the asphalt (a sure sign of neglect), so it hadn't been open all that summer, at least. Yet after we settled across the highway at the Western Motel, we looked over at the tall sign reading Swiss Inn. It was still lighted, even to the bright red neon of the "NO VACANCY" sign below, and small white lights outside each door welcomed . . . nobody.

I could only guess it had been a sudden and unresolved closing—like if the owner had died (the previous time a gray-haired old lady checked us in), and no one had got around to shutting things down yet.

It was the second time this tour we had observed that . . . motel entropy. (Title!) Whenever I am riding from the Eastern U.S. toward Toronto, I like to stop for the night in Cape Vincent, New York, on the south bank of the St. Lawrence River. In the morning, we take a little ferry across to Wolfe Island, Ontario (with the world's smallest border-crossing facility), around it to a larger ferry over to Kingston, then ride on into work. Over several years, I stayed twice at the Buccaneer Inn, a small motel in Cape Vincent run by an elderly couple—but the second time I noticed the man had suffered a stroke. He was doddering around and *trying* to be helpful, while his wife followed, taking care of everything—letting him pretend to help. Sadder yet was the next visit, seeing the place dark and empty.

Clearly the Swiss Inn had been somebody's dream—conceived and nurtured with love. But maybe it's not over—maybe the "right person" will come along and keep that dream alive a little longer. Anything can happen. (I was tempted to put in an offer myself—and make Michael stay there and run it . . . )

*Il Maestro*, Paul Rudd

The next early morning (quite a series now) carried us over Monarch Pass, at 11,312 feet—where Brian Catterson and I had experienced a blizzard, almost exactly five years before (in July!), riding from the Swiss Inn to Denver. Following the same route, Michael, Wes, and I descended into the grassy basin known as South Park, and, as Brian and I had done, stopped for breakfast at a rustic café in Fairplay—one of the "models" for the enduringly brilliant animated series *South Park*. (Perfect coincidence that my bandmates had dined with Matt Stone and his wife in Boulder the previous night.)

Then a short, easy run to the arena in Denver, where I started my show-day duties by changing the oil in both my motorcycles. My older Canadian bike, Geezer VI, would be going on the trailer for the last time, and eventually to my home in Quebec for winter storage—with clean oil. My American bike, Geezer VII, would be trucked back to California after the last show—and after one final easy ride across the backroads of Kansas. Nothing too daring or demanding, a simple valedictory speech—a parade lap.

A *victory* lap.

Which brings us back to the beginning—er, the end.

The final show in Kansas City.

See how I did that?

Because this way, it's over.

But it's never over . . .

# 16

# ANGELS LANDING

NOVEMBER 2013

Zion National Park, Utah

**To open on a positive note**—or positive *chord*, more like, G Major perhaps—this is a portrait of a happy man. And we do not use the word "happy" lightly. The attainment of where he is standing (Angels Landing) will be recounted soon, but the backstory is important, too. The rock combo he had played in for thirty-nine years was on "indefinite hiatus," and his bandmates (the Guys at Work) had agreed not to even *talk* about work for at least a year.

(Just after the band's tour ended, he was enjoying one of the pleasures of being home, the Sunday crossword, and saw this clue: "Rush job?" The answer was "rockconcert," which made him smile—nice tribute!—but also think, "Not for a while!")

So for the first time in over a year, he wasn't counting down the days until his next departure. For the first time in *ten* years, he was free of work obligations and schedules, and for these few days, he was even free of family commitments. Some months ago his wife,

Carrie, announced that she was planning a trip to Chicago and New York City with her mother and their daughter to visit friends of hers, and she asked him to join them. When he thought about airports, luggage, hotels, and big cities, he said, "You know what? I've had enough of all that for a while. You girls go and have a good time. I'll stay home—maybe go on a roadtrip for a few days."

Now I was on the second day of a five-day journey through Southwestern Utah in my new Aston Martin Vanquish. (Ordered the previous year, it was delivered during a break in the tour, so I had only been able to put a few hundred miles on it.) I paused to spend a day hiking in both Zion and Bryce Canyon National Parks, and altogether would drive over 1,500 miles and hike about fifteen—enjoying both to their fullest.

Quoth the Raven,
"Nevermore"

A passing hiker at Angels Landing courteously took my out-stretched camera and snapped the opening shot. While snacking on an apple and some cheese and enjoying the hard-won view, I had heard him speaking German with his two hiking companions. Other people around us spoke French, or had British accents, among the many European and Asian visitors I encountered. They must have been as grateful as I was that the State of Utah had undertaken to reopen its national parks, despite the shameful government "shut-down." I had been planning my visit for a month, and had a backup plan if the national parks remained closed. But what did these for-eigners think of a country in which a few mean-spirited creeps could hold the entire country hostage—all for the principle of denying mercy to the suffering (because it *might* be "their own fault"—hardly a Christian objection), while also denying its citizens (and "resident aliens," as this Canadian is classified) access to *their* property? (A flash-ing sign inside Bryce Canyon National Park put it nicely: "WELCOME TO BRYCE. ENJOY YOUR PARK.")

These foreign visitors, like the American seniors who also visit the national parks outside the summer months, might have waited all their lives for this one opportunity. And there are tens of thousands of Americans, especially in the West, whose livelihoods are tied to the national parks. (One county in Utah, San Juan, claims seventy percent of its residents depend on the parks for their family income.) As one Utah official said, "It's not like we can miss October and make it up in January."

For this reporter, the politics are one thing—but now it was *per-sonal*. Compacting what could easily become a rant into a brief blast, clearly those few miserable, damaged egos (I almost said "souls," but

Virgin River, Zion

no) in Congress didn't care about any damn foreigners—or their own people. Like renegade bikers and surly rednecks, they ought to wear DILLIGAF T-shirts. Their message is the same: "Do I Look Like I Give a Fornication?"

(The world would be a far better place if their *parents* hadn't!)

That is an expression of pure evil, and those who profess it might as well be vaporized on sight. Apparently about one in every hundred humans is a sociopath—a scary thought. And just such grandiose, cynical, and merciless semi-humans are the ones who would seek power and abuse it.

One way to fight back is to set a better example. During my recent downtime, while I enjoyed spending time at my desk writing stories, I had quietly pledged to try to do something for someone else every day. A former belief in karma got hammered out of me about sixteen years ago, but as I have written since, "Any undamaged individual knows how good it can feel to help others." In this case, nothing big, but a host of small favors. Letters to neglected friends who will appreciate the thought, thank-you notes to strangers for gifts I received on the road, an introduction to brother Danny's book of poetry, or friend Gavin Harrison's book of drum transcriptions, auditioning niece Hannah's "indie acoustic" music and trying to give her some worthwhile encouragement—interactivities like that which demanded time and attention to do properly, and willingly. Because *my* T-shirt and my heart say, "IGAF."

The date of my climb to Angels Landing was October 15, 2013, exactly fifteen years less a day since my one previous visit to the national parks of Southwestern Utah, on my *Ghost Rider* travels. As part of my planning this time, I reread those passages in the book, especially the letters to Brutus and Mendelson Joe from Zion and Bryce Canyon. I had not looked at those pages for many years, ever more unwilling to relive those times, so I was hesitant. Not long ago the book's publisher asked me to record the audiobook, and I said no—I knew it would be an awful task for me. Even auditioning other potential narrators was tough, and a few paragraphs of each were all I could take. I just picked one that seemed good and gave the project my blessing.

Approaching Zion

The scars remain tender. Never, ever healed, but only lightly scabbed over. Time does not heal all wounds, but only allows us to adapt, if we can, to a life that is forever altered. Some wounds are like physical disabilities that will *never* heal, but can only be compensated for, adapted to. Now when I think back to the dark years of the late '90s, I feel far away in time, even unto building a new life and new memories, and my *Ghost Rider* persona seems ever more distant—unknowable. I have come to think of that book's author in the third person—another character in another life. Sometimes I feel the way Robert Pirsig portrays his memories of the man he was before electroconvulsive therapy in *Zen and the Art of Motorcycle Maintenance.*

But opening *Ghost Rider* in the middle, to a time and place with at least *some* positive resonance, and of immediate interest, was tolerable. The tone is somber and occasionally desperate, but not without humor. The style is easy and natural, especially because that part of the book consists mostly of handwritten letters to a "captive audience"—Brutus in a federal prison near Buffalo. (That fall of 1998, he had just been arrested for trying to import a large quantity of herbal remedies from Mexico through the United States into Canada. These days, as ever more states and countries "decriminalize" that herb, we may look upon Brutus as something of a medical pioneer. A regular Jonas Salk.)

It has long puzzled me why *Ghost Rider* is by far my most popular book, when all the others are much cheerier. But at least it has a happy ending (though as remarked in previous stories, that doesn't change what came before—just, at best, "illuminates" it). A friend of

Carrie's lost both her parents within one year, while also learning that her infant son had a rare condition that would severely delay his physical and mental development. When consulting a psychiatrist about how to cope with these tragedies, one of his prescriptions was *Ghost Rider*.

Its author has mixed feelings about that. It is nice to be considered helpful to others on a road I had to travel, but . . . that's one road I could have lived without.

Not looking down

The setting of this story's opening photograph, Angels Landing, is a vertiginous outcropping of rock at 5,875 feet. It is reached by a narrow, perilous trail along a slender sandstone "fin," with drops of over a thousand feet on each side. This photo shows the chains that are bolted into the rock in many sections, as much-needed handholds. Lose your step here and you will fall a long way. A sign at the trailhead offered a grim warning, "Since 2004, six people have died falling from the cliffs on this route."

That gives a cruel twist to Angels Landing.

On first looking over the map of hiking trails and their descriptions in Zion National Park, I recalled that all those years ago I had chosen the trail to Observation Point. Snapshot memories brought back images of climbing high up the canyon wall to the rim, over rounded contours of eroded pink, cream, and brown stone. Waves of rock were smoothed and symmetrically grooved by eons of moving water, where tumbling stones in flashfloods had engraved the sandstone. The all-important lunch stop at Observation Point had offered a stunning view down over the valley floor, where the bends of the Virgin River (a modest stream compared to the torrents that formed that canyon) shone through leafy cottonwoods, green with airbrush bursts of autumn yellow. Nearly always I choose a hike to a high vantage point, whether a summit or an overlook, to enjoy lunch with a view. (And to go *downhill* on the way back.)

This time, my first notion was to repeat that same hike, and why not? But when I looked over the park's other offerings, I saw a trail called Angels Landing—too tempting, following on the recent end of our *Clockwork Angels* tour, and an earlier story titled "The Better Angels." I like themes.

A section of the trail leads over a razor's edge of rock to the summit in the background, 1,400 feet straight down to the valley floor on both sides. Tiny steps have been cut into the sandstone (the trail has been maintained, and traveled, since the 1920s—apparent where

the chains have worn grooves in the rock, like the action of stones in moving water). Those heavy chains on stanchions were *very* welcome, even indispensable. (I wouldn't have tried it without them.) Hauling myself upward with shoulders, arms, and legs made a full-body workout, and I was glad I had been back into my Y routine for a few weeks. (After the tour, I allowed myself a month or so of zero-exertion, but soon *needed* to be active again.) As I climbed, I did not look down, or to either side, just held on and watched where my feet and hands should go.

The trail was fairly crowded, and sometimes it was necessary to pause at a wider point and let other hikers make their way by. (Plenty of chances to do something nice for others that day.) If the experience became too "uncomfortable," I was mentally prepared to turn around and go back, as many people report doing. The cutoff before that last harrowing quarter-mile is called Scout Lookout, also nicknamed "Chicken-Out Point." Other hikers have reported feeling overwhelmed by fear, and one woman said she tackled the climb in the hope of conquering her fear of heights. She made it, but would never do it again.

Finally reaching the end viewpoint, a capstone peninsula like an "island in the sky," I found a space among the dozen or so other people to sit down for a few minutes. Rather than stopping for lunch and a rest as I usually would, I was keen to head down that trail—get back to "Chicken-Out Point" and put that dangerous section behind me. Lunch could wait.

View from Angels Landing

From Scout Lookout down, the way was steep—including one set of something like twenty-one switchbacks called Walter's Wiggles (named after an early park superintendent who helped lay out the route). By noon, many more people were on their way up, though I noticed it wasn't a steady stream, but waves, with quiet periods between. I realized it was because of the trams. Since my visit fifteen years before, the main road through the park had been closed to private vehicles during busy times, and sightseers and hikers were ferried around the park on tandem buses they called trams. I had first encountered that solution to overcrowding and pollution at Denali National Park in Alaska in the late '90s, then soon after at Grand Canyon and Yosemite. The system was well organized for convenience and access, and that morning I had caught a smaller bus from my motel into the village of Springdale, where I bought my provisions for the hike. Crossing a footbridge into the park, I took the tram to the trailhead at the Grotto (a collapsed cave with waterfall).

On the way down, I had lunch near the Grotto, then caught the two trams back to my motel. I felt weary and a little sore, but happy to have made it to Angels Landing (and back!). I was looking forward to a shower, a generous measure of The Macallan, and steak for dinner. As my friend Mendelson Joe says, "Every day is Thanksgiving Day."

Just before sunrise the next morning, I drove up out of Zion Canyon on an incredibly "loopy" bit of road. Some long curving tunnels necessitated open windows and a gratuitous downshift to hear that wonderful V12 music. (The Aston Martin engineers deliberately designed "baffles" in the mufflers that open on startup, or above a certain RPM, to enhance the "auditory experience.") I paused often at overlooks to watch the light fading up on the immense cliffs behind me, the Towers of the Virgin and the Court of the Patriarchs. The canyon was too deep and narrow to admit the sun until much later in the morning, so it wasn't a "sunrise" so much as a "lightrise." The air was cold, but tasted fresh and clean, fragrant with pine, juniper, and sage.

The road flattened out onto the plateau above the canyon, part of a vast geological upheaval called the Grand Staircase, rising strata of different eras of sedimentary rocks stretching from Zion Canyon through Bryce to Grand Canyon. (The National Park Service groups those three parks into what they call the Grand Circle, which makes sense now that I understand the geology.) Even on the plateau, the sun wasn't quite over the horizon yet, but the light was full over the open sage and juniper rangeland. The temperature was in the twenties, and under the center-pivot irrigation sprinklers blinding white frost had collected on the fields, making a surreal sight.

At that time of morning, I had been watching for deer and saw a few, so I kept my speed down. Ahead of me, two mule deer were standing on the right side of the road, feeding, and facing away from me. I slowed down even more and blipped off a downshift to give a menacing roar—"Loud Downshifts Save Lives." As I came alongside

the two deer, they started moving in the same direction as me, then suddenly—*whoomp!*—they dived right into me!

As I jammed on the brakes, I heard the sound of a heavy body landing on carbon fiber (everybody knows *that* sound) as one of them fell on top of the hood, then slid to the ground. Shocked and disbelieving, I watched it lay there, hooves scrabbling against the pavement, for a horrible moment. My mind was racing in spirals, trying to process what was happening, and what I should do if it was hurt badly. (Unlike Michael in *Far and Away*'s "Every Road Has Its Toll," where he had to put a wounded deer out of its misery with a bullet, I wasn't carrying.) I was mighty relieved to see it rise to its feet and hobble away to the other side of the road. It would surely be stiff and sore for a few days, and probably say some bad words, but I hoped it would be okay. I drove on, shaken and shaking my head. Even Britain's millions of sheep aren't *that* dumb!

Capitol Reef
National Park

At such a slow speed, it was more like the deer ran into me than the other way around—so I didn't expect any damage. However, when I stopped later and looked, I saw a star-shaped crack, the size of a fist, right through the middle of the front bumper. The only way I can imagine a slow impact causing that kind of damage is a hoof. Probably on purpose—taking out its fear, and resulting anger, on the car. Because you would, wouldn't you?

I was not unduly bothered by the damage to the car, because no car that is driven through the great world, however carefully, is ever going to be perfect. That reality was accepted long ago, and I would rather drive a car with a few cosmetic flaws than keep it showroom perfect—especially on a drive like this one. I would get it fixed . . . sometime.

Which brings me to a choice I had to make about *displaying* the car in this story. I always avoid showing, or writing much about, the material possessions I have been fortunate enough to acquire. Part of that is native Canadian modesty—not wanting to seem to brag—but part of it is the wish not to arouse envy. It is a sadly common human trait to resent fine things others have, or begrudge their success or attractiveness. Envy is said to be motivated by primal instincts of com-

petitiveness, and if *schadenfreude* is feeling pleasure from another's pain, plain old envy is feeling pain from another's pleasure. I have felt those poisons myself, as a youth, convincing myself I disliked someone when it was really envy, and it is an ugly emotion to have or receive. Having grown out of such bad instincts to the point where I envy no one (okay, maybe Jay Leno for his garage!), I equally have no wish to be disliked, even by strangers, for such negative reasons.

Joshua forest,
Mojave Desert

However, the car was as much a part of this story as my motorcycle is in others. So, despite the many gorgeous photos I captured of the car ("autoporn") against the stunning rock formations and autumn colors, I decided I would just show it from the back, as part of the scenery.

A quote from T.S. Eliot resonates with me: "For us, there is only the trying. The rest is not our business."

That includes envy, politics, sociopaths, haters, DILLIGAFs, and suicidal deer . . .

On the first morning of this long-awaited road trip, I rose eagerly in the pre-dawn darkness. I aimed to get across the forty-mile width of Los Angeles before its usual weekday gridlock. My exit was smooth and swift, and by sunrise I was cruising into my beloved high desert, the Mojave. My route from there was undecided, for I had all day to reach Zion National Park, roughly 500 miles whichever route I chose, and I wanted to "improvise" a little. At Barstow, I turned onto Interstate 40 instead of the direct route through Vegas on I-15. Following a whim, at Newberry Springs I turned off again, onto the "old road," the National Trails Highway, formerly the legendary Route 66.

John Steinbeck called it the "Mother Road" in *The Grapes of Wrath*, set in the 1930s, and by the late '40s it was a place to "get your kicks."

*If you should plan to motor west*
*Travel my way, take the highway that is best*
*Get your kicks on Route 66.*

The song was written by Bobby Troup in 1946, with lyrics that were partly a travelogue of his own post-war journey west "from Chicago to L.A." (from Pennsylvania, in his case). It became an immediate hit for Nat King Cole that same year, and has since been recorded by countless artists, from the Rolling Stones to Depeche Mode. (Seriously.) In the early '60s, a TV series called *Route 66* portrayed the adventures of two young men with the all-American names of Buz and Tod. They drove around the country in an all-American Corvette, having adventures and helping people. (A worthy approach to life, then and now.)

By the 1980s, the Mother Road had been entirely replaced by Interstate 40 and was decommissioned in 1985. (The number was then given to an unromantic stretch of interstate in Maryland.) Only vestiges remain of Old 66 now, service roads here and there, though there is an arc through Arizona that is evocative, and a fairly long section across the Mojave, where I was driving, through brown desert and green creosote. The characterful motels and diners, like Roy's, are all but gone, ghosts of a time before faceless chains and styrofoam food.

The first thirty miles east to Ludlow were very rough, the pavement crumbling and lumpy, but from there on it was smooth and empty. It occurred to me that driving Route 66 today is probably *much* nicer than it was during its heyday, when every truck and car traveling between Chicago and L.A. would have filled its two lanes in a slow, creeping parade. Today it is a joyride—back then it was probably . . . not.

And *dangerous?* There were so many wrecks that it was sometimes called "Bloody 66."

As always, I paused at Roy's Motel for a photo, and I was determined to capture one of the big Route 66 signs painted on the road. (The only way to mark the route, because the actual metal signs are always stolen. Route 66 has been heavily fetishized, both by nostalgic Americans and romantic Europeans.)

I have written about Roy's Motel before, particularly in *Ghost Rider*. During the *Test for Echo* tour, in early 1997, Brutus and I stayed there one night. On a couple of previous stops for gas or lunch, we made friends with the owner, Walt. When we came to stay overnight, we brought wine to share with him and his mysterious chef, a Mexican-American who had cooked in some fancy places (if his stories were true) like Palm Springs and San Diego—but was now hiding in a burger joint in the desert. When I dropped by Roy's again in 1998, on the *Ghost Rider* journey, Walt told me he was hoping some soon-to-visit "money men" would invest in the place—build a swimming pool, even a golf course. That obviously didn't happen, and over the years when I have driven or motorcycled by (it's in the middle of some of my favorite Mojave routes), I saw the place continue to crumble. The cabins to the right, where we stayed, are no longer habitable—windowpanes broken, furniture gone. I sometimes wonder what became of Walt. Maybe still waiting for the money men . . .

Onward across the Mojave, up Kelbaker Road to the Kelso Depot (so many stories in these apparently "deserted" places), the patterned creosote rolled away gently for miles in every direction, to distant brown mountains. Northeast on the Cima Road, I turned onto a little-traveled strip of crumbling pavement through a fairy-tale land of wondrous Joshua trees.

This was a time to hook up the radar detector, to avoid any "surprises." On a straight, empty desert backroad it was safe and sensible to travel faster than the posted limit, and the odds of being ticketed were low. It would be a matter of bad luck there, while on the interstate, if they were trying to catch you, they would. That's why they call it a "trap." So I don't bother trying to speed there. As one of the band's professional drivers once said, "All a radar detector will tell you is when you are about to be pulled over."

Then it was back on I-15, the main route to Vegas. (I know now, but seem not to have known in the *Ghost Rider* years, that it is always just Vegas, *never* Las Vegas. Who decides these things? Like when San Francisco used to be "Frisco," but you can't call it that anymore.)

Driving through Vegas in the early morning, I decided it should be called "Ahhh, Vegas." A note of sadness for what it *could* have been, I guess. Its baroque immensity and spectacle were undeniably exciting to see from a distance, especially at night—but up close, not so much.

Regarding previous remarks about the U.S. government's current misdeeds, the arrogance and cold-hearted spite of a vocal few, I would not say that "Americans get the government they deserve." That's just

Passing Kelso Dunes

mean. But it must be true that Americans get the *entertainment* they deserve. If they want to watch people humiliate themselves, or each other, that's what they're going to get—you cannot blame the "providers." Following the same reasoning, it must be true that Americans get the Vegas they deserve.

These days I am more tolerant of human . . . frailty than was "that other guy" fifteen years ago (hey—he had good *reason* to hate the world!), but I understand how Vegas offended his delicate sensibilities then. And the remark he made that people in the national parks were "half the size, with twice the vitality." That remains true.

But as with all the world's complaints about humanity offered by the rest of humanity, what the hell are you going to do about it?

Capitol Reef
National Park

Shut up and drive, I guess.

Driving out of Zion that morning, I stopped for breakfast in Panguitch (just for the name!), then carried on north through irrigated hayfields and pastures. Several big magpies caught my eye, vivid in their black and white plumage, like flying pinwheels.

Once again I followed a whim, and turned off for Capitol Reef National Park. As ever, I was pleased to display my annual pass for the national parks—it felt like a membership card to an *excellent* club. After stopping at the visitor center for a passport stamp and some gifts for Olivia (always good shopping for children's books and such in the national parks), I followed the scenic drive down through the park. It is centered on a geological uplift called the Waterpocket Fold (the name like something out of Tolkien). As in Zion, sedimentary rocks were eroded into colorful ramparts, domes (like the namesake Capitol), arches, and branching canyons. The overall impression is "grandeur."

Backtracking a little to Torrey, I headed south on Utah 12, a winding delight of stunning views and little traffic. Some sections resembled a two-lane version of the trail to Angels Landing, a narrow, winding isthmus plunging away on both sides, seemingly at pavement's edge. As on that trail, I kept my eyes on the road. The day's ultimate destination was Bryce Canyon National Park, which was only about 100 miles from Zion—but I managed to stretch it to a very enjoyable 350 miles.

Stopping at the Bryce visitor center, I bought a few things and talked a little with the sweet lady behind the counter. In line with my "doing something nice for others" pledge, on my travels around Utah I was responding to those who seemed like they wanted to pass the time of day—a relaxed openness that my concert-tour schedule didn't always allow. I asked her if everybody around there was as happy as I was to have the parks open again, and she replied, "Well, I certainly am—but most of all for all of *you*, to be able to see these wonderful places."

I told her I had just driven down from Capitol Reef, and she said, "That highway 12—I never get tired of that beauty."

I mentioned that my backup plan, if the national parks had remained shuttered, had been to visit Kodachrome Basin State Park, and she said, "I live between here and there, and that was a *lot* of people's backup plan. Including all the bus tours."

Oh yes, hadn't thought of that. Such bus tours were bringing many of the visitors to the area, foreigners and natives alike, on the "Grand Circle Tour" of Zion, Bryce, and Grand Canyon.

Alas, I would encounter many of them that evening in the hotel dining room—where my heart sank to witness a crowded mass around the tables and a lineup of about forty people at the door. However, Ruby's resort had been doing this for a long time (since the 1920s) and could handle it. The line moved quickly, the service was good (as my waitress reported, "We are used to it like this"), and the food was . . . good enough, under the circumstances.

Capitol Reef

However, the second night at Bryce I drove into nearby Tropic (just for the name—Tropic, Utah) and found a pleasant little restaurant. (Even served wine, which you can't always expect in Mormon Utah.) Both the menu and the small-town diner atmosphere suited me better than the resort experience.

My personal dining companions on that trip were my journal and a book, *Weir's World*, sent to me during the European tour by a Scottish fan. (Thanks, Daniel!) It was a nicely written, nature-based autobiography published in 1994 by Tom Weir (1914–2006), a Scottish mountaineer, bird-lover, environmental activist, broadcaster, and sometime drummer. Later in life, he had been a popular television host, traveling around his country and "visiting" people, talking to

Bryce Amphitheater

them. (Another admirable way of life.) *Weir's World* recounted his background as a musician, climber, ornithologist, and explorer, both far and near—with occasional drams of whisky.

A man after my own heart. I enjoyed the book very much, and it suited my present surroundings and mindset perfectly.

This is the view that etched itself on my memory fifteen years before, and sustained my impression that it was perhaps the most fantastic place I had ever seen. It is named for a pioneer rancher, Ebenezer Bryce, and the story goes that when he was asked what it was like to live around there, he said, "It's a hell of a place to lose a cow."

Fairyland Canyon

(Mormon sources change that to "heck.")

A glance at the trail map reminded me right away that the hike I did last time was called Fairyland Loop, and I remembered it as living up to that description. In the park newspaper, it was listed under "Strenuous Hikes (steep grades with MULTIPLE elevation changes)" and described this way: "See the China Wall, Tower Bridge, and tall hoodoos on this spectacular, less-crowded trail."

They had me at "spectacular" and "less-crowded"—I would take it again.

(Hoodoos, incidentally, are the individual spires and pinnacles that make up that intricate landscape. It is from a similar root as "voodoo," and likewise has to do with "spell casting." Those hoodoos certainly are spell*binding*. Paiute myths say the hoodoos were "Legend People," turned to stone by the trickster god Coyote.)

(Love those tricksters—like Loki and Raven.)

The plateau above Bryce Canyon rises to over 9,000 feet, and the overnight temperatures were in the twenties. Sheltered walls of the higher overlooks showed a dusting of snow. Looking out in the early morning, I saw my car covered in sparkling white frost. So I took my time over breakfast and gathering my provisions for the day, seeing no reason not to let the morning warm up a little.

Wearing a windbreaker over a fleece jacket, gloves, scarf, and toque, I headed down from Fairyland Point. Almost immediately I stopped and took out my camera, pointing it in every direction. A smile spread across my face and stayed there for a long time. It seemed that every few minutes, around every bend in the trail, I was stopping

The Acropolis

to take more photos. As I had reported back in 1998, I took more pictures in Bryce Canyon than I had ever taken anywhere, and the same was true this time. It was impossible to get one image that was "emblematic," as might be done in most areas of natural splendor—Zion, Grand Canyon, Yosemite, Monument Valley, Yellowstone, even Death Valley from Dante's View. So many panoramas offered completely different impressions.

I don't know if "The Acropolis" is the official name of this formation, but it's certainly what I thought of. (On the map it appears to be "Boat Mesa.") Other groups of hoodoos and eroded fins suggested pagodas, castles, melted ice-cream cakes, or sculpted bricks of wax. Around another corner would be a massive coral reef across from an array of gothic battlements, towers, and spires. Curving amphitheaters suggested a spectral choir, armored giants turned to stone (by a trickster), or the gigantic female figures that support the Parthenon —caryatids.

A larger, or deeper, analogy occurred to me the first evening, outside my motel at Zion. I stood with my post-drive single-malt whisky and watched the evening light play on the mighty gray walls around me. The light seemed to penetrate the gigantic slabs of rock, or radiate from them. The power of that light seemed amplified by the sheer scale of those cliffs, and I sensed a kind of "hum." Or maybe something more like a steady "*om*," a vibrating chant of power and endurance. The words came to me: frozen music. Nothing mystical or psychedelic, just the notion that this was how frozen music *would* look, especially great symphonies and operas.

(Though I remembered a comparison I once made about the Grand Canyon's visual impact being like "a power chord.")

Zion might be Beethoven, and perhaps Puccini, grand and impassioned, while Bryce might be Bach, an intricate monument. Somehow Capitol Reef suggested Mahler. I wrote in my journal, "Those rocks are not *eternal*, except compared to us—but they *speak* of eternity."

Sing of it, maybe.

Fairyland Trailhead

Wonderful to reflect that it's all *water* music, too—all those formations created by either moving water or ice. The fins and hoodoos of Bryce were gradually shaped by the cycle of frost and thaw in their crevices.

I learned something new from the recorded narration on the Zion park tram, too—that these massive slabs of sandstone had been formed not only by immense pressure from above (from ancient mountains and plateaus that had long eroded away), but also by a chemical reaction with minerals leaching through it, forming a kind of cement.

The Fairyland Trail was the opposite of my usual preference—descending at first, with several ups and downs ("MULTIPLE elevation changes"), then a steep climb to the rim trail. I prefer to attack the hard part of a hike first, when I'm fresh, then have a "homeward cruise" downhill at the end, when I'm tired. And have lunch at the top. But never mind. The scenery was clearly worth it, and could only be experienced that way.

Another factor at nearly 9,000 feet was the thinness of the air, apparently providing only seventy percent of the oxygen at sea level. I felt that on the uphill part, breathing deeply and steadily. (I noticed I used the same rhythm I do for long-distance swimming—three paces per breath.) I was glad to meet the Rim Trail, and know the climbing was over, but on the three-mile return on a more-or-less level section, my legs and feet seemed to ache more than they usually would. Perhaps the diminished oxygen affects recovery time, too. Surely it couldn't be my . . . "tender years" . . .

That phrase has a worthy connection with another recent adventure. Just a week or two prior to this journey, in early October, I drove up the Pacific Coast Highway to Drum Workshop. They had asked me to try out a new line of drums and see what I thought, and I was looking forward to doing some "aimless playing." For the first time in five years or so (see "Autumn Serenade" in *Far and Away*), I would sit behind the drums without serious intent, not rehearsing, recording, or performing, just playing.

On my way there, as I drove into the farming country around Camarillo and Oxnard, I saw a number of fields groomed into brown blankets of bare earth—lying fallow to regenerate their nutrients. I smiled to think that during my own period of rest, my mind was allowed to be fallow—to refill the aquifer and simply absorb energy to promote new growth. I was trying very hard *not* to have any ideas. Just a few minutes later, some idle train of thought led me across the phrase "tender years," and a spark lit up in my mind: "*song title!*" (Thinking with a dark smile, "You're not supposed to be *doing* that yet.")

"Tender years" refers to youth, typically, but I was struck by the larger application—because *all* our years are tender, aren't they?

From first to last.

Finally trudging my way back to Fairyland Point, I was relieved to climb into the car. I cruised easily (in both senses!) down the scenic road once more, thinking I would visit a few viewpoints I hadn't stopped at the previous day. Along with a few other vehicles, I paused to watch a herd of pronghorns feeding at the roadside. Sometimes wrongly called antelopes, they did display that characteristic delicacy and grace, and I had never seen so many together. "Prongers" had been headed for extinction in the previous century, and in thirty years of traveling America's backroads by bicycle, motorcycle, and car, I had never seen more than two at a time, and that rarely. Now they were on the rebound, largely thanks to the national parks.

I was still looking for the one overlook I remembered so well from fifteen years ago. I had a hunch it might be the one named after Ebenezer Bryce, so I parked there and walked toward the edge—hobbling at first

From the Rim

until my legs unstiffened again. Out on the fenced-in point, I looked out and . . . there it was.

I looked left toward Inspiration Point, and around the indelible scene of what in my mind's eye I had thought of as the Heavenly Choir. (More frozen music.)

Three boys aged ten to twelve or so, with the clean-cut "whiteness" and sturdy clothing of Mormon children (in Utah, after all), were fooling around on the edge. One of them was kneeling down with his smartphone, then on his elbows, pretending to take "artful" photographs. He directed his two buddies, or brothers, in increasingly bizarre poses, and they all giggled.

With a smile, I held out my camera to him and said, "Could I get you to take one of me, please? You seem to be the photographic expert around here."

The boy looked down modestly and said, "Aw, I was just foolin' around."

I was left smiling to myself and thinking, "No! Really?"

Kids don't always get grown-up humor—I remember.

The boy took my camera and stood back, carefully composing the frame, then took a few shots. He still didn't seem satisfied and continuing eyeing the composition, until I said, "Thank you, I'm sure that's got it."

Bubba in Fairyland

I took back my camera, smiling again. Maybe someday that boy will see this and know that he helped me to capture the frozen music.

Early the following morning, at dark o'clock, the Ghost Driver loaded his luggage into the frost-covered car and fired it up. (He had considerately parked away from the rows of motel rooms, knowing he would be leaving at an "antisocial hour." No DILLIGAF here.)

Headlights on bright, he drove into the cold night, heading for home, feeling good, and watching for deer. Over the mountains on a dark, winding two-lane, then onto the interstate and breakfast at Denny's in St. George. Down through Vegas and across the wide Mojave, the Vanquish handled it all with alacrity and comfort. A ten-hour drive was no strain in that car, truly a Grand Tourer, and the 1,500 miles had been an absolute joy, as were the fifteen miles of hiking. Altogether, a memorable experience—one of his favorite road trips ever.

Now he was aiming for home, and the following night his wife and daughter would be returning from New York. He wanted to be waiting when they opened the door.

Angels Landing.

# 17

# Bubba And The Professor

FEBRUARY 2014

**Can't you just picture** the '60s sitcom, or wacky road movie, that would follow that title? Why, I can hear the theme music. The story would hinge on the classic "odd couple" setup, where a methodical, high-minded would-be aesthete and intellectual is handcuffed to an easygoing Neanderthal everythingaholic drummer.

Or a Nabokovian, Jekyll-Hyde twist, where the two polar sides of one character are tricked into sharing a long, difficult journey?

Oh wait—that's my life.

What tales our nicknames can tell. The two in this title have been conferred upon one individual—your reporter—at different times in his life. You may imagine they come with a story or two.

I often think back to a "road lesson" involving one of my oldest friends, Jimmy Johnson. He and I met around 1968, when J.J. joined my second band, the Majority (ha—our booking agency's genius slogan was "Join the Majority!"), as a "roadie." A few tumultuous years later (for both of us), when I joined Rush, J.J. became Alex's guitar tech for many years—many *hilarious* years. The two of them were a fine comedy duo.

(For the past couple of decades, J.J. has been performing the same job for Styx, and making them laugh, too, I'm sure.)

But way back in the Olden Days (when dinosaurs walked the earth), in the mid-'70s, Jimmy affected a mustache (as many of us did—I sported a full-on handlebar, myself). However, in the eyes of his fellow crew members, Ian and Liam, J.J. seemed to move beyond the pale when he started wearing a small scarf around his neck, knotted with a ring. They dubbed him "Tony Orlando," and the rest of us laughed and started using it, too.

J.J. blurted out a line that has resonated for decades: "But I don't *want* to be called Tony Orlando!"

Oh, we laughed and laughed.

Finally somebody put him wise: *"You don't get to pick your own nickname!"*

It was the same way with Bubba—I didn't pick it, and probably wouldn't have. It came from Andrew MacNaughtan, the band's main photographer from around 1989 until his tragically early death in 2011. During those years Andrew shot us casually and formally all over the world, including the portrait that opens this story (with expert Photoshop work from Hugh Syme), my all-time favorite. (Bubba's, anyway.) In the early '90s, Andrew also traveled with us on a couple of tours as a personal assistant. (Poor guy.)

Back in those days, early in a friendship that would deepen over the years, Andrew started calling me Bubba. Originally Southern slang for "brother," that title has grown to convey a "good ol' boy" stereotype—even "redneck." I could only assume Andrew was calling me that because I was pretty much the "Anti-Bubba" (I *hope* that's what he was thinking), because, you know, I had read books, and written them, and cared about art, and cooked for my family, arranged flowers, and was friends with people who are gay and people who have brown skin.

(That duality amused me when I named "Bubba's Book Club," for example—a counterpoint to Oprah's. Later, the invention of "Bubba's Bar 'n' Grill" merely aimed to teach other Bubbas how to cook "Good Simple Food.")

An even earlier nickname given to me, "The Professor," had an equally ironic root. It was not, as many strangers assumed, some reflection of admiration from the Guys at Work for my intellect and learning. Oh no. Nor did it reflect an actual university degree, as some rumors

1974 Crew—Liam, Ian, J.J.

held. No, the Guys at Work were simply equating my demeanor with the character on *Gilligan's Island* played by Russell Johnson.

Not *terribly* insulting—but not exactly *cool*, either.

(In the middle of writing this story, Russell Johnson suddenly appeared in the news, because he had *died*. However, he was eighty-nine, so not a bad run. And for almost fifty years his only real claim to fame had been that role as the Professor—he had "dined out on it," as the Brits would say.)

The screwball sitcom *Gilligan's Island* only aired for three seasons in the mid-'60s, but for decades after it was widely syndicated. During the show's first season, Professor Roy Hinkley, Ph.D., was not even included in the opening theme song—the five other characters were mentioned by name, but he and Mary Ann were lumped into "and the rest."

(Bubba suggests that our sitcom should be retitled *Bubba . . . and the Rest*.

The dry-humored Professor sniffs, "Hi-*lar*-ious, Chucklehead.")

Early episodes revealed that the Professor was a research scientist and "well-known Scoutmaster." (I do hope that wasn't a veiled stereotype inserted to explain his seemingly "unnatural" lack of interest in sultry, sophisticated Ginger or sweet, virginal Mary Ann.) Cynical viewers have long noted, "Isn't it odd that the Professor could make a radio out of a coconut, but couldn't fix a hole in a boat?"

So . . . a question arises that has honestly never occurred to me before: which is the "real me"? The Professor, or Bubba?

Whoa. Perhaps that duality is like what a writer for *Spy* magazine once described as a metaphor of morality for people who grew up in the era of Disney cartoons: above one shoulder is the "Good Goofy," an angel, and above the other is the "Bad Goofy," a devil. (Though Bubba is not really a devil, and the Professor is certainly no angel.)

The Bubba side of the doppelgänger, as he is shown in the opening photo, would surely say, "Let me pour you another drink and we'll talk about it. Have some laughs."

But the Professor would cut in, "No, no, that won't do. We are on *sabbatical*. We have to *achieve* something."

Ah, sweet sabbatical. The Professor's first intention was to begin this story with a rumination on that subject—wanting to open with the following photo of the night sky and spontaneous couplet. Bubba wanted to call the story "Black Sabbatical"—because that made him chuckle.

However, that title was ultimately doomed to fail, simply because

Bubba's California Twilight [Inspiring an
accidental poem by the Professor]
*Venus, cypress, crescent moon with earthshine*
*Royal palm, fan palms, Norfolk Island pines*

there was nothing *dark* about that time—quite the opposite. Even in December, the California night sky sparkled with light and hope, and we can think of few times in our life that have been brighter. ("*Some days were dark . . . some nights were bright.*") But somehow "Golden Sabbatical" didn't make Bubba smile the same way.

Later, when the Professor pitched his "high concept" for the *Bubba and the Professor* sitcom, Bubba could only agree.

However, it turns out the words "sabbatical" and "sabbath" *do* have similar roots. An ancient Hebrew word (yes, *Shabbat*) means "a ceasing." The worthy Wiki gives us this nice clarification: "In recent times, 'sabbatical' has come to mean any extended absence in the career of an individual in order to achieve something. In the modern sense, one takes sabbatical typically to fulfill some goal, e.g., writing a book or traveling extensively for research."

Oh yes, that works for us. Again we offer our definition of the perfect life: "a working vacation." As we happen to be taking an "extended absence" from our career, and aim to spend that time well, the truly key words in that definition are "*in order to achieve something.*"

Well, yes. That's the difference between a sabbatical and a vacation—something more like recreation than rest. (Though rest is nice, too, of course.)

"Traveling extensively for research" takes on a different meaning when your *work* involves traveling extensively. We were thinking of something more like "staying home extensively for research."

"Achievement" can be broadly interpreted to include spending time with our four-year-old daughter, Olivia. Out of the many church signs we have collected and held up for ridicule over the years, a vanishing few have reflected the kind of deep, ancient wisdom that transcends faith and offers timeless human truth.

"HOW DOES A CHILD SPELL LOVE? T-I-M-E."

Bubba and the Professor always try to remember that. At some point in every day, we are summoned to be the "quick sketch artist" for Olivia's fantastic visions. She will announce, "Mater, I want you to *draw* something." (Yet another nickname! After the Bubba-like tow truck in the *Cars* movies, voiced by Larry the Cable Guy. We won't go too deeply into that.)

Fetching our Sharpie, we sit on the floor by her little work table and roll out a fresh sheet of paper, then stick it down with blue tape. Olivia describes what she wants—in this case, various characters from the *Cars* movies as "rainbow fairies," including one of her own invention called

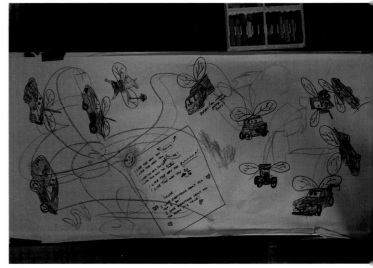

Art with Olivia

Roger the Rainbow Garbage Truck Fairy. (Ha—Pixar never thought of *that*.) A couple of the cars had to have dipstick-shaped headgear, like Dipsy from *Teletubbies*. (That's where the laughing sun comes from, too.) Olivia the pig dances ballet in the air, wearing mermaid shells, fairy wings, and a wand shaped like Mater, the UFO in *Mater's Tall Tales*. Because, well—obviously!

It's Olivia's world! We just live in it . . .

Olivia dictates every detail as she envisions it, every facial expression and gesture. We draw what she directs as closely as we can, then she colors it in. Here Olivia has also added "zoom lines," some Joan Miró swoops, and Cy Twombly–style decorations.

In the middle, we printed a new verse for a song we had been working on, "I Love Everything About You," so we wouldn't forget it. We already had two verses and a chorus, and it was certainly one of our finest collaborations.

In a medium swing feel, the first verse went like this [*with accompanying choreography*]:

*I like the way you think* [point to temples and sing cymbal ride,
    "ding-de-ding, ding-de-ding"]
*I like the way you talk* [make hand puppet talking]
*I like the way you da-a-a-ance* [add frantic choreography]
*I like the way you walk* [add walking fingers]

*I like the way you si-i-i-i-ing* [falsetto long and loud!]
*I like the way you do* . . . [shrug] . . . *everything*
*'Cau-au-ause* [long rising note, over tempo shift to medium shuffle]
*I love everything about you*
*Yes I do*
*I love everything about you*
*You know it's true*

(Unfortunately, we realized later that the chorus melody echoes
"Tell Him," by the Exciters—"*I know something about love*"—from 1962,
so we'll have to adjust that before we start recording.)

Then into the second verse, back to the medium swing feel:

*I like the way you count* [two, three, four, five]
*I like the way you spell* [a, b, c, d]
*I like the way you bou-ou-ounce* [jump up and down three times
    saying, "Boing, boing, boing"]
*I like the way you* . . . [long sniff] . . . *smell*

*I like the way you ru-u-u-un* [dash quickly around the kitchen counter]
*I like the way you have fun−*

[Repeat chorus]

That October day, we worked out the third verse, while refining
our graphic arts. All through the later months of 2013, and into 2014,
our sabbatical time included that kind of "creative play."

Looking forward to our sabbatical year, and gradually formulating
our goals, in early January we outlined our plans for what we hoped
to achieve, in a letter to our friend Craiggie. He only lives across town
in South Pasadena, and we had seen him just a few days before—
with our families, attending "Bandfest," as we have for the past three
years. (A few days before the Rose Festival parade, selected marching
bands from around the world perform on a football field. Many of the
bands, with dazzling costumes, spinning flags and batons, and nimble

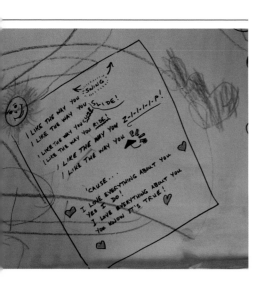

footwork, create a wondrous combination of music and choreography that is much more artful than they can deliver "on the march," as it were.)

Like many of our friends, and ourselves, Craiggie writes long old-fashioned letters. Often these are employed as "sounding boards," when we're thinking something through for ourselves.

("How do we know what we think until we see what we write?")

Here is part of what we wrote to Craiggie that morning, "at the gate of the year," describing our hopes for a sabbatical 2014.

Watching Bandfest

This isn't a time to "do nothing," but quite the opposite—a precious opportunity to do *different* things.

Work has been going forward on the *Clockwork Angels* graphic novel, and I'm getting pretty excited about it. I have been drawn into being more involved with the project, especially the artwork, loving the opportunity to see *my* vision of Crown City and the steamliners portrayed. (That's where we are so far, in the first issue.)

The live-show rear-screen stuff was much more generic steampunk, sometimes of the more dystopian genre, which is opposite to the truly fantastic and rather splendid way I see Albion, with the darker scenes to come in Poseidon—"on the waterfront."

(Did you know Poseidon was the mythical capital of Atlantis? That's why I liked giving it the darker spin, an outlaw port full of scoundrels and misfits.)

The rear-screen stuff is not my department, and I can't supervise *everything*, so I just let that go. Hugh's artwork was always totally in sync with my vision, and now this is a chance to really nail every detail of the different settings.

The artist, Nick Robles, is quite excellent, at both characters and outlandish architecture, and takes "direction" well. Kevin [Anderson] is writing the script—I am surprised to learn that he basically maps out the whole thing, panel by panel, even dictating their relative sizes, and the artist "just" fills them in.

Interesting that Nick has previously been most active in "hard" sci-fi illustration, and later admitted he wasn't that familiar with the steampunk aesthetic. Thus his first renderings of Crown City were much more generic—the typical setting that resembles Victorian London. Oh no, not *my* Crown City! It is something entirely more monumental and fantastically exotic. I had to steer him back toward the "grandeur" of sci-fi cityscapes, something more awesome, spacious, and—yes—Utopian.

Then I'm thinking it's time to publish another collection of stories. Although the title of the calendar was conceived only for that purpose, I'm starting to like it for a book. Maybe *Far and Near: On Days Like These*.

Owen arrives in
Crown City

The cover image in my mind is still that North Yorkshire one, so that would work. (One thing I loved right away about the title "On Days Like These" is that it works for *every* image, and every day!) Then a variety of scenic photos on the back, as in *Far and Away*, to suggest the extent of the settings within.

I would like to collect one more story, maybe of February in Quebec (a recurring theme!), then would want to write new intro and outro pieces for it.

Putting together a book, even of existing stories, is no small undertaking, collecting all the elements for publication, supervising the layout and proofreading, and preparing all the "ancillary" material—the "front matter," they call it.

However, it is certainly rewarding to hold the finished product in your hands—and send it to all your friends!

A proper sabbatical year should include both other modes of study, and travel (for "research"), and a chance to delve deeper into your own "specialty"—in my case, hitting things with sticks. I have already talked with Peter Erskine about working with him again, maybe around springtime. Something worthwhile is sure to come out of that . . .

All of a sudden today I am jonesing for a long motorcycle ride. Over the past few months I kind of consciously put that aside, deliberately wanting to make everything about my everyday life *different*, and give the usual daily activities in my recent life—drumming and motorcycling—a rest.

That has been good, but this morning as I backed the car out of the garage to head for the Y, I glanced at my shiny red GS sitting there, and—a *spark* went off in my brain.

Probably in the so-called "reptile brain," a pre-literate grunt, "Want. To. Ride."

So I'm letting that desire float up into the higher levels of cognition, to figure out how to satisfy that primitive urge in some creative way.

At the time of writing that letter to Craiggie, we hadn't yet had the divine inspiration for *Bubba and the Professor*, but that final passage is a perfect example of how we work together. Bubba has an urge; the Professor finds an intelligent way to scratch it.

The Professor was busy with his own itches in late 2013, because one unexpected achievement was an outpouring of "educational" writing. (The quotes seem necessary, because that quality can only be hoped for, not assured.)

North Yorkshire—Bubba at "centre stage"

First a British drum magazine asked for some thoughts on our solo excursions on the *Clockwork Angels* DVD. (They seem to have choked on the carefully wrought 4,000 word response, for we've heard nothing back from them!)

The faithful steed awaits

Then the author of a book called something like *By Drummers for Drummers* asked for some thoughts on recording. Perhaps a book will be a more suitable medium for the 4,000 words we gave him—though we haven't heard back yet.

A music scholar contacted us about a "senior comprehensive research paper" he was writing on the teachings of Freddie Gruber. He sent us a detailed questionnaire, which Bubba insisted we ignore, and we proceeded to tell the story *our* way—improvising around the questions in a way similar to the way we describe practicing in that essay: Just start playing, and work the exercises into whatever the day's "story" becomes. So we sent him about 3,000 words on that worthy subject—no word back on that one, either.

But never mind—we'll find some place to publish it, for the excellent cause of keeping Freddie's memory, and his teachings, alive.

All that writing kept the Professor fairly busy, while Bubba played with his cars.

On the subjects of soloing and recording, and studying, too, we realize that we have been preoccupied by all those pursuits for over forty years—so we have a great number of experiences, and a little advice, to share. And given the time—a *sabbatical* time—it seemed worth doing.

Truth be told, that kind of writing is not as entertaining or rewarding as these little "open letters" always are—no pleasure of reading them over at the end of the day with a double-old-fashioned glass clinking with ice and amber nectar. (A true Bubba-meets-the-Professor moment if there ever was one!) There are no surprises from a day's work, like the unexpected directions "undisciplined" writing can reveal. Those technical essays were more of a chore, and were simply "worth doing." Still, we couldn't help chipping away at those tasks with the approach to work and life drilled into us early by our father.

"If a thing is worth doing, it's worth doing well."

Bubba chimes in with a snort, "You mean, it's worth beating yourself up day and night *trying* to get it right!"

The Professor adds with a dark laugh, "And worth beating yourself up about forever after—because you *didn't* get it right."

But that's just me.

I mean, him . . .

A more creative and satisfying undertaking for both Bubba and the Professor was putting together a new calendar for Bubba's Bar 'n' Grill—something they could *both* get their teeth into. As we have noted before, few activities are as enjoyable and rewarding as *making things*—meaning things you can hold in your *hands*, with pride, and even look at on your wall all year, with pleasure. (Bubba and the Professor agree that pride and pleasure are a good combination. Both in moderation, of course. We are Canadian.)

Back in the autumn of 2011, we had a little time at home, and a little ambition (sometimes a *great* combination), and with our lifetime art director, Hugh Syme, put together Bubba's first calendar. We were sure we had created something beau-

Freddie and me (us) at his eightieth birthday party, 2007, watching Joey Heredia play

tiful, entertaining, cool, and *affordable*—surely everyone would want one, and to buy lots more for their friends at Christmas.

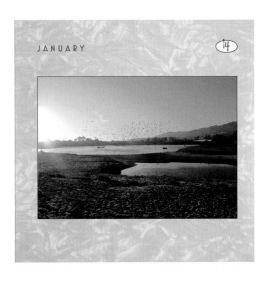

But alas, sales were disappointing—we gave away more copies than we sold. The world let us down again. (As it still does often enough to keep us humble . . . )

The following autumn we were out on the *Clockwork Angels* tour, so didn't have the leisure to try to match the first calendar's combination of carefully chosen images and text blocks. However, this past September we were just settling into our sabbatical frame of mind and were inspired to try another calendar. Brother Danny, who has been our prose editor for the past couple of years, helped in selecting the images and text passages, and once again Hugh Syme stepped up with a *brilliant* design.

The front cover combined a "far and away" shot taken by Brutus in Germany (we titled it "Der Zigzags"), with Hugh's additions of a more dramatic sky, and the shapely rear of Bubba's 1963 Split-Window Corvette.

On the back cover, we were delighted to have another chance to present that all-time favorite portrait—or at least *Bubba's* favorite—the one that opens this story.

Nice things happened to make this calendar rewarding. One day in October, we were visiting Don Lombardi up at Drum Channel and mentioned that we had put the calendar up for sale online, but early orders were disappointing. As a good friend and booster (and the founder of Drum Workshop), Don immediately picked up the phone and called the president of Guitar Center—a national chain of almost 300 stores that sell musical instruments. After some consultations, they eventually agreed to order 1,200 calendars to spread around their stores. The bad news was that the price would not be enough even to match my costs, and they are on a "sale or return" basis, so we will see an unknown quantity coming back. But never mind—at least people would have a *chance* to find them.

And there were other rewards—many grateful recipients of the copies we sent to friends wrote to thank us. One day we received a note from Jamie Borden, who combines the unlikely Vegas careers of dedicated cop by day and passionate rock drummer by night. (We smell another sitcom!)

Jamie told us he had arrived home from a trip just before Christmas and found his whole extended family baking up a storm, with decorations everywhere, and his home filled with every true spirit of the season. Amid all that, he opened our calendar and went through it, describing to his loved ones what he knew about the stories behind the images, and reading some aloud.

Naturally, that was exactly the kind of heartfelt appreciation from a dear friend that could make the project feel entirely worthwhile.

In a letter (probably to Craiggie) just after Christmas, we were reviewing that hectic season, the three weeks we had dedicated to shopping for gifts, getting them shipped, planning menus for Chef Bubba, shopping for groceries, and cooking for large gatherings on Christmas Eve (ten guests) and Day (fifteen—with a Flintstones-sized turkey).

We concluded with what felt like the "score."

"Me: Grateful.

Others: Grateful to me."

That seemed like a fair result.

## Always be yourself
## Unless you can be a pirate
## Then always be a pirate.

Okay, that surreal segue comes with a smile, and courtesy of friend Craiggie. It delights us to imagine it on a sign in front of a church.

As a career choice, piracy didn't work out for us (too much competition, these days!), so we're going to keep on being Bubba and the Professor. (Not that we have any choice.)

Fortunately, one thing we do have in common is that both of us like road trips, the longer the better, on two wheels or four. In early January, wife Carrie expressed interest in a two-night family trip to San Francisco, wanting especially to see the David Hockney exhibition at the de Young Museum. While the girls preferred to travel by air, Bubba and the Professor willingly chose the 850-mile return drive in their Aston Martin Vanquish. Interstate 5 is typically the quickest way north, by an hour or so, but California 101 is more scenic and "characterful." Best of all, if time permits, there's Highway 1 between San Luis Obispo through Big Sur to Monterey—one of the world's greatest stretches of road.

However, that route pretty much demands an overnight somewhere along that sublime coast, so this time we would be satisfied with six hours or so on 101, to get to the hotel in San Francisco before the girls. No problem. Leaving in the pre-dawn darkness and heading up the coast as the sky pearled into light over the calm Pacific, the miles passed pleasantly. North through Ventura, Santa Barbara, and San Luis Obispo, we decided to pause for lunch at the In-N-Out Burger in Salinas (John Steinbeck's hometown, with its "National Steinbeck Center," described in *Ghost Rider*).

In that midwinter season, the hills of Central California should have been velvety green from the winter rains, but they wore their midsummer brown (what we once called the "lion-colored hills"), looking parched and shriveled. Through December and January, we should have received much of a year's worth of rainfall—but there had been almost none. The drought in California was off the charts—not something like half or three-quarters, but a mere single-digit percentage of average amounts. The worst in recorded history.

The Professor's DB5,
Pacific Coast Highway–2008

In the Los Angeles Basin, the dreaded Santa Anas, or "devil winds," had been sweeping in from the high desert, growing hotter and drier as they descended. In a time of such drought, they vastly increased the danger of wildfires. A couple of bad ones had already flared up, and it was likely only the beginning of a dangerous season.

(Some wag once defined the four seasons in Southern California as drought, wildfire, flood, and mudslide. This year we were only getting the first two—so far.)

The smoke in the air also worsened the effects of the Santa Anas. In the opening of *Traveling Music*, we told about the unpleasantness of the devil winds—rasping in your sinuses, your throat, your eyes, your skin, and your mood.

In the novel *Red Wind*, Raymond Chandler defined the Santa Anas for all time:

> There was a desert wind blowing that night. It was one of those hot dry Santa Anas that come down through the mountain passes and curl your hair and make your nerves jump and your skin itch. On nights like that every booze party ends in a fight. Meek little wives feel the edge of the carving knife and study their husbands' necks. Anything can happen.

The climate of the Bay Area, 400 miles north, was cooler and usually wetter—though they had their own "devil winds," the Diablos, from time to time. And their drought at that time was equally severe. A friend living in the nearby Santa Cruz Mountains told us they usually received seventy inches of rain—that year they'd had *five*.

During our visit to Tony Bennett's "city by the bay," we had cool, sunny weather, and all had a good time—a great playground in Yerba Buena Gardens for Olivia, and an unforgettable meal for Mom and Dad at Michael Mino's restaurant.

And there was the uplifting experience of viewing *A Bigger Exhibition*, a monumental installation of recent works (this century) by David Hockney. British born (1937), Yorkshire bred, and a long-time resident of California, Hockney rose to prominence in the pop art school of the '60s, then grew into his own mature style of what Bubba and the Professor (amateur art critics who know the lingo) might call "representational expressionism." Over the years we had seen his work at the Tate Gallery in London, and at the Los Angeles County Museum of Art, and had always enjoyed it, in a lukewarm way. However, after viewing this exhibition, we came away convinced David Hockney is the greatest living visual artist—a worthy heir in skill, range, and vision to his self-described hero, Picasso.

The works on display at the de Young represented an immense variety and quantity of art—yet covered just over a decade, by an artist in his seventies. That alone was inspiring. Works were grouped according to medium, across the full spectrum of an obviously passionate, even *obsessed* graphic artist—entire galleries of charcoal sketches, watercolors, oils, acrylics, and color sketches created on iPads and iPhones. (In one of the descriptions he relates an anecdote: The neighbors in his Yorkshire village jokingly asked if it was true he was making art on his mobile phone. He replied that no, he simply sometimes used his sketchpad as a telephone.)

Those creations were gorgeously printed out on scales ranging from small studies to multi-canvas assemblages that filled whole walls—overwhelming to stand before. Some of the combinations echoed his longtime fascination with cubism—famously expressed during the '70s by collages assembled from multiple Polaroids and, later, high quality prints arranged to depict a fragmented but entire view. He called them "joiners." We could see that approach echoed in more recent filmworks, in which he used multi-camera digital videos on gallery-sized grids of screens to show fragmented views of driving through a Yorkshire landscape, or of jugglers practicing.

David Hockney, *Yosemite I*, October 16, 2011. iPad drawing printed on paper (six sheets)

Hockney's recent visual preoccupations were apparent in several series of portraits, and many vast landscapes of Yosemite and East Yorkshire. Being familiar with both of those areas, we could only wonder what the experience was like for those who weren't—did those great paintings evoke the same degree of appreciation if you hadn't seen the "source material"—the actual landscapes they attempted to capture?

Bubba opined, "Hmm, no—other folks just can't see it like we do. 'Cause we can say, 'That is *exactly* how a Yorkshire lane looks on a rainy day.' It's one thing to say a piece of art is beautiful, but a whole lot greater to say it's beautiful and *true*."

The Professor said, "Whoa, Bubba—you are *deep* today."

Early next morning, at 5:30, we were on the way back south from San Francisco. We drove through the endless dark suburbs to San Jose, then, as the red disk of sun inched up before us, into the farmlands of the Salinas Valley. We stopped in Salinas again, for breakfast at the Black Bear Diner, a Western chain of traditional small-town eateries with nostalgic décor, music, and menus. Always friendly and good, in our experience.

Interstate 5—brown dirt, white sky

(Roadcraft tip: As professional travelers, we have suffered more intestinal distress from undercooked eggs than any other cause. We love soft-boiled, sunny-side-up, and especially poached eggs, but we make those at home. When traveling, we recommend over-medium or scrambled.)

Just over a week later, we set off on another long road trip, this time 500 miles north, to a dot on the map called Willows, California. This would be a different kind of "traveling extensively for research." Once again we started north along the dark coast through Malibu and Ventura County, then turned inland to Ojai, and one of our all-time favorite roads: California State Route 33. On two wheels or four, that little road has just about everything, and rarely do we share it with any other traffic. The first seventy miles or so are a looping, challenging delight, winding through the chaparral and pines of the Santa Ynez Mountains and Los Padres National Forest.

Up toward Maricopa, the country flattens out into irrigated hay-fields, then a long stretch of oilfields—the old-fashioned kind of "nodding bird" pumps. Somehow such an old-tech industry had a quirky charm, and certainly didn't blight that dusty landscape. No doubt the dreaded, more modern fracking is going on beneath the surface.

That stretch of Route 33 is not especially scenic, but the driving is fine, on a straight, empty two-lane. In good conditions, that kind of desert road can sensibly be driven at 80 mph—but of course the signs dictate otherwise. So we put up our radar detector, to stand guard against "surprises" from the California Highway Patrol. A speed trap was unlikely, but the odd time you might encounter a randomly patroling cruiser coming the other way. We hate that conversation.

The crossroads of Blackwells Corners has been billed as "James Dean's Last Stop." On September 30, 1955, while driving his Porsche Spyder to a racetrack in Salinas, he apparently bought gas, ciga-rettes, and an apple. A few miles farther on, at the intersection with California 46, he was killed by a Ford sedan, when its driver failed to see the tiny silver car in a glaring sun. Dean was only twenty-five—and none of the three movies that would make him an enduring legend (*Rebel Without a Cause*, *East of Eden*, and *Giant*) had even been released.

Around there, at the quaintly named town of Kettleman City, we surrendered to the "mileage disposal unit"—Interstate 5. We had cov-ered half the journey, 250 miles, on the backroads, and now needed to make some time. We also changed defensive tactics: instead of the radar detector, we turned on the cruise control. In previous Roadcraft references, we have advised that speeding on American interstates is generally a losing gamble. Just set the cruise at an acceptable "eight over" and relax.

A bleak Central Valley interstate scene makes a good contrast to other images we have shown of "idyllic" California—the evening sky with palm trees and the Coast Highway. In the heart of the Central Valley (which grows something like thirty percent of America's pro-duce), the drought left the fields, leafless orchards, and hills nearby parched and brown. Occasional amateurish signs along the freeway pleaded "STOP THE CONGRESS-CREATED DUST BOWL."

We knew those signs, and many others with similar messages, referred to the constant struggle over water rights in such "lands of little rain." In semi-desert regions like the Central Valley (all of

Southern California, for that matter), the combination of unlimited sunshine with a supply of irrigation water was a treasure beyond price. As Mark Twain explained, "Whisky is for drinking. Water is for fighting over."

As we cruised along I-5 at *precisely* 78 mph, we saw the farther hills on both sides, and the sky above, were ghostly white. That was the smoke drifting downwind from the big Colby fire, in the San Gabriels near Glendale—about 200 miles away. The sun burned through, but the light was harsh and glaring on windshields in the opposite lanes.

The brown, twiggy balls of tumbleweed that would usually cluster along the windward fences had been gathered into enormous stacks. That made a monstrous image of what they *really* represented—not a romantic symbol of the Old West, but an invasive species and pest. Another monstrous presence loomed over a few enormous cattle feedlots, which give off one of the vilest stenches on earth. Driving by them on the leeward side, we try to hold our breath. Mile after mile, the overall impression was of a flat, arid, rather bleak landscape subjugated by vast factory farms and intricate irrigation canals.

Still, it was what it was, and for us, the drive was a perfectly enjoyable way to spend a day. Traveling for research. And the destination was inspiring, too—Thunderhill Raceway, for the next day's Aston Martin club trackday. A racetrack is where a car like the Vanquish can properly "express itself," of course—not on a freeway or suburban boulevard. (Not that it isn't nice to drive there, too!) On winding roads along the coast or in the mountains, and on racetracks, the car has a "sporting" character, powerful and responsive. Yet it also excels as a "grand tourer"—after a 500-mile drive, we climb out feeling fresh and free of pain. A little bleary-eyed and stiff, of course, but not hurting anywhere. When people ask us what the Vanquish is like, we simply reply, "It is everything it *ought* to be."

Our friend Matt Scannell once said he liked how when a stranger looked at one of our cars admiringly and described it as his (and sometimes her) "dream car," we would simply say, "Mine, too."

Because of course these *are* all dream cars to Bubba and the Professor, who both admire them and *use* them—long journeys and racetrack outings for the "modern supercar," and plenty of backroad

Pasadena wildfire, 2009

exercise for the "classics." (We have put over 20,000 miles on the DB5 alone, in six or seven years—which included long absences while touring and recording, and a year off the road for a mechanical rebuild.)

Regular readers will notice that we have reversed the stance put forth in the previous story, "Angels Landing." We had decided only to picture the Vanquish from the rear, as part of the scenery, not to excite any negative reactions. Wearing his editorial hat, Brother Danny pointed out, and Bubba and the Professor have come to agree, that the spirit of "sharing" that inspires these stories does not need to be concerned about those who are *incapable* of sharing the joys of others.

Regarding such dark souls, insert your own expletive of dismissal . . .

For Bubba and the Professor, our first experience on a racetrack was in the mid-'80s, at the Circuit Mont-Tremblant in Quebec. We attended the Jim Russell Racing School (still operating, we are glad to note), one year for the Formula 1600 course, the next for the Formula 2000 class (with more power and aerodynamic wings that made the car a *whole* lot quicker and more serious—scary, even).

Bubba and the Professor at play

To readers with zero interest in motorsports, we promise to be as brief and considerate as possible. (After this latest trackday, we scribbled in our notebook, "Such an experience, such a *scene*, to try to describe without being *boring!*") First of all, a roadrace track is different from the common stereotype of, say, a NASCAR oval. Sometimes when we tell people we were at a trackday, they will say, "How fast did you go?" That's not what it's about. The typical layout might be two or three miles of loops and bends, a highly technical combination of turns in varying radii and camber, plus elevation changes (ups and downs). Short straightaways might allow you to accelerate beyond 100 mph for a few seconds, but then you'll be braking hard into the next turn and balancing the car to take it as quickly as you can. On faster tracks, like Willow Springs, you carry a lot of speed through several bends and have to brace yourself accordingly. After a long day of those "lateral Gs," we will hurt for days.

On a trackday, there is no racing between drivers (or at least,

not "officially"). The cars are sent out at intervals, with passing only permitted in specific "safe zones." You race against yourself and the track—which, unlike most public roads, is not designed to work for you, but against you. The tricks have names like "off-camber," meaning the corner banks *away* from you, or "decreasing radius," where a turn suddenly gets sharper instead of opening up. As you push your car, and its tires, to the limits of friction, smoothness is key—every input with hands and feet has to be "delicately deliberate." At best, it's a dance on the edge of control, and when you string together a series of smooth, fast laps, it feels very good.

Comparable to our drum studies—or early motorcycle training— the basics we learned at the beginning continued to be supplemented by other instructors. (For example, on two wheels, we attended the Freddie Spencer High Performance Riding School in Vegas, described in *Ghost Rider*. Which reminds us that we had another kind of split personality then—*three* ways, as we recall—traveling on that journey, and attending the school, under the alias John Ellwood Taylor.)

After moving to California in 2000, we discovered that informal trackdays for cars or bikes were common and inexpensive, and started attending one or two every year. (The Professor insisted that the risk of injury on a racetrack was too high on two wheels, so we

Off-camber in a dry country

stayed with cars.) Expert instructors were usually on hand, and we always liked to have them ride with us for a few laps—often in the early afternoon, after we'd had a chance to try it "our way" for a while. Inevitably they would give us enough little tips to make the rest of our day quicker and raise our game for the next time.

Over the years, we had the opportunity to challenge most of California's racetracks, like Laguna Seca, Willow Springs, the Auto

DB5 storming
Thunderhill, 2013

Club Speedway in Los Angeles, and our favorite, Thunderhill Raceway in Northern California. The Aston Martin club event is always held there, and in January, when we are never touring ("Because, um, motorcycling?" as explained before), so we haven't missed one since 2006.

As always, this one was a learning experience. ("For research," again.) As we have moved up through successive modern Aston Martins, from the DB9 to the DBS, and now the Vanquish (the old DB5 was a one-time "parade" outing), we have to admit we have reached our peak of capability—maybe a little beyond. In one late morning session, we "overcooked" it on one corner, and the car went sliding sideways across the track (what Brit moto-journalists would call a "lurid slide"). We corrected it enough to drive straight off into the dirt infield, rather than spin-ning, but as we went slewing into the dusty gravel (throwing up a mighty cloud of dust, we know from witnessing other "off-track excursions"), we were feeling plenty . . . "alert."

Trying to steer or brake would only make things worse, so it was necessary to counter that natu-ral instinct. We just held on, mentally repeating, "Don't do anything, don't do anything," until the gravel slowed the car enough to let us steer back onto the track.

We made sure *that* didn't happen again. For the rest of the day, we kept the car on the track and reeled off some satisfyingly consistent laps.

Bubba gets high on the adrenalin; the Professor likes the concen-tration and precision. They both have a *very* good time.

The longtime organizer of the Aston Martin event is George Wood, a district attorney up in the Bay Area. (We bought our DB5 from him, back in 2006.) In his DB9, George is a very enthusiastic participant himself, and once crowed, "I *live* for trackdays!"

Bubba and the Professor would *almost* agree—but between the two of us, we live for so many things. Cars, motorcycles, birds, words, music, landscapes, cooking, family, art, learning, roadtrips, and . . . single malt whisky.

After all these years, now that we are a sexa- genarian, it's still rather amazing that we can find enough "common ground" to coexist. You could say the same about an enduring marriage (or rock band!), and perhaps the same qualities apply: we are just enough alike to be willing to share the same time and space, but different enough to sometimes *surprise* each other.

Twenty years ago, Andrew MacNaughtan col- laborated on another portrait, for the *Roll the Bones* tourbook. We hoped it might represent what we vaguely felt were different facets of our character. Back then we weren't thinking of ourselves as Bubba and the Professor, but of course that's exactly what Andrew captured. The Professor held up Aristotle's *Poetics*, regarding the camera with a look of wry tolerance, or resignation, while in the background Bubba danced like a maniac.

That's us—I mean *me*.

When Bubba and the Professor were kids, it would have been Bubba who said, "I want to play the drums!"

The Professor would have replied, "Fine, but we're going to study and practice hard, and be as good as we can get. And never stop try- ing."

And so they united in a common goal. A few years later, it was Bubba who complained, "I want to quit school and be a full-time musician."

The Professor would have said, "Fine, but we're going to give it everything and more, even chase across the ocean and be poor and desperate, until we get established. Then we're going to get the edu- cation we're missing now."

Still later, Bubba said, "I want to ride motorcycles all over the place!"

The Professor said, "Fine, but we're going to learn to do it well, and wear all the proper gear, all the time. And *I'll* pick the destinations and routes—where we might *learn* something."

Some years passed, and Bubba said, "I want a '63 Corvette Sting Ray, like we used to dream of when we were ten! Remember how we used to draw that car all over our schoolbooks—until we started drawing Keith Moon's drumset instead?"

The Professor said, "Fine, but first we get an Aston Martin DB5—because that's what we dream of *now*."

And so it came to pass that "on days like these," when the day starts to fade toward late afternoon, and it's time to pause and read over the day's work, you can always count on Bubba to say, "Hey, Perfessor—how about a drink?"

The Professor will reply, "That would be nice, Bubba. I'll join you."

# 18

# NOT ALL DAYS
# ARE SUNDAYS

**MARCH 2014**

**The title is a West African saying,** describing what in that part of the world is a cultural ambivalence toward life's . . . vagaries. Some good days, some bad days. Into each life a little rain must fall. Ski trails may turn to ice. Every silver cloud has a dark lining. Not all days are Sundays.

Interesting that the "Sunday" metaphor seems to be fairly universal, not only in the West, but in many regions of Africa and Asia where Christian missionaries have been active. Despite choosing a different day of the week, the tradition is maintained among Jews and many Muslims—an ideal day of rest and ease, and sometimes prayer. I defer to Aldous Huxley's father, who said a walk in the mountains was the

Return of the
Snowdancer

equivalent of going to church. This reporter would maintain that the same equation applies to other pleasurable activities in nature, like the display of devout snowshoeing in the opening photo.

That day, though, *was* a Sunday, in every sense. It was early February, in the Laurentian Mountains of Quebec—a day that was everything that season, in that place, ought to be. Over two feet of snow covered the ground and clotted on the trees, the sky was pearly gray in a light overcast (often a harbinger of snow, like the proverbial "white sky"), and the temperature was in the single digits Fahrenheit. Cold, but not *bitter* cold.

Breaking trail

Neighbor Charles and I tramped happily into the backland across the road from our houses. We entered a vast territory of roadless, uninhabited forest, where a few old logging roads and survey lines made cleared passages. We could explore them almost limitlessly for miles to the east and south, away from the inhabited lakes.

We took turns breaking trail through deep powder and talked about the trees around us, the animal tracks in the snow, and our lives. In our local woods, Charles and I are particularly fond of the hemlocks, *les prûches*, the largest, most majestic, and shapeliest of our trees, especially in winter. Often the hemlocks stand together in small groves, over a hundred feet tall, with trunks over a foot thick. Yet they are surrounded by the bare gray spindles of much younger hardwoods or comparatively ragged-looking spruce and fir. Our area had been logged over twice, in the late nineteenth century and in the mid-twentieth, so the bush we explored was all third-growth—only the hemlocks seemed at all "venerable."

The once-mighty forests across Southern Quebec and Ontario had originally been dominated by lofty oaks and white pines, but after the first cut the oaks didn't grow back (they could not compete against the faster-growing birches and poplars). Cedars and maples are among the other common trees that can grow to a good size. The tall white pines, the monarchs of the north, remain rare in our area—mostly on the small islands, for some reason. Perhaps that made them harder to cut and transport in the horse-drawn era, yet it should have been easy enough the second time around—the logging industry was well motorized by the 1950s.

I was told the loggers spared the hemlock groves because they camped under them, but being efficient pillagers of the earth, you'd think they would have hacked them down before moving on. After all,

every tree represented a few pieces of silver. In any case, for Charles and me, the presence of those old hemlocks is one of the *sweeter* mysteries of our woods.

And talking of the horse-drawn era, and mysteries, one day I was snowshoeing alone, far back in the woods on an old logging track, and noticed an unnaturally symmetrical object about nine feet up in a yellow birch. Someone must have found it the previous summer or fall (I was sure it hadn't been there last winter; I would have noticed it) and thrown it high into a tree for a "ringer." However that hundred-year-old horseshoe arrived there, I can say it signified a good-luck omen for me that February—though similarly tarnished by the weight of years, hard weather, and loss.

If this year did not quite offer "The Best February Ever" I crowed about back in 2008 (mostly to do with the weather, which has its own vagaries, of course), it was still pretty great. I was able to spend the entire month there and, in the middle, welcomed Carrie and Olivia for a week. Four-and-a-half-year-old Olivia would finally experience her *true* Canadian half—winter!

Among the hemlocks

(We had tried to bring her there the previous year, but to my disappointment, she was afflicted with the childhood cliché of ear infections, and couldn't fly.)

So often when I am in Quebec in winter, I think of the evocative line by French-Canadian poet Gilles Vigneault: "*Mon pays ce n'est pas un pays; c'est l'hiver.*" My country is not a country, it is winter. The thought marries well to a line delivered by Canada's then–Governor General, Roméo LeBlanc, when my bandmates and I—the Guys at Work—were awarded the Order of Canada, in 1996. Speaking of the qualities and experiences that unite all Canadians, regardless of culture or language, he said, "We all know what it's like to be alone in the snow."

The Merida of snowshoes

If we Canadians know what it's like to be alone in the snow, we also know what it's like to be *together* in the snow. It was an extreme delight for me to introduce Olivia to a whole new world of quaint Canadian customs *dans l'hiver*.

It begins, of course, with taking half an hour to get dressed—putting on all the layers, the boots, the scarf, the mittens, the balaclava (Olivia *loved* to say that word), hat, and sunglasses.

Then to walk outside and feel the shock of the cold—even if only on the two inches of face left exposed, but also in the nostrils and lungs. Cold fresh air like that is definitely a mild narcotic—just as I once described my favorite drink as "February in Quebec." Olivia climbed the snowbanks, slid down them, dived into the deep powder, rolled in it, swam in it and, finally, tasted it. She said, "I *love* snow!" My heart melted.

The next day I got Olivia strapped into her new pink snowshoes, and she took to it right away. (One great thing about that sport is its natural technique—if you can walk, you can snowshoe.) We took a lap around the house to get the hang of it, then climbed down the steep bank to the open whiteness of the lake. Several feet of snow lay over an equal thickness of ice, and Olivia was fascinated by the concept, stepping boldly out onto the immaculate surface.

It was my natural instinct to want to pave her way—to go ahead and pack down the trail for Olivia. I told her, "It will be easier if you follow in my tracks and let me break trail."

She said, "I want to break trail!" and marched off across the lake beside me.

Pointing to the line of trees on the far shore, perhaps a half-mile distant, she said, "Let's go all the way across." I loved her spirit but wanted to make sure this first time on snowshoes was *positive*—didn't want her getting sore or tired. I turned us back halfway, knowing we still had that steep bank to climb. Sure enough, there was some slipping and falling, but no complaining. When we got to the top, I told her, "You are really good on snowshoes—very strong and very brave."

She burst out with "I am the Merida of snowshoes!" (The Scottish princess from the Disney movie *Brave*, see.)

Another day we all went tobogganing and sledding at a small abandoned ski hill nearby. In my former life, it was a great family place on weekends, with a T-bar lift and a small chalet serving hot chocolate and fries with gravy. I have many happy memories of winter afternoons there with my lost Selena in the '80s, when she was eight or ten. Riding up the T-bar, she was so small that when the crossbar fitted behind her butt, as it should, it had to be behind my *knees*.

All that is long gone, but the hillside remained clear for cross-country skiers and sledders. Olivia liked tobogganing, nestled between my knees as I steered us down the hill with my boots, but she especially loved piloting her own little red plastic sled. Like cross-country skiing, the thing about tobogganing is you don't just ride down the hill—you have to climb up it, too. But Olivia was game, and we made many spectacular runs, together and separately.

After, we drove home, got out of all our wet clothes, and I taught her how to build a fire. (She loved the word "kindling.") I made hot chocolate (the *proper* kind, with whole milk, chocolate syrup, whipped cream, and shavings of dark chocolate), while the fire flared up and snowflakes whirled outside the windows, bluing into evening. Olivia's previous idea of snowstorms had been the little glass snow globes her grandmother gave her every Christmas, and she said, "It's like someone shook up the world!"

Indeed, dear daughter . . .

One snowy afternoon, Olivia and I bundled up and went out to fill the birdfeeders, "Bubba's Seeds 'n' Suet." The blue jays clean out the mixed seeds almost daily—I call them the "crackheads" of the bird world. Mobs of them flock to the feeder, all edgy and screechy, nodding their blue crests

Filling Bubba's
Seeds 'n' Suet

and flapping their wings to chase away all the friendly little chicka-dees. (Blue jays actually imitate the call of the red-tailed hawk, to make them seem scary—like punks imitating gangsters for status.) Twitchy and nervous, they use their bills to sweep the seeds waste-fully aside and onto the ground to get at the choice ones they want. With their cheeks full, they flock to hide seeds for future days. (I read once that jays can remember up to 10,000 hiding places.)

SkiCam™—perfect trail ahead

Blue jays are clever and attractive, all right, but their *character* is not very appealing to this bird-lover. It occurred to me that just as you might say you like people, but not *all* of them, the same is true of birds. Crows and blue jays, say, bullies and robbers, repre-sent the bad kind of people, too. The chickadees are cheerful and social, innocent pacifists, and let them-selves be shouldered out—but the woodpeckers don't fear the jays, nor do the smaller nuthatches, white- and rose-breasted. They simply ignore them and carry on feeding.

I noticed there were no redpolls around this year, or juncos—often the weather farther north dictates which birds are driven south to feed at Bubba's.

One unusual visitor puzzled me, as it had once years ago, I eventually realized. It was the size of a finch or sparrow, dove-gray, black wings barred with white. I thought I knew all the local species, but I just couldn't think what this one was. I finally identified it as a female goldfinch in her plain winter plumage—the one variation that is seldom illustrated in the bird books. In the following days there were five or six of them, including a few males, which are more yellowish, and thus more identifiable.

To my surprise, they didn't even touch their summer favorite, the Niger seeds (let's pronounce it like the country in French, "*nee-jzhair*"), but went for the fattier sunflower seeds. Similarly, some seed-eating birds eat insects only during breeding season—for the protein. Vegans become carnivores during that critical time. (Like pregnant human females you hear about, tearing up their PETA cards and diving into burgers.)

Before and after the family week, I had ten days on my own for reading, writing, cross-country skiing, and snowshoeing. Mornings and evenings were spent with books and words, quiet and studious (two favorites of the month: *Sacré Bleu* by Christopher Moore and

*TransAtlantic* by Colum McCann), while afternoons lured me out into the snowy woods. There was only one day I didn't go out—in freezing rain, a useless kind of weather—and one day I *shouldn't* have gone out, in the aftermath of that ice storm. Later I was writing about that day to my little email circle, the "Breakfast Club for Cuties"— Brutus in Calgary, brother Danny in Vancouver, and Craiggie in South Pasadena—and immediately thought of that West African quote for the title of my message to them, "Not All Days Are Sundays."

The ice storm struck on a Friday, when the temperature rose a few degrees above freezing. Typically freezing rain or ice pellets are caused by a warm air mass flowing in, so the precipitation falls as rain, then either freezes on the way down, or when it reaches the ground. At its most extreme, an ice storm brings down trees like matchsticks, and electrical pylons are crumpled like so much tinfoil.

Ice storm

This storm wasn't that severe, but driving or even walking on wet ice is near impossible. I went out to fill the birdfeeders (cursing the crackhead blue jays) and could hardly keep my feet under me—had to hang onto the front porch pillars to make it out to the softer snow.

That night, the temperature shot down into the deep freeze again, and the briefly softened snow hardened into a solid crust. That was fine for snowshoeing, even sometimes quite good—it prevents sinking in so much—but it is not suitable for cross-country skiing. In order to move forward, the skis must grip the snow briefly, with the aid of temperature-sensitive waxes. (Cross-country ski waxes range from various purples and reds for warm temperatures through blue and green for colder, with many variations and hybrids in between, each with specific ranges for air temperature and freshness of the snow. It's a kind of alchemy.)

The following Monday promised at least a dusting of new snow, so I decided to try an old favorite ski trail—a ten-kilometer (six-mile) loop with rolling terrain to change up the rhythm, and some pleasant variations in the passing woods. In some areas, bare gray branches stood against the open sky; in others, shadowy evergreens arched over me—it was like skiing through a tunnel. Thirty years before, it had been the first proper trail I ever skied, and I had done it dozens of times since, so I was looking forward to an enjoyable "rendezvous."

It started out all right, with a flat stretch along the old railway alignment, then up a long, steep climb (the same old ski hill where I had tobogganed with Carrie and Olivia). Then I came to the first gentle, curving descent, and it swept me downhill faster than I liked, skis clattering over the crusty surface. I couldn't gain any "bite" to steer, to make a snowplow of my skis and push against the crust for control, and the light new snow had not penetrated the trees enough to help.

A still steeper section swooped down and to the left, and I couldn't make the turn—I had to bail out by sitting down. (Trailcraft: I have learned it is better to choose when you're going to fall, rather than to hold on a little too long and take a "headlong flight"—quite possibly into a tree.) As I slid along the icy crust, it pushed up my jacket and underlayers and scraped the skin raw above my beltline. That unyielding surface also offered no purchase for the wax, which needs crystals to grip and push against, then release into the glide part of the motion. Again and again, a slight misstep or icy bump made one ski slide away under me, triggering a sudden animal bellow as I scrambled to stay upright. The freezing rain had also brought down twigs, dry leaves, and needles, to litter the trail and drag on one ski or the other, so the amount of slip or grip was unpredictable. Soon those sudden bellows of fear were laced with shouted profanities of rage, and I was becoming . . . "discouraged" . . .

SkiCam™—imperfect trail ahead

Later, above a crusty, littered, and wretched trail, I encountered a yellow sign that warned of a steep downhill approaching. That day, it meant I would have to stop, take off my skis, and walk down the hill until the trail was navigable again. Tracks in the snow told me that the one skier who had preceded me that day had done that, and I decided to follow that sensible example. Steep climbs required the same desperate measure, because there was nothing for a herringboned ski to edge itself against—it just slipped back with a sandpaper rasp and threatened to upset me in a particularly unpleasant, spread-eagled way. More animal bellows and curses rang through the silent forest—with no one to hear. Other than that single set of tracks—*boot* tracks—I didn't see one other skier that day, and no wonder. In thirty years of cross-country skiing, it was the worst conditions I had ever known. More fool me—I had dared to hope.

There was no turning around because, unusually, that particular trail was a one-way arrangement. Its steep, narrow slopes could not be safely climbed and descended by two skiers at the same time. The downhill skier would be moving too fast, with no view ahead, and the uphill skier had nowhere to get out of the way, so there was a risk of painful collisions. Instead, I chose a shorter loop back toward my trailhead. Still, even that was a difficult, "dynamic" trail, and I had to take off my skis and walk for at least ten climbs and descents. I had never had to walk so much—nearly as far as I skied—and it was a long, hard, unrewarding three hours before I made it back to my car.

Brother Danny offered me a suitable quote, from Shakespeare's *Richard II*:

> These high wild hills, and rough uneven ways
> Draw out our miles, and make them wearisome

SnowshoeCam™—better trail ahead

Weary indeed, and sore all over, I hobbled around the house at my evening chores. After sitting for a while, I rose stiffly to my feet with a groan. I chuckled at how *wrecked* I felt—amused now, because it was over, and I had *endured* it.

I decided to wait for new snow on the ski trails, and the next afternoon went snowshoeing instead—a much more stable mode of travel for those conditions.

Later that day and overnight, a few inches of new snow gladdened my heart, and I decided to try the "skinny sticks" again. I knew one trailhead that would give me several options—a long, more-or-less flat cruise, or various loops with more challenging terrain. That way I could make a decision *after* I saw how things were. Live and learn.

As I set out—again following only one other skier—the snow was soft, pliant, and grippy under me, and I fell into the easy rhythm of kick-and-glide. Where the old railway alignment tended slightly downhill, I was able to get into the double-poling stride (or "kick double pole," technically), perhaps the most graceful of cross-country cadences. You reach forward with both poles and plant them, push back as you kick with one ski, then glide a fair distance as you bring the poles forward again, then push and kick with the other ski. There are only a few areas where I can ever get that groove going, and only if the conditions are right.

Without thinking much about it, a plan seemed to "crystallize," and I found myself turning off to take the *long* way. That trail represented my "benchmark" loop, usually about a three-hour circuit, with every kind of terrain in pleasantly varying rhythms.

About one third into it, I realized that not only had I not fallen, I hadn't once lost control. No animal bellows or flights of roared profanity disturbed the peaceful winter forest. In fact, I realized, I was

"Expert Skiers Only"

making very good time. Over the years, I had made notes of my best times on some of the local trails, and that day I happened to notice I had started at 12:50, so I decided to see what sort of time I could post. Not racing, but skiing steadily, without pause, I climbed the uphill pitches, strode smoothly along the flats, and glided downhill with perfect control against that yielding cushion of snow.

Back home, showered and changed and feet up by the fire, I saw that some years ago I had recorded two hours and twenty minutes, and in 2011 cut that to two hours seventeen minutes, in what I described as "very good conditions—light snow, –4°C [25°F]." That day's time was two hours and thirty minutes—close enough to my "personal best," without half trying, and I felt *great* after.

How easy it is to exercise hard for two or three hours every day when it's something you *enjoy*—not stuck in a gym pumping grimly at some machine that merely *imitates* the actual sport. (Without the scenery, or the air.) That was why I liked starting my tour preparations that way—using February as the launching pad for the spring's fitness programs and rehearsals. No better, or more enjoyable, way to get fit.

The following day I returned to the trail that had so brutalized me on Monday. It was payback time. Even more new snow had fallen overnight, making conditions truly ideal, and that day I even dared to take on the "Black Diamond" sectors of the trail, which I usually took a longer loop to avoid. Just before one of those stretches, a sign warned off all but expert skiers—which did *not* refer to this indomitable enthusiast. I am too gangly and graceless to actually be anything like an "expert" at skiing, and as with other endurance sports like bicycling and swimming, it is just that I can *do* it for a long time. The photo shows that once again only one set of tracks preceded me on the trail that day, and that the new snow lay deep and powdery—easy to push against for steering and braking.

In the distance, the trail crests and then descends sharply out of view, the first of a series of steep, curving descents, twisting narrowly left and right between the trees on either side. I had always thought of that section as "The Chutes," and with something more than respect. Call it fear. It was like a luge or snowboard run, swooping downhill with concave banks on either side, and over the years I had fallen there many and many a time—usually bailing out intentionally, when I was going too fast and realized I could no longer steer or stop.

On that first crest, I paused and took a deep breath, then let gravity sweep me downhill, skis edged out in a wide, triangular "piece of pie" (as the ski instructors teach kids) against the loose snow. Hallelujah—I was steering! I was slowing down when I wanted to!

"Sweat-sicles"

However, the deadliest part of the Chutes was the end—hurtling downhill on the steepest pitch yet, then facing a sharp left turn. (What is *wrong* with the people who designed that trail?) I have almost never made that turn, and this day was no exception—gathering speed, feeling the edge of control approaching, and seeing that sharp turn looming ahead, I leaned back and sat down. I went tumbling to a halt in a jumble of limbs, skis, and poles, but unhurt. It was the only time on the entire ten-kilometer (six-mile) loop when I had to bail out that day, and I was okay with that.

I was more than okay—I was *ecstatic*.

Not for the first or last time that February, I repeated my friend Mendelson Joe's mantra, "Every day is Thanksgiving Day."

Perhaps not *every* day—but certainly all Sundays!

This photo was taken at the end of that three-hour ski, in flurries of snow at about 15 degrees below freezing. My sweat had soaked the balaclava, then leaked out to freeze in the cold air and form the "sweat-sicles" across my brow.

That Friday was my last day in Quebec, before flying back to the very different winter of Southern California (see "Winter Latitudes"). It was even colder that day, and although I was determined to go out

Atop a beaver lodge

into the winter woods one last time, I went on snowshoes instead. More stable, and almost no chance of a bad fall leaving you stranded.

Over the weeks, I had tramped out a decent network of snowshoe trails, sometimes with Charles (silent "s"), and once the two of us with another neighbor, Robert (silent "t"). The packed-down tracks made for easier walking, even in fresh snow, so every time out I had pushed back a little farther into the trackless woods, following old logging roads or survey lines. I was able to explore areas I hadn't visited for years, or even *ever*.

Far back in those deep woods was where the bigger animals took refuge through the winter, and I was pleased to see where a moose had been resting. The number and pattern of tracks showed that it had foraged and "nested" in the shelter of a bank of conifers—for a few days, it appeared, but not since the last snowfall. Its steps were marked by plate-sized holes in the snow, sometimes sinking deep enough to show the rounded depression of its body.

I was also happy to see some wolf tracks—a sure sign that our *wilderness* endured.

Keeping an eye on the time, in that season of brief daylight, I turned around after an hour and a half. The return journey was easy, over an increasingly well-tracked trail. I felt strong and fit—felt it in every muscle and joint—and was grateful for another wonderful season in the snow, and the sweat-sicle on my sunglasses . . .

Not all days are Sundays, and not all Februarys are perfect. Much as I might resist having to modulate into a sad minor key, it is a part of our music—a part of our world—like it or not. As it is described so enduringly in the movie *Down by Law*, "It's a sad and beautiful world."

Smack in the middle of the month, a dear friend—a *brother*—was felled by a heart attack, just after his sixty-first birthday. My age. Steven was the elder brother of my late wife, Jackie. His twin brother, Keith, had looked after my Quebec homes for almost twenty years. We had been friends since our teens, back in St. Catharines, Ontario, when Keith and Steve worked at the local record store, and I was a struggling musician. Naturally, a struggling musician was going to hang around the record store (in those days, anyway!). At the time I joined Rush, in 1974, I was living in a farmhouse with Steve, Keith, and Wayne "the Bear" Lawryk.

In later years, Steven and I shared the *worst* times in our lives—in England after Selena's death, looking after Jackie through her decline (her *surrender*) in London, Toronto, and Barbados. When I was at my lowest, Steven was my rock. After the wrench of Jackie's passing, Steven met me on my Ghost Rider travels to help "kill Christmas" (the worst time of year when your family is shattered)—one year in Belize, with his wife, Shelly, the next year pounding through Baja in his father-in-law's Hummer. A few years later, Steven lost his teenage son, Kyle, to stupid cancer, and I was able to be there for him. (The "walking wounded," we called ourselves.) He was a good man, a good friend, and a good brother—I felt his loss keenly. His brother Keith was *devastated*. They had talked on the phone every day, and now there was a big hole in Keith's life—"Like half of me has died," he said.

At least I was glad to be around for Keith for a little while. All too experienced in the ways of grief and loss, I am not uncomfortable in the face of it, as those who have never known death up close can sometimes be. When my girls had flown back to California, I invited Keith over for dinner. He said he wasn't feeling very hungry, and I understood, but when he dug into Chef Bubba's penne rigate bolognese with Reggiano, he ate it all up. I sent him home with a container of leftovers for another good meal.

Sometimes there's nothing more you can do for someone than

cook for them—and the bonus of a little company is good, too. Of course there was nothing I could *really* do or say—there never is—just feed Keith a few more dinners, take him on the "Steven Memorial Snowshoe Hike," and encourage him to share the *good* memories, so that he might eventually learn to smile at them.

The Quebec woods in winter forever remind me of the friend who introduced me to cross-country skiing, over thirty years ago. Robbie Whelan was the assistant engineer at nearby Le Studio, which hosted an amazing variety of artists during the late '70s and '80s—Tina Turner, Wilson Pickett, Cat Stevens, David Bowie, the Police, Ritchie Blackmore, Keith Richards, Asia, and many more. In those years, the Guys at Work and I recorded at Le Studio many times and became good friends with all the staff, perhaps especially Robbie. He was an enthusiastic member of the recording team, fully into the music and the technical side of it, and was equally fired up in our late-night volleyball games.

Steven Taylor
February 4, 1953-February 15, 2014

> *I remember*
> *How we talked and drank into the misty dawn*
> *I hear the voices*
> *We ran by the water on the wet summer lawn*
> *I see the footprints*
> *I remember*
> *("Afterimage," 1983)*

In the spring of 1983, Robbie was killed in a car accident right near the studio, while the band was touring in Europe. It was the first "unnatural" death I had ever experienced—unlike the more-or-less timely passing of grandparents and elderly relatives, this was someone *young*, a friend. Now I consider the thirty years of my life before that as "Life Before Death"—because from then on my outlook was necessarily darker, especially as more and more deaths piled up around me.

The song I wrote about Robbie, "Afterimage," has enduring resonance for me—true again and again, death after death. Another specific memory of Robbie in that song was him leading me down "The Chutes" for the first time. As I waited at the crest, not knowing what was ahead of me, I heard his whoops of fear and excitement ahead.

*I remember*
*The shouts of joy, skiing fast through the woods*
*I hear the echoes*
*I learned your love for life,*
*I feel the way that you would*
*I feel your presence*
*I remember*

The song's opening lines came back to me when I was asked what to put on the "souvenir card" (ouch) for Selena's funeral.

*Suddenly*
*You were gone*
*From all the lives*
*You left your mark upon*

Those lines have been true a dozen times since, and were true again with Steven.

When I was young, caught up in the solipsistic angst and insecurities of my teens and twenties, I truly believed life must get *easier* as you got older. Surely it must smooth out into some kind of plane, or groove, or even a *rut*. But of course I learned the opposite is true—the longer you last, life will just break your heart again and again.

All I know is that we really have no choice but to keep on breaking trail. Or, if we are fortunate, to follow in the tracks of those who have gone before, or of the young.

For now, at least, they remain immortal . . .

"Skiing fast through the woods"

"I want to break trail!"

19

# TELESCOPE
# PEAK REVISITED

APRIL 2014

Dante's View

**After riding up** the steep switchbacks to the mile-high lookout of Dante's View, in Death Valley National Park, I straddled my motorcycle at the edge, looking west, and thumbed the kill switch. All was suddenly quiet and still, and I sat for a few minutes, facing that majestic vista, seeing it—and *feeling* it—as I had so many times before. For seven hours and almost 500 miles, I had been wandering the backroads of California's Mojave Desert, so I was a little sore and tired, and ready to "get there." But I would not have missed that unparalleled viewpoint, and hadn't even considered passing by the winding little road up to Dante's View.

Eighteen years and dozens of visits had not dulled its radiance. If anything, knowing the place so well made it *more* alive, with memories

358

of viewpoints, hiking trails, mountaintops, and perhaps most vital of all, so many *stories*, personal and historic. Since my first sight of Death Valley, under a full moon in late 1996, to two days of filming scenes for my instructional DVD, *Taking Center Stage*, in various locations around the park in early 2011, my senses have been thrilled and my imagination inspired by one of my favorite landscapes.

Though it's not really a landscape so much as a *dreamscape*. (I like the word the late great art critic Robert Hughes used to describe the paintings of Giorgio de Chirico: "oneiric"—dreamlike. And de Chirico, an early surrealist who founded the *scuola metafisica*, might be one artist who could have rendered Death Valley in paint.)

Zabriskie Point

Death Valley is powerfully surreal and overwhelmingly strange, otherworldly. In some previous stories about spectacular views in the American West, I have resorted to musical metaphors—describing the sensory experience of standing before Grand Canyon as like a power chord, and the monumental rock formations of Zion Canyon as "frozen music," specifically an orchestral G major. Seen from this elevation, Death Valley struck a mighty chord as well, but the harmonic convergence included a slight dissonance, a disturbing harmony, an eeriness.

From lower down, like sitting on the terrace of the Furnace Creek Inn at sea level, looking across the shimmering valley floor to the dark, chiseled Panamint Range, the music changes to a steady, thick drone of gradually shifting harmonies. I think of *2001: A Space Odyssey*—that choral piece "Lux Aeterna" (eternal light, fittingly) by György Ligeti, like voices from purgatory (likewise suitably "Dantean").

The vast, sunken basin is the hottest, driest place in North America and typically thrums with almost visible heat. Even on that early April day, it was 103°F at Furnace Creek. The stark bareness of it all—the white swirls of the "chemical desert," the brown folds of bare rock in the Panamints behind—were the very definition of naked geology.

Looking out from Dante's View, at 5,475 feet, is overwhelming to the senses, and the topography is endlessly fascinating—even just considering the numbers. From my mile-high vantage, I looked down at Badwater Basin, almost 300 feet *below* sea level, and across the valley floor to the chocolate-brown alluvial fans of eroded debris (called *bajadas* when they join), and the wrinkled brown shoulders of the Panamints. The view centered on Telescope Peak, the highest summit in Death Valley National Park, at 11,049 feet.

The snowy streaks visible in the opening photograph mark the area surrounding Telescope Peak, and seeing that made my heart sink a little. My plan for the following day was to hike up Telescope Peak and view that scene in reverse—from there to here. Now that might not be possible. (At such a moment, you wish you could hold a defiant fist up to a skygod and shout, "Hey, man—I *trained* for this!")

I had last stood on that summit almost fifteen years before, in October 1999. All unexpectedly, that place and time had marked a major turning point in my life—a hinge of fate, as it were. In writing my story of that time, in *Ghost Rider*, I came to realize that the hike up Telescope Peak was an important "plot point." Dramatic. Symbolic.

Desert race—two wheels will win (as soon as I put away this camera)

Five and a half years later, in April 2005, I planned a second attempt on Telescope Peak, but was warned by the park rangers that the higher elevations had too much snow and ice to climb without winter mountaineering gear—crampons and ice axes and such. I didn't have any of those on my motorcycle. (Note to self: a man of your age and station ought to possess an ice axe.) So that day I hiked up nearby Wildrose Peak instead, at only 9,064 feet, and still had to work around or through a fair amount of snow.

This time, looking out from Dante's View in April 2014, I saw that snow and knew that, like my motorcycle route that day, the next day's hiking plans would have to be . . . improvised.

Before setting out from home at dark o'clock that morning, I had not let myself decide anything about the route I would take, even the general direction. My only plan was to arrive at Stovepipe Wells in Death Valley by late afternoon—cocktail time—and there were many pleasant ways to accomplish that modest goal. After eighteen years of rambling around the Mojave, I knew its roads, major and minor, pretty thoroughly. Having lived in Southern California for over fourteen years, the desert was part of my "neighborhood," like the majestic Sierras around Kings Canyon and Sequoia National Parks, or the Pacific Coast Highway up through Big Sur and the redwoods. So I could improvise a route at will—the most "liberated" of journeys.

In a choice between exploring a new route with map and GPS, or simply wandering among familiar favorite roads and turning at "whim-points," the odds seem to favor the latter—much higher chances of having a great ride. Because experience.

Before publishing *Roadshow* in 2005, I had collected notes in 1996 and '97 for a similar book I was going to call *American Echoes: Landscape With Drums*. Its writing was interrupted when some jealous deity or other worked in mysterious ways and took my family "to a better place"—but I found this passage from that draft, describing my first "enlightenment" about the Western deserts.

Until this time, I had never considered myself to be much of a "desert person." As a nature-lover, I appreciate all kinds of landscapes, from seashore to farmland to prairie, but as already stated, my favorite is always forested mountains. Not necessarily big, majestic mountains like the Alps or the Rockies, but nice rolling land with trees and rivers or lakes, like the Black Forest, or my beloved Laurentians. It's the dynamic topography, the foliage, the smells, the sheltered little roads, and the trees reflected in water.

However, the desert was starting to grow in my "soulscape." The colors of tan and gray under wide blue skies, the hardy shrubs and cacti, but more than anything, it was a response to all that *space*. Brutus had spent a few years living near El Paso, and he told me that when he first went there he wasn't too impressed by the landscape. It seemed bleak and empty; there was nothing there. Later he would come to realize that this was the point—there was so *much* nothing there—and now this understanding was starting to creep into me.

For humans, perhaps the greatest luxury in the world is simply space, in all its forms. This is increasingly true on our ever-more-crowded planet (and the idea first occurred to me in China, and then again while sharing an eighteen-seat African bus with forty people), but it has been true since ancient times. Big buildings and big rooms have always been symbols of importance and prestige, and whether these extremes of "personal space" were built to house a king, a god, or a tycoon, their size is not necessarily a reflection of ego, but rather to provide and display the luxury of space. Even simple manifestations of this impression, like a magazine layout with generous blankness around its text and illustrations, play to the same sensibility in the viewer. Unlike other elements, the space is not there to do a job; it's not "working," it's just plain, luxurious space.

When the horizon is low and flat on every side, like in the middle of an ocean or a desert, the sky cannot get any bigger. Mountains that seem clear and close are actually a hundred miles away, the full length of a train is stretched along the horizon in tiny blocks of color, and at night, the lights of an approaching town take forever to reach.

So the desert has space, it has nice air, it has good roads with stunning vistas of mountains and rugged cliffs, and it has little traffic. On this, our second crossing of the Mojave, I was feeling the desert in a way I never had before. Certainly the motorcycle had something to do with that.

Joshua trees

That morning, as I wheeled the bike out of the garage into the dark streets of Westside Los Angeles, it seemed suddenly clear that I should ride east on Interstate 10. Once through the megacity and past Palm Springs, into the open desert, I should turn off at Joshua Tree National Park. Heading north from there, I would have a choice of several two-lane routes through the Mojave, the high desert, in the general direction of Death Valley.

In early April, the weather was likely to be relatively cool, and I was looking forward to seeing the wildflowers in bloom. It wasn't something you could ever count on—not a regular occurrence in that harsh environment, and even then short-lived—but it was something you could *hope* for. (A metaphor in there somewhere.)

(clockwise from top) Ocotillo, desert marigold, Brittlebush, Mojave aster

Years ago I had been surprised to learn that the busiest season for visitors in Death Valley is March and April. Because flowers. Perhaps the attraction can be compared to the autumn "leaf-peepers" who crowd the Northeast—New England, Ontario, Quebec—every October, in cars, minivans, SUVs, and bus tours. Both seasons offer a short, spectacular display, but the wildflower bloom in the Mojave is more subtle—and elusive. In fact, it only *really* shows off maybe once every twenty years, when the rain is timed and measured exactly right.

The rains had certainly been good for a sacred datura I pulled over to photograph—the largest, liveliest plant of its kind I have ever seen in the Mojave. It glorified the roadside just outside Joshua Tree National Park, with Twentynine Palms in the background, and I saw several like it that day.

In other years, I had sometimes noticed a white, trumpet-shaped flower or two, lying pale and limp beside its dark stems and leaves in the roadside gravel. But this was a spirited-looking bloom indeed, the white petals standing proud and delicately tinted around the outside with lavender. (Note the tiny yellow desert dandelions thriving in its shade.)

Sacred datura

Many years ago, a cab driver in Tucson told me sacred datura was a hallucinogen, and something about his manner said he spoke from experience. However, the entire plant is highly poisonous, and one description of a Zuni rite of manhood that included ingesting a drink made from sacred datura ends chillingly: "Not all of the boys survived."

The plant is holy to some Native Americans (hence the name), and its observed effects gave rise to the disrespectful name "Indian whisky." Also called jimsonweed, angel trumpet, moon lily and, in Spanish, *yerba del Diablo*—devil's weed—it is used for the traditional "vision quest" ritual, when hallucinations are said to reveal the animal whose spirit dwells within you.

Spirit vision quest

In the late '60s and early '70s, a popular series of "spiritual" books was written by Carlos Castañeda. (Now *there's* a story—not just the books, but the author. After selling twenty-eight million books in seventeen languages, Castañeda retired from public life in 1973. He bought a mansion in Los Angeles, and started his own cult—"Fellow Travelers of Awareness"—with three female friends, who gave up their identities, families, and friends. Even his death, in 1998, was secret, and went unreported for two months. Later, the remains of one of the women was found near Death Valley.) Leading off with *The Teachings of Don Juan: A Yaqui Way of Knowledge*, in 1968, Castañeda's books were notorious among the '60s hippies for his experiments with psychedelics, especially peyote—but it was apparently datura tea he consumed on the vision quest when he reported turning into a crow and actually flying.

Coincidentally, in another vision quest, just the previous week, friend Craiggie had fooled around with a photo from a hike I did in Topanga State Park with Greg Russell, and created this remarkable "hallucination." I liked that it seemed to reveal my spirit as a ferruginous hawk—not some showy, vainglorious eagle, you understand, but just one step below, the largest of hawks. That would be cool.

However, I think I'll take a pass on the datura tea, thanks anyway. Because poison.

In my years of desert travels on various vision quests, I have observed that in such a demanding, unforgiving environment, roads are demonstrably a *good* thing—not just for motorcycling and driving, but for the natural flora. Any rain that falls on the strips of pavement runs off to the side, bringing just enough extra moisture that the roadside shrubs are markedly larger than those in open country. In spring, the wildflowers thrive along the pavement's edge.

Mile after mile, with rarely another vehicle in sight, I rode through the Mojave's vast, oceanic sweep, distant brown peaks framing wide, gently undulating seas of patterned creosote. The creosote bushes grow in colonies, each a careful distance apart (either poisoning the soil around them with chemicals in their roots, or simply absorbing every drop of moisture—scientists are not sure), and collectively they are the oldest living organisms on Earth—some colonies over 10,000 years. A few of the creosote branches displayed their tiny yellow flowers, and I rode between tall, spindly ocotillos studded with blossoms like red jewels, and the fetching gesticulations of the Joshua trees. All the while, my eyes glanced down at the evanescent wildflowers to either side—shy flecks of yellow, white, red, orange, and purple. Brittlebush, asters, desert paintbrush, datura, lupins, and a few others were familiar. Many others I couldn't identify, but they delighted me just the same.

Route 66

Riding out of Joshua Tree, I paused in Twentynine Palms for gas, then continued up the Amboy Road to Old 66. I stopped to take a Ghost Rider shot—one of many in a sixteen-year series—looking west toward Amboy, Roy's Motel in the distance, and the Amboy Crater to the left. Pretty well every time I pass that way, by motorcycle or car, I pause to set up a shot like this. I hope I always will.

Because memory.

Ahead of me, I still had some attractive route options to consider and was reminded of another advantage to carrying my spare gas can, apart from emergencies: my choice of roads was less restricted by the location of gas stations. I turned north on Kelbaker Road, with a choice to make at Kelso Depot—at that fork I could stay left on the straight-through route up to Baker and Death Valley, or turn right onto the shunpikers' choice, into the wilder parts of the Mojave National Preserve.

I shunpiked.

At the next fork, at Cima, I turned north to the intersection with Interstate 15, where I fueled up again. The temperature had climbed into the eighties, heading for the nineties, so I stripped off a few layers of gear, then crossed the freeway and rode back into open desert.

A neglected, overgrown track of rough pavement called the Excelsior Mine Road curved west, traversing the remote, mostly abandoned mines of the Kingston Range. It climbed to a narrow, rocky little pass named for the next town, Tecopa, and I knew things could get difficult there. It was my third time passing that way: the first time the unpaved pass had been rough, the next time it was even worse, and I was worried that by now it might have deteriorated to impassibility.

Excelsior Mine Road

One flash flood could do it. However, the Tecopa Pass had obviously been graded recently, which meant there was some kind of economic activity continuing around there—because it still followed my basic definition of a road's purpose: "Money at one end, a bank at the other."

In the desert hamlet of Shoshone (population thirty-one in 2010, down from fifty-two in 2000), just outside Death Valley National Park, I decided to pause at the bar and grill called the Crowbar (heh-heh). Over the years, I have often enjoyed their fine cheeseburgers and lemonade (I like how they serve it in Mason jars). As I stood outside by the bike, getting myself organized to head inside, I looked over at the gas station across the road. A gathering of numerous green dual-sport motorcycles clustered around the pumps, and I knew who they must be. Moto-journalist friend Brian Catterson had told me he would be around Death Valley that week, attending a press introduction of the latest Kawasaki KLR-650 (long the benchmark for single-cylinder dual-sport bikes—meaning on- and off-pavement—since their introduction in 1987, so not exactly a "new model intro").

Even from across the road, I recognized Brian's pyramid of thick hair above his gray Aerostich suit, and a moment later he looked over, saw me, and ambled across. When he got close, he grinned and said, "I recognize that gas can!" (He always likes to kid me for carrying that, as I always do between the Mississippi and the Coastal Ranges.) We shared a hug that was necessarily big and manly, both still encased in armored riding suits.

I knew the Kawasaki group was staying at the Furnace Creek Inn—part of the reason I had found that longtime favorite destination to be short of good rooms. In any case, I had already decided to stay at the budget-priced Stovepipe Wells property—still perfectly acceptable to this desert rat, and twenty-five miles closer to my hoped-for trailhead the following morning.

Stovepipe Wells is more or less in the middle of Death Valley, near the Mesquite Flat Sand Dunes (said to be the most photographed dunes in the world). A rambling compound of single-storey motel units (with park-in-front-of-your-door convenience), it offers a decent restaurant, a "saloon," and a general store (mostly souvenirs) with gas pumps (Regular only). It did not boast the beauty or luxury of Furnace Creek Inn—or the spectacular "Lux Aeterna" view over the valley floor and across to the Panamints—but I had enjoyed those features numerous times before. This trip, Stovepipe Wells would be perfectly comfortable.

Emigrant Canyon

Brian suggested we get together later, but I said no, I'd just stay where I was—"with the poor people," I laughed. I should have explained that the reason I didn't want us to get together was that we were staying twenty-five miles apart, on motorcycles, so it wouldn't be a good idea.

Because alcohol.

Of course I am a drinking man, but strict about it with regard to motorcycling. "No drinking and riding. Not even one."

I made a mental note to explain that to Brian later, so he wouldn't take it personally.

Early the next morning, I was riding up through Emigrant Canyon, into the higher-elevation meadows of sage and grasses. Wildflowers were especially plentiful there, in patches of yellow, white, blue, and dark red. I was aiming for the higher trailheads to Wildrose and Telescope Peaks. I figured I would just see how things were up there, then decide what would be *possible*. (Might be another metaphor in there.)

I am not one to believe in omens, but I do like symbols, and the idea of hiking up that trail to Telescope Peak again, almost fifteen years later, seemed heavily symbolic to me. The first time had come to represent a ragged line between a bad *old* life (ended badly, and that's all that counts for a long time) and a hopeful *new* life—between feeling completely disengaged from the world, then rejoining it.

Back in 2001, when I was in Toronto with the Guys at Work and trying to start on lyrics for a new album, naturally I had lots of "baggage" to work through. Some of that made it into songs; much did not. One of the lyrics I wrote for the *Vapor Trails* sessions was titled "Telescope Peak," and though at the time it didn't "sell" to the other guys, I still kind of like it. (I'm not bitter, because "Ghost Rider" got put to music and, with coproducer Paul Northfield's encouragement, recorded, so at least one of my "songs of the American road" saw the light of performance. Good enough!)

But here was me in 2001, thinking back to October 1999 and wanting to write a song called "Telescope Peak." The words still "sing" to me—an uptempo rocker in the verses, then hanging on the line "On the last lonely day" before dropping into a grinding groove for the bridges. The choruses, naturally, in gentler half-time. (When I'm writing lyrics, I always have an imaginary tempo and melody in mind, but never share that with the Guys at Work—just let them take it where it leads them. Good things happen that way.)

> *Looking back to the lowest low from the highest high*
> *Way down to the burning white desert from the clear blue sky*
> *On Telescope Peak, salvation just a day away*
> *On Telescope Peak, I could have said goodbye to yesterday*
> *—On the last lonely day*
>
> *So many dreams are buried there*
> *In ghost towns and abandoned mines*
> *So many dreams are carried there*
> *In the sound of the wind in the pines*
> *—On the last lonely day*
>
> *It's the end of something*
> *It's the start of something too*
> *It's the end of something*
> *It's the start of something new*
> *The last lonely day*

Then into the second verse, which opens with a line inspired by a Swahili saying I had collected in my African travels. It still often resonates with me:

"Hyena says, 'I am not lucky, but I am always on the move.'"

Oh, that echoes deep for me, year after year. Like so much African wisdom in the oral tradition, the insight is as chiseled and nuanced as anything by Aesop or Aristotle.

Telescope Peak

*Well, I may not be too lucky, but I'm always on the move*
*Now I've got nothing to lose, I've got nothing to prove*
*One thing I have learned—you can't tell yourself how to feel*
*Surrender to the notion the irrational is no less real*
*—On the last lonely day*

*So many things I've buried there*
*In ghost towns and abandoned mines*
*So many things I've carried there*
*That I will leave behind*
*—On the last lonely day*

Telescope Peak, October 1999

An observant fan of songs by the Guys at Work will notice that I recycled the "can't tell yourself how to feel" idea into another song on *Vapor Trails*, "How It Is," and the "lowest low and the highest high" into "Ghost Rider."
Because salvage!
(I actually call my file of leftover lyrical ideas the "Scrapyard.")
This excerpt from a letter to Brutus in *Ghost Rider* describes that first ascent, starting with the motorcycle approach.

And that was just to get to the trailhead, at 8,000 feet. Then seven miles on foot up to the summit, through ascending ranges of sage, then juniper, then pinyon pine, mountain mahogany (another tree, like the giant sequoias and ponderosa pines, that needs fire to germinate), limber pine above 9,000 feet, and finally the ancient bristlecone pines, above 10,000 feet.

The summit itself was pretty much bare, jagged rock (though it felt pretty comfortable to lay on by the time I got there), with only a few grasses, but the view, of course, was stupendous. The whole valley so far down, the white floor around Badwater (the part they call the "chemical desert"), and the oasis of Furnace Creek just a tiny green smudge. And far below to the west, Panamint Valley, with its brown furrowed mountains, heaping of sand dunes at one end, the highway across it invisible except to my imagination, and somewhere way over there, Father Crowley Overlook.

Now, though, I'm tired and sore. Coming down was once again nearly as tough as going up—except it was easier to breathe, at least. At one point I was enumerating my pains as I walked: neck, shoulders, back, lower back, hips, thighs, hamstrings, knees, calves, ankles, and, especially, feet. (Waaah!) But I made it without needing a helicopter rescue.

This time, on April 9, 2014, I rode up the graded gravel track to the Wildrose trailhead, beside the Charcoal Kilns (see "December in Death Valley," in *Far and Away*). The road was dry, but patches of snow remained among the pinyon pines to either side. (Death Valley has a double treeline—the usual upper limit beyond which trees will not grow, and a lower line, defined by heat and dryness, below which no trees live.) Climbing from there, a sign warned that high-clearance four-wheel drive might be required. The track became narrower, steeper, and badly rutted, with solidified mud and gravel studded with larger rocks. I switched the motorcycle's traction control setting to "Enduro," to allow for some wheelspin, then stood on the pegs and bounced up another mile or so. I parked near the Mahogany Flats campground, at 8,113 feet.

Changing from riding gear into hiking clothes and shouldering my daypack, I stopped at the register for the Telescope Peak trailhead. It was like a raised metal desk with a lid, and inside was a pad of paper and assorted pens and pencils. The most recent entry, dated two days before by "two adults," said, "We summited!" I took that as encouragement. Not an omen, but a glimmer of . . . possibility.

I picked up a pencil and signed in below.

4/9/14 Bubba 9:10

A couple of miles later, maybe a thousand feet higher, I rounded a point among the limber pines and saw the view of distant Telescope Peak. And all that *snow*. The expression in my self-portrait echoes the "Are You Serious?" theme used before about cross-country skiing self-portraits, skimming downhill in a blizzard at 0°F. This time I mentally added an expletive to that rhetorical question—for extra emphasis.

Are you serious?

Because it sure didn't look good.

(Despite all of that precipitation apparent just above Death Valley, the valley floor had received just one third of an inch of rain that year—less than two inches since the previous spring. Whatever moisture got by the barrier of the Sierras to the west, the Panamints intercepted, leaving Death Valley in a double rainshadow.)

Without giving it much thought, I decided to set out and keep going upward as long as possible, then turn around. Hard to quarrel with that plan—except perhaps with the debatable line of what defined "possible." Farther along that difficult trail, I would discuss that line with myself more than once—wondering if perhaps I had reached it.

Below one snowfield, I looked up and saw three tiny figures coming the other way—animals, I thought at first, but they turned out to be three hikers, young guys. I gave them a wave and a smile, but did not pause in my determined march. Two of them seemed to be together, maybe Europeans, for they wore sports clothes—like soccer or rugby uniforms, and athletic shoes—rather than hiking gear (yes, I'm the fashion police when it comes to backcountry hiking, cross-country skiing, or motorcycling), and carried no packs. Where the snowfield ended (for them—began for me), the third guy moved wide to pass around us, then broke into a trot. He appeared to be a Trail Runner (I'm sure he capitalized and adopted the

name in his social media). Below his man-bun and poetic facial hair, he was dressed collar to cuffs in tight lycra, with a yoke-like affair over his shoulders carrying bottles of water. He was wearing those funny little shoes with the separate toes (I noticed from his tracks in the deep snow after that—must have been cold).

Later, following their tracks upward, smiling darkly at the toe-shaped ones, I saw where Trail Runner had fallen. The thin, waffle-patterned sole and toes had slipped down the icy surface a fair distance, ending where his curled-up body shape was pressed into the white slope, shoulders and knees facing downhill. Snow can be treacherous—*dangerous*.

Apparently there is some debate about how many words the Inuit actually have for frozen water, but as a native Canadian, I can attest that snow has many, many different manifestations upon the earth. Powdery soft to rock hard, blinding white to shadowy blue, fairy-tale woods to gray city slush.

A few stories ago, I was grappling with some large, slippery concept—something do to with the way people's impressions of an alien landscape, like, say, "the desert" or "the mountains," was always simplistic and reductive. I introduced the existential notion that "Nothing is ever just one thing."

Later I was surprised to see the great *New York Times* columnist Maureen Dowd use that *exact* phrase, and I wondered, "Hey—where'd she get that?" Then I learned that a master writer got there before either of us: Virginia Woolf, in *To the Lighthouse*, "For nothing was simply one thing."

Well, yeah. Because complicated.

Long digression short, to say that nothing is simply one thing is abundantly true of snow.

Where the trail followed the ridges and saddles (one with the great name of Arcane Meadows—"secret, mysterious, known to only a few"), I could either sidestep the drifts—some up to two feet deep—or labor through them, as I saw previous hikers had done. However, that surface was not *reliable*; sometimes I could make a few steps on top of the drift, then suddenly one boot would sink deep, tripping me up and needing extra effort to get out and move on. Breathing was difficult in the thin air, so every lungful was guarded and precious. (Somewhere I learned only to think about the *exhale*, because you're going to breathe in naturally anyway, and that always works for me.)

Another hazard was that after a few such deep plunges, the loose snow gathered around my boot tops and wicked down into my socks, until they were soaked through. Now I worried about blisters—I still had a long way to walk, even if I turned around before the top.

On steeper pitches, as shown above, I could kick my toes into the softer snow and lever upwards. But occasionally the snow *wasn't* soft, but icy and unyielding, and that wasn't nice to kick. Sometimes I could "herringbone" my boots, edging them into the snow with toes out and heels in, as in cross-country skiing. But with either technique, too many times the snow gave way under my weight, and I would slide back down a step, and that was discouraging. I would have to work harder to regain my balance, often crying out in surprise and frustration, and would lose that precious step upward. Falling was a worse fear, especially around exposed rocks—they were often sharp-edged blocks of gneiss, which could cause a serious injury, especially to a vulnerable knee. Even falling into the yielding snow was tough, because of the effort of struggling up again. I paused often to catch my breath (I mean look at the view!), and altogether it was becoming a challenge on the edge of my determination.

Had I reached that line yet?

Looking upward, the steep snowfield between jagged rocks and weathered trees seemed to rise so high above me. And I couldn't know if that visible edge actually represented the summit, or if I would arrive there to find another arduous slope of rock and snow. Body straining, my mind grew dim and fanciful. Maybe I should turn around—hell, I could even claim to have made it, no one would know. Those three guys probably hadn't made it all the way up. (I hadn't asked, not wanting to be discouraged.) Perhaps, two days ago, when the two hikers wrote, "We summited!" in the trail register, they had *lied*. Or maybe that day the snow had been easier, firmer underfoot on those steeper pitches. All I knew was, this was getting to be . . . too much.

But I kept climbing, one foot in front of the other, for a long time. (I am very bad at giving up—must work on that.) By then, the hours had become an arc of effort—it felt like I had started the hike straining for the first couple of miles, then settled into a steady groove for a while, but now—surely toward the *end*—it was punishingly hard again. That reminded me of other such ordeals, like what bicyclists call a

"Century," where you ride 100 miles in one day. In the '80s and '90s I had done a number of Centuries, and always found that the first ten or twenty miles seemed hard, and it was impossible to contemplate the entire distance from that tender beginning. Then a groove would take over for sixty or seventy miles—the endorphins and dopamine, I guess—erasing time and distance. Those miles fell behind easily. Then, as if in withdrawal from those sustaining drugs, the last ten miles crashed down on me. Weariness and discouragement turned those final miles into a dark slog.

Sometimes cyclists choose to do a "Metric Century" instead, meaning 100 kilometers, or 62.5 miles. I smiled to think that *I* was almost a metric century, at 61.5 years, so no wonder this climb felt so tough. The last time I had done it was fifteen years ago, after all, when I was a mere forty-six—a *child*!

Bristlecone pine

Though compared to the ancient bristlecone pines that clung to the highest elevations around me, we were *all* children. Unborn cells, really. Apart from creosote colonies, bristlecones are the oldest *individual* organisms on earth—as much as 5,000 years, dating to the time of the pharaohs. The example pictured here, with the Panamint Valley and the white line of the snow-crested Sierra Nevada behind, is actually still *alive*, despite being cruelly blasted by millennia of harsh weather and lightning.

Finally, finally, finally, I crested the peak. It *was* a "false summit," but I remembered that a short saddle led to the actual top. (I didn't see any recent tracks in the snow there, so I wondered if the three young sportsmen had turned around a little too soon.) The actual summit was a roughly circular pedestal of barren, square-faulted rock, with only a few hardy grasses in the cracks. An old metal ammunition box rested at an angle, and you could leave a note if you wanted. I didn't.

Because tired.

Telescope Peak was climbed and named in 1861 by Dr. Samuel George. He said he could see so far that it reminded him of looking through a telescope. Nicely played, Doc.

I eased myself down onto those sharp-edged rocks and stretched my legs out toward a lingering snowdrift, facing down over Death Valley. One slab of rock offered a decent angle, and I leaned back against it, feeling nothing but relief. (Though always with an undercurrent of anxiety, still facing the long, perilous descent.) Taking my time, I looked around at the 360-degree view, drank some water, ate an apple, a stick of cheese, and a chocolate wafer bar.

BootCam™

My feelings were certainly "elevated," though hardly ecstatic—I knew I still had a long, hard walk back to my motorcycle. But I had made it to that summit. Even at the ripe old age of a Metric Century. And that *did* feel good.

The ammunition box came in handy as a camera stand, for a self-timer shot of my summit triumph.

Taking up my pack again and heading down, the steep, snowy pitch was nearly as hard to descend as it had been to climb, and just as dangerous. Mostly I followed my previous trail, now kicking my heels into the snow, and traversing across the steepest patches. Sometimes I held onto a rock or grabbed at a limber pine branch (great smell they have, as do the high-elevation sages), feeling my legs aching and occasionally quivering with the strain. I plodded, slogged, and marched across the saddles, the wind driving in from the west in powerful gusts that pushed me sideways. (People on mountain ledges get killed that way, too—blown off by unexpected winds. Good thing I was "well weighted.")

"Don't ever do this again!"

Mostly my eyes were down on the trail, watching my footing (that's why bandanas are my preferred hiking headgear, to absorb sweat while allowing me to see ahead), but occasionally I paused and stood looking around at the view—west to Panamint Valley and the distant Sierras, east over the pale expanse of Death Valley, the dark Funeral Mountains, and the far-off, snow-tipped White Mountains in Nevada.

My thoughts churned away, but at nothing in particular. I have always found that when I am exerting maximum *will*, my thinking is not imaginative. (Somewhere Isak Dinesen wrote about the reverse conclusion: ". . . the freedom of the artist, who has no will, who is free of will." That explains a lot about *tragic* artists, that's for sure.) Exercising in a gym, riding a bicycle or motorcycle, or hiking in the mountains has never produced a *creative* thought for me. (Drumming is the only activity in my life that combines athletic activity with creative thinking—and that's plenty.) Typically, during an ordeal like that hike, the best my mind can do is work at "writing exercises"—trying to observe and put what I see and feel into sentences, then remember it for when I try to write it, to *share* it.

Dark imaginings of falling and hurting myself badly, or being struck down by some cardiovascular "event," made me think of hypothermia—as in "dying of." That reminded me of a word I had just learned, "hyperthymia." It is basically defined this way: "Hyperthymic

The way the wind blows

people have so much energy, do so many things, and get so much done that it annoys other people."

Oh dear. Some who know me well will laugh at that—others will be annoyed. Because truth.

In fact, ahem, well, if I do say—it's so true that I even often annoy *myself*. Like on that hike, there was a moment when I thought of something simple and important enough that I paused to write it down: "Don't ever do this again."

Later I added a joke, "No more suffering on *purpose*, okay?"

Brother Danny offered a suitable quote (as always) from British mountaineer C.F. Meade: "Whatever agonies and miseries the sufferer may endure on his pilgrimage to the heights, and however often he may swear never to return there, longing to do so is certain to recur."

The previous week, I spent an afternoon at Drum Channel, borrowing a little drumset in the studio for some casual "explorations." It was gratifying to learn that my technique remained "ingrained" (I said to Don Lombardi, "The machine still works!"), and that having stepped away from the *routine* of it allowed me to think in surprisingly fresh ways. It was an enjoyable, rewarding few hours—but after, I thought about doing that every day, like rehearsing for a tour. The idea did not appeal. The same with the 950-mile motorcycle ride to Death Valley and back, and all the packing and unpacking—it did not make me want to go back to doing that every day.

But that decision is far in the future—we'll see which way the wind blows then. Perhaps, as the man said, "Longing to do so is certain to recur."

On that endless march down from Telescope Peak, every time my eyes followed the trail curving far around a ridge ahead, I hoped it would be the last one. But those long ridges went on and on, until I wondered if I had somehow got on the wrong trail. There was only one trail up there—it had just grown longer since I climbed it a few hours before. My body was a tired, aching slave, and my mind was a dark, empty engine of will. I kept going because there was nothing else to do.

(One helpful consolation of old journals and writings is that they can help correct some illusions of memory. Like the common refrain that something hard was ever easy—the truth is that you just *forget* over time! Recall my list of aches from the '99 hike: "neck, shoulders, back, lower back, hips, thighs, hamstrings, knees, calves, ankles, and, especially, feet." Nothing different fifteen years later!)

At last I reached the trailhead and stopped to sign out in the register. (I noticed the three sportsmen had been too cool for that precaution—or *courtesy*, you might say. To save others worry and trouble.)

> 4/9/14 Bubba 9:10
> 4:45
> Tough going, fair bit of snow.
> But got 'er done.

That's the way Bubba would say it.

My motorcycle waited alone in the parking lot, I was glad to see, with the shadows growing long. Earlier, when I was setting out, a late-model SUV had been parked there, its sides dusty and badly scraped by branches (probably a rental, to be abused so recklessly!), and one campsite had been occupied with a tent and four-wheeler. That may have accounted for the three hikers I encountered, coming down so early, but the place was deserted now. The nearest people were at the

Wildrose Campground far below, so if anything nasty had happened, it would have been at least a day before someone noticed my abandoned motorcycle and finally came looking for me. Almost certainly too late, in that extreme exposure.

I struggled out of my hiking boots and back into my riding gear, the effort of bending over and getting boots on and off enough to set me groaning and grumbling. Swinging a leg over the saddle (ouch!) and standing on the pegs for the first rough descent was also a strain for my weary legs. I was glad to get back to pavement, settle back and just *cruise* the rest of the way to Stovepipe Wells.

I was thinking along predictable lines. There will be whisky. There will be a hot shower. There will be steak. There will be red wine. There will be sleep—early and long.

So let it be written; so let it be done.

Before sunrise, I was up and quietly packing the bike, aiming to ride out through the other "classic" point of entry, Townes Pass. So many stories attach themselves like flags to places all over Death Valley for me—even that pass. One shining memory is riding in that way for the first time, in autumn 1996, with Brutus—earlier pausing at Father Crowley Overlook above Panamint Valley as the moon rose, then over Townes Pass and into Death Valley, seeing the place for the first time like that.

Another story tells of a Chicago businessman named Albert Johnson who visited early in the twentieth century and found relief for his health in the arid heat. In the 1920s, he and his wife, Bessie, constructed a massive Mission-style mansion in Grapevine Canyon. He employed a character named Death Valley Scotty to look after the place (it soon came to be known locally as Scotty's Castle, which suggests a tale or two), and the story spins out from there. In 1943, Bessie was killed in a car accident in Townes Pass.

My entire journey to Death Valley this time had become a pilgrim-

Death valley sunrise

age of sorts, not only to Telescope Peak, but to the place itself. Even choosing to ride in through Death Valley Junction to Dante's View, rather than the equally scenic Salsberry Pass route out of Shoshone and past Badwater, had been deliberate—to make this visit *emblematic*. Not just memorable, but a summary of *all* of my memories of the place, and a symbol of what I hoped I could share with others.

Because magic.

# ON NIGHTS LIKE THESE

**"Magic exists,** but it often requires some planning." If there is one germ of hard-won wisdom I wish these tales might impart, that could be it. (That, and order your eggs well cooked.)

When reviewing the stories to prepare this book, many times I came across a passage of description, action, or conversation and thought, "I would never have remembered that." Sobering to reflect that if a time and place do not exist in memory or in art, they might as well never have happened. (Ah—except for the *moment*, right? At least the experience was golden—that must be worth something in this crazy mixed-up world.)

Sometimes it's nice just to relive an experience without the rain, as it were. However, many of these times and places jump up readily

and vividly on my mental screen, simply because my most treasured memories live in these stories. They recall what Wallace Stegner called "the very richness of that past," and I hope they can sing of it. At least I can say I am thankful I took the time and trouble to collect the notes, mental and written, and the photographs, both carefully planned and spontaneous, and put them together when the experiences were fresh.

Life caught on the fly that way aims at immediacy and emotional resonance, both high and low. And, alas, in real life there are always lows. No one would say he or she was "fortunate" to have suffered tragedy and loss, but it is human nature at its best to profit from dark experiences—in building what is called "character," and in an everyday sense of being more present, appreciating everything with just a little more engagement. Referring again to the genuine essence of that "in the moment" mantra, I return to Mendelson Joe: "Every day is Thanksgiving Day."

To which I might add, with a tinge of regret, "And every day is Memorial Day."

But yes, I am thankful. Thankful for these days and nights, for these people and places, for these experiences and memories.

Now I will take my bows—three, as I do at the end of every show: right, left, and center (meaning to you, and you, and you)—and say good night.

Let us all remember how it felt to be this alive . . .

On days like these, on nights like these.

## Photo Credits

All photos by the author, except those contributions noted below:

Michael Mosbach: xii, 13, 15, 18, 19, 23 (top), 26, 46, 48, 51 (top), 55, 59, 60 (top), 64 (top), 65, 107, 110, 111, 112, 113, 115, 116 (bottom), 117, 119, 121, 122, 123, 124, 126, 127, 128, 130, 137 (top), 141, 145, 146, 148, 149, 151, 157, 159, 160, 162, 170, 173, 174, 205, 206, 207, 208, 209, 215 (bottom), 216, 218, 219, 221, 222, 223 (bottom), 225 (top), 227, 251, 257, 259 (top), 261 (bottom), 262, 266, 267, 268, 269, 271, 272, 274, 277, 280, 283, 284, 285, 286, 288, 293, 295, 297, 298 (top)

Rob Wallis: 1, 5, 12

Tracie Moore: 7

Tom Marinelli: 66

Brian Catterson: 68, 70, 74 (top), 75

Patrick McCoy: 69

Brutus: 27, 29, 30, 33, 34, 36, 37, 38, 40, 45, 135 (bottom), 150 (bottom), 231, 233, 234, 235, 236, 237, 238, 239 (bottom), 240, 241 (top), 242, 244, 246, 247, 250, 252, 253, 255, 256 (bottom), 329 (top)

John Arrowsmith: 21, 72, 74 (bottom), 143, 179 (bottom), 181 (top), 182 (bottom), 228 (top), 230, 254, 270, 290, 299, 382

Andrew MacNaughtan: 71, 73, 321, 341

Lorne Wheaton: 82

Craig Renwick: 22, 84, 132, 151, 180, 181 (bottom), 210, 212, 213, 215 (top), 232, 281, 282, 291, 327, 337

Joe Testa: 85

Christian Stankee: 89, 291

Robert Knight: 91

Tom Sandler: 94, 96, 98, 99

George Pimentel: 100

Steve Hardy: 101

Ben Surman: 103

John Myers: 166 (top)

Paul Beaulieu: 106 (bottom)

Pam Myers: 167

Charles Voisin: 185, 189, 190 (top), 343, 344, 345 (top), 354

Doug Webber: 195 (top)

Greg Russell: 196, 197, 198, 199, 200, 364 (with raptor enhancement by Craig M. Renwick)

Matt Scannell, Esquire: 201, 333

Michael Bertolli: 228 (bottom)

Donovan Lundstrom: 229

Lashawn Lundstrom: 273

Arthur (Mac) McLear: 279

A foreigner in Utah: 300

Ryan Poyer: 318

A kid in Utah: 320

Richard Fegley: 322

Artwork by Nick Robles: 328

Rebecca Truszkowski: 330 (top)

Art by David Hockney: 334

Head-On Photos: 338, 340

Loris Ourieff: 339

Carrie Nuttall: 347 (bottom)

Shelly Bade: 356

## Permissions

"Art for Art's Sake" (Gouldman/Stewart) Copyright © 1975 by Man-Ken Music Ltd. Used by Permission. All Rights Reserved.

"Big Rock Candy Mountains" Reprinted with the permission of the Estate of Harry K McClintock; Published by Harry K McClintock Publishing (ASCAP). Copyright 1928.

"Blues in the Night" Lyrics by Johnny Mercer. Music by Harold Arlen. © 1941 WB Music Corp. Used by Permission of Alfred Music. All Rights Reserved.

"Coombe Gallows" Words and Music by Caleb Quaye Copyright © 1971 UNIVERSAL/DICK JAMES MUSIC LTD. Copyright Renewed All Rights in the U.S. and Canada Administered by UNIVERSAL - POLYGRAM INTERNATIONAL PUBLISHING, INC. All Rights Reserved. Used by Permission. *Reprinted by Permission of Hal Leonard Corporation 2.*

"Eve of Destruction" Words and Music by P.F. Sloan and Steve Barri Copyright © 1965 UNIVERSAL MUSIC CORP. Copyright Renewed. All Rights Reserved. Used by Permission. *Reprinted by Permission of Hal Leonard Corporation.*

"Mississippi Goddam" Words and Music by Nina Simone. © 1964 (Renewed) WB Music Corp. Used by Permission of Alfred Music. All Rights Reserved.

"Mon Pays" Paroles et musique: Gilles Vigneault. Used by Permission. All Rights Reserved.

"On Days Like These" Music by Quincy D. Jones. Lyric by Donald Black. Copyright © 1969 Sony/ATV Music Publishing. All Rights Reserved. Reprinted by permission of Sony/ATV Publishing LLC.

"Route 66" by Bobby Troup. Copyright © 1946, Renewed 1973, Assigned 1974 to Londontown Music. All Rights Outside the U.S.A. controlled by Edwin H. Morris & Company, A Division of MPL Music Publishing, Inc. International Copyright Secured. All Rights Reserved. *Reprinted by Permission of Hal Leonard Corporation.*

"Strange Fruit" Words and Music by Lewis Allan. Copyright © 1939 (Renewed) by Music Sales Corporation (ASCAP). All Rights for the United States controlled by Music Sales Corporation (ASCAP). International Copyright Secured. All Rights Reserved. Reprinted by Permission.

"Sweet Home Alabama" Words and Music by Ronnie Van Zant, Ed King and Gary Rossington Copyright © 1974 SONGS OF UNIVERSAL, INC., EMI LONGITUDE MUSIC, UNIVERSAL MUSIC CORP. and FULL KEEL MUSIC. Copyright Renewed. All Rights Controlled and Administered by SONGS OF UNIVERSAL, INC. and UNIVERSAL MUSIC CORP. All Rights Reserved. Used by Permission. *Reprinted by Permission of Hal Leonard Corporation.*

"The Stars Fell on Alabama" Music by Frank Perkins. Lyric by Mitchell Parish. © 1934 (Renewed) EMI Mills Music, Inc. Exclusive Print Rights Administered by Alfred Music. All Rights Reserved. Used by Permission.

Every effort has been made to contact the copyright holders; in the event of an inadvertent omission or error, please notify the publisher.